1,000,000 Books

are available to read at

www.ForgottenBooks.com

Read online
Download PDF
Purchase in print

ISBN 978-0-331-76003-3
PIBN 11056082

Forgotten Books is a registered trademark of FB &c Ltd.
Copyright © 2018 FB &c Ltd.
FB &c Ltd, Dalton House, 60 Windsor Avenue, London, SW19 2RR.
Company number 08720141. Registered in England and Wales.

For support please visit www.forgottenbooks.com

SESSIONAL PAPERS

VOL. XLVI.—PART IV.

THIRD SESSION

OF THE

THIRTEENTH LEGISLATURE

OF THE

PROVINCE OF ONTARIO

SESSION 1914

TORONTO:
Printed and Published by L. K. CAMERON, Printer to the King's Most Excellent Majesty
1914

Printed by
WILLIAM BRIGGS,
29-37 Richmond Street West,
TORONTO.

LIST OF SESSIONAL PAPERS

Presented to the House During the Session.

Title.	No.	Remarks
Accounts, Public	1	Printed.
Agricultural College, Report	30	"
Agricultural and Experimental Union, Report	32	"
Agricultural Societies, Report	42	"
Agriculture, Department of, Report	29	"
Almonte High School, correspondence	103	Not Printed.
Algonquin Park Forest Reserve	72	Printed.
Archivist, Report	51	"
Auditor, Statement of	54	"
Bee-Keepers', Report	37	Printed.
Bilingual Schools, correspondence with Bishop Fallon	101	Not Printed.
Bilingual Schools, correspondence with Bishop Scollard	102	"
Births, Marriages and Deaths, Report	20	Printed.
Canada Temperance Act, attitude of officials in Welland	76	Not Printed.
Children, Dependent, Report	27	Printed.
Coal supply for Public Institutions	74	Not Printed.
Colcock, N.B., moneys advanced to	60	"
Cole's Report, Mining Engineer T. & N.O.	88	Printed.
Common Gaols, official regulations	92	"
Consolidated Revenue Fund, Orders-in-Council	63	Not Printed.
Corn Growers' Association, Report	35	Printed.
Dairymen's Association, Report	38	Printed.
Division Courts, Report	5	"
Division Courts, Revised Rules and Orders	71	"
Education, Report	17	Printed.
Education, Orders-in-Council	55	"
Education, grants to rural public schools	77	Not Printed.
Education, investigation by Dr. Merchant	86	"
Education, grants withheld	98	"
Education, correspondence, Almonte School	103	"
Education, authorized text-books	104	"

TITLE.	No.	REMARKS.
Elections, return from Records	50	*Printed.*
Electric Railways, Report for or against	62	"
Employers' Liability, for Compensation to Employees..	53	"
Entomological Society, Report	36	..
Epileptics Hospital, ·Report	23	..
Estimates ....·.........	2	..
Factories, Report	46	*Printed.*
Farmers' Institutes, Report	40	"
Feeble-minded, Report ....·.	24	"
Forest Reserves—Pembroke Lumber Company	72	· "
Friendly Societies, Report	11	*Printed.*
Fruit Growers', Report	44	"
Fruits of Ontario ....·........	33	"
Game and Fish, Report	14	*Printed.*
Goodman, prosecution of correspondence ·············	59	*Not Printed.*
Good Roads Commission, Report	84	*Printed.*
Grand River, overflow, correspondence	58	*Not Printed.*
Guelph Prison Farm, buildings erected	75	"
Hamilton Athletic Association, correspondence	79	*Not Printed.*
Health, Report	21	*Printed.*
Health, Special Report	21a	"
Highway Improvement, Report	15	"
Horticultural Societies, Report	43	"
Hospitals and Charities, Report	25	"
Hospitals and Charities, Regulations	91	"
Hydro-Electric Power Commission, Report	48	
Hydro-Electric Power Commission, moneys spent on line from Morrisburg to Prescott	87	*Not Printed.*
Idiots and Epileptics, Report	23	*Printed.*
Industrial Farms, Official Regulations	93	"
Industries, Report of Bureau	45	"
Insane Hospitals, Report	22	
Insane Hospitals, Regulations	95	..
Insane Hospitals, Bulletin	56	
Insurance, Report	10	..
Kenora, action against, correspondence	70	*Not Printed.*
Labour, ·Report	16	*Printed.*
Lands, Forests and Mines, Report	3	"
Legal Offices, Report	6	"
Library, Report .....·...........................	52	*Not Printed.*

Title.	No.	Remarks.
Liquor License Acts, Report	28	*Printed.*
Liquor License Holders in Toronto	69	*Not Printed.*
Live Stock Associations, Report	39	*Printed.*
Loan Corporations, Statements	12	"
Local Option, convictions	89	*Not Printed.*
Mercer Reformatory, Regulations	90	*Printed.*
Meredith, Sir William R., moneys paid to	80	*Not Printed.*
Murray, Mather & Co., option to	82	"
Mines, Report of Bureau	4	*Printed.*
Municipal Drainage, Order-in-Council	85	"
McKelvie, Overseer, conduct of	59	*Not Printed.*
Northern Ontario, road construction in	73	*Printed.*
Ontario Homes Company, charter of	99	*Not Printed.*
Ontario Hospitals, Regulations	95	*Printed.*
Ontario Railway and Municipal Board, Report	49	"
Ontario Reformatory, Regulations	94	"
Ontario Vegetable Growers', Report	34	
Pembroke Lumber Company	72	*Printed.*
Power Commission Act, Orders-in-Council	97	*Not Printed.*
Prison Farm, buildings on	75	"
Prisons and Reformatories, Report	26	*Printed.*
Provincial Auditor, Statements	54	"
Provincial Conference, Proceedings	67	
Provincial Municipal Auditor, Report	8	"
Provincial securities sold	64	*Not Printed.*
Public Accounts, 1913	1	*Printed.*
Public Health, Report	21	"
Public Institutions, coal for	74	*Not Printed.*
Public Works, Report	13	*Printed.*
Queen Victoria N. F. Park, Report	9	*Printed.*
Railway and Municipal Board, Report	49	*Printed.*
Registrar-General, Report	20	"
Registry Offices, Report	7	"
Road Construction in Northern Ontario	73	
Rondeau Provincial Park, Regulations	57	
Secretary and Registrar, Report	19	*Printed.*
Smuck, William, license application	66	*Not Printed.*
Statute distribution	96	"
Surrogate Court, Orders-in-Council	61	"

TITLE.	No.	REMARKS.
Taylor, Scott & Co., amount received from	68	*Not Printed.*
Taylor, Mr., evidence of	83	"
Text-books, authorized	104	"
Timber Limits, sold	65	"
Timiskaming & N. O. Ry. Commission, Report	47	*Printed.*
Timiskaming & N. O. Ry., Cole's Report	88	"
Timiskaming & N. O. Ry., settlers' effects, over	100	*Not Printed.*
Toronto Liquor License Holders	69	"
Toronto University, Report	18	*Printed.*
Toronto University, cost of heating plant	78	*Not Printed.*
Toronto University, *re* deficit	81	"
Vegetable Growers', Report	34	*Printed.*
Veterinary College, Report	31	"
Whitson's Report on road construction in New Ontario.	73	*Printed.*
Women's Institutes, Report	41	"
Workmen's Compensation, Report	53	"

LIST OF SESSIONAL PAPERS

Arranged in Numerical Order with their Titles at full
length; the dates when presented to the Legislature;
the name of the Member who moved the same,
and whether ordered to be Printed or not.

CONTENTS OF PART I.

No. 1   Public Accounts of the Province for the year ending 31st October, 1913. Presented to the Legislature, 3rd March, 1914. *Printed.*

No. 2   Estimates—Supplementary, for the service of the Province for the year ending 31st October, 1913-14. Presented to the Legislature, 27th February and 9th April, 1914. *Printed.* Estimates for the year ending 31st October, 1915. Presented to the Legislature, April 21st, 1914. *Printed.*

CONTENTS OF PART II.

No. 3   Report of the Department of Lands, Forests and Mines for the year 1913. Presented to the Legislature, April 15th, 1914. *Printed.*

No. 4   Report of the Bureau of Mines for the year 1913. Presented to the Legislature, April 1st, 1914. *Printed.*

No. 5   Report of the Inspector of Division Courts for the year 1913. Presented to the Legislature, March 11th, 1914. *Printed.*

No. 6   Report of the Inspector of Legal Offices for the year 1913. Presented to the Legislature, April 1st, 1914. *Printed.*

No. 7   Report of the Inspector of Registry Offices for the year 1913. Presented to the Legislature, April 17th, 1914. *Printed.*

No. 8   Report of the Provincial Municipal Auditor for the year 1913. Presented to the Legislature, April 16th, 1914. *Printed.*

No. 9   Report of the Commissioners for the Queen Victoria Niagara Falls Park for the year 1913. Presented to the Legislature, April 15th, 1914. *Printed.*

CONTENTS OF PART III.

No. 10   Report of the Department of Insurance for the year 1913. Presented to the Legislature, March 20th, 1914. *Printed.*

No. 11   Report of the Registrar of Friendly Societies for the year 1914. Presented to the Legislature, March 20th, 1914. *Printed.*

CONTENTS OF PART IX.

CONTENTS OF PART X.

No. 37   Report of the Bee-Keepers' Association for the year 1913. Presented to the Legislature, April 22nd, 1914. *Printed.*

No. 38   Report of the Dairymen's Association for the year 1913. Presented to the Legislature, April 22nd, 1914. *Printed.*

No. 39   Report of the Live Stock Associations for the year 1913. Presented to the Legislature, March 3rd, 1914. *Printed.*

No. 40   Report of the Farmer's Institutes for the year 1913. Presented to the Legislature, April 9th, 1914. *Printed.*

No. 41   Report of the Women's Institutes for the year 1913. Presented to the Legislature, April 9th, 1914. *Printed.*

No. 42   Report of the Agricultural Societies of the Province for the year 1913. Presented to the Legislature, April 9th, 1914. *Printed.*

No. 43   Report of the Horticultural Societies of the Province for the year 1913. Presented to the Legislature, April 22nd, 1914. *Printed.*

No. 44   Report of the Fruit Growers' Association for the year 1913. Presented to the Legislature, April 22nd, 1914. *Printed.*

No. 45   Report of the Bureau of Industries for the year 1913. Presented to the Legislature, April 23rd, 1914. *Printed.*

No. 46   Report of the Inspectors of Factories for the year 1913. Presented to the Legislature, April 22nd, 1914. *Printed.*

CONTENTS OF PART XI.

No. 47   Report of the Timiskaming and Northern Ontario Railway Commission for the year 1913. Presented to the Legislature, March 23rd, 1914. *Printed.*

No. 48   Report of the Hydro-Electric Power Commission for the year 1913. Presented to the Legislature, March 16th, 1914. *Printed.*

CONTENTS OF PART XII.

No. 49   Report of the Ontario Railway and Municipal Board for the year 1913. Presented to the Legislature, April 24th, 1914. *Printed.*

No. 50   Return from the Records of the Bye-elections held on the second day of June, the fourteenth day of July, the eighth day of September, and the twenty-seventh day of November, 1913. Presented to the Legislature, February 18th, 1914. *Printed.*

No. 51   Report of the Provincial Archivist for the year 1913. Presented to the Legislature, April 15th, 1914. *Printed.*

CONTENTS OF PART XIII.

New Liskeard, Ont., or the dismissal of the said McKelvie from his position. 3. The prosecution of one Eli Tibbs in November, 1912, for illegal possession of furs. 4. The prosecution of any party or parties for illegal possession of furs seized by the said McKelvie from one Angus Wabi. Presented to the Legislature, February 27th, 1914. Mr. *Elliott.* *Not Printed.*

No. 60 A Return to an Order of the House of the 15th April, 1913, for a Return showing:—1. In detail the persons to whom the sum of $19,946.18, appearing an page 323 of the Public Accounts, 1912, was advanced by N. B. Colcock, and the purposes for which the same was advanced. 2. In detail the persons to whom the sum of $11,060.85, appearing on page 372 of the Public Accounts was paid by N. B. Colcock, and the purposes for which the same was paid. Presented to the Legislature, March 3rd, 1914. Mr. *Anderson (Bruce).* *Not Printed.*

No. 61 Copies of Orders-in-Council authorizing payments out of Surrogate of the Counties of York and Simcoe in accordance with the provisions of the Surrogate Courts Act. Presented to the Legislature, March 10th, 1914. *Not Printed.*

No. 62 Return to an Order of the House of the 11th March, 1913, for a Return showing for what Municipalities was the Report of the Lieutenant-Governor in Council in favour of, or against, building an electric railway for such Municipalities. Presented to the Legislature, March 16th, 1914. Mr. *Elliott.* *Printed.*

No. 63 Copies of Orders in Council in accordance with the provisions of sec. 2, cap. 2, 2 George V, An Act for raising money on the Credit of the Consolidated Revenue Fund of Ontario. Presented to the Legislature, March 16th, 1914. *Not Printed.*

No. 64 Return to an Order of the House of the 2nd March, 1914, for a Return showing:—1. What securities have been sold by the Province since October 31st, 1912. 2. What was the date of the sales. 3. What are the names of the purchasers. 4. What are the prices at which such securities were sold. Presented to the Legislature, March 16th, 1914. Mr. *Sinclair.* *Not Printed.*

No. 65 Return to an Order of the House of the 27th February, 1914, for a Return showing:—1. What timber limits, or areas, have been sold by the Government since the first day of January, 1913. and the total area of each. 2. The price at which each such limit, or area, was sold. 3. The names of the respective purchasers and if any were sold at public auction. 4. And if any were so sold at auction, which limit or area was so sold, and the dates on which the several sales took place. Presented to the Legislature, March 18th, 1914. Mr. *Mageau.* *Not Printed.*

66 | Return to an Order of the House of the 6th March, 1914, for a Return showing:—1. Application for license of William Smuck of the Township of Bayham in the electoral district of East Elgin for the year 1913-14; the granting thereof; the withdrawal of such application; all correspondence between the ·Department and any officer thereof and the said Smuck, or the License Inspector or other residents of East Elgin in reference thereto. 2. The application of the said Smuck to be appointed License Inspector for East Elgin, and all protests against his appointment. 3. All letters, reports or communications in reference to the health or work by the former License Inspector, Mr. W. R. Andrews. 4. The resignation of the former License Inspector or Notice of the Termination of his employment. 5. All protests or complaints during the years 1912, 1913 and 1914 from residents of Aylmer or other citizens of East Elgin in reference to the lack of enforcement of the License Law and the conduct of the hotels in Aylmer or of license officials of East Elgin. Presented to the Legislature, March 27th, 1914. Mr. *Rowell. Not Printed.*

. 67 | Minutes of the Proceedings in Conference of the Representatives of the Provinces, October, 1913. Presented to the Legislature, March 19th, 1914. *Printed.*

. 68 | Return to an Order of the House of the 2nd March, 1914, for a Return showing:—1. What amount was received by the Government from Messrs. Taylor, Scott & Co. for the work done by prisoners from Central Prison under its contract with Taylor, Scott & Co., dated 1st September, 1905, for each year during which the contract was in force. 2. How long was the contract in force. 3. What amounts were paid by the Government for debt, damages or costs respectively in connection with or arising out of the said contract. 4. To whom were such amounts paid. 5. Was the agreement between Taylor, Scott & Co. and the Government changed after the agreement had been submitted to the House and approved by it. 6. If it were changed, were such changes embodied in an agreement in writing between the parties. 7. If it was changed, was such change or modified agreement submitted to the House for approval. Presented to the Legislature, March 23rd, 1914. Mr. *Bowman. Not Printed.*

. 69 | Return to an Order of the House of the 18th March, 1914, for a Return showing:—1. The names of the license holders under the Liquor License Act in the City of Toronto for the year from 1st May, 1908, to 1st May, 1909, and the place or places of business in which each license holder carried on business. 2. The names of those license holders under the said Act, and the location of the premises in which they carried on business, whose licenses were cut off or were not renewed in the year

1909 in Toronto. 3. The names of the license holders in Toronto whose licenses were transferred with the approval of the Board of License Commissioners in the years 1909, 1910, 1911, 1912 and 1913; the places in which they carried on business; the names of the persons to whom licenses were transferred; and the locations of the premises in which the persons to whom the licenses were transferred carried on business. Presented to the Legislature, March 23rd, 1914. Mr. *Proudfoot.* *Not Printed.*

No. 70   Return to an Order of the House of the 26th March, 1913, for a Return showing:—1. All the correspondence (including telegrams) passing between the Prime Minister, the Attorney-General, the Minister of Crown Lands or any other member or official of the Government and the Counsel or Solicitors for Keewatin Power Company, or the Counsel or Solicitors for the Hudson's Bay Company with reference to the action brought by these Companies against the Town of Kenora for a declaration that they and not the Crown were the owners of the water power on the East Branch of the Winnipeg River, and that the lease from the Crown to the Town of Kenora was invalid. 2. A copy of the telegram (if any) sent by the Prime Minister to the Counsel for the Keewatin Power Company advising him that the Government did not desire to defend its own title to the water power or be added as a party to the action. 3. All correspondence (including telegrams passing between the Town of Kenora or the Counsel or Solicitors for the Town of Kenora, and the Government or any Minister or official thereof with reference to these actions, and particularly all communications requesting the Crown to take part in the defence of its own title to the water power. 4. Copies of all correspondence (including telegrams) passing between the Prime Minister, Attorney-General, the Minister of Crown Lands or any other Minister or official of the Government, and Mr. W. H. Hearst, acting as Counsel for the Government, in reference to these actions. 5. Copy of the judgments of the Trial Judge and the Court of Appeal. Presented to the Legislature, March 24th, 1914. Mr. *Rowell. Not Printed.*

No. 71   Revised Rules, Orders and Forms of the Division Courts of the Province of Ontario. Presented to the Legislature March 26th, 1914. *Printed.*

No. 72   Correspondence and Papers relating to timber in the Algonquin Park Forest Reserve. Presented to the Legislature, March 27th, 1914. *Printed.*

No. 73   Whitson's Report upon Road Construction in Northern Ontario. Presented to the Legislature, March 30th, 1914. *Printed.*

. 74 | Return to an Order of the House of the 27th February, 1914, for a Return showing:—1. The names of the tenderers for the supply of coal for Government Institutions, in Toronto, during the years 1910, 1911, 1912 and 1913, respectively. 2. The amount of each tender for each of such years. 3. The names of the contractor or contractors for each of such years. 4. The amount of coal supplied under each contract during each year. 5. The prices at which the coal was purchased. Presented to the Legislature, March 31st, 1914. *Mr. Bowman. Not Printed.*

. 75 | Return to an Order of the House of the 27th February for a Return showing:—1. What buildings have been erected by the Province at the Prison Farm at Guelph. 2. What has been the total cost to the Province of each building. 3. Were any of these buildings built by prison labour in whole or in part. 4. If so, what buildings, and what class of prison labour was employed. 5. And if the statement of cost makes any allowance for the prison labour employed, if any. Presented to the Legislature, March 31st, 1914. *Mr. Atkinson. Not Printed.*

. 76 | Return to an Order of the House of the 18th March, 1914, for a Return showing:—1. Whether the Minister of Agriculture or any officer or official of his Department, or the Minister of Education or any officer or official of his Department, communicated with the district representative of Agriculture within the County of Welland with reference to his attitude to the Canada Temperance Act or the vote to be taken thereon on the 29th January last. 2. And if any communication was made, was such communication verbal or in writing. 3. And who was the officer making the same, and what was the date thereof. Presented to the Legislature, March 31st, 1914. *Not Printed.*

. 77 | Return to an Order of the House of the 27th March, 1914, for a Return showing:—1. The conditions upon which grants are made to rural public schools. 2. Were the grants to rural public schools of Ontario in 1913 less per school in 1913 than they were in the year 1912. If so, how much. 3. Has the Department of Education notified the Boards of Public School Trustees of Rural Schools, or any of them, that they cannot pay the grant provided for by the regulations. 4. If such notice has been given, upon what their ground for refusing to pay the grants. 5. Has the Department of Education notified the School Boards of Rural Schools, or any of them, that the grants this year would be cut down 28 *per cent.,* or any amount whatever. If so, how much. Presented to the Legislature, April 1st, 1914. *Mr. Kohler. Not Printed.*

78 | Return to an Order of the House of the 30th March, 1914, for a Return showing:—1. What was the estimated cost of the heating plant for the Toronto University. 2. What was the actual cost of the plant when fully completed. 3. Has the total amount

been paid; if not, what amount, if any, is held in reserve. 4. And if the heating plant is giving satisfaction. Presented to the Legislature, April 1st, 1914. Mr. *Bowman. Not Printed.*

No. 79 Return to an Order of the House of the 1st April, 1914, for a Return of copies of all correspondence, resolutions or other documents received by, or on behalf of any Member of the Government in any way relating to the Hamilton Athletic Association regarding which certain legislation is sought for during the current Session. Presented to the Legislature, April 2nd, 1914. Mr. *Studholme. Not Printed.*

No. 80 Return to an Order of the House of the 1st April, 1914, for a Return showing:—1. What sum of money has Sir William Meredith, the Chief Justice of Ontario, received from the Government in addition to his salary as Chief Justice, since January 1st, 1909, to date. 2. In what capacity did Chief Justice Sir William Meredith receive such sum or sums, and what amount was received with respect to each capacity in which he received any sum or sums as aforesaid. Presented to the Legislature, April 2nd, 1914. Mr. *Anderson (Bruce). Not Printed.*

No. 81 Return to an Order of the House of the 27th March, 1914, for a Return showing:—1. If there was a deficit in the financial operations of the Provincial University for the fiscal year ending 1912. If so, how much. 2. Was there a deficit in the financial operations of the Provincial University for the fiscal year 1913. If so, how much. 3. If there have been deficits during the years 1912-13, or either of them, how have these deficits been provided for. 4. What is the estimated expenditure of the Provincial University for the current fiscal year. 5. What is the estimated revenue of the University for the current fiscal year. Presented to the Legislature, April 2nd, 1914. Mr. *Marshall. Not Printed.*

No. 82 Return to an Order of the House of the 27th March, 1914, for a Return showing:—1. If there was an option given to the firm of Murray, Mather & Co. to purchase certain Government securities during the calendar year 1913. 2. If so, what was the date of the option, and what were the character, amount and price of the securities covered by it. 3. Was such option, if any, exercised; and if so, to what extent. Presented to the Legislature, April 3rd, 1914. Mr. *Sinclair. Not Printed.*

No. 83 Return to an Order of the House of the 27th March, 1914, for a Return showing:—1. Copy of evidence of Mr. Taylor, of Messrs. Taylor, Scott & Co., given before the Dominion Penitentiary Investigation Commission, of which Mr. G. M. Macdonald, K.C., of Kingston, is Chairman, and which was taken in Shorthand by a Stenographer provided by Dr. Gilmour,

Warden of the Central Prison, such evidence or a copy thereof being now in the custody or control of the Provincial Secretary, or of some of the officers or officials of his Department, or of the institutions under the control of his Department. 2. Copies of all correspondence passing between the Provincial Secretary, or any officer or official of his Department, or any officer or official of any of the institutions under the charge of his Department, and Mr. Joseph Downey, in reference to the said evidence or the production thereof. Presented to the Legislature, April 3rd, 1914. Mr. *Bowman. Not Printed.*

. 84 Report of the Good Roads Commission. Presented to the Legislature, April 7th, 1914. *Printed.*

. 85 Copy of an Order-in-Council approved by His Honour the Lieutenant-Governor, under the provisions of 552 of sec. 18 of the Municipal Drainage Act. Presented to the Legislature, April 8th, 1914. *Printed.*

. 86 Return to an Order of the House of the 2nd March, 1913, for a Return showing:—1. Copies of all correspondence between the Minister of Education or any other member or official of the Government and any other person or persons during 1910, 1911 and 1912, relating to the investigation made by Dr. Merchant of the bi-lingual or French-English Schools in Ontario. 2. Copies of all correspondence between the Minister of Education or any other member or official of the Government and any other person or persons during the year 1912, relating to Regulation No. 17. Presented to the Legislature, April 9th, 1914. Mr. *Mageau. Not Printed.*

o. 87 Return to an Order of the House of the 7th April, 1914, for a Return showing:—1. How much the Hydro-Electric Power Commission has spent in building the trunk line from Morrisburg to Prescott, and from Morrisburg to Winchester and Chesterville. 2. Did the Hydro-Electric Power Commission enter into an agreement with the New York and Ontario Power Company, or any person on their behalf, for a supply of power for transmission on this line, to be developed at Waddington or elsewhere; and if so, what is the date of such agreement. 3. Was it a term of any such agreement that the Directors of the New York and Ontario Power Company became personally liable if power was not supplied within a certain defined time. 4. Has the Hydro-Electric Power Commission entered into any agreement with the Rapids Power Company for the supply of power; if so, what is the date of such agreement. Presented to the Legislature, April 9th, 1914. *Not Printed.*

. 88 Coles' Report, Mining Engineer, Timiskaming and Northern Ontario Railway Company. Presented to the Legislature, April 28th, 1914. *Printed.*

No. 89 | Return to an Order of the House of the 8th April, 1914, for a Return showing:—1. The number of convictions for intoxication in Local Option Municipalities. 2. Convictions for other offences against Local Option Law during the license year 1912-13. Presented to the Legislature, April 14th, 1914. Mr. *McPherson*. *Not Printed.*

No. 90 | Official Regulations for the Government of the Andrew Mercer Reformatory. Presented to the Legislature, April 16th, 1914. *Printed.*

No. 91 | Official Regulations for the Government of the Hospitals and Public Charities of Ontario. Presented to the Legislature, April 16th, 1914. *Printed.*

No. 92 | Official Regulations for the Government of Common Gaols of Ontario. Presented to the Legislature, April 16th, 1914. *Printed.*

No. 93 | Official Regulations for the Government of Industrial Farms in Ontario. Presented to the Legislature, April 16th, 1914. *Printed.*

No. 94 | Official Regulations for the Government of the Ontario Reformatory. Presented to the Legislature, April 16th, 1914. *Printed.*

No. 95 | Official Regulations of the Ontario Hospitals. Presented to the Legislature, April 17th, 1914. *Printed.*

No. 96 | Statement of Statute distribution for 1913. Presented to the Legislature, April 21st, 1914. *Not Printed.*

No. 97 | Return to an Order of the House of the 27th March, 1913, for a Return showing:—Copies of all Orders in Council passed under Section 8, of the Power Commission Act, as amended by the Power Commissions Act, 1912. Presented to the Legislature, April 21st, 1914. Mr. *Mageau*. *Not Printed.*

No. 98 | Return to an Order of the House of the 1st April, 1914, for a Return showing:—1. All the schools in the Province, both public and separate, from which the Government grant has been withheld during the years 1912 and 1913 respectively. 2. The grounds upon which such grants have been withheld from the said schools respectively. 3. The grounds upon which County Councils are required to withhold from schools the moneys raised by taxation from the people. Presented to the Legislature, April 21st, 1914. Mr. *Racine*. *Not Printed.*

No. 99   Return to an Order of the House of the Twenty-first day of April
         instant for a Return of a Copy of the Letters, or Charter, of the
         " Ontario Homes Company, Limited," giving the Corporation
         license to promote a company for the purpose of engaging in
         the business of the purchase of real estate in manufacturing
         localities and showing what, if any, returns have been made to
         the Department and if the company is still doing business.
         Presented to the Legislature, April 22nd, 1914. Mr. *Studholme.*
         Not Printed.

No. 100   Return to an Order of the House of the 16th April, 1914, for a
          Return showing:—The quantity of settlers' effects delivered
          over the T. & N. O. Railway at New Liskeard and Cochrane,
          respectively, and carried as such under the regulations of the
          said Railway, for the financial year ending October 31st, 1913.
          Presented to the Legislature, April 24th, 1914. Mr. *Atkinson.*
          Not Printed.

No. 101   Return to an Order of the House of the 17th February, 1913, for
          a Return of: Copies of all correspondence between Bishop
          Fallon, of London, and the Provincial Secretary, the Minister
          of Public Works or any Member of the Government regarding
          the Bi-lingual Schools in the Province of Ontario, since the first
          day of May, 1910. Presented to the Legislature, April 24th,
          1914. Mr. *Evanturel. Not Printed.*

No. 102   Return to an Order of the House of the 17th February, 1913, for a
          Return of Copies of all correspondence between Bishop Scollard,
          of Sault Ste. Marie, and the Government, regarding the
          Bi-lingual Schools of the Province of Ontario, since the first
          day of March, 1907. Presented to the Legislature, April 24th,
          1914. Mr. *Evanturel. Not Printed.*

No. 103   Return to an Order of the House of the 16th April, 1914, for a
          Return showing:—1. All correspondence between the Depart-
          ment of Education and any officer or official thereof and the
          Board of Trustees of the Almonte High School. 2. All corre-
          spondence between the Department of Education and any officer
          or official thereof and any of the teachers in the Almonte High
          School. 3. All correspondence between the Department of Edu-
          cation and any officer or official thereof and Miss Eade with
          reference to an application by her for a position in the Almonte
          High School. Presented to the Legislature, April 28th, 1914.
          Mr. *Marshall. Not Printed.*

No. 104   Return to an Order of the House of the 21st April, 1914, for a
          Return showing:—1. The present practice of the Department
          of Education in regard to the number of text-books authorized
          for use in each subject in the Course of Studies. 2. The number
          of text-books authorized for use in the elementary and secondary

schools of Ontario issued since the date of the last return laid
before this House, March 20th, 1911, and the methods adopted
to keep these books up to the requirements of the schools. 3. The
cost to the Province of each of these books in the form of payments to authors, printers and electrotypers. 4. The estimated
saving to purchasers of all text-books in elementary and second-
ary schools on all the books as compared with previous prices of
the same. 5. The amount annually paid in royalties by the Department of Education to writers of authorized text-books. 6.
The cost to the Province of the preparation, editing, and printing of supplementary readers authorized for use in the schools.
7. The amount paid annually by publishers to any official of
the Department of Education on text-books authorized for use in
the schools of this Province. 8. What Ontario books have
been adopted in other Provinces. Presented to the Legislature,
April 28th. 1914. Mr. *Musgrove. Printed.*

LOAN . CORPORATIONS STATEMENTS

BEING

FINANCIAL STATEMENTS MADE BY

BUILDING SOCIETIES, LOAN COMPANIES, LOANING LAND
COMPANIES, AND TRUSTS COMPANIES

FOR THE YEAR ENDING

31st DECEMBER, 1913.

PRINTED BY ORDER OF
THE LEGISLATIVE ASSEMBLY OF ONTARIO

TORONTO:
Printed and Published by L. K. CAMERON, Printer to the King's Most Excellent Majesty
1914

Printed by
WILLIAM BRIGGS,
29-37 Richmond Street West,
TORONTO.

To His Honour Sir JOHN MORISON GIBSON, Knight Commander of the Most Distinguished Order of St. Michael and St. George, a Colonel in the Militia of Canada, etc., etc., etc., Lieutenant-Governor of the Province of Ontario.

MAY IT PLEASE YOUR HONOUR:

The undersigned has the honour to present to your Honour the Report of the Registrar of Loan Corporations for the Province of Ontario for the year ended 31st December 1913.

Respectfully submitted,

J. J. FOY,

Attorney-General.

Toronto, 2nd April, 1914.

To the Honourable J. J. Foy, K.C., M.P.P., etc.,

Attorney-General,

Toronto.

Sir,—I have the honour to present herewith the sixteenth Report of the Annual Statements made by Loan Corporations under the Act (Loan and Trust Corporations Act, 2 Geo. V., Chap. 34). Prefixed to these statements-will be found a copy of the official blank form.

The Companies included in the Report are classified (as in the Act) into:

Loan Companies.

Loaning Land Companies.

Trusts Companies.

The Loan Companies forming the first mentioned class are further subdivided into:

A. Companies having only permanent stock.

B. Companies having terminating as well as permanent stock, or having withdrawable stock only.

I have the honour to be, Sir,

Your obedient servant,

A. R. Boswell,

Registrar of Loan Corporations.

Parliament Buildings.
Toronto, 30th March, 1914.

[4]

CONTENTS

[5]

NOTE

Section 112 of The Loan and Trust Corporations Act (R.S.O. 1914, Chap. 184) provides as follows:—

112.—(1) No corporation shall under the penalty of becoming disentitled to registry or of having its registry suspended or cancelled make, print, publish, circulate, authorise or be a party or privy to the making, printing, publishing, or circulating of any statement or representation that its solvency or financial standing is vouched for by the Registrar or that the publication of its statement in his report is a warranty or representation of the solvency of the corporation, or of the truth or accuracy of such statement in any particular.

FORM OF ANNUAL STATEMENTS

SUPPLIED TO LOAN CORPORATIONS FOR PURPOSES OF THIS REPORT.

[7]

FORM OF ANNUAL STATEMENT.

The following is a copy of the form supplied to each Loan Corporation for purposes of its Annual Statement for the year ending 31st December, 1913.

[The Annual Statement and Duplicate (each duly completed, with its schedules) are to be filed with the Registrar of Loan Corporations for Ontario (Department of Insurance, Parliament Buildings), Toronto, on or before the *first day of March, 1914*, subject to a penalty of $50 for each day of default in filing, as provided by *The Loan and Trusts Corporations Act*, R.S.O., 1914, Chap. 184, Section 110. In each of the statements there should be enclosed a certified copy of any statement or statements made by the Directors to the Shareholders during or relating to the year 1913, including a certified copy of the Auditors' Report. Ibid., Secs. 103, 110 (6); Also copies of all notices calling general meetings of the corporation during such year.]

[The above duplicates should be accompanied by a cheque for $5 (filing fee) drawn payable to the Provincial Treasurer of Ontario.]

ANNUAL STATEMENT

Of the condition and affairs of the (Name of Corporation) ....of..................
at the 31st December, 1913, and for the year ending on that day, made to the Registrar of Loan Corporations for the Province of Ontario, pursuant to the laws of the said Province.

The Corporation was incorporated under the laws of..................on the ....
day of ....18..................

The Head Office of the Corporation is at No. ....(Name of Street)..........in the (City, Town or Village)..................of..................in the (Province, State, etc.)..................of..................

The Chief Agency for Ontario (if Corporation's Head Office is elsewhere than in Ontario) is situate at No. ....(Name of Street) ....Street in the (City, Town, etc.)..........of..................in the Province of Ontario.

The Chief Agent and Attorney for Ontario (if Corporation's Head Office is elsewhere than in Ontario) is (Name)..................and his address is..................in the Province of Ontario.

The Board is constituted of............Directors, holding office for the term of..........years.

The Directors and Chief Executive Officers of the Corporation at the 31st December, 1913, were as follows:

NAMES OF DIRECTORS AND CHIEF EXECUTIVE OFFICERS.	DESIGNATION OF OFFICE.	ADDRESS.	CURRENT TERM OF OFFICE.	
			Began (Date).	Will end (Date).
	President Vice-President Directors Manager Secretary			

A. Permanent Capital Stock: Total amount authorised, $ .... Total amount subscribed, $ ....
as more particularly set out in Schedule A hereto. (Page 7 of this form.)

B. Terminating or Withdrawable Stock.

SUBSCRIBED SHARES OF TERMINATING OR WITHDRAWABLE STOCK.	FULLY PAID.		PREPAID.		INSTALMENT.		Total.
	No.	Amount.	No.	Amount.	No.	Amount.	
Number and amount in force at 31st December, 1912							
" " issued during 1913							
Gross total in force at any time in 1913							

	No. of shares.	Amount					
Deduct as follows: Withdrawn and paid off during 1913. Retired by Corporation during 1913. Converted into Permanent Stock during 1913							
Forfeited and lapsed during 1913							
Total deductions							

Net total remaining in force at 31st December, 1913........

Summary of Terminating or Withdrawable Stock in force 31st December, 1913.

Totals as above. No. of Shareholders Of which there has been credited to loan fund.

Shares Fully Paid Stock at......$ per Share....$ on which Shareholders have paid in $
Shares "Prepaid" Stock (other than above) ....$ per Share....$ on which " " paid $
Shares Instalment Stock (payable by fixed periodical payments) at $ per Share....$ on which " " paid $

Totals..................
Total amount distributed or credited to Terminating or Withdrawable Stock in 1913.
(1) As interest ....$
Rate of such interest, per cent. per annum ....
(2) As dividends out of profits ....$
Rate or rates per cent. of such dividends ....

[9]

BALANCE SHEET AS AT 31st DECEMBER, 1913.

Dr.   CAPITAL AND LIABILITIES.

CAPITAL (LIABILITIES TO STOCKHOLDERS OR SHAREHOLDERS).

	$	c.	$	c.

Item No.

*A.—Permanent Capital Stock or Shares.

1. (a) Ordinary Joint Stock Capital, fully called: Total called, $........Total paid thereon.
2. (b) Ordinary Joint Stock Capital, ...% called: Total called, $.......Total paid thereon.
3. (c) Ordinary Joint Stock Capital, ...% called: Total called, $.......Total paid thereon.
    (cc) Joint Stock Capital paid in advance of calls†
4. (d) Dividends declared in respect of (1), (2) or (3), but not yet paid
5. (e) Unappropriated profits in respect of (1), (2) or (3)
6. (f) Reserve Fund in respect of (1), (2) or (3)
7. (g) Contingent Fund in respect of (1), (2) or (3)
8. (h) Instalment Permanent Stock (payable by fixed periodical payments): Total subscribed, $.... on which has been paid
9. (i) Dividends declared on (8), but not yet paid
10. (j) Unappropriated profits on (8)
11. (k) Reserve Fund in respect of (8)
12. (l) Contingent Fund in respect of (8)
13. (m) Instalments or premiums on (8), paid in advance†

NOTE.—Liabilities reported in 1912 under A, but written off in 1913 (not extended), $.....................

*B.—Terminating Capital Stock or Shares.

14. (a) Fully paid stock, less shown in (24): Total in force....shares at $.... per share carried to Loan Fund
15. (b) Profits or accrued interest on (14), less shown in (25) and credited or appropriated but not yet paid
16. (c) Profits or accrued interest on (14), less shown in (25), and not credited or appropriated
17. (d) Prepaid Stock, less shown in (24): Total in force....shares at $....per share, on which has been paid into Loan Fund
18. (e) Profits or accrued interest on (17), less shown in (25) and credited or appropriated, but not yet paid
19. (f) Profits or accrued interest on (17), less shown in (25), and not credited or appropriated
20. (g) Instalment Stock, less shown in (24): Total issue now in force....shares at $....per share, on which has been paid in all $....of which sum there has been paid into the Loan Fund
21. (h) Profits or accrued interest on (20), less shown in (25), and credited or appropriated, but not yet paid
22. (i) Profits or accrued interest on (20), less shown in (25), and not credited or appropriated
23. (j) Instalments or premiums paid on (20). in advance†

NOTE.—Liabilities reported in 1912 under B, but written off in 1913 (not extended), $.....................

24, 25. Liability in respect of Terminating Stock or Shares (Fully paid, Prepaid or Instalment), other than shown in (14), (17) and (20), as to which the Corporation has received notice of withdrawal, but at 31st December, 1913, has not been paid off, viz.:
24. Principal sum due by Corporation
25. Interest, Profits or Dividends due by Corporation

C.—Liabilities to Stockholders or Shareholders other than as shown under A or B, viz.:
26. ....

LIABILITIES TO THE PUBLIC.

27. Deposits (including unclaimed deposits). Right reserved to require 30 days' notice on any withdrawal
28. Interest on deposits, due or accrued, or capitalised
    (a) Interest due or accrued on 3 (cc); or on 13 (m); or on 23 (j)
29. Debentures issued in Canada
30. Interest due and accrued on (29)
31. Debentures issued elsewhere than in Canada
32. Interest due and accrued on (31)
33. Debenture Stock issued in Canada
34. Interest due and accrued on (33)
35. Debenture Stock issued elsewhere than in Canada
36. Interest due and accrued on (35)
37. Owing to Banks (including interest due or accrued)
38. Due on Bills payable other than (37), including interest due or accrued..
39. Due on Loans in process of completion or to pay assumed mortgages......
40. Unclaimed dividends (enclosing memo giving names and amounts)
41. Other liabilities to the public, viz.:
42.   (a) ....
43.   (b) ....
44.   (c) ....
    Total actual liabilities ....

N.B.—Section I. (showing liabilities for which the Corporation is absolutely liable) is to be balanced independently of Section II. (which shows contingent liabilities).

BALANCE SHEET AS AT 31st DECEMBER, 1913.—*Continued.*

DR.—*Continued.*

	$	c.	$	c.
CONTINGENT LIABILITIES.				
45. Claims against the Corporation not acknowledged as debts, viz.:				
46. (a)				
47. (b)				
48. (c)				
49. Money for which the Corporation is contingently liable, viz.:				
50. (a) Principal guaranteed				
51. (b) Interest guaranteed				
52. (c) Trust Funds invested, but not guaranteed:				
53. 1. Principal				
54. 2. Interest				
55. (d) Trust Funds uninvested, not bearing interest and not guaranteed..				
56. (e) Other contingent liabilities				
Total Contingent Liabilities				
NOTE.—Contingent liabilities reported in 1912, but written off in 1913 (not extended).				
Gross Total Liabilities, Actual and Contingent				

* Increase or decrease of authorised Permanent Capital Stock in 1913....
Authority for said increase or decrease ....
† Under what authority, and upon what terms have such advances been received by Company? Ans..

CR.

I.—ASSETS OF WHICH THE CORPORATION IS THE BENEFICIAL OWNER.	$	c.	$	c.
A. Immovable Property Owned Beneficially by the Corporation:				
Item No.				
1. (a) Office premises situated as follows:				
2. (I) At ....held in freehold..........				
3. (II) At ....held in hold..........				
4. (III) At ....held in hold..........				
5. (b) Freehold land (including buildings) other than foregoing *				
6. (c) Leasehold land (including buildings) other than foregoing *				
7. (d)				
8. (e)				
B. Debts secured by Mortgages of Land.				
9. (a) Debts (other than item 10) secured by mortgages of land				
10. (b) Debts secured by mortgaged land held for sale †..................				
(bb) Debts secured by land held by the Company as Mortgagee in possession, or secured by land for the rents and profits of which the Company is accountable				
11. (c) Interest due or accrued on items 9 and 10, and not included therein †..				
12. (d) Of the debts mentioned in items 9, 10 and 11, the sum of $....... is due by directors or officers of the Corporation (not extended), $....				
C. Debts not above enumerated, for which the Corporation holds securities, as follows:				
13. (a) Debts secured by accepted Bills of Exchange				
14. (b) Debts secured by Municipal Bonds or Debentures				
15. (c) Debts secured by Public School Debentures				
16. (d) Debts secured by Loan Corporations' Debentures				
17. (e) Debts secured by Dominion Government Stock or Bonds				
18. (f) Debts secured by Stock or Bonds of any of the Provinces of Canada..				
19. (g) Debts secured by Stock or Bonds of other Governments				
20. (h) Debts secured only by Permanent Stock or Shares of the Corporation‡..				
21. (i) Debts secured only by Terminating Stock or Shares of the Corporation..				
22. (j) Debts secured by				
23. (k) Debts secured by				
24. (l) Debts secured by } Particulars given in Schedule I., page 5b.				
25. (m) Debts secured by				
26. (n) Interest due or accrued on items 14 to 25, and not included therein.....				
D. Unsecured Debts.				
27. (a)				
28. (b)				
29. (c)				
30. (d) Interest due or accrued on items 27 to 29, and not included therein....				

BALANCE SHEET AS AT 31st DECEMBER, 1913.

Ox.—Continued.

	$	c.	$	c.
I.—ASSETS OF WHICH THE CORPORATION IS THE BENEFICIAL OWNER.—Con.				
E. Cash.				
81. (a) On hand				
82. (b) In bank as follows :—				
83. (I) In the...................Bank at				
84. (II) In the...................Bank at				
85. (III) In the...................Bank at				
86. (IV) In the...................Bank at				
F. Assets not herein before mentioned.				
87. (a)				
88. (b)				
89. (c) .... Particulars given in Schedule I. p. 5b				
40. (d)				
41. (e)				
42. (f)				
Total of assets owned beneficially by Corporation				
Note.—Assets reported in 1912, but written off in 1913 (not extended) $..............				
N.B.—Section I. (containing assets of which the Corporation is beneficial owner) is to be balanced independently of Section II. (containing assets not so owned).				
II. ASSETS NOT OWNED BENEFICIALLY BY CORPORATION, BUT FOR WHICH THE CORPORATION IS ACCOUNTABLE.				
A. As Guarantor				
(a) Mortgage securities :—				
43. (I) Principal.........				
44. (II) Interest due and accrued...........................				
(b) Other securities :—				
45. (I) Principal.				
46. (II) Interest due and accrued.....................................				
B. As Trustee, Representative, Guardian or Agent (without Guarantee).				
(a) Mortgage securities :—				
47. (I) Principal..............				
48. (II) Interest due and accrued....................				
(b) Other securities :—				
49. (I) Principal..............				
50. (II) Interest due and accrued.................... ...:				
51. (c) Unsecured debts........................				
52. (d) Uninvested Trust Funds...................................				
Total Assets II...................				
Note.—Assets reported in 1912, but written off in 1913 (not extended) $..............				
Gross Total of Assets I and II				

* Embracing properties vested in the Company by foreclosure, or by conveyance, or under quit-claim deed.

† Including rent of properties held under power of sale.

‡ As to limit of such loans, see Loan and Trust Corp. Act, R.S.O. 1914, chap. 184.

CASH ACCOUNT.
RECEIPTS FOR THE YEAR ENDING 31st DECEMBER, 1913.

	Amount carried to earnings, maintenance, or contingent account. (Column 1.)		Amount carried to Capital Account.					
1.—RECEIVED BY THE CORPORATION FOR ITS OWN USE.			Terminating Capital. (Column 2.)		Permanent Capital, including Reserve. (Column 3.)		Total. (Column 4.)	
A.—Balances from 31st December, 1912.	$	c.	$	c.	$	c.	$	c.

Item No.
1. Cash...
2.   (i) On hand.....................................
3.   (ii) In bank ....

   B.—Sums received Wholly or Partly on Capital Stock.

4. (a) Calls on Joint Stock Permanent Capital..................
  (aa) Joint Stock Capital received in advance of calls ....
5. (b) Premiums on (4)..........................
6. (c) Sales of fully paid Building Society Stock ....
7. (d) Sales of prepaid Building Society Stock ....
8. (e) Dues on Instalment Building Society Stock.............
9. (f) Premiums on (6), (7) and (8)...........................

   C.—Receipts on Account of Investments, Loans or Debts.

  (a) On Mortgages of Realty:
10.   (i) Principal.................................
11.   (ii) Interest.................................
  (b) On other securities:
12.   (i) Principal.................................
13.   (ii) Interest or dividends......................
  (c) Unsecured debts:
14.   (i) Principal.................................
15.   (ii) Interest ....

   D.—Receipts from Real Estate Owned Beneficially by Corporation.

16. (a) Sales (not included in any of the foregoing items)............
17. (b) Rents †.......................................

   E.—Miscellaneous.

18. (a) Commission, Brokerage (or Remuneration as Corporate Agents, Trustees, etc.)..........................
19. (b) Premium or Bonus on Loans......................
20. (c) Membership or Entry Fees (being income of Corporation)....
21. (d) Fines.......................................
22. (e) Forfeiture or Lapses. (Extend into Column 1)............
23. (f) Revivals of Terminating Stock. (Extend into Column 2)....
24. (g) Conversion of Terminating Stock into Permanent Stock. (Extend into Column 3)..........................

   F.—Borrowed Money.

25. (a) Bank or other advances, discounts or overdrafts. ....
26. (b) Borrowed by taking deposits........................
27. (c) Borrowed on Debentures..........................
28. (d) Borrowed on Debenture Stock......................
29. (e) Borrowed otherwise, viz.:—

   G.—Receipts from Other Sources, viz.:

30. (a)..
  (b)..
  (c)..

    Totals..

* Under what authority and upon what terms have such advances been received by company ?

Ans..

† Includes rents of property acquired by purchase or exchange, or by foreclosure, or by quit claim deed.

RECEIPTS FOR THE YEAR ENDING 31st DECEMBER, 1913.—*Continued.*

	Amount carried to earnings, maintenance or contingent account.	Carried to Capital Account.	Total.

N.B.—Section I. (showing cash received by the Corporation for its own use) is to be balanced independently of Section II. (showing cash received as corporate trustee, etc.)

II.—RECEIVED AS CORPORATE TRUSTEE, REPRESENTATIVE, GUARDIAN OR AGENT, IN TRUST.

A.—Balance from 31st December, 1912.

Item No.			$	c	$	c.
31.	(a) Capital Account..........					
	(b) Cash (not included in 31)...........					
32.	(i) On hand...........					
33.	(ii) In bank...........					

B.—Received on Account of Investments, Loans or Debts:—

34.	(a) On Mortgages: Principal, $........... Interest, $...........
35.	(b) On other securities: Principal, $........... Interest, $...........
36.	(c) On Unsecured Debts: Principal, $........... Interest, $...........

C.—Receipts from Real Estate.

| 37. | (a) Sales (not included in foregoing items)........... |
| 38. | (b) Rents †........... |

D.—Receipts from Other Sources, viz.:

39.	(a).....
40.	(b)...........
41.	(c)...........

Totals...........

† Includes rents of property acquired by purchase or exchange, or by foreclosure, or by quit claim deed.

CASH ACCOUNT.

EXPENDITURE FOR THE YEAR ENDING 31st DECEMBER, 1913.

I.—EXPENDED ON CORPORATION ACCOUNT. A.—Sums Loaned or Invested on Capital Account.	Amount carried to earnings, maintenance or contingent account. (Column 1.)		Amount carried to Capital Account.		Total. (Column 4.)	
			Terminating Capital. (Column 2.)	Permanent Capital, including Reserve. (Column 3.)		
Item. No.	$	c.	$ c.	$ c.	$	c.
1. (a) Loaned on Mortgages of Realty (including Item 7 (e) if no separate account therefor)						
(b) Loaned on or invested in other Securities, viz.:						
2. (i)						
3. (ii)						
4. (iii)						
5. (iv)						
6. (c) Real Estate purchased						
7. (d) Incumbrance on Realty paid off						
(e) Insurance or taxes advanced on property mortgaged to the Corporation						
B.—Expended on Stock Account.						
8. Dividends paid on Permanent Stock. (Extend into Col. 1).— (a) Interest paid on Joint Stock Capital received in advance of calls. (Extend into Column 1)						
9. Dividends paid on Terminating Stock. (Extend into Col. 1)						
10. Interest paid on Terminating Stock. (Extend into Col. 1).						
11. Paid for Terminating Stock withdrawn. (Extend into Col. 1 or 2 or divide between 1 and 2 as the case may be).						
12. Paid for Terminating Stock matured. (Extend as in 11).						
13. Profits paid on (11) and (12). (Extend as in 11).						
14. Paid for Terminating Stock retired. (Extend into Col. 2)						
15. Terminating Stock forfeited or lapsed. (Extend into Col. 2)						
16. Terminating Stock converted into Permanent. (Extend into Column 2)						
17. Terminating Stock revived. (Extend into Col. 1)						
C.—Borrowed money (other than foregoing) or interest thereon Paid, viz.:						
18. (a) Bank Account (Principal and Interest)						
19. (b) Deposits Principal, $............Interest, $....						
20. (c) Debentures issued in Canada: Principal, $....Interest						
21. (d) Debentures issued elsewhere: Principal, $....Interest, $						
22. (e) Debenture Stock issued in Canada: Principal, $..... Interest, $						
23. (f) Debenture Stock issued elsewhere: Principal, $...... Interest, $						
24. (g) Guarantees paid: Principal, $........Interest, $.....						
D.—Management Expenses (other than foregoing):						
25. (a) Salaries, Wages and Fees						
26. (b) Commission or Brokerage						
27. (c) Advances to Agents						
28. (d) Stationery, Postage, Printing and Advertising						
29. (e) Law Costs						
30. (f) Fuel, Rent, Taxes (other than in 7 and 32) and Rates.						
31. (g) Travelling Expenses						
32. (h) Registration Fees						
33. (i) Other Management Expenditure						
E.—Other Expenditures, viz.:						
34. (a)						
35. (b)						
36. (c)						
F.—Balance.	$	c.				
37. (a) Cash on hand						
(b) Cash in various banks as follows:						
38. (i)						
39. (ii)						
40. (iii)						
41. (iv)						
Totals						

N.B.—Section I. (showing cash paid by the Corporation for its own debts) is to be balanced independently of Section II. (showing cash paid as Corporate Trustees, etc.)

EXPENDITURE FOR THE YEAR ENDING 31st DECEMBER, 1913.—*Continued.*

II.—EXPENDED ON TRUST OR AGENCY ACCOUNT. A.—Loaned or invested on Capital Account.	Amount carried to earnings, maintenance or contingent account.		Amount carried to capital account.		Total.	
Item. No.	$.	c	$	c.	$	c
42. (a) Loaned on Mortgages of Realty....................						
(b) Loaned or invested on, or in other securities, viz.:						
43. (i)						
44. (ii)						
45. (iii)						
46. (iv)						
47. (a) Real Estate purchased						
(b) Incumbrances on Realty paid off, viz.:						
48. (i) Principal						
49. (ii) Interest						
B.—Other Expenditures.						
50. (a) Commission or Remuneration paid for Management of Estate, Trust or Agency (including item 26)						
51. (b) Rent, Taxes and Rates						
52. (c) Debts or obligations wholly or partly paid: Principal, $......Interest, $....................						
53. (d)						
C.—Balance.	$	c.				
54. (a) Cash on hand						
55. (b) Cash in various banks, as follows:						
55. (i)						
56. (ii)						
57. (iii)						
Totals						

SCHEDULE I.

PARTICULARS OF CERTAIN ASSETS. (Supra p. 3.)

Assets (Items No. 22 to 25; and No. 37 to 42).

Miscellaneous Statement for the year ending 31st December, 1913.

1. Amount of Debentures maturing in 1914: Issued in Canada, $............
   Issued elsewhere, $............
2. Amount of other existing obligations which will mature in 1914, $............,....
3. Amount of Securities held by the Corporation which will mature and become payable to the Corporation in 1914, $............
4. Average rate of interest per annum paid by the Corporation during 1913, on deposits...........on debentures..........on debenture stock...........
5. Average rate of interest per annum received by the Corporation during 1913:
   (a) On mortgages of realty, (b) on other securities:
   (i) Owned beneficially by the Corporation (a).........(b)........
   (ii) Not owned beneficially (a)...........(b)........
6. Of the mortgages owned beneficially by the Corporation, $.........is on realty situate in Ontario, and $.........is on realty situate elsewhere.
7. Of the mortgages not owned beneficially by the Corporation, $......... is on realty situate in Ontario, and $........... is on realty situate elsewhere.
8. Loans written off or transferred to real estate account during 1913: (i) funds or securities owned beneficially, $.......... (ii) not so owned, $.........
9. Number and aggregate amount of mortgages upon which compulsory proceedings have been taken by the Corporation in 1913:
   (i) Owned beneficially, No...........Amount, $............
   (ii) Not so owned, No.............Amount, $............
10. Aggregate market value of land mortgaged to the Corporation:
    (i) Mortgages owned beneficially.........(ii) Not so owned.......
11. How often are the securities held by the Corporation valued?
12. (a) Specify the officers of the Corporation who are under bond, and for what sum respectively

    (b) Are the said bonds executed by private sureties or by Guarantee Companies?
13. Date when the accounts of the Corporation were last audited?
14. Names and addresses of the auditors respectively for 1913 and for 1914 (if appointed). For 1913...........For 1914
15. What were the dividend days of the Corporation in 1913, and what rate or rates of dividend were paid on those days respectively?
16. What is the date appointed for the Annual Meeting?
    Date of last Annual Meeting?
17. Special General Meetings held in 1913: Dates

County of

We,   , President, and   , Secretary.
of the Loan Corporation known as
severally make oath and say, and each for himself says, that we are the above described
officers of the above Corporation, and that we have each of us individually the means of
verifying the correctness of the Statement within and above contained of the affairs of
the said Corporation, and that on the 31st December, 1913, the issues and holdings of
the Capital Stock of the said Corporation were as shown on the Schedule "A" hereto
annexed, also that all the within described assets were the absolute property of the said
Corporation, free and clear from any liens or claims thereon, except as hereinbefore
stated, and that the statement of the unclaimed balances as set forth on page 5a is correct in every particular, and, we are satisfied that the said statement, with the schedules
and explanations herein contained and hereunto annexed, are a full and correct exhibit
of all the liabilities and assets, and of the income and expenditure, and of the general
condition and affairs of the said Corporation on the 31st day of December, 1913, and
for the year ending on that day; also that the said Statement was on the   day
of   191   , at a meeting of the Board of Directors of
the said Corporation, held on that day, considered by the said Board, and was, by a
Resolution duly passed in that behalf, adopted as the Statement of the said Board, a
certified copy of which Resolution is hereinbelow indorsed.

Sworn before me at the
in the County of
this   day of
A.D. 1914.

....*President*

....*Secretary*

....

....

CERTIFIED COPY OF RESOLUTION.

Referred to in Foregoing Affidavit—R.S.O. 1914, Chap. 184, S. 110 (2).

I, undersigned, the ....of the....................
hereby certify that at a meeting of the Board of Directors of the said Corporation held
at .... on the .... day of .... 19....
the following Resolution was passed (pursuant to the statute in that behalf) adopting
the Statement within and above made as the Statement of the said Board.

Moved by ...., seconded by ....and
Resolved that the Statement of the Company for the year ending the thirty-first day of
December, made to the Registrar of Loan Corporations and to be verified by the affidavit
of ....as President, and ....
as Secretary of the said Company .... be and the same is this
.... day of .... adopted as the Statement of the Board
of directors of the said Company pursuant to the enactment in that behalf of the Province
of Ontario, R.S.O. 1914, Chap. 184, S. 110 (2).

....

....

Attach to this Annual Statement a certified copy of each notice calling a General
Meeting of the Corporation during the year ending 31st December, 1913, and a certified
copy of the Statement or Statements furnished to Shareholders during or relating to the
said year; also a certified copy of Auditors' Report—*Loan and Trust Corporations Act,*
R.S.O. 1914, Chap. 184, sections 103, and 110 (6).

2 L.C.

I. LOAN COMPANIES

DETAILED REPORTS OF THE SEVERAL COMPANIES

THE BROCKVILLE LOAN AND SAVINGS COMPANY, LIMITED.

Head Office, Brockville, Ontario.

CONSTATING INSTRUMENTS.

Incorporated by declaration filed 11th May, 1885, with the Clerk of the Peace for the United Counties of Leeds and Grenville. The declaration was made by virtue of the "Building Societies Act," R.S.O. 1877, c. 164, continued by R.S.O. 1887, c. 169, and superseded by 60 V. c. 38 (O.), now R.S.O. 1897, c. 205.

The lending and borrowing powers are derived from the above public General Acts

---

ANNUAL STATEMENT

Of the condition and affairs of the Brockville Loan and Savings Company, Limited, of Brockville, Ontario, at the 31st December, 1913, and for the year ending on that day, made to the Registrar of Loan Corporations for the Province of Ontario, pursuant to the laws of the said Province.

The head office of the Corporation is at No. 4 Court House Avenue, in the Town of Brockville, in the Province of Ontario.

The Board is constituted of seven directors, holding office for one year.

The directors and chief executive officers of the Corporation at the 31st December, 1913, were as follows, together with their respective terms of office:

W. H. Cole, President, Brockville; February 5th, 1913; February 4th, 1914.
D. W. Downey, Vice-President, Brockville; " "
W. A. Gilmour, Director, Brockville; " "
D. Derbyshire, Director, Brockville;
John H. Fulford, Director, Brockville;
Edwin Abbott, Director, Brockville;
L. C. Dargavel, Managing-Director, Brockville; "
L. Sturgeon, Secretary-Treasurer, Brockville; "

A. Permanent capital stock; total amount authorized, $500,000; total amount subscribed, $350,000, as more particularly set out in Schedule A hereto.

SCHEDULE A.

Class I.—Fixed and Permanent Capital Stock created by virtue of Building Society Acts.

Last call made: Date 30th June, 1903; rate per cent., 10 per cent.
Gross amount, $35,000; amount paid thereon, $21,862.50.

Description.	No. of shares.	Par value.	Total amount held.	Total amount paid thereon.	Total remaining unpaid and constituting an asset of the Corporation.
		$	$	$ c.	$ c.
2. 60 per cent. called	7,000	50	350,000	194,945 00	113,707 50
4. Paid in advance of calls	....	....	....	41,347 50	....
Totals..............	7,000	50	350,000	236,292 50	113,707 50

LIST OF SHAREHOLDERS AS AT 31st DECEMBER, 1913.

(Not printed.)

BALANCE SHEET AS AT 31st DECEMBER, 1913.

Dr.   **Capital and Liabilities.**

Capital (Liabilities to Stockholders or Shareholders.)

A.—Permanent Capital Stock or Shares.

2. (b) Ordinary joint stock capital, 60 per cent. called; total called, $210,000.00; total paid thereon	$194,945	00
3. (cc) Joint stock capital paid in advance of calls........	41,347	50
4. (d) Dividends declared in respect of (2) and (3), but not yet paid	7,047	27
6. (f) Reserve fund in respect of (2) and (3)	56,000	00
7. (g) Contingent fund in respect of (2) and (3)	1,510	01
	$300,849	78

Liabilities to the Public.

27. Deposits, right reserved to require 30 days' notice in any withdrawal, including interest to December 31st, 1913	$256,415	21
37. Owing to banks (including interest due or accrued).....	44,622	22
	301,037	43
Total liabilities	$601,887	21

Cr.   **Assets.**

I.—Assets of which the Corporation is the Beneficial Owner.

B.—Debts secured by Mortgages of Land.

9. (a) Debts (other than item 10) secured by mortgages of land	$552,361	61
10. (b) Debts secured by mortgaged land held for sale......	2,861	31
11. (c) Interest due and accrued on items 9 and 10 and not included therein	39,677	36
	$594,900	28

C.—Debts not above enumerated for which the Corporation holds securities, as follows:

20. (h) Debts secured only by Permanent Stock or Shares of the Corporation	5,278	23

E.—Cash.

31. (a) On hand	1,427	95

F.—Assets not hereinbefore mentioned.

37. (a) Office furniture	280	75
Total assets	$601,887	21

CASH ACCOUNT.

Receipts for the year ending 31st December, 1913.

· Received by the Corporation for its Own Use.

A.—Balance from 31st December, 1912.

2.	(1) On hand	$1,291 87

B.—Sums Received Wholly or Partly on Capital Stock.

4. (a) Calls on Joint Stock Permanent Capital:	(aa) Joint stock capital received in advance of calls	8,430 00

C.—Receipts on account of Investments, Loans or Debts.

(a) On Mortgages of Realty:

10.	(i) Principal	49,893 51
11.	(ii) Interest	37,859 58

(b) On other securities:

12.	(i) Principal stock loans	2,200 00
13.	(ii) Interest	142 92

F.—Borrowed Money.

25. (a) Bank or other advances, discounts or overdrafts		44,622 22
26. (b) Borrowed by taking deposits		322,483 10

G.—Receipts from other Sources.

30. (a) Rent safety deposit boxes		$20 50	
(b) Interest on bank balances		497 05	
			517 55
Total			$467,440 75

CASH ACCOUNT.

Expenditure for the year ending 31st December, 1913.

I.—Expended on Corporation Account.

A.—Sums Loaned or Invested on Capital Account.

	Total (Col. 4).
1. (a) Loaned on mortgages of realty	$156,453 78
(b) Loaned or invested in other securities:	
2. (1) On permanent stock	4,100 00

B.—Expended on Stock Account.

8. Dividends paid on permanent stock	13,758 74

C.—Borrowed money (other than foregoing) or interest thereon paid, viz.:

18. (a) Bank account: Principal, $6,760.13; interest, $520.97	7,281 10
19. (b) Deposits: Principal, $268,864.63, and interest, $9,331.46	278,196 09

CASH ACCOUNT.—Continued.

Expenditure for the year ending 31st December, 1913.

D.—Management Expenses (other than foregoing).

25. (a) Salaries, wages and fees	$3,017 49	
26. (b) Commission or brokerage	1,346 70	
27. (c) Auditors' fees	240 00	
28. (d) Stationery, postage, printing and advertising	436 26	
29. (e) Law costs	128 18	
30. (f) Fuel, rent, taxes (other than in 7 and 32) and rates..	442 84	
31. (g) Travelling expenses	130 10	
32. (h) Registration fees	203 20	
33. (i) Other management expenditure	276 32	
		$6,223 09

F.—Balance.

37. (a) Cash on hand		1,427 95
Total		$467,440 75

MISCELLANEOUS STATEMENT FOR THE YEAR ENDING 31ST DECEMBER, 1913.

1. Amount of debentures maturing in 1914: Issued in Canada, none. Issued elsewhere, none.
2. Amount of other existing obligations which will mature in 1914, none.
3. Amount of securities held by the Corporation which will mature and become payable to the Corporation in 1914, none.
4. Average rate of interest per annum paid by the Corporation during 1913: On deposits, 4%; on debentures, none; on debenture stock, no debentures issued.
5. Average rate of interest per annum received by the Corporation during 1913:
    (a) On mortgages of realty; (b) On other securities.
    (i) Owned beneficially by the Corporation: (a) 7%; (b) 6%.
    (ii) Not owned beneficially: (a) All owned beneficially.
6. Of the mortgages owned beneficially by the Corporation, $594,900.28 is on realty situate in Ontario, and none is on realty situate elsewhere.
7. Of the mortgages not owned beneficially by the Corporation, none is on realty situate in Ontario, and none is on realty situate elsewhere. All owned beneficially.
8. Loans written off or transferred to real estate account during 1913, viz.:
    (i) Funds or securities owned beneficially, $300.72.
    (ii) Not so owned. All owned beneficially.
9. Number and aggregate amount of mortgages upon which compulsory proceedings have been taken by the Corporation in 1913, viz:
    (i) Owned beneficially, No. 9; amount, $8,247.96.
    (ii) Not so owned, none; amount, none.
10. Aggregate market value of land mortgaged to the Corporation:
    (i) Mortgages owned beneficially, $1,000,000.00.
    (ii) Not so owned, none.
11. How often are the securities held by the Corporation valued? Yearly.
12. (a) Specify the officers of the Corporation who are under bond and for what sum respectively: Managing Director, $10,000.00; Secretary-Treasurer, $3,000.00.
    (b) Are the said bonds executed by private sureties or by Guarantee Companies? Guarantee Company.
13. Date when the accounts of the Corporation were last audited. Audited monthly.
14. Names and addresses of the auditors respectively for 1913 and for 1914 (if appointed):
    For 1913: James Reynolds and Albert E. Foxton.
    For 1914: James Reynolds and Albert E. Foxton.
15. What were the dividend days of the Corporation in 1913, and what rate or rates of dividend were paid on those days respectively? January 15th, 1913, 6%; July 15th, 1913, 6%.
16. What is the date appointed for the Annual Meeting? February 4th, 1914. Date of last Annual Meeting: February 5th, 1913.
17. Special General Meetings held in 1913: Dates, none.

CANADA LANDED AND NATIONAL INVESTMENT COMPANY, LIMITED.

Head Office, Toronto, Ontario.

CONSTATING INSTRUMENTS

This Company was in 1891 constituted by an amalgamation of (1) The Canada Landed Credit Company with (2) The National Investment Company of Canada (Limited), and the re-incorporation of the amalgamated Company. Of the two Companies so amalgamated:

1. The Canada Landed Credit Company had been incorporated in 1858 by special Act of the Province of Canada, 22 V. c. 133; a special Act of 1859, 22 V. c. 105, increased the capital; the two foregoing Acts were amended by 29.30 V. (1866-7), c. 125. In 1873, an Act of Ontario, 36 V. c. 122, amended 22 V. c. 133, supra; in 1874 the powers of the Company were extended by 38 V. c. 73 (O.); in 1875.6 the capital was further increased by 39 V. c. 97 (O.); in 1882 the special Acts of 1858 and 1859 supra were amended by 45 V. c. 72 (O.). In 1882 the special Act of Canada, 45 V. c. 110, extended the Company's operations to Manitoba and the Northwest Territories. In 1890 the special Act of Ontario, 53 V. c. 128, authorized the Company to issue debenture stock to become amalgamated with other companies, etc. In 1871, Letters Patent of Canada, dated January, 1891, authorized the amalgamation of the Company with the National Investment Company of Canada. In 1891, Letters Patent of Ontario, dated 12th February, authorized the same amalgamation.

2. The National Investment Company of Canada had been incorporated by Letters Patent of Canada, dated 21st August, 1882, issued under 40 V. c. 43 (D.).

For the powers of the amalgamated Company, see the Letters Patent above cited; see also R.S.O., 1886, secs. 88.98, and sec. 101; see also the Loan and Trust Corporations Act, R.S.O. 1914, chap. 184.

ANNUAL STATEMENT

Of the condition and affairs of the Canada Landed and National Investment Company, Limited, Toronto, at 31st December, 1913, and for the year ending on that day, made to the Registrar of Loan Corporations for the Province of Ontario, pursuant to the laws of the said Province.

The head office of the Corporation is at 23 Toronto Street, in the City of Toronto, in the Province of Ontario.

The Board is constituted of eight directors, holding office for one year.

The directors and chief executive officers of the Corporation at 31st December, 1913, were as follows, together with their respective terms of office:

John Hoskin K.C., LL.D., D.C.L., President, Toronto; 12th Feb., 1913: 11th Feb., 1914.
D. E. Thomson, K.C., LL.D., Vice-President, Toronto;   "   "
J. Kerr Osborne, Director, Toronto;   "   "
James Playfair, Director, Midland;   20th Aug., 1913;   "
Newman Silverthorn, Director, Summerville;   12th Feb., 1913;   "
  G. T. Ferguson, Director, Toronto;   "   "
  F. W. Harcourt, K.C., Director, Toronto;   "
Edward Saunders, Managing Director, Toronto;   "

A. Permanent capital stock; total amount authorized, $4,000,000; total amount subscribed, $2,410,000, as more particularly set out in Schedule A hereto.

Class 2.—Fixed and permanent capital stock created by virtue of Joint Stock Companies' Act or Private Acts.

Last call made: Date, 2nd December, 1912; rate per cent., 50; gross amount, $402,000; amount paid thereon, $201,000.

Description.	No. of shares.	Par value.	Total amount held.	Total amount paid thereon.	Total remaining unpaid calls.
		$	$	$	
2. 50 per cent called	24,100	100	2,410,000	1,205,000	None

LIST OF SHAREHOLDERS AS AT 31st DECEMBER, 1913.

(Not printed.)

BALANCE SHEET AS AT 31st DECEMBER, 1913.

Dr.   Capital and Liabilities.

Capital (Liabilities to Stockholders or Shareholders).

A.—Permanent Capital Stock or Shares.

2. (b) Ordinary joint stock capital, 50 per cent. called; total called, $1,205,000; total paid thereon $1,205,000 00		
4. (d) Dividends declared in respect of (2), but not yet paid	27,112 50	
5 (e) Unappropriated profits in respect of (2)	8,007 69	
6. (f) Reserve fund in respect of (2) 1,000,000 00		
		$2,240,120 19

Liabilities to the Public.

29. Debentures issued in Canada ....$ 312,179 50		
30. Interest due and accrued on (29)	2,614 37	
31. Debentures issued elsewhere than in Canada 3,923,159 35		
32. Interest due and accrued on (31)	21,479 00	
39. Due on loans in process of completion or to pay assumed mortages	2,004 00	
40. Unclaimed dividends	1,361 87	
41. Other liabilities to the public, viz.:		
42. (a) Sundry Creditors	1,746 47	
		4,264,544 56

Total liabilities $6,504,664 75

Cr.   Assets.

I.—Assets of which the Corporation is the Beneficial Owner.

Subject to the terms of trust deed dated 6th April, 1894, to secure debenture-holders.

A.—Immovable Property Owned Beneficially by Corporation.

1. (a) Office premises, situate as follows:		
2. (i) At Toronto, held in freehold ....$	35,000 00	
5. (b) Freehold land (including buildings) other than foregoing	2,416 00	
		$ 37,416 00

BALANCE SHEET.—Continued.

Cr.   Assets.

B.—Debts secured by Mortgages of Land.

9. (a) Debts (other than item 10) secured by mortgages
       of land $5,848,079 08
10. (b) Debts secured by mortgaged land held for sale.....   1,947 65
11. (c) Interest due or accrued on items 9 and 10 and not
       included therein 103,325 61
                                                              ————————
                                                              $5,953,352 34

C.—Debts not above enumerated for which the Corporation holds securities as follows:

14. (b) Municipal Bonds or Debentures owned by the
       Company ....$ 133,328 47
15. (c) Public School Debentures owned by the Company.... 120,228 10
18. (f) Stocks or Bonds of any of the Provinces of Canada
       owned by the Company 2,000 00
22. (j) Ontario Government Scrip owned by the Company...   19,667 70
23. (k) Electric Light Company's Bond owned by Company..   1,000 00
24. (l) Electric Development Bonds owned by the Company..   4,437 23
25. (m) Loans on collateral security of stocks............   65,678 10
26. (n) Interest due or accrued on items 14 to 25 and not
       included therein 7,227 37
                                                              ————————
                                                              353,566 97

E.—Cash.

31. (a) On hand ....$ 3,190 72
32. (b) In banks in Canada 152,655 47
35. (iii) National Bank of Scotland, London 4,483 25
                                                              ————————
                                                              160,329 44
                                                              ————————
       Total assets $6,504,664 75

CASH ACCOUNT.

Receipts for the year ending 31st December, 1913.

I. Received by the Corporation for its own use.

A.—Balance from 31st December, 1912.

(b) Cash not already shown under (1):
                                                         Col. 4 (Total).
2.   (i) On hand ....$ 1,270 81
3.   (ii) In bank 59,517 55
                                                              ————————
                                                              60,788 36

C.—Receipts on Account of Investments, Loans or Debts.

(a) On Mortgages of Realty:
10.   (i) Principal 587,641 78
11.   (ii) Interest 416,871 66
(b) On other securities:
12.   (i) Principal 56,188 76
13.   (ii) Interest or dividends 21,074 84

D.—Receipts from Real Estate Owned Beneficially by Corporation.

17. (b) Rents 3,025 11

CASH ACCOUNT.—Continued.

Receipts for the year ending 31st December, 1913.

F.—Borrowed Money.

27. (c) Borrowed on debentures 825,814 43

G.—Receipts from other sources.

30. (a) Bank interest 1,729 50
    (c) Gain on exchange 144 78

      Totals $1,978,279 22

CASH ACCOUNT.

Expenditure for the year ending 31st December, 1913.

I.—Expended on Corporation Account.

A.—Sums Loaned or Invested on Capital Account.

1. (a) Loaned on mortgages of realty, including insurances or taxes
      advanced on property mortgaged to the Corporation $689,687 67
    (b) Loaned or invested in other securities:
3.   (ii) Debentures purchased 9,506 09
5.   (iv) Loans on stocks 1,744 50
7. (d) Incumbrances on realty paid off 782 06

B.—Expended on Stock Account.

8. Dividends paid on permanent stock 127,422 03

C.—Borrowed Money (other than foregoing) or interest thereon paid, viz.:

18. (a) Bank account (principal and interest) 38,177 06
20. (c) Debentures issued in Canada: Principal, $60,010.00; interest
    $13,734.11 .... 73,744 11
21. (d) Debentures issued elsewhere: Principal, $649,899.52; interest,
    $159,391.34 .... 809,290 86

D.—Management Expenses (other than foregoing).

25. (a) Salaries, wages and fees 42,512 00
26. (b) Commission or brokerage 13,737 21
28. (d) Stationery, postage, printing and advertising 1,915 09
30. (f) Fuel, rent, taxes (other than in 7 and 32) and rates 3,974 90
31. (g) Travelling expenses 1,317 60
32. (h) Registration fees 280 00
33. (i) Other management expenditure 1,261 10

E.—Other Expenditure.

35. (b) Government and business taxes 2,183 65
36. (c) Repairs to Company's buildings 413 85

F.—Balance.

37. (a) Cash on hand and in banks 160,329 44

      Total $1,978,279 22

1. Amount of debentures maturing in 1914: Issued in Canada, $44,105.00; issued elsewhere, $816,432.00
2. Amount of other existing obligations which will mature in 1914, none.
3. Amount of securities held by the Corporation, which will mature and become payable to the Corporation in 1914, $847,813.74.
4. Average rate of interest per annum paid by the Corporation during 1913: On deposits, no deposits taken; on debentures, 4.102; on debenture stock, none.
5. Average rate of interest per annum received by the Corporation during 1913 (a) on mortgages of realty, (b) on other securities.
    (i) Owned beneficially by the corporation (a) 6.84%; (b) 5.12%.
    (ii) Not owned beneficially; (a) none, all funds are held beneficially; (b) none, all funds are held beneficially.
6. Of the mortgages owned beneficially by the Corporation, $2,242,610.11 is on realty situate in Ontario, and $3,609,832.62 is on realty situate elsewhere.
7. Of the mortgages not owned beneficially by the Corporation, none is on realty situate in Ontario, and none is on realty situate elsewhere.
8. Loans written off or transferred to real estate account during 1913, viz.:
    (i) Funds or securities owned beneficially, $416.00.
    (ii) Not so owned, none.
9. Number and aggregate amount of mortgages upon which compulsory proceedings have been taken by the Corporation in 1913, viz.:
    (i) Owned beneficially, No. 6; amount, $7,170.
    (ii) Not so owned, none; amount, none.
10. Aggregate market value of land mortgaged to the Corporation:
    (i) Mortgages owned beneficially, $12,100,000.
    (ii) Not so owned, none.
11. How often are the securities held by the Corporation valued? Annually in the case of doubtful loans.
12. (a) Specify the officers of the Corporation who are under bond and for what sum respectively. All officers are under bonds from $2,000 to $5,000, amounting in all to $41,000.
    (b) Are the said bonds executed by private sureties or by Guarantee Companies? Guarantee Companies.
13. Date when the accounts of the Corporation were last audited? Audited to 31st December, 1913.
14. Names and addresses of the auditors respectively for 1913 and for 1914 (if appointed):
    For 1913: T. Watson Sime, C.A., G. U. Stiff, F.C.A., Toronto; J. B. Pepler, Winnipeg.
    For 1914: Not yet appointed.
15. What were dividend days of the Corporation in 1913 and what rate or rates of dividend were paid on those days respectively? January 2nd, 4% for half-year April 1st, 2¼%; July 2nd, 2¼%; October 1st, 2¼%.
16. What is the date appointed for the Annual Meeting? 11th February, 1914. Date of last Annual Meeting? 12th February, 1913.
17. Special General Meetings held in 1913: Dates, none.

CANADA PERMANENT MORTGAGE CORPORATION.

Head Office, Toronto, Ont.

CONSTATING INSTRUMENTS.

This Company was under the provisions of the special Act of Ontario, 63 V. c. 129, formed by the amalgamation of the Canada Permanent Loan and Savings Company, the Western Canada Loan and Savings Company, the Freehold Loan and Savings Company, and the London and Ontario Investment Company: 63 V., c. 129 (Ont.) See also special Act of Canada, 62 V., c. 101 (D).

ANNUAL STATEMENT

Of the condition and affairs of the Canada Permanent Mortgage Corporation of Toronto, at the 31st December, 1913, and for the year ending on that day, made to the Registrar of Loan Corporations for the Province of Ontario, pursuant to the laws of the said Province.

The head office of the Corporation is No. 14-18 Toronto Street, in the City of Toronto, in the Province of Ontario.

The board is constituted of ten directors holding office for one year.

The directors and chief executive officers of the Corporation at 31st December, 1913, were as follows, together with their respective terms of office:

W. G. Gooderham, President, Toronto;
W. D. Matthews, 1st Vice-President, Toronto;
G. W. Monk, 2nd Vice-President, Toronto;
F. Gordon Osler, Director, Toronto;
R. S. Hudson, Director, Toronto,
E. R. C. Clarkson, Director, Toronto;
John Massey, Director, Toronto;
Albert E. Gooderham, Director, Toronto;
J. H. G. Hagarty, Director, Toronto;
John Campbell, Director, Edinburgh,
       Scotland;
R. S. Hudson; } Joint General Managers;
John Massey,   }
George H. Smith, Superintendent of Branches and Secretary, Toronto.

A. Permanent capital stock; total amount authorized, $30,000,000; total amount subscribed, $6,000,000, as more particularly set out in Schedule A hereto.

SCHEDULE A.

Fixed and Permanent Capital Stock.

Description.	No. of shares.	Par value of shares.	Total amount held.	Total amount paid thereon.	Total remaining uncalled.
1. Fully called and paid...	600,000	$ 10	$ 6,000,000	$ 6,000,000	....

LIST OF SHAREHOLDERS AS AT 31st DECEMBER, 1913.

(Not printed.)

BALANCE SHEET AS AT 31st DECEMBER, 1913.

Dr.   Capital and Liabilities.

Capital (Liabilities to Stockholders or Shareholders).

A.—Permanent Capital Stock or Shares.

1. (a) Ordinary joint stock capital fully called; total called
         and total paid thereon $6,000,000 00
4. (d) Dividends declared in respect of (1), but not yet
         paid 150,000 00
5. (e) Unappropriated profits in respect of (1) 130,654 51
6. (f) Reserve Fund in respect of (1) 4,250,000 00
                                                                    ———————— $10,530,654 51

Liabilities to the Public.

27. Deposits (including unclaimed deposits), right reserved
         to require 30 days' notice of any withdrawal).....$5,337,452 67
28. Interest on deposits due or accrued or capitalized 92,932 47
29. Debentures issued and payable in Canada 2,855,456 47
30. Interest due and accrued on (29) 32,885 99
31. Debentures issued in Canada, payable elsewhere 12,471,259 00
32. Interest due and accrued on (31) 68,133 32
33. Debenture stock issued in Canada, payable elsewhere.... 419,136 80
34. Interest due and accrued on (33) ....·.... 8,404 71
41. Other liabilities to the public, viz.:
     (a) For commissions, unpaid accounts, etc. 10,302 43
                                                                    ———————— 21,295,963 86

         Total liabilities $31,826,618 37

───

Cr.   Assets.

───

I.—Assets of which the Corporation is the Beneficial Owner.

A.—Immovable Property Owned Beneficially by Corporation.

1. (a) Office premises situate as follows:
2.   (i) At Toronto, held in freehold $181,855 11
             Winnipeg, Man., held in freehold 125,000 00
             Vancouver, B.C., held in freehold 75,000 00
             St. John, N.B., held in freehold 40,000 00
             Edmonton, Alta., held in freehold 75,000 00
             Regina, Sask., held in freehold ....·.. 125,000 00
                                                                    ———————— $621,855 11

B.—Debts secured by Mortgages of Land.

9. (a) Debts (other than item 10) secured by mortgages of land........ 28,355,791 17

C.—Debts not above enumerated for which the Corporation holds securi-
         ties, as follows:

14. (b) Debts secured by municipal bonds or debentures,
         $711.46; owned by Corporation, $186,124.77 .... $186,836.23
15. (c) Public School Debentures owned by Corporation... 3,040 90
16. (d) Debts secured by Loan Corporations' Debentures.... 1,016 38
17. (e) Debts secured by stock or bonds, other than 14 and
         16, purchased by ·Corporation 467,590 10
20. (h) Debts secured only by Permanent Stock or Shares
         of the Corporation 180,623 93
22. (j) Debts secured by advances on bonds and ·stocks not
         owned by Corporation 109,087 72
                                                                    ———————— $948,195 26

BALANCE SHEET.—Continued.

Cr.   Assets.

E.—Cash.

31. (a) On hand $57,523 27
32. (b) In banks in Canada and in England 1,843,253 56
                                                                    1,900,776 83

    Total assets $31,326,618 37

CASH ACCOUNT.

Receipts for the year ending 31st December, 1913.

I.—Received by the Corporation for its Own Use.

A.—Balances from 31st December, 1912.

2.   (i) On hand $70,170 06
3.   (ii) In bank 862,026 26
                                                                    $932,196 32

C.—Receipts on account of Investments, Loans or Debts.

    (a) On mortgages of realty:—
10.   (i) Principal and charges 4,085,591 69
11.   (ii) Interest 2,089,801 24
    (b) On other securities:—
12.   (i) Principal 395,016 88
13.   (ii) Interest or dividends 23,027 37

D.—Receipts from Real Estate Owned Beneficially by Corporation.

17. (b) Corporation's premises, rent and expense account 46,568 59

F.—Borrowed Money.

26. (b) Borrowed by taking deposits 10,657,699 15
27. (c) Borrowed on debentures 1,456,671 78

G.—Receipts from other sources.

30. (a) Bank interest and exchange 18,589 52

    Totals $19,655,162 54

CASH ACCOUNT.—Continued.

Expenditure for the year ending 31st December, 1913.

I.—Expended on Corporation Account.

A.—Sums Loaned or Invested on Capital Account.

1. (a) Loaned on mortgages of realty $3,440,516 08
    (b) Loaned or invested in other securities:
2.   (i) Loaned on bonds and stocks 228,078 77
3.   (ii) Loans on this Corporation's stock 56,932 36
4.   (iii) Bonds and stocks purchased 240,290 10
6. (c) Real estate purchased and additions to buildings at Vancouver,
      Edmonton and Regina 67,784 83

CASH ACCOUNT.—Continued.

Expenditure for the year ending 31st December, 1913.

B.—Expended on Stock Account.

8. Dividend paid on permanent stock $585,000 00

C.—Borrowed Money (other than foregoing) or interest thereon paid, viz.:
18. (a) Bank interest and exchange 18 02
19. (b) Deposits: Principal and interest 11,060,684 33
20. (c) Debentures payable in Canada: Principal, $532,487.93; interest,
    $121,762.64 . . . . 654,250 57
21. (d) Debentures payable elsewhere: Principal, $498,434.08; interest,
    $497,891.89 . . . . . . 996,325 97
22. (e) Debenture stock issued elsewhere; interest 16,809 42

D.—Management Expenses (other than foregoing).

26. (a) Salaries, wages and fees 231,877 26
27. (c) Advances to agents for commission and charges 60,345 55
28. (d) Stationery, postage, printing, advertising, etc. ....↲.......... 53,440 58
29. (e) Law costs 534 77
31. (g) Travelling expenses and inspection 10,012 85
32. (h) Registration fees, Municipal and Government taxes and fees.... 13,191 29

E.—Other Expenditures, viz.:

34. (a) Corporation's premises, rent and expenses account.............. 36,842 64
35. (b) Furniture for office 1,450 32

F.—Balance.

37. (a) Cash on hand and in bank 1,900,776 83

Totals $19,655,162 54

MISCELLANEOUS STATEMENT FOR THE YEAR ENDING 31ST DECEMBER, 1913.

1. Amount of Debentures maturing in 1914: Issued in and payable in Canada, $693,-248.32; Issued in Canada, payable elsewhere, $2,415,752.42.
2. Amount of other existing obligations which will mature in 1914: Excluding deposits, none.
3. Amount of securities held by the Corporation which will mature and become payable to the Corporation in 1914: Approximately, $6,000,000.00.
4. Average rate of interest per annum paid by the Corporation during 1913: On deposits, 3.5334%; on debentures, 4.08%; on debenture stock, 4%.
5. Average rate of interest per annum received by the Corporation during 1913:
   (a) On mortgages of realty; (b) On other securities:
   (i) Owned beneficially by the Corporation: (a) 7.02%; (b) 5½ to 6½%.
   (ii) Not owned beneficially: (a) None; (b) none.
6. Of the mortgages owned beneficially by the Corporation, $8,938,031.78 is on realty situate in Ontario, and $19,417,759.39 is on realty situate elsewhere.
7. Of the mortgages not owned beneficially by the Corporation, —— is on realty situate in Ontario, and —— is on realty situate elsewhere.
8. Loans written off or transferred to real estate account during 1913, viz.:
   (i) Funds or securities owned beneficially, none.
   (ii) Not so owned, none.
9. Number and aggregate amount of mortgages upon which compulsory proceedings have been taken by the Corporation in 1913, viz.:
   (i) Owned beneficially: Number, 86; Amount, $121,535.00.
   (ii) Not so owned: Number, ——; Amount, ——.
10. Aggregate market value of land mortgaged to the Corporation:
    (i) Mortgages owned beneficially, ——.
    (ii) Not so owned: Approximately, $54,500.00.

11. How often are the securities held by the Corporation valued? Once a year.
12. (a) Specify the officers of the Corporation who are under bond and for what sum respectively. All officers and employees holding responsible positions give bonds or security to Corporation for $1,000 to $5,000 each.
    (b) Are the said bonds executed by private sureties or by Guarantee Companies? Largely Guarantee Companies, some by private individuals.
13. Date when the accounts of the Corporation were last audited. As at 31st December, 1913.
14. Names and addresses of the auditors respectively for 1913 and for 1914 (if appointed):
    For 1913: A. E. Osler and Henry Barber, Chartered Accountants.
    For 1914: Same as 1913.
15. What were the dividend days of the Corporation in 1913, and what rate or rates of dividend were paid on those days respectively?- January 2nd at 2¼%; April 1st, July 2nd, October 1st at 2½%.
16. What is the date appointed for the Annual Meeting? February 4th, 1914. Date of last Annual Meeting: February 3rd, 1913.
17. Special General Meetings held in 1913: Dates, ——.

THE CANADIAN MORTGAGE INVESTMENT COMPANY.

Head Office, Toronto, Ontario.

Incorporated under special Act of Canada, 62.3 Vict., c. 103. (Decl. Book II., 92).

ANNUAL STATEMENT

Of the condition and affairs of the Canadian Mortgage Investment Company, of Toronto, Ont., at the 31st December, 1913, and for the year ending on that day, made to the Registrar of Loan Corporations for the Province of Ontario, pursuant to the laws of the said Province.

The head office of the Company is at No. 10 Adelaide Street East, in the City of Toronto, in the Province of Ontario.

The Board is constituted of seven directors holding office for one year.

The directors and chief executive officers of the Corporation on the 31st December, 1913, were as follows, together with their respective terms of office:

L. A. Hamilton, President, Lorne Park; January 1st, 1913; December 31st, 1913.
H. S. Osler, K.C., Vice-President, Toronto; " "
S. G. Beatty, Director, Toronto; " "
D. B. Hanna, Director, Toronto;
Joseph Henderson, Director Toronto
Hon. Wallace Nesbitt, K.C., Director, Toronto; "
F. W. G. Fitzgerald, Managing Director, Toronto; "

A. Permanent capital stock: Total amount authorized, $5,000,000; total amount subscribed, $1,504,500, as more particularly set out in Schedule A hereto.

SCHEDULE A.

Class 2.—Fixed and permanent Capital Stock created by virtue of Joint Stock Companies' Acts or Private Acts.

Description.	Total amount issued and subsisting at 31st December, 1913.		Total amount of actual payments thereon.	Total amount unpaid and constituting an asset of the Corporation.
	No. of shares.	Par value of shares. —		
		$	$	$ c.	$
1. Fully called.......	8,883	100	888,300	888,300 00	....
2. 50% called.........	4,621	100	462,100	231,085 00	231,015 00
4. Shares payable at fixed dates.......	1,541	100	154,100	75,089 61	79,010 39
Totals...........	15,045	....	1,504,500	1,194,474 61	310,025 39

LIST OF SHAREHOLDERS AS AT 31st DECEMBER, 1913.

(Not printed.)

BALANCE SHEET AS AT 31st DECEMBER, 1913.

Dr.   Capital and Liabilities.

Capital (Liabilities to Stockholders or Shareholders).

A.—Permanent Capital Stock or Shares.

1. (a) Ordinary joint stock capital fully called; total called, $888,300.00; total paid thereon	$888,300 00	
2. (b) Ordinary joint stock capital, 50 per cent. called; total called, $231,050.00; total paid thereon......	231,085 00	
3. (cc) Accrued dividends on (2)	6,009 30	
4. (d) Dividends declared in respect of (1), (2), but not yet paid	33,441 94	
8. (h) Instalment permanent stock (payable by fixed periodical payments); total subscribed, $154,100; on which has been paid	75,089 61	

Note.—Liabilities reported in 1912 under A, but written off in 1913 (not extended), $828.02.

C.—Liabilities to Shareholders other than already shown under A or B.		
26. Profit and loss	19,165 98	
Reserve fund	300,000 00	
		$1,553,091 83

Liabilities to the Public.

29. Debentures issued in Canada	$56,897 77	
31. Debentures issued elsewhere than in Canada............	615,780 29	
33. Interest due and accrued on (31)	3,660 93	
37. Owing to banks (including interest due or accrued)....	27,297 97	
40. Unclaimed dividends	15 00	
42. (a) Accounts payable ....:.........................	5,626 50	
		709,278 46
Total liabilities		$2,262,370 29

Cr.   Assets.

I.—Assets of which the Corporation is the Beneficial Owner.

A.—Immovable Property Owned Beneficially by Corporation.

1. (a) Premises acquired for office purposes, including fittings:		
2. (i) At Toronto, held in freehold	$257,210 24	
		$257,210 24

B.—Debts secured by Mortgages of Land.

9. (a) Debts (other than item 10) secured by mortgages of land	$1,704,827 22	
10. (b) Debts secured by mortgaged land held for sale......	22,697 53	
11. (c) Interest due and accrued on item 9 and not included therein	74,856 03	
		1,802,390 78

C.—Debts not above enumerated for which the Corporation holds securities as follows:

20. (h) Debts secured only by permanent stock or shares of the Corporation		2,222 63

BALANCE SHEET.—Continued.

Cr.   Assets.

E.—Cash.

31.	(a) On hand	$455 79	
32.	(b) In banks in Toronto and elsewhere	34,888 63	
			$35,344 42

F.—Assets not hereinbefore mentioned.

37.	(a) Fully paid stocks and bonds owned by the Company.	$161,598 88	
38.	(b) Rents receivable	1,753 34	
39.	(c) Accounts receivable	1,950 00	
			165,302 22
	Total assets		$2,262,370 29

Note.—Assets reported in 1912, but written off in 1913 (not extended),
$9,336.51.

CASH ACCOUNT.

Receipts for the year ending 31st December, 1913.

I.—Received by the Corporation for Its Own Use.

A.—Balance from 31st December, 1912.

		(Col. 1),	(Col. 2)	(Col. 3)	(Col. 4)
2.	(i) On hand	....	....	$206 40	
3.	(ii) In bank	....	....	33,889 54	

B.—Sums received wholly or partly on Capital Stock.

8.	(e) Received on account of stock payable by fixed instalments	....	....	9,813 79	

C.—Receipts on account of investments, loans or debts.

(a) Mortgages of Realty:

10.	(i) Principal	....	....	221,730 39	
11.	(ii) Interest	$172,662 85			

(b) On other securities:

12.	(i) Principal	....	....	13,463 98	
13.	(ii) Interest or dividends...	7,109 11			

D.—Receipts from Real Estate Owned Beneficially by Corporation.

16.	(a) Sales	....	....	1,560 00	
17.	(b) Rents	18,640 03			

E.—Miscellaneous.

18.	(a) Commission, brokerage, etc...	2,775 36	

F.—Borrowed Money.

CASH ACCOUNT.—Continued.

Receipts for the year ending 31st December, 1913.

	(Col. 1)	(Col. 2)	(Col. 3)	(Col. 4)
25. (a) Bank or other advances, discounts or overdrafts	....	27,297 97		
27. (c) Borrowed on debentures	....	59,193 06		
G.—Receipts from other sources, viz.:				
30. (a) Transfer fees	58 00			
(b) Borrowers' insurance, taxes, etc.	....	....	15,381 76	
Sundry accounts	10 00			
Totals	$201,235 35	$86,491 03	$296,045 86	$583,772 24

CASH ACCOUNT.

Expenditure for the year ending 31st December, 1913.

Expended on Corporation Account.

A.—Sums loaned or invested on Capital Account.

	(Col. 1)	(Col. 2)	(Col. 3)	(Col. 4)
1. (a) Loaned on mortgages of realty	....	....	$295,860 87	
(b) Loaned or invested in other securities, viz.:				
2. (i) Debentures issued in Canada	....	....	17,759 11	
3. (ii) Loans on Permanent stock	....	....	650 00	
7. (e) Insurance or taxes advanced on property mortgaged to the Corporation	$983 63	....	29,975 34	
B.—Expended on Stock Account.				
8. Dividends paid on permanent stock	64,952 00			
C.—Borrowed Money (other than foregoing) or Interest thereon paid, viz.:				
18. (a) Bank account	....	47,198 41		
20. (c) Debentures issued in Canada: Principal, nil; Interest ..	2,516 20			
21. (d) Debentures issued elsewhere: Principal, $13,505.00; Interest, $25,720.61	25,720 61	13,505 00		
D.—Management expenses (other than foregoing).				
25. (a) Salaries, wages and fees	21,445 58			
26. (b) Commission to agents	5,506 92			
28. (d) Stationery, postage, printing and advertising	3,322 15			
29. (e) Law costs	1,767 36			
30. (f) Taxes (other than in 7 and 32) and rates	572 03			

CASH ACCOUNT.—Continued.

Expenditure for the year ending 31st December, 1913.

	(Col. 1)	(Col. 2)	(Col. 3)	(Col. 4)
31. (g) Travelling expenses	3,163 85			
32. (h) Registration fees and Government taxes	1,336 67			
33. (i) Other management expenditure: Commission on funds loaned and borrowed ...	2,883 70			
E.—Other Expenditure, viz.:				
34. (a) Expense of Corporation premises	8,093 14	....	$476 23	
35. (b) Sundry expense	738 97			
F.—Balance.				
37. (a) Cash on hand in banks	....	....	35,344 42	
Totals	$143,002 81	$60,703 41	$380,066 02	$583,772 24

MISCELLANEOUS STATEMENT FOR THE YEAR ENDING 31ST DECEMBER, 1913.

---

1. Amount of Debentures maturing in 1914: Issued in Canada, $2,700.00; Issued elsewhere, $197,927.33.
2. Amount of other existing obligations which will mature in 1914, none.
3. Amount of securities held by the Corporation which will mature and become payable to the Corporation in 1914, none; a portion of principal repayable monthly.
4. Average rate of interest per annum paid by the Corporation during 1913: On deposits, none; on debentures, 4½%; on debenture stock, none.
5. Average rate of interest per annum received by the Corporation during 1913:
   (a) On mortgages of realty; (b) On other securities.
   (i) Owned beneficially by the Corporation: (a) 9%; (b) 5%.
   (ii) Not owned beneficially: (a) None; (b) none.
6. Of the mortgages owned beneficially by the Corporation $122,263.19 is on realty situate in Ontario, and $1,657,420.07 is on realty situate elsewhere.
7. Of the mortgages not owned beneficially by the Corporation none is on realty situate in Ontario, and none is on realty situate elsewhere.
8. Loans written off or transferred to real estate account during 1913, viz.:
   (i) Funds or securities owned beneficially, $5,373.37.
   (ii) Not so owned.
9. Number and aggregate amount of mortgages upon which compulsory proceedings have been taken by the Corporation during 1913, viz.:
   (i) Owned beneficially: Number, 27; amount, $31,000.00.
   (ii) Not so owned: Number, none; amount, none.
10. Aggregate market value of land mortgaged to the Corporation:
    (i) Mortgages owned beneficially, $5,900,000.00.
    (ii) Not so owned, none.
11. How often are the securities held by the Corporation valued? Revalued in all doubtful cases.
12. (a) Specify the officers of the Corporation who are under bond and for what sum respectively: All officers and other employees holding important positions give bonds and securities satisfactory to the company.
    (b) Are the said bonds executed by private sureties or by Guarantee Companies? Guarantee Companies and approved private sureties.
13. Date when the accounts of the Corporation were last audited 31st December, 1913.
14. Names and addresses of the auditors respectively for 1913 and for 1914 (if appointed):
    For 1913: Price, Waterhouse & Co., C.A., Toronto.
    For 1914: Price, Waterhouse & Co., C.A., Toronto.
15. What were the dividend days of the Corporation in 1913, and what rate or rates of dividend were paid on those days respectively? 2nd January and 2nd July, 6%.
16. What is the date appointed for the Annual Meeting? 4th February, 1914. Date of last Annual Meeting? 5th February, 1913.
17. Special General Meetings held in 1913: Dates, none.

THE CENTRAL CANADA LOAN AND SAVINGS COMPANY.

Head Office, Peterborough, Ontario.

CONSTATING INSTRUMENTS.

The former Provincial Company, incorporated 1884, 7th March, L.P. of Ontario. (Lib. 16, No. 67.)

1890, 53 V. c. 129 (O.); fixes the capital stock at $5,000,000, divided into 50,000 shares of $100 each; (sec. 1), confirms the purchase of the assets of the Peterborough Real Estate Investment Co., Limited; secs. 2-4 sanction the issue of debenture stock; secs. 5-12 authorize agencies in the United Kingdom; (13) defines the limit of borrowing powers.

1893, 8th June, Letters Patent of Ontario amending the foregoing Letters Patent.

1897, May 6th, Letters Patent of Ontario so amending the foregoing Letters Patent as to give the Company the status of a Loan Company (and not the status of a Loaning Land Company) under the Loan and Trust Corporations Act.

Dominion Company of same name incorporated by 61 V. c. 97 (D.), assets of Provincial Company transferred to Dominion Company by 63 V. c. 130 (Ontario).

ANNUAL STATEMENT

Of the conditions and affairs of the Central Canada Loan and Savings Company at the 31st December, 1913, and for the year ending on that day, made to the Registrar of Loan Corporations for the Province of Ontario, pursuant to the laws of the said Province.

The head office of the Corporation is at No. 437 George Street, in the City of Peterborough, in the Province of Ontario.

The Board is constituted of eleven directors, holding office for one year.

The directors and chief executive officers of the Corporation at the 14th January, 1914, were as follows, together with their respective terms of office:—

Hon. George A. Cox, President, Toronto;   January 14th, 1914; January 13th, 1915.
E. R. Wood, Vice-President and Managing
    Director, Toronto;   "   "
Sir Thomas W. Taylor, Director, Hamilton;
E. W. Cox, Director, Toronto;   "
Richard Hall, Director, Peterborough, Ont.;   "
F. C. Taylor, Director, Lindsay, Ont.;   "
H. C. Cox, Director, Toronto;   ..
Sir Wm. MacKenzie, Director, Toronto;
Hon. Robt. Jaffray, Director, Toronto;   '
J. H. Housser, Director, Toronto;   "
G. A. Morrow, Ass't Manager & Director, Toronto;   "
W. S. Hodgens, Secretary, Toronto.

A. Permanent capital stock: Total amount authorized, $5,000,000; total amount subscribed, $2,500,000, as more particularly set out in Schedule A hereto.

SCHEDULE A.

Class 2.—Fixed and permanent capital stock created by virtue of Joint Stock Companies' Acts or Private Acts.

Description.	No. of shares.	Par value.	Total amount held.	Total amount paid thereon.
		$	$	$
1. Fully called..........	15,625	100	1,562,500	1,562,500
2. 20 per cent. called....	9,375	100	937,500	187,500
Totals..............	25,000	....	2,500,000	1,750,000

LIST OF SHAREHOLDERS AS AT 31ST DECEMBER, 1913.

(Not printed.)

BALANCE SHEET AS AT 31st DECEMBER, 1913.

Dr. Capital and Liabilities.

Capital (Liabilities to Stockholders or Shareholders).

A.—Permanent Capital Stock or Shares.

1. (a) Ordinary joint stock capital fully called; total called, $1,562,500; total paid thereon	$1,562,500 00	
2. (b) Ordinary joint stock capital, 20 per cent. called, $187,500; total paid thereon	187,500 00	
4. (d) Dividend declared in respect of (1) and (2), but not yet paid	43,750 00	
5. (e) Unappropriated profits in respect of (1) and (2)....	43,623 18	
6. (f) Reserve fund in respect of (1) and (2)	1,750,000 00	
		$3,587,373 18

Liabilities to the Public.

27. Deposits, right reserved to require 30 days' notice of any withdrawal	$1,560,292 26	
29. Debentures issued in Canada	1,783,983 14	
30. Interest due and accrued on (29)	35,572 29	
31. Debentures issued elsewhere than in Canada	2,933,323 88	
32. Interest due and accrued on (31)	17,052 52	
		6,330,224 09
Total liabilities		$9,917,597 27

Cr. Assets.

I.—Assets of which the Corporation is the Beneficial Owner.

A.—Immovable Property Owned Beneficially by Corporation.

1. (a) Office premises situate as follows:		
2. (1) At Toronto, and other real estate with rents due, held in freehold		$180,494 75

B.—Debts secured by Mortgages of Land.

9. (a) Debts (other than item 10) secured by mortgages of land	$1,274,468 40	
11. (c) Interest due or accrued on item (9), not included therein	58,299 03	
		1,332,767 43

C.—Debts not above enumerated for which the Corporation holds securities, as follows:

22. (j) Debts secured by collateral security of bonds and stocks	$2,490,791 62	
26. (n) Interest due or accrued on item (22) and not included therein	18,030 19	
		2,508,821 81

E.—Cash.

31. (a) On hand		$183,803 98
32. (b) In banks and Loan Company:		
In Canada	$647,536 31	
Less overdraft	124,455 62	
	523,080 69	
		706,884 67

BALANCE SHEET.—Continued.

Cr.   Assets.

F.—Assets not hereinbefore mentioned.

37. (a) Securities owned beneficially by Company...........$5,159,074 46
        Interest 29,554 15
                                                                            5,188,628 61

        Total assets $9,917,597 27

CASH ACCOUNT.

. Receipts for the year ending 31st December, 1913.

I.—Received by the Corporation for its Own Use.

A.—Balance from 31st December, 1912.

Cash (not already shown under (1)):
2.   (i) On hand $131,732 46
3.   (ii) In bank 557,354 00
                                                                        $689,086 46

C.—Receipts on account of Investments, Loans or Debts.

(a) On mortgages of realty:
10.   (i) Principal 110,085 04
11.   (ii) Interest, including interest on loans on stocks $270,702 25
        (iii) Insurance, taxes, etc., advanced by Company. 8,190 99

(b) On other securities, viz.: Bonds, stocks and deben-
    tures owned by Company:
12.   (i) Principal 264,430 52
13.   (ii) Interest or dividends and special profits on
            bonds and stocks purchased and sold......   384,568 56
                                                                        655,270 81

(c) Loans on bonds, stocks and debentures:
14.   (i) Principal 4,819,116 08
15.   (ii) Interest, included in item 11, part (ii).

D.—Receipts from Real Estate Owned Beneficially by Corporation.

16. (a) Sales (not included in any of the foregoing items). $368 93
17. (b) Rents 36 00
                                                                        404 93

F.—Borrowed Money.

26. (b) Borrowed by taking deposits $14,268.491 53
27. (c) Borrowed on debentures (currency) 102.589 56
28. (d) Borrowed on debentures (sterling) 598,752 79
                                                                        14,969,833 88

        Totals $21,516,418 71

CASH ACCOUNT.

Expenditure for the year ending 31st December, 1913.

Expended on Corporation Account.

A.—Sums Loaned or Invested on Capital Account.

		(Col. 4.)
1. (a)	Loaned on mortgages of realty	$88,565 03
(b)	Loaned or invested in other securities:	
2.	(i) Loans on security of bonds, stocks and debentures	4,969,604 80
3.	(ii) Purchase of bonds, stocks and debentures	165,770 28
6. (c)	Real estate purchased	8,348 33
7. (e)	Insurance or taxes advanced on property mortgaged to the Corporation	8,794 53

B.—Expended on Stock Account.

8.	Dividends paid on permanent stock	175,000 00

C.—Borrowed Money (other than foregoing) or interest thereon paid, viz.:

19. (b)	Deposits: Principal, $14,225,873.78; interest, $60,146.39	$60,146 39	14,225,873 78
20. (c)	Debentures issued in Canada: Principal, $206,297.82; interest, $72,860.52	72,860 52	206,297 82
21. (d)	Debentures issued elsewhere: Principal, $597,745.21; interest, $124,384.99	124,384 99	597,745 21
			257,391 90

D.—Management Expenses (other than foregoing).

25. (a)	Salaries, wages and fees and special tax	$45,427 25	
26. (b)	Commission or brokerage expenses re money borrowed or loaned	12,107 58	
28. (d)	Stationery, postage, printing and advertising	13,260 43	
29. (e)	Law costs	102 02	
30. (f)	Fuel, rent, taxes (other than 7 and 32) and rates...	9,895 08	
32. (h)	Registration fee	350 00	
33. (i)	Directors' compensation for 1913	25,000 00	
			106,142 36

F.—Balance.

37. (a)	Cash on hand and in bank and Loan Company	706,884 67
	Total	$21,516,418 71

MISCELLANEOUS STATEMENT FOR THE YEAR ENDING 31ST DECEMBER, 1913.

1. Amount of Debentures maturing in 1914: Issued in Canada, $22,550.01; Issued elsewhere, £113,397 5s. 11d.
2. Amount of other existing obligations which will mature in 1914, none. No securities maturing in 1914 but stock.
3. Amount of securities held by the Corporation which will mature and become payable to the Corporation in 1914. Loans amounting to $2,508,821.81, subject to call.
4. Average rate of interest per annum paid by the Corporation during 1913: On deposits, 3½%; on debentures, currency, 4%, sterling, 4.203%; on debenture stock.
5. Average rate of interest per annum received by the Corporation during 1913: (a) On mortgages of realty; (b) On other securities.
   (i) Owned beneficially by the Corporation: (a) 5.718%; (b) Fluctuates.
   (ii) Not owned beneficially: (a) None; (b) None.
6. Of the mortgages owned beneficially by the Corporation, $1,124,300.81 is on realty situate in Ontario, and $150,312.00 is on realty situate elsewhere.

7. Of the mortgages not owned beneficially by the Corporation, none is on realty situate in Ontario, and none is on realty situate elsewhere.

8. Loans written off or transferred to real estate account during 1913, viz.:
   (1) Funds or securities owned beneficially, $922.00.
   (ii) Not so owned, none.

9. Number and aggregate amount of mortgages upon which compulsory proceedings have been taken by the Corporation in 1913, viz.:
   (1) Owned beneficially: Number, 2; Amount, $3,417.65.
   (ii) Not so owned: Number, none; Amount, none.

10. Aggregate market value of land mortgaged to the Corporation:
   (1) Mortgages owned beneficially, $3,352,189.50.
   (ii) Not so owned, none.

11. How often are the securities held by the Corporation valued? Doubtful loans watched closely; bonds and stocks and loans on stocks watched daily.

12. (a) Specify the officers of the Corporation who are under bond and for what sum respecively. All officers and clerks, in sums ranging from one to ten thousand dollars, amounting in all to $122,000.00.
   (b) Are the said bonds executed by private sureties or by Guarantee Companies? Guarantee Companies.

13. Date when the accounts of the Corporation were last audited? December 31st, 1913, and receiving monthly audit during the year.

14. Names and addresses of the auditors respectively for 1913 and for 1914 (if appointed):
   For 1913: Walter Sterling, Toronto; Jas. A. Hall, Peterboro.
   For 1914: Walter Sterling, Toronto; Jas. A. Hall, Peterboro.

15. What were the dividend days of the Corporation in 1913, and what rate or rates of dividend were paid on those days respectively? 10% dividend, paid quarterly, on 1st January, April, July, and October.

16. What is the date appointed for the Annual Meeting? January 14th, 1914. Date of last Annual Meeting? January 15th, 1913.

17. Special General Meetings held in 1913. Dates. none.

THE CREDIT FONCIER FRANCO-CANADIEN.

Head Office, 35 St. James Street, Montreal.

As to the Paris Board of Management ("Paris Committee,"), sec. 43.4 V., cap. 60 (Q.), secs. 30.35, 47 V., c. 62 (Q.), Sched. A, Art. 51, enacts as follows: "The general meetings shall be held before the 31st day of May in each year, either at the head office or at Paris in France, according as there may be more shares to order held and stock certificates to bearer deposited in the Province of Quebec or in France, thirty days before the meeting."

By resolution passed at a special general meeting of the Company, held pursuant to article 52 of the by-laws at Paris, France, on the 12th December, 1907, the directors were authorized to increase the capital stock from 25,000,000 franc ($5,000,000) to 40,000,000 ($8,000,000) by the issue of 30,000 new shares of 500 francs ($100) each.

Agent for Ontario: William Edwin Long, Toronto.

CONSTATING INSTRUMENTS.

43.4 V., c. 60, Province of Quebec: An Act to incorporate the Company. Schedule A to the Act contains the original constitution and laws of the Company: See Act of Quebec (1884), 47 V., c. 52, infra.

44 V., c. 58, Dominion of Canada. Section 13 defines the Company's borrowing powers. (See also 62.63 Vic., c. 41 (D.), s. 20.)

44 V., c. 51, Province of Ontario, empowers the Company to establish branch offices in Ontario, to lend money, hold real estate in the Province, etc.

45 V., c. 84, Province of Quebec, amends 43.4 Vic., c. 60 (Q.).

46 V., c. 85, Dominion of Canada, assimilates the powers of the Company to those of other Loan Companies.

47 V., c. 62, Province of Quebec. Schedule A to the Act contains the revised constitution and laws of the Company.

55.56 V., c. 29 (D. Criminal Code, 1892), by sec. 205 (6 d) exempts the Company from the general law prohibiting lotteries.

63 V. (1900), c. 74, Province of Quebec. An Act to amend the Charter of the Credit Foncier Franco-Canadien.

ANNUAL STATEMENT

Of the condition and affairs of the Credit Foncier Franco-Canadien (Loan Company) of Montreal, at the 31st December, 1913, and for the year ending on that day, made to the Registrar of Loan Corporations for the Province of Ontario, pursuant to the laws of the said Province.

The head office of the Corporation is at No. 35 St. James Street, in the City of Montreal, in the Province of Quebec.

The chief agency for Ontario is situated at 42 Victoria Street, in the City of Toronto, in the Province of Ontario.

The chief agent and attorney for Ontario is Wm. Edwin Long, and his address is 42 Victoria Street, Toronto, in the Province of Ontario.

The board is constituted of eleven directors holding office for three years.

The directors and chief executive officers at the 31st December, 1913, were as follows, together with their respective terms of office:

J. H. Thors, President, Paris, France;	May, 1912;	May, 1915.
Hon. J. A. Ouimet, Vice-President, Montreal;	" 1912;	" 1915.
Hon. Sir A. R. Angers, Director, Montreal;	" 1912;	" 1915.
Rene Brice, Director, Paris, France	" 1913;	" 1916.
Count Moise de Camondo, Director, Paris, France;	" 1913;	" 1916.
A. Denfert Rochereau, Director, Paris, France;	" 1911;	" 1914.
H. Laporte, Director, Montreal;	" 1911;	" 1914.
J. E. Moret, Director, Paris, France;	" 1913;	" 1916.
Dr. E. Persillier, Lachapelle, Director, Montreal;	" 1912;	" 1915.
Ch. Cahen d'Anvers, Director, Paris, France;	" 1912;	" 1914.
L. Escoffier, Director, Paris, France;	" 1913;	" 1915.
M. Chevalier, General Manager, Montreal.		
T. R. Nelson, Assistant Manager, Montreal.		
J. Theo. Leclerc, Secretary, Montreal.		

A. Permanent capital stock: Total amount authorized, Fcs. 50,000,000—$9,647,667.19; total amount subscribed, Fcs. 50,000,000—$9,647,667.19, as more particularly set out in Schedule A hereto.

SCHEDULE A.

Class 2.—Fixed and permanent capital stock created by virtue of Joint Stock Companies Act or Private Acts.

Description.	No. of shares.	Par value of shares.	Total amount held.	Total amount paid thereon.	Total remaining unpaid on calls.
2. 50 per cent called	100,000	Francs. 500	Francs. 50,000,000	$ 4,823,833 59	....
	100,000	....	$9,647,667 19	4,823,833 59	....

LIST OF SHAREHOLDERS AS AT 31st DECEMBER, 1913.
(Not printed.)

BALANCE SHEET AS AT 31st DECEMBER, 1913.

Dr.   Capital and Liabilities.

Capital (Liabilities to Stockholders or Shareholders).

A.—Permanent Capital Stock or Shares.

2. (b) Ordinary joint stock capital 50 per cent. called; total called, total paid thereon....	$4,823,833 59	
4. (d) Dividend declared in respect of (2), but not yet paid	9,181 67	
5. (e) Unappropriated profits in respect of (2)	1,006,722 48	
6. (f) Reserve fund in respect of (2)	2,519,918 08	
		$8,359,655 82

Liabilities to the Public.

31. Debentures issued elsewhere than in Canada	$39,330,589 55	
32. Interest accrued on (31)	319,954 36	
39. Due on loans in process of completion or to pay assumed mortgages	299,097 69	
41. Other liabilities to the public, viz.:		
42. (a) Due on debentures and coupons not yet presented..	198,379 38	
44. (c) Sundries	155,619 69	
		$40,303,640 67

Total liabilities $48,663,296 49

BALANCE SHEET.—Continued.

Cr.　　　　　　　　　　　　　　　Assets.

I.—Assets of which the Corporation is the Beneficial Owner.

A.—Immovable Property Owned Beneficially by the Corporation.

1. (a) Office premises situate as follows:—		
At Montreal, Quebec, held in freehold	$200,000 00	
2.　　(i) At Quebec, Quebec	10,000 00	
3.　　(ii) At Vancouver, British Columbia	200,461 49	
4.　　(iii) At Edmonton, Alta	50,000 00	
(iv) At Regina, Saskatchewan	60,000 00	
5. (b) Freehold land (including building) other than		
foregoing	11,311 99	
		$531,773 48

B.—Debts secured by Mortgages of Land.

9. (a) Debts (other than item 10) secured by mortgages		
of land $40,152,633 02		
11. (c) Interest due on item 9 and not included therein...	252,608 05	
Interest accrued on item 9, but not yet due	268,723 36	
		40,673,964 43

C.—Debts not above enumerated for which the Corporation
holds securities as follows:

14. (b) Debts secured by municipal bonds or debentures ..	$159,280 55	
15. (c) Debts secured by Public School debentures	278,761 72	
16. (d) Debts secured by Loan Corporation debentures....	774,899 99	
20. (h) Debts secured only by permanent stock or shares of		
the Corporation	3,593 74	
22. (j) Call loans	786,238 72	
33. (k) Debts secured by debentures of incorporated com-		
panies	3,019,209 94	
		5,021,984 66

E.—Cash.

31. (a) On hand	23,590 08	
32. (b) In banks	2,360,103 05	
		2,383,693 13

F.—Assets not hereinbefore mentioned.

42. (f) Sundries ..../.......................................		51,880 79
Total assets $48,663,296 49		

CASH ACCOUNT.

Receipts for year ending 31st December, 1913.

For the Province of Ontario only.

I.—Received by the Corporation for its Own Use.

A.—Balance from 31st December, 1912.

	(Col. 3)	(Col. 4)
2. Cash on hand and in banks ....…		$12,214 81

CASH ACCOUNT.—Continued.

Receipts for the year ending 31st December, 1913.

C.—Receipts on account of Investments, Loans or Debts.

    (a) On mortgages of realty:

10.	(i) Principal	$336,601 85	
11.	(ii) Interest	211,773 17	
	(iii) Insurance, etc., advanced borrowers, and repaid	5,568 90	
	(b) On other securities:		
12.	(i) Principal	1,000 00	
			554,943 92

E.—Miscellaneous.

18.	(a) Commission	292 11	
19.	(b) Premium on bonus on loans	1,342 41	
			1,634 52

G.—Receipts from other sources.

30.	(a) Received from Head Office	792,965 15

	Total	$1,361,758 40

CASH ACCOUNT.

Expenditure for the year ending 31st December, 1913.

For the Province of Ontario only.

I.—Expended on Corporation Account.

A.—Sums Loaned or Invested on Capital Account.

		(Col. 3)	(Total Col. 4.)
1.	(a) Loaned on mortgages of realty	$1,145,424 45	
	(b) Loaned or invested in other securities, viz.:		
2.	(i) On Stocks	143,800 00	
			$1,289,224 45
7.	(e) Insurance, etc., advanced on property and mortgage to the Corporation		3,767 65

D.—Management Expenses (other than foregoing).

		(Col. 1.)	
25.	(a) Salaries, wages and fees	$8,285 94	
26.	(b) Commission or brokerage............	8,629 20	
28.	(d) Stationery, postage, printing and advertising	1,062 23	
30.	(f) Fuel, rent, taxes (other than in 7 and 32) and rates	2,730 59	
31.	(g) Travelling expenses	442 11	
32.	(h) Registration fees	300 00	
33.	(i) Ontario Government tax.............	1,955 20	
			$23,405 27

F.— Balance.

37.	(b) Cash on hand and in banks	45,361 03

	Total	$1,361,758 40

MISCELLANEOUS STATEMENT FOR THE YEAR ENDING 31ST DECEMBER, 1913.

1. Amount of debentures maturing in 1914: Issued in Canada, none; issued elsewhere, a certain number are retired each year by drawing.
2. Amount of other existing obligations which will mature in 1914: None.
3. Amount of securities held by the Corporation which will mature and become payable to the Corporation in 1914: No special account kept of loans maturing each year.
4. Average rate of interest per annum paid by the Corporation during 1913: On deposits, none; on debentures, 5%; on debenture stock.
5. Average rate of interest per annum received by the Corporation during 1913: (a) on mortgages of realty; (b) on other securities; (i) owned beneficially by the Corporation; (a) 6.68%; (b) approximately 6%; (ii) not owned beneficially; (a) all securities are owned beneficially.
6. Of the mortgages owned beneficially by the Corporation, $3,835,522.31 is on realty situate in Ontario, and $36,317,110.71 is on realty situate elsewhere.
7. Of the mortgages not owned beneficially by the Corporation: none is on realty situate in Ontario, and none is on realty situate elsewhere.
8. Loans written off or transferred to real estate account during 1913, viz.:
   (i) Funds or securities owned beneficially in Ontario, $1,600.00.
   (ii) Not so owned.
9. Number and aggregate amount of mortgages upon which compulsory proceedings have been taken by the Corporation in 1913, viz:
   (i) Owned beneficially in Ontario: No. 1; amount, $1,600.00.
   (ii) Not so owned: None.
10. Aggregate market value of land mortgaged to the Corporation:
    (i) Mortgages owned beneficially, $80,400,000.
11. How often are the securities held by the Corporation valued: At no regular period.
12. (a) Specify the officers of the Corporation who are under bond and for what sum respectively: General manager, to the extent of 100 shares of the Company, and the Directors to the extent of 50 shares each. (b) Are the said bonds executed by private sureties or by guarantee companies?
13. Date when the accounts of the Corporation were last audited: 28th February, 1913.
14. Names and addresses of the auditors respectively for 1913 and for 1914 (if appointed):
    For 1913: J. O. Gravel and P. Bienvena, both of Montreal.
    For 1914: J. O. Gravel and P. Bienvena, both of Montreal.
15. What were the dividend days of the Corporation in 1913, and what rate or rates of dividend were paid on those days respectively? 1st June, 1913, on base of 9½%.
16. What is the date appointed for the annual meeting? May, 1914. Date of last annual meeting? 19th May, 1913.
17. Special general meetings held in 1913: Dates.

CROWN SAVINGS AND LOAN COMPANY.

Head Office, Petrolea, Ontario.

CONSTATING INSTRUMENTS.

Incorporated under the Building Societies Act, R.S.O. 1877, c. 164, by declaration filed with the Clerk of the Peace for the County of Lambton, 30th January, 1882.

The lending and borrowing powers of the Company are now governed by the Loan and Trust Corporations Act, R.S.O., 1914, Chap. 184.

ANNUAL STATEMENT

Of the condition and affairs of the Crown Savings and Loan Company of Petrolea at the 31st December, 1913, and for the year ending on that day, made to the Registrar of Loan Corporations for the Province of Ontario, pursuant to the laws of tho said Province.

The head office of the Corporation is at the Town of Petrolea in the Province of Ontario.

The Board is constituted of nine directors holding office for one year.

The directors and chief executive officers of the Corporation at the 31st December, 1913, were as follows, together with their respective office:

J. H. Fairbank, President, Petrolea;   Feb. 6, 1913; Feb. 5, 1914.
J. L. Englehart, Vice-President, Toronto;   "   "
Charles Egan, Director, Petrolea;   "   "
C. 'O. F. Fairbank, Director, Petrolea;
Joseph McCormick, Director, Kertch;
W. English, Director, Petrolea
John Hunter, Director, Petrolea;
Robert Jackson, Director, Petrolea;
B. P. Corey, Director, Petrolea;
Wm. English, Manager, Petrolea;

A. Permanent capital stock: Total amount authorized, $1,000,000; total amount subscribed, $226,450, as more particularly set out in Schedule A hereto.

SCHEDULE A

Class I.—Fixed and permanent capital stock created by virtue of Building Society Acts.

Description.	Total amount issued and subsisting at 31st December, 1913.			Total amount of actual payments thereon.	Total amount unpaid and constituting an asset of the Corporation.
	No. of shares.	Par value.			
Fully called	4,529	$50	$226,450	$226,450	....

LIST OF SHAREHOLDERS AS AT 31ST DECEMBER, 1913.

(Not printed.)

4 L.C.

BALANCE SHEET AS AT 31st DECEMBER, 1913.

Dr.   Capital and Liabilities.

Capital (Liabilities to Stockholders or Shareholders).

A.—Permanent capital stock or shares.

1. (a) Ordinary joint stock capital fully called; total called, total paid thereon	$226,450 00	
5. (e) Unappropriated profits	4,363 35	
6. (f) Reserve fund in respect of (1)	67,000 00	
		$297,813 35

Liabilities to the Public.

27. Deposits, right reserved to require 30 days' notice of any withdrawal	$41,663 84	
29. Debentures issued in Canada	184,678 73	
		226,342 57
Total liabilities		$524,155 92

Cr.   Assets.

I.—Assets of which the Corporation is the Beneficial Owner.

B.—Debts secured by Mortgages of Land.

9. (a) Debts (other than item 10) secured by mortgages of land	$496,459 03

C.—Debts not above enumerated for which the Corporation holds securities as follows:

14. (b) Debts secured by municipal bonds or debentures	574 79

E.—Cash.

33.	(1) In bank	27,122 10
	Total assets	$524,155 92

CASH ACCOUNT.

Receipts for year ending 31st December, 1913.

I.—Received by the Corporation for its Own Use.

A.—Balance from 31st December, 1912.

	(Col. 3.)	(Col. 4.)
1 Cash.		
3. (ii) In bank	$4,136 24	
B.—Sums received wholly or partly on Capital Stock.		
4. (a) Calls on joint stock permanent capital	$100 00	
5. (b) Premiums on (4)	20 00	

CASH ACCOUNT.—Continued.

Receipts for the year ending 31st December, 1913.

C.—Receipts on account of Investments, Loans, or Debts.

		(Col. 1.)	(Col. 3.)	(Col. 4, Total.)
(a) On mortgages of realty:				
10.	(i) Principal		$90,819 59	
11.	(ii) Interest	$28,559 03		
(b) On other securities:				
12.	(i) Principal		653 34	
	(ii) Interest	24 75		
F.—Borrowed Money.				
26. (b)	Borrowed money by taking deposits..		25,549 93	
27. (c)	Borrowed on debentures		39,150 00	
	Totals	$28,583 78	$160,429 10	$189,012 88

CASH ACCOUNT.

Expenditure for the year ending 31st December, 1913.

I.—Expended on Corporation Account.

A. Sums Loaned or Invested on Capital Account:

		(Col. 1.)	(Col. 3.)	(Col. 4, Total.)
1. (a)	Loaned on mortgages of realty.......	....	$76,988 02	
B.—Expended on Stock Account.				
8.	Dividends paid on permanent stock	$13,585 50		
C.—Borrowed Money (other than foregoing) or interest thereon paid, viz.:				
18. (a)	Bank account (principal and interest)	....	....	
19. (b)	Deposits: Principal, $16,511.17; interest, $1,102.11	1,102 11	16,511 17	
20. (c)	Debentures issued in Canada: Principal, $42,731.95; interest, $8,426.58.	8,426 58	42,731 95	
D.—Management Expenses (other than foregoing).				
25. (a)	Salaries, wages and fees	1,326 00		
28. (d)	Stationery, postage, printing and advertising	132 55		
30. (f)	Fuel, rent, taxes (other than in 7 and 32)	365 73		
32. (h)	Registration fees	227 55		
33. (i)	Other management expenditure	114 72		
E.—Other expenditures, viz.:—				
34. (a)	General interest	373 85		
F.—Balance.				
37. (a)	Cash in bank	....	27,122 10	
	Totals	$25,659 64	$163,353 24	$189,012 88

1. Amount of debentures maturing in 1914: Issued in Canada, $99,450.00; issued elsewhere, none.
2. Amount of other existing obligations which will mature in 1914: None.
3. Amount of securities held by the Corporation which will mature and become payable to the Corporation in 1914: Estimated $80,000.
4. Average rate of interest per annum paid by the Corporation during 1913: On deposits, 3.15%; on debentures, 4½%; on debenture stock, none.
5. Average rate of interest per annum received by the Corporation during 1913: (a) On mortgages of realty; (b) on other securities;
    (i) Owned beneficially by the Corporation: (a) 5.60%; (b) 4.40%.
    (ii) Not owned beneficially: (a) none; (b) none.
6. Of the mortgages owned beneficially by the Corporation, $496,459.03 is on realty situate in Ontario, and none is on realty situate elsewhere.
7. Of the mortgages not owned beneficially by the Corporation, none is on realty situate in Ontario, and none is on realty situate elsewhere.
8. Loans written off or transferred to real estate account during 1912, viz.:
    (i) Funds or securities owned beneficially, none.
    (ii) Not so owned,
9. Number and aggregate amount of mortgages upon which compulsory proceedings have been taken by the Corporation in 1913, viz.:
    (i) Owned beneficially, none; amount, none.
    (ii) Not so owned, none; amount, none.
10. Aggregate market value of land mortgaged to the Corporation:
    (i) Mortgages owned beneficially: Estimated, $1,500,000.
    (ii) Not so owned, none.
11. How often are the securities held by the Corporation valued? Annually.
12. (a) Specify the officers of the Corporation who are under bond and for what sum respectively. Manager, $5,000; clerk, $1,000.
    (b) Are the said bonds executed by private sureties or by Guarantee Companies? Guarantee Companies.
13. Date when the accounts of the Corporation were last audited: Dec. 31, 1913.
14. Names and addresses of the auditors respectively for 1913 and for 1914 (if appointed):
    For 1913: J. M. Fowler, A. M. McQueen.
    For 1914: J. M. Fowler, A. M. McQueen.
15. What were the dividend days of the Corporation in 1913 and what rate or rates of dividend were paid on those days respectively? June 30, 1913, 3%; Dec. 31, 1913, 3%.
16. What is the date appointed for the annual meeting? February 5th, 1914. Date of last annual meeting? February 6th, 1913.
17. Special general meeting held in 1913: Dates, none.

THE DOMINION SAVINGS AND INVESTMENT SOCIETY.

Head Office, London, Ontario.

Incorporated under Chapter 53 of the Consolidated Statutes of Upper Canada as a Permanent Building Society, by declaration filed with the Clerk of the Peace for the County of Middlesex, 20th April, 1872.

The lending and borrowing powers are governed by the Loan and Trust Corporations Act, R.S.O. 1914, chap. 184.

ANNUAL STATEMENT

Of the condition and affairs of the Dominion Savings and Investment Society of London, Ontario, at the 31st December, 1913, and for the year ending on that day, made to the Registrar of Loan Corporations for the Province of Ontario, pursuant to the laws of the said Province.

The head office of the Corporation is at No. 371 Richmond Street, in the City of London, in the Province of Ontario.

The Board is constituted of seven directors, holding office for one year.

The directors and chief executive officers of the Corporation at 31st December, 1913, were as follows, together with their respective terms of office:

Thomas H. Purdom, K.C., Pres., London, Ont.;   10th Feb., 1914-9th Feb., 1915.
John Ferguson, Vice-President, London, Ont.;   "   "
W. J. McMurtry, Director, Toronto, Ont.;   "   "
John Purdom, Director, London, Ont.;
Samuel Wright, Director, London, Ont.;
John Milne, Director. London, Ont.;   "
Nathaniel Mills, Managing-Director, London, Ont.;   "

A. Permanent capital stock; total amount authorized, $1,500,000; total amount subscribed, $1,000,000, as more particularly set out in Schedule A hereto.

SCHEDULE A.

Class 1.—Fixed and permanent capital stock created by virtue of Building Society Acts.

Description.	No of shares.	Par value of shares.	Total amount held.	Total amount paid thereon.	Total amount unpaid and constituting an asset of the Corporation.
		$	$	$ c.	$ c.
Fully called stock.	20,000	50	1,000,000	934,750 07	65,249 93

LIST OF SHAREHOLDERS AS AT 31st DECEMBER, 1913.

(Not printed.)

BALANCE SHEET AS AT 31st DECEMBER, 1913.

Dr.   Capital and Liabilities.

Capital (Liabilities to Stockholders or Shareholders).

1. (a) Ordinary joint stock capital fully called; total called; total paid thereon	$934,300 00	
2. (b) Ordinary joint stock capital; ....% called; total called; total paid thereon	450 07	
4. (d) Dividends declared in respect of (1), (2), but not yet paid	23,357 50	
6. (f) Reserve fund in respect of (1), (2)	200,000 00	
7. (g) Contingent fund in respect of (1), (2)	4,416 88	
		$1,162,524 45

Liabilities to the Public.

27. Deposits (right reserved to require 30 days' notice of any withdrawal, including interest)	$703,717 81	
29. Debentures issued in Canada	103,424 51	
30. Interest due and accrued on (29)	1,796 08	
31. Debentures issued elsewhere than in Canada	306,985 63	
32. Interest due and accrued on (31)	1,616 00	
		1,117,540 03
Total liabilities		$2,280,064 48

Cr.   Assets.

I.—Assets of which the Corporation is the Beneficient Owner.

B.—Debts secured by Mortgages of Land.

9. (a) Debts (other than item 10) secured by mortgages of land	$1,566,046 83	
10. (b) Debts secured by mortgaged land held for sale	94,591 50	

C.—Debts not above enumerated for which the Corporation holds securities as follows:

14. (b) Debts secured by municipal bonds or debentures	829 00	
16. (d) Debts secured by Loan Corporations debentures	9,500 00	
20. (h) Debts secured only by permanent stock or shares of the Corporation	46,679 05	
22. (j) Debts secured by stocks and bonds	473,399 28	

E.—Cash.

31. (a) On hand	5,521 47	
32. (b) In banks in Canada	75,008 23	
In banks in England and Scotland	8,489 12	
Total assets		$2,280,064 48

CASH ACCOUNT.

Receipts for the year ending 31st December, 1913.

I.—Received by the Corporation for its Own Use.

A.—Balance from 31st December 1912.

	Total (Col. 4).
(a) Cash not already shown under (1):	
2. (i) On hand	$3,560 44
3. (ii) In banks	38,211 17

BALANCE SHEET.—Continued.

Receipts for the year ending 31st December, 1913.

C.—Receipts on account of Investment, Loans, or Debts.

(a) On mortgages of realty:
10.	(i) Principal	294,576 25
11.	(ii) Interest	117,455 36

(b) On other securities:
12.	(i) Principal	18 999 37
13.	(ii) Interest or dividends	27,404 10

F.—Borrowed Money.

26. (b)	Borrowed by taking deposits	1,315,063 12
27. (c)	Borrowed on debentures	114,044 02

	Total	$1,929,313 83

CASH ACCOUNT.

Expenditure for the year ending 31st December, 1913.

I.—Expended on Corporation Account.

A.—Sums Loaned or Invested on Capital Account.

Total (Col. 4).
1. (a)	Loaned on mortgages of realty	$242,214 94
	(b) Loaned and invested in other securities, viz.:	
3.	(ii) On stocks, bonds and debentures	69,271 99

B.—Expended on Stock Account.

8.	Dividends paid on permanent stock	42,043 50

C.—Borrowed Money (other than foregoing) or interest thereon paid, viz.:

19. (b)	Deposits: Principal, $1,331,817.06; interest, $24,962.11	1,356,779 17
20. (c)	Debentures issued in Canada: Principal, $39,683.84; interest, $4,133.43	43,817 27
21. (d)	Debentures issued elsewhere: Principal, $59,495.00; interest, $12,490.18	71,985 18

D.—Management Expenses (other than foregoing).

25. (a)	Salaries, wages and fees	9,141 00
26. (b)	Commission or brokerage	1,153 91
28. (d)	Stationery, postage, printing and advertising	1,827 87
30. (f)	Fuel, rent, taxes (other than 7 and 32) and rates	1,052 19
31. (g)	Travelling expenses	39 30
32. (h)	Registration fee	150 00

CASH ACCOUNT.—Continued.

Expenditure for the year ending 31st December, 1913.

E.—Other Expenditures, viz.:

34. (a)	Telephone and telegraph	$135 44
36. (c)	Sundries	683 25

F.—Balance.

37. (a)	Cash on hand and in bank	39,018 82

	Totals	$1,929,313 83

MISCELLANEOUS STATEMENT FOR THE YEAR ENDING 31ST DECEMBER, 1913.

1. Amount of debentures maturing in 1914: Issued in Canada, $28,304.50; Issued elsewhere, $45,454.66 (£9,340).
2. Amount of other existing obligations which will mature in 1914: Exclusive of deposits, none.
3. Amount of securities held by the Corporation which will mature and become payable to the Corporation in 1914: $512,490.62.
4. Average rate of interest per annum paid by the Corporation during 1913: On deposits, 3.748%; on debentures, 4.22%; on debenture stock, none.
5. Average rate of interest per annum received by the Corporation during 1913: (a) On mortages of realty; (b) On other securities:
   (i) Owned beneficially by the Corporation: (a) 6.082%; (b) 5.744%.
   (ii) Not owned beneficially: (a) None; (b) None.
6. Of the mortgages owned beneficially by the Corporation: $1,635,169.95 is on realty situate in Ontario, and $25,468.38 is on realty situate elsewhere.
7. Of the mortgages not owned beneficially by the Corporation: None is on realty situate in Ontario and none is on realty situate elsewhere.
8. Loans written off or transferred to real estate account during 1913, viz.:
   (i) Funds or securities owned beneficially: None.
   (ii) Not so owned: None.
9. Number and aggregate amount of mortgages upon which compulsory proceedings have been taken by the Corporation in 1913, viz.:
   (i) Owned beneficially: Number, 2; amount, $3,990.46.
   (ii) Not so owned: Number, none; amount, none.
10. Aggregate market value of land mortgaged to the Corporation:
    (i) Mortgages owned beneficially: $3,105,181.50.
    (ii) Not so owned: None.
11. How often are the securities held by the Corporation valued? Annually.
12. (a) Specify the officers of the Corporation who are under bond and for what sum respectively: Manager, $10,000.00; Accountant, $5,000.00; Teller, $5,000.00.
    (b) Are the said bonds executed by private sureties or by Guarantee Companies? Guarantee Company except Accountant, by private individual.
13. Date when the accounts of the Corporation were last audited? 31st December, 1913.
14. Names and addresses of the auditors respectively for 1913 and for 1914 (if appointed):
    For 1913: John Lochead and Francis B. Ware.
    For 1914: John Lochead and Francis B. Ware.
15. What were the dividend days of the Corporation in 1913 and what rate or rates of dividend were paid on those days respectively? January 1st, July 1st, at rate of 4% per annum and bonus of ¼ of 1%.
16. What is the date appointed for the Annual Meeting? 10th February, 1914. Date of last Annual Meeting? 11th February, 1913.
17. Special General Meetings held in 1913: Dates, none.

EAST LAMBTON FARMERS' LOAN AND SAVINGS COMPANY.

Head Office, Forest, Ontario. (Company's By-law No. 29.)

CONSTATING STATEMENTS.

Incorporated under the Building Societies Act, R.S.O. 1887, c. 169, by declaration filed with the Clerk of the Peace for the County of Lambton, 19th December, 1891.

The lending and borrowing powers are governed by the Loan and Trust Corporations Act, R.S.O. 1914, chap. 184.

ANNUAL STATEMENT

Of the condition and affairs of the East Lambton Farmers' Loan and Savings Company of Forest, Ontario, at 31st December, 1913, and for the year ending on that day, made to the Registrar of Loan Corporations for the Province of Ontario, pursuant to the laws of the said Province.

The head office of the Corporation is at No. 74, south side King Street, in the Town of Forest, in the Province of Ontario.

The Board is constituted of eight directors, holding office for two years.

The directors and chief executive officers of the Corporation at 31st December, 1913, were as follows, together with their respective terms of office:

James Hutton, M.D., President, Forest;	Feb. 28th, 1913,	Feb. 28th, 1915
R. J. McCormick, M.P.P., Vice-Pres., Walford, R.R. No. 2;	" 1914,	" 1916
P. Cairns, Director, Forest	" 1913,	" 1915
Duncan Weir, Director, Forest;	" 1913,	" 1915
John McE. Shaw, Director, Forest;	" 1913,	" 1915
Wm. N. Ironside, Director, Thedford;	" 1914,	" 1916
D. P. Campbell, Director, Thedford;	" 1914,	" 1916
Thos. Sutcliffe, Director, Forest;	" 1914,	" 1916
N. Tripp, Manager-Secretary, Forest.		

A.—Permanent capital stock: Total amount authorized, $500,000; total amount subscribed, $200,000, as more particularly set out in Schedule A hereto.

SCHEDULE A.

Class 1.—Fixed and permanent capital stock created by virtue of Building Societies Act.

Description.	Total amount issued and subsisting at 31st December, 1913.			Total amount of actual payments thereon.	Total amount unpaid and constituting an asset of the Corporation.
	No. of shares.	Par value of shares.	—		
1. Fully called stock	4,000	$ 50	$ 200,000	$ c. 200,000 00	$ c. ....

LIST OF SHAREHOLDERS AS AT 31st DECEMBER, 1913.

(Not printed.)

BALANCE SHEET AS AT 31st DECEMBER, 1912.

Dr.   Capital and Liabilities.

Capital (Liabilities to Stockholders or Shareholders).

A.—Permanent Capital Stock or Shares.

1. (a) Ordinary joint stock capital fully called; total called, $200,000; total paid thereon	$200,000 00	
4. (d) Dividends declared in respect of (1), but not yet paid	6,000 00	
6. (f) Reserve fund in respect of (1)	43,457 03	
		$249,457 03

Liabilities to the Public.

27. Deposits (right reserved to require 30 days' notice of any withdrawal)	$169,944 71	
29. Debentures issued in Canada	81,125 00	
30. Interest due and accrued on (29)	1,410 60	
		252,480 31
Total liabilities		$501,937 34

Cr.   Assets.

I.—Assets of which the Corporation is the Beneficial Owner.

A.—Immovable Property Owned Beneficially by Corporation.

1. (a) Office premises situate as follows:		
2. (1) At Forest, Ont., held in freehold		$2,500 00

B.—Debts secured by Mortgages of Land.

9. (a) Debts (other than item 10) secured by mortgages of land	$280,607 87	
11. (c) Interest due and accrued on item (9) and not in cluded therein.	14,071 66	
		294,679 53

C.—Debts not above enumerated for which the Corporation holds securities as follows:

14. (b) Debts secured by municipal bonds or debentures	$117,675 95	
15. (c) Debts secured by Public School debentures	67,591 15	
20. (h) Debts secured only by permanent stock or shares of the Corporation	7,337 85	
26. (n) Interest due and accrued on items (14), (15) and (20) and not included therein	6,641 99	
		199,246 94

E.—Cash.

31. (a) On hand and in Bank		5,510 87
Total assets		$501,937 34

CASH ACCOUNT.

Receipts for the year ending 31st December, 1913.

I.—Received by the Corporation for its Own Use.

A.—Balance from 31st December, 1912.

(b) Cash:

2.   (i) On hand $2,567 56

B.—Sums Received Wholly or Partly on Capital Stock.

4. (a) Calls on Joint Stock permanent capital 100 00

C.—Receipts on account of Investments, Loans or Debts.

(a) On mortgages of realty:

10.	(i) Principal	$38,499 50	
11.	(ii) Interest on items 10, 12, 13 and 14	27,156 19	

(a) On mortgages of realty:

12.	(i) Principal, municipal debentures	7,559 78	
13.	(ii) North West school debentures	8,993 33	

(c) Other debts:

14.	(i) Principal, loans on stock	6,012 15	88,220 95

D.—Receipts from Real Estate Owned Beneficially by Corporation.

17. (b) Rents 97 50

F.—Borrowed Money.

26. (b) Borrowed by taking deposits	$136,201 33		
27. (c) Borrowed on debentures	22,825 00	159,026 33	

Total $250,012 34

CASH ACCOUNT.

Expenditure for the year ending 31st December, 1913.

I.—Expended on Corporation Account.

	(Col. 1.)	(Col. 4.)
1. (a) Loaned on mortgages of realty	$21,900 00	
(b) Loaned on other securities:		
2. (i) On municipal debentures	9,674 40	
3. (ii) N. W. school debentures	10,085 20	$41,659 60

B.—Expended on Stock Account.

8. Dividends paid on permanent stock 10,994 50

C.—Borrowed Money (other than foregoing) or interest thereon paid, viz.:

18. (a) Bank account, interest	$ 549 76	
19. (b) Deposits: Principal, $150,004.97; interest, $5,955.54	155,960 51	
20. (c) Debentures issued in Canada: Principal, $29,600.00; interest, $2,548.50	32,148 50	188,658 77

CASH ACCOUNT.—Continued.

Expenditure for the year ending 31st December, 1913.

D.—Management Expenses (other than foregoing).

25. (a) Salaries, wages and fees	$1,500 00	
28. (d) Stationery, postage, printing and advertising	31 21	
30. (f) Fuel, rent, taxes (other than 7 and 32) and rates...	290 26	
32. (h) Registration fees, including filing fee	80 00	
33. (i) Other management expenditure	85 08	
		$1,986 55

E.—Other Expenditures, viz.:

34. (a) Repaid overdraft in bank of 1912	227 00

F.—Balance.

37. (a) Cash on hand and in Bank	6,485 92
Total	$250,012 34

MISCELLANEOUS STATEMENT FOR THE YEAR ENDING 31ST DECEMBER, 1913.

1. Amount of Debentures maturing in 1914: Issued in Canada, $39,000; issued elsewhere, none.
2. Amount of other existing obligations which will mature in 1914, none.
3. Amount of securities held by the Corporation which will mature and become payable to the Corporation in 1914, $32,440.
4. Average rate of interest per annum paid by the Corporation during 1913: On deposits, 3.55; on debentures, 4%; on debenture stock none.
5. Average rate of interest per annum received by the Corporation during 1913:
    (a) On mortgages of realty; (b) on other securities.
    (i) Owned beneficially by the Corporation: (a) 5.22%; (b) 5.70%.
    (ii) Not owned beneficially: (a) none, (b) none.
6. Of the mortgages owned beneficially by the Corporation, $273,457.87 is on realty situate in Ontario, and $7,150.00 is on realty situate elsewhere.
7. Of the mortgages not owned beneficially by the Corporation, none is on realty situate in Ontario, and none is on realty situate elsewhere.
8. Loans written off or transferred to real estate account during 1913, viz.:
    (i) Funds or securities owned beneficially, none.
    (ii) Not so owned, none.
9. Number and aggregate amount of mortgages upon which compulsory proceedings have been taken by the Corporation in 1913, viz.:
    (i) Owned beneficially, none; amount, none.
    (ii) Not so owned, none; amount, none.
10. Aggregate market value of land mortgaged to the Corporation:
    (i) Mortgages owned beneficially, $548,800.00.
    (ii) Not so owned, none.
11. How often are the securities held by the Corporation valued? Yearly.
12. (a) Specify the officers of the Corporation who are under bond, and for what sum respectively: Manager, $5,000.
    (b) Are the said bonds executed by private sureties or by Guarantee Companies? Guarantee Company.
13. Date when the accounts of the Corporation were last audited: February 11th, 1914.
14. Names and addresses of the auditors respectively for 1913 and for 1914 (if appointed):
    For 1913: A. Williams and J. M. McKenzie.
    For 1914: A. Williams and A. Jamieson.
15. What were the dividend days of the Corporation in 1913, and what rate or rates of dividend were paid on those days respectively? June 30th, at 5½%; December 31st, at 6%.
16. What is the date appointed or the Annual Meeting? Third Saturday in February. Date of last Annual Meeting? February 21st, 1914.
17. Special General Meetings held in 1913: None.

THE FRONTENAC LOAN AND INVESTMENT SOCIETY.

Head Office, Kingston, Ont.

CONSTATING INSTRUMENTS.

Incorporated under the Building Societies' Act, Consolidated Statutes of Upper Canada, chap. 53, by declaration filed with the Clerk of the Peace for the County of Frontenac, 13th August, 1863.

The lending and the borrowing powers are governed by the Loan and Trust Corporations Act, R.S.O., 1914, chap. 184.

ANNUAL STATEMENT

Of the condition and affairs of the Frontenac Loan and Investment Society of Kingston, Ontario, on the 31st December, 1913, and for the year ending on that day, made to the Registrar of Loan Corporations for the Province of Ontario, pursuant to the laws of the said Province.

The head office of the Corporation is at No. 87 Clarence Street, in the City of Kingston, in the Province of Ontario.

The Board is constituted of five directors, holding office for one year.

The directors and chief executive officers of the Corporation at 31st December, 1913, were as follows, together with their respective terms of office:

Lieut.-Col. Henry R. Smith, C.M.G., President, Ottawa, Ont.; March, 1913; March, 1914.
Dr. R. C. Cartwright, Vice-President, Napanee, Ont.; March, 1913; March, 1914.
W. H. Moutray, Director, Stella, Ont.; March, 1913; March, 1914.
Lieut.-Col. A. B. Cunningham, Director, Kingston, Ont.; March, 1913; March, 1914.
W. F. Nickle, M.P., K.C., Director, Kingston, Ont.; March, 1913; March, 1914.
Lieut.-Col. S. C. McGill, Manager, Kingston, Ont.; March, 1913; March, 1914.

A.—Permanent capital stock: Total amount authorized, unlimited; total amount subscribed, $200,000, as more particularly set out in Schedule A hereto.

SCHEDULE A.

Class 1.—Fixed and permanent capital stock created by virtue of Building Society Acts.

Description.	Total amount issued and subsisting at 31st December, 1913.			Total amount of actual payments thereon.	Total amount unpaid and constituting an asset of the Corporation.
	No. of shares.	Par value of shares.	—		
Fully called	4,000	$ 50	$ 200,000	$ 200,000	....

LIST OF SHAREHOLDERS AS AT 31st DECEMBER, 1913.

(Not printed.)

BALANCE SHEET AS AT 31st DECEMBER, 1913.

Dr.   Capital and Liabilities.

Capital (Liabilities to Stockholders or Shareholders).

A.—Permanent Capital Stock or Shares.

1.	(a)	Ordinary joint stock capital, fully called; total called, $200,000.00; total paid thereon.................	$200,000 00
4.	(d)	Dividends declared in respect of (1), but not yet paid	5,224 75
6.	(f)	Reserve fund in respect of (1).....................	30,000 00
7.	(g)	Contingent fund in respect of (1).................	11,050 00

$246,274 75

Liabilities to the Public.

27.	Deposits, including unclaimed deposits (right reserved to require 30 days' notice of any withdrawal).....	$77,065 85
29.	Debentures issued in Canada...........................	8,000 00
30.	Interest due or accrued on (29).......................	160 00

85,225 85

Total liabilities $331,500 60

Cr.   Assets.

I.—Assets of which the Corporation is the Beneficial Owner.

A.—Immovable Property Owned Beneficially by Corporation.

1.	(a)	Office premises situate as follows:	
2.		(i) At Kingston, Ont., held in freehold...........	$4,981 91
5.	(b)	Freehold land (including buildings) other than foregoing..	915 58

$5,897 49

B.—Debts secured by Mortgages of Land.

9.	(a)	Debts (other than item 10) secured by mortgages of land...	$225,534 32
10.	(b)	Debts secured by mortgaged land held for sale.......	12,131 61

237,665 93

C.—Debts not above enumerated for which the Corporation holds securities as follows:

20.	(h)	Debts secured only by permanent stock or shares of the Corporation and accrued interest...........	$19,428 78
22.	(j)	Debts secured by bonds............................	10,013 50
23.	(k)	Debts secured by preferred stocks, etc., etc..........	37,723 46
24.	(l)	Debts secured by life assurance policy..............	4,000 00
25.	(m)	Debts secured by Society's debentures..............	858 32

72,024 06

E.—Cash.

31.	(a)	Cash on hand	$421 01
32.	(b)	In banks	15,392 11

15,813 12

F.—Assets not hereinbefore mentioned.

38.	(b)	Office furniture	100 00

Total assets $331,500 60

CASH ACCOUNT.

Receipts for the year ending 31st December, 1913.

I.—Received by the Corporation for Its Own Use.

A.—Balance from 31st December, 1912.

(1) Cash not already shown under (1):

2.	(i) On hand	$1,702 65
3.	(ii) In bank	10,307 20
		$12,009 85

C.—Receipts on account of Investments, Loans or Debts.

(a) On mortgages of realty:

10.	(i) Principal }	
11.	(ii) Interest }	46,412 25
	(b) On other securities:	
12.	(i) Principal........................ .. ..•......	2,611 33
13.	(ii) Interest or dividends	2,709 03

D.—Receipts from Real Estate Owned Beneficially by Corporation.

17. (b)	Rents............:....	240 00

F.—Borrowed Money.

26. (b)	Borrowed by taking deposits.....................................	97,033 01
27. (c)	Borrowed on debentures	8,000 00

G.—Receipts from other Sources.

30. (a)	Solicitors' charges	56 60
	Totals..	$169,072 07

CASH ACCOUNT.

Expenditure for the year ending 31st December, 1913.

I.—Expended on Corporation Account.

A.—Sums Loaned or Invested on Capital Account.

		Total (Col. 4.)
1. (a)	Loaned on mortgages of realty.................................	$24,861 32
	(b) Loaned or invested in other securities:	
2.	(i) Shareholders' stock	2,000 00
3.	(ii) Bonds................................	5,061 47

B.—Expended on Stock Account.

8.	Dividend paid on permanent stock....................................	9,974 50

C.—Borrowed Money (other than foregoing) or interest thereon paid, viz:

19. (b)	Deposits: Principal, $99,801.79; interest, $27.53..................	99,829 32
20. (c)	Debentures issued in Canada: Principal, $7,500; interest, $300....	7,800 00

CASH ACCOUNT.—Continued.

Expenditure for the year ending 31st December, 1913.

D.—Management Expenses (other than foregoing).

25. (a) Salaries, wages and fees	$2,647	50
26. (b) Commission or brokerage	53	54
28. (d) Stationery, postage, printing and advertising	132	40
30. (f) Fuel, rent, taxes (other than in 7 and 32) and rates	372	47
32. (h) Registration fees	295	00
33. (i) Other management expenditure	66	25

E.—Other Expenditure, viz.:

34. (a) Advanced on real estate	38	98
35. (b) Repairs	34	11
36. (c) Written off office furniture	92	09

F.—Balance

37. (a) Cash on hand and in banks	15,813	12
Totals	$169,072	07

MISCELLANEOUS STATEMENT FOR THE YEAR ENDING 31ST DECEMBER, 1913.

1. Amount of debentures maturing in 1914: Issued in Canada, $5,000.00; Issued elsewhere, none.
2. Amount of other existing obligations which will mature in 1914: None.
3. Amount of securities held by the Corporation which will mature and become payable to the Corporation in 1914: None.
4. Average rate of interest per annum paid by the Corporation during 1913 on deposits, 3%; on debentures, 4%; on debenture stock, none.
5. Average rate of interest per annum received by the Corporation during 1913 (a) On mortgages of reality; (b) On other securities; (i) Owned beneficially by the Corporation; (a) 5.60%; (b) 6 %; (ii) Not owned beneficially; (a) None; (b) None.
6. Of the mortgages owned beneficially by the Corporation, $184,767.40 is on realty situate in Ontario, and $52,898.53 is on realty situate elsewhere.
7. Of the mortgages not owned beneficially by the Corporation, none is on realty situate in Ontario, and none is on realty situate elsewhere.
8. Loans written off or transferred to real estate account during 1913, viz: (i) funds or securities owned beneficially, none; (ii) not so owned, none.
9. Number and aggregate amount of mortgages upon which compulsory proceedings have been taken by the Corporation in 1913, viz: (i) Owned beneficially, No. — ; Amount, none.
10. Aggregate market value of land mortgaged to the Corporation: (i) Mortgages owned beneficially, $399,426 approximately.
11. How often are the securities held by the Corporation valued? When loan is applied for and when necessary.
12. (a) Specify the officers of the Corporation who are under bond and for what sum respectively; Cashier, $2,000.
   (b) Are the said bonds executed by private sureties or by Guarantee Companies? Private.
13. Date when the accounts of the Corporation were last audited, February, 1914.
14. Names and addresses of the auditors respectively for 1913 and for 1914 (if appointed): For 1913, J. H. Birkett and James F. Lesslie. For 1914, Not appointed
15. What were the dividend days of the Corporation in 1913 and what rate or rates of dividend were paid on those days respectively: 2½% each on 6th January, 1913, and 4th July, 1913.
16. What is the date appointed for the Annual Meeting? 18th March, 1914. Date of last Annual Meeting? 19th March, 1913.
17. Special General Meetings held in 1913. Dates, none.

THE GUELPH AND ONTARIO INVESTMENT AND SAVINGS SOCIETY.

Head Office, Guelph, Ontario.

Incorporated under the Buildings Societies Act (Consol. Statutes U.C., chap. 53), by declaration filed with the Clerk of the Peace for the County of Wellington, 19th January, 1876.

The lending and the borrowing powers are governed by the Loan and Trust Corporations Act, R.S.O. 1914, chap. 184.

ANNUAL STATEMENT

Of the condition and affairs of The Guelph and Ontario Investment and Savings Society of Guelph, Ontario, at the 31st December, 1913, and for the year ending on that day, made to the Registrar of Loan Corporations for the Province of Ontario, pursuant to the laws of the said Province.

The head office of the Corporation is on corner of Cork and Wyndham Streets, in the City of Guelph, in the Province of Ontario.

The Board is constituted of six directors holding office for one year.

The directors and chief executive officers of the Corporation at 31st December, 1913, were as follows, together with their respective terms of office:

Alexander Baine Petrie, President, Guelph;   February, 1913; February, 1914.
Henry Howitt, M.D., 1st Vice-President, Guelph;   "   "
George D. Forbes, 2nd Vice-President, Hespeler;   "   "
Charles E. Howitt, Director, Guelph;   "
George Shortreed, Director, Guelph;
J. E. McElderry, Man. Dir. and Sec. Treas., Guelph;   "

A. Permanent capital stock: total amount authorized, $1,000,000; total amount subscribed, $1,000,000, as more particularly set out in Schedule A hereto.

SCHEDULE A.

Class I.—Fixed and Permanent capital stock created by virtue of Building Society Acts.

Description.	Total amount issued and subsisting.			Total amount of actual payments thereon.	Total amount unpaid and constituting an asset of the Corporation.
	No. of shares.	Par value of shares.	—		
		$	$	$	$
1. Fully called stock.....	9,727	50	486,350	486,350	....
2. Partly "	9,400	50	470,000	94,000	376,000
3. Instalment Stock	873	50	43,650	14,020	29,630
(payable by fixed periodical payments and still in process of payment)					
Totals............	20,000	....	1,000,000	594,370	405,630

LIST OF SHAREHOLDERS AS AT 31st DECEMBER, 1913.

(Not printed.)

5 L.C.

BALANCE SHEET AS AT 31st DECEMBER, 1913.

Dr.   Capital and Liabilities.

Capital (Liabilities to Stockholders or Shareholders).

A.—Permanent Capital Stock or Shares.

1. (a) Ordinary joint stock capital fully called; total called, $430,000; total paid thereon	$430,000 00
2. (b) Ordinary joint stock capital, 20 per cent. called; total called, $94,000; total paid thereon	94,000 00
4. (d) Dividends declared in respect of (1) and (2), but not yet paid	26,200 00
5. (e) Unappropriated profits in respect of (1) and (2)...	13,646 36
6. (f) Reserve fund in respect of (1) and (2)	524,044 00
8. (h) Instalment permanent stock (payable by fixed periodical payments; total subscribed, $100,000.00; on which has been paid	70,370 00
9. (i) Dividends declared on (8) but not paid	3,456 67
10. (j) Unappropriated profits on (8)	
11. (k) Reserve fund in respect of (8) } Included in items (5), (6).	
13. (m) Instalments or premiums on (8) paid in advance: Instalments, $50,370.00; premiums, $27,357.00.	

$1,161,717 03

Liabilities to the Public.

27. Deposits (including unclaimed deposits), right reserved to require 30 days' notice of any withdrawal....	$483,252 54	
28. Interest on deposits, due or accrued or capitalized	7,314 67	
29. Debentures issued in Canada	1,543,841 80	
30. Interest due and accrued on (29)	32,362 92	
31. Debentures issued elsewhere than in Canada	183,489 49	
32. Interest due and accrued on (31)	3,898 74	

2,254,160 16

Total liabilities $3,415,877 19

Cr.   Assets.

I.—Assets of which the Corporation is the Beneficial Owner.

A.—Immovable Property Owned Beneficially by Corporation.

1. (a) Office premises at Guelph, Ont. (held in freehold).............. $20,000 00

B.—Debts secured by Mortgages of Land.

9. (a) Debts (other than item 10) secured by mortgages of land, including accrued interest 3,179,346 82

C.—Debts not above enumerated for which the Corporation holds securities as follows:

14. (b) Municipal bonds or debentures owned by Society....	$76,336 84	
15. (c) Public School debentures owned by Society	2,000 00	
16. (d) Debts secured by Loan Corporation debentures	14,401 53	
20. (h) Debts secured only by permanent stock or shares of the Corporation	4,580 87	
26. (n) Interest due and accrued on items (14) to (20) and not included therein	1,147 92	

98,467 16

BALANCE SHEET.—Continued.

E.—Cash.

31. (a) On hand	$6,859 25	
32. (b) In bank, Guelph, Ont.	97,207 10	
In bank, London, England	13,696 86	
		117,763 21

F.—Assets not hereinbefore mentioned.

37. (a) Rents accrued	$300 00
Total assets	$3,415,877 19

CASH ACCOUNT.

Receipts for the year ending 31st December, 1913.

I.—Received by the Corporation for Its Own Use.

A.—Balance from 31st December, 1912.

	(Col. 1.)	(Total Col. 4.)
2. (i) On hand	$8,307 71	
(ii) In bank	76,651 89	
		84,959 60

B.—Sums Received Wholly or Partly on Capital Stock.

4. (a) Calls on joint stock permanent capital	$20,000 00	
(aa) Joint stock received in advance of calls..........	50,370 00	
5. (b) Premiums on (4)	38,044 00	
		108,414 00

C.—Receipts on account of Investments, Loans or Debts.

(a) On mortgages of realty (including renewals):		
10. (i) Principal	$481,832 14	
11. (ii) Interest	226,164 81	
(b) On other securities:		
12. (i) Principal	14,428 78	
13. (ii) Interest or dividends	3,810 13	
		726,235 86

D.—Receipts from Real Estate Owned Beneficially by Corporation.

17. (b) Rents of portion of office building............................	1,379 46

F.—Borrowed Money.

26. (b) Borrowed by taking deposits, including interest capitalized	$976,032 29	
27. (c) Borrowed on debentures, currency	628,062 16	
28. (d) Borrowed on debentures, sterling	51,474 72	
		1,655,569 17

G.—Receipts from Other Sources.

30. (a) Interest on bank deposits, etc., net	$4,452 23	
(b) Exchange, collection charges, etc., net.............	706 53	
		5,158 76
Total		$2,581,716 84

CASH ACCOUNT.

Expenditure for the year ending 31st December, 1913.

I.—Expended on Corporation Account.
A.—Sums Loaned or Invested on Capital Account.

		(Col. 1.)	(Total Col. 4.)
1.	(a) Loaned on mortgages of realty, including renewals..	$715,239 64	
	(b) Loaned or invested on other securities:		
2.	(i) On Loan Corporation's debentures	12,582 00	
3.	(ii) On Loan Corporation's permanent stock.......	2,020 00	
			$729,841 64

B.—Expended on Stock Account.

8. Dividends paid on permanent stock...............................	54,674 74

C.—Borrowed Money (other than foregoing) or interest thereon paid, viz.:

19.	(b) Deposits: Principal, $1,021,626.92; interest, $14,757.36.$1.036,384 28	
20.	(c) Debentures payable in Canada: Principal, $502,893.80; interest, $64,471.00	567,364 80
21.	(d) Debentures payable elsewhere: Principal, $38,772.73; interest, $7,940.20	46,712 93
		1,650,462 01

D.—Management Expenses (other than foregoing).

25.	(a) Salaries, wages and fees	$17,101 15	
26.	(b) Commission and expenses in connection with moneys borrowed and lent	4,657 22	
27.	(c) Caretaking, etc.	454 00	
28.	(d) Stationery, postage, printing and advertising	1,790 31	
29.	(e) Law costs	31 65	
30.	(f) Fuel, rent, taxes (other than in 7 and 32) and rates.	2,072 45	
31.	(g) Travelling expenses and land valuations	1,058 10	
32.	(h) Registration fees	234 00	
33.	(i) Other management expenditure	594 69	
	(j) Repairs office building and vault fittings...........	453 20	
			28,446 77

E.—Other Expenditure, viz.:

34.	(a) Taxes, insurance and repairs on portion of office building leased	528 47

F.—Balance.

37.	(a) Cash on hand and in banks in Canada and in Britain..........	117,763 21
..	Total	$2,581,716 84

MISCELLANEOUS STATEMENT FOR THE YEAR ENDING 31ST DECEMBER, 1913.

---

1. Amount of Debentures maturing in 1914: Issued in Canada, $272.108.48, including overdue debentures; issued elsewhere, $20,609.17, including overdue debentures.
2. Amount of other existing obligations which will mature in 1914: Other than deposits, none.
3. Amount of securities held by the Corporation which will mature and become payable to the Corporation in 1914, $936,169.69.
4. Average rate of interest per annum paid by the Corporation during 1913: On deposits, 2.8764%; on debentures, 4.551%; on debenture stock, none.

5. Average rate of interest per annum received by the Corporation during 1913:
   (a) On mortgages of realty; (b) on other securities.
   (i) Owned beneficially by the Corporation: (a) 7.4815%; (b) 3.959%.
   (ii) Not owned beneficially: (a) None; (b) none.
6. Of the mortgages owned beneficially by the Corporation $491,111.93 is on realty situate in Ontario, and $2,688,234.89 is on realty situate elsewhere.
7. Of the mortgages not owned beneficially by the Corporation, none is on realty situate in Ontario, and none is on realty situate elsewhere.
8. Loans written off or transferred to real estate account during 1913, viz.:
   (i) Funds or securities owned beneficially, none.
   (ii) Not so owned, none.
9. Number and aggregate amount of mortgages upon which compulsory proceedings have been taken by the Corporation in 1913, viz.:
   (i) Owned beneficially: Number, 32; amount, $43,033.75.
   (ii) No so owned: Number, none; amount, none.
10. Aggregate market value of land mortgaged to the Corporation:
    (i) Mortgages owned beneficially, $7,334,645.00.
    (ii) Not so owned, none.
11. How often are the securities held by the Corporation valued? The mortgages are inspected annually.
12. (a) Specify the officers of the Corporation who are under bond and for what sum respectively: Managing directors, $10,000.00; other officers, $14,000.00; some of the solicitors are also under bond.
    (b) Are the said bonds executed by private sureties or by Guarantee Companies? By Guarantee Companies with one exception.
13. Date when the accounts of the Corporation were last audited? As at 31st December, 1913.
14. Names and addresses of the auditors respectively for 1913 and for 1914 (if appointed):
    For 1913: J. W. Kilgour, Guelph, and J. M. Scully, F.C.A., Berlin.
    For 1914: J. W. Kilgour, Guelph, and J. M. Scully, F.C.A., Berlin.
15. What were the dividend days of the Corporation in 1913, and what rate or rates of dividend were paid on those days respectively? 2nd of January and 2nd of July, at 10% per annum.
16. What is the date appointed for the Annual Meeting? February 18th, 1914. Date of last Annual Meeting? February 19th, 1913.
17. Special General Meetings held in 1913: Dates, none.

THE GREY AND BRUCE LOAN COMPANY.

(Formerly the Owen Sound, Grey and Bruce Loan and Savings Company.)

Head Office, Owen Sound, Ontario.

CONSTATING INSTRUMENTS.

Incorporated under the Building Societies Act, R.S.O., 1887, c. 169, as a permanent Building Society under the name of the Owen Sound, Grey and Bruce Loan and Savings Company, by Declaration filed with the Clerk of the Peace for the County of Grey, 10th May, 1889.

The corporate name was by Order in Council of Ontario, 15th September, 1897, changed to the Grey and Bruce Loan Company.

The lending and borrowing powers of the Company are governed by the Loan and Trust Corporations Act, R.S.O. 1914, Chap. 184.

ANNUAL STATEMENT

Of the condition and affairs of The Grey and Bruce Loan Company, of Owen Sound, Ont., at the 31st December, 1913, and for the year ending on that day, made to the Registrar of Loan Corporations for the Province of Ontario, pursuant to the laws of the said Province.

The head office of the Corporation is at No. 861, Second Avenue East, in the Town of Owen Sound, in the Province of Ontario.

The Board is constituted of ten directors, holding office for one year.

The directors and chief executive officers of the Corporation as at 31st December, 1913, were as follows, together with their respective terms of office:

S. J. Parker, President, Owen Sound;   Feb. 5th, 1913;   Feb. 4th, 1914.
Capt. Robt. McKnight, Vice-Pres., Owen Sound;   "   "
Robert Wightman, Director, Owen Sound;   "   "
John Armstrong, Director, Owen Sound;   "
W. H. Taylor, Director, Owen Sound;   "
John McDonald, Director, Chatsworth;
Wm. Thomson, Director, Grimston;
W. J. Paterson, Director, Owen Sound;
H. B. Smith, Director, Owen Sound;
John Parker, Director, Owen Sound, Ont.;
Wm. P. Telford, Manager, Owen Sound;

A.—Permanent capital stock: Total amount authorized, $500,000; total amount subscribed, $500,000, as more particularly set out in Schedule A hereto.

SCHEDULE A.

Class 1.—Fixed and permanent capital stock created by virtue of Building Societies Acts.

Description.	Total amount issued and subsisting at 31st December, 1913.			Total amount of actual payments thereon.	Total amount unpaid and constituting an asset of the Corporation.
	No. of shares.	Par value of shares.	—		
		$		$	
1. Fully called stock.....	8,843	50	442,150	442,150	....
2. Partly called stock .	1,157	50	57,850	580	....
Totals...............	10,000	....	500,000	442,730	....

LIST OF SHAREHOLDERS AS AT 31st DECEMBER, 1913.

(Not printed.)

BALANCE SHEET AS AT 31st DECEMBER, 1913.

Dr.   Capital and Liabilities.

Capital (Liabilities to Stockholders or Shareholders).

A.—Permanent Capital Stock or Shares.

1. (a) Ordinary joint stock capital fully called; total called, $442,150; total paid thereon, $442,150	$442,150 00	
2. (b) Ordinary joint stock capital, total called, $57,850; total paid. thereon, $580	580 00	
		$442,730 00
4. (d) Dividends declared in respect of (1) and (2), but not yet paid	....	13,268 60
5. (e) Unappropriated profits (balances to carry over)	....	32 18
6. (f) Reserve fund in respect of (1) and (2)	....	45,900 00

Liabilities to the Public.

27. Deposits (right reserved to require 30 days' notice of any withdrawal	$35,344 04	
29. Debentures in Canada	143,856 00	
30. Interest due or accrued on (29)......................	2,306 63	
		181,506 67
41. Other Liabilities to the Public, viz.:—		
42. (a) Overdraft at Merchants Bank, Dec. 31, 1913..................		13,889 39
Total liabilities		$697,326 84

Cr.   Assets.

I.—Assets of which the Corporation is the Beneficial Owner.

A.—Immovable Property Owned Beneficially by Corporation.

1. (a) Office premises situate as follows:		
3. (1) At Owen Sound, held in freehold...............	$22,000 00	
7. (d) Office furniture and safety deposit boxes...........	671 00	
8. (e) Rents, accrued	1,612 50	
		$ 24,283 50

B.—Debts secured by Mortgages of Land.

9. (a) Debts (other than item 10) secured by mortgages of land	$623,254 53	
(b) Insurance premiums and other mortgage charges ..	564 13	
11. (c) Interest due and accrued on item (9), not included therein	16,243 76	
		640,062 42

C.—Debts not above enumerated for which the Corporation holds securities as follows:

20. (h) Debts secured by permanent stock or shares of the Corporation	$29,956 28	
26. (n) Interest due and accrued on item (20) and not included therein	2,137 74	
		32,094 02

E.—Cash.

31. (a) On hand		$86 90
Total assets		$697,326 84

CASH ACCOUNT.

Receipts for the year ending 31st December, 1913.

I.—Received by the Corporation for Its Own Use.

    A.—Balance from 31st December, 1912.

    (b) Cash not already shown under (1):

2.	(i) On hand	$2,125 97	
3.	(ii) In Bank	9,714 98	
			$ 11,840 95

    B.—Sums received wholly or partly on Capital Stock.

4. (a)	Calls on joint stock permanent capital	$ 1,850 00	
5. (b)	Premiums on (4)	322 00	
9.	Transfer fees	9 70	
			2,181 70

    C.—Receipts on account of Investments, Loans or Debts.

    (a) On mortgages of realty:

10.	(i) Principal and insurance premiums, etc.......	$74,716 67	
11.	(ii) Interest	34,852 77	
			109,569 44

    (b) In other securities:

12.	(i) Principal: stock loans repaid	$ 4,270 05	
13.	(ii) Interest on stock loans	673 46	
			4,943 51

D.—Receipts from Real Estate Owned Beneficially by Corporation.

17. (b) Rent of part of office premises................................		695 00

F.—Borrowed Money.

26. (b)	Borrowed by taking deposits	$127,089 61	
27. (c)	Borrowed on debentures	63,581 00	
29. (e)	Overdraft in Merchants Bank (Dec. 31, 1913)	13,889 39	
			204,560 00

G.—Receipts from other Sources.

36. (a) Rents of safe deposit boxes		47 00
Total		$333,837 60

CASH ACCOUNT.

Expenditure for the year ending 31st December, 1913.

I.—Expended on Corporation Account.

A.—Sums Loaned or Invested on Capital Account.

1. (a)	Loaned on mortgages of realty	$ 86,152 89	
	(b) Loaned or invested in other securities, viz.:		
2.	(i) On Company's stock	10,956 83	
7. (e)	Insurance and taxes advanced on property mortgaged to the Corporation	660 59	
			$ 97,770 31

CASH ACCOUNT.—Continued.

Expenditure for the year ending 31st December, 1913.

B.—Expended on Stock Account.

8. Dividends paid on permanent stock .... $ 25,912 41

C.—Borrowed Money (other than foregoing) or interest
thereon paid, viz.:

18. (a) Bank account: (Principal and interest)—Interest paid bank....		199 23
19. (b) Deposits: Principal, $126,943.80; interest, $1,104.71.	$128,048 51	
20. (c) Debentures payable in Canada: Principal, $69,590.00; interest, $7,129.62	76,719 62	
		204,768 13

D.—Management Expenses (other than foregoing).

25. (a) Salaries, wages and fees	$ 2,340 00	
28. (d) Stationery, postage, printing and advertising	132 43	
30. (f) Fuel, rent, taxes (other than in 7 and 32) and rates..	1,224 18	
32. (h) Registration and filing fees and Provincial tax	366 65	
33. (i) Other management expenditure	237 36	
		4,300 62

F.—Balance.

37. (a) Cash on hand	886 90
Totals	$333,837 60

MISCELLANEOUS STATEMENT FOR THE YEAR ENDING 31ST DECEMBER, 1913.

1. Amount of debentures maturing in 1914: Issued in Canada, $54,245.00; issued elsewhere, none.
2. Amount of other existing obligations which will mature in 1914: None.
3. Amount of securities held by the Corporation which will mature and become payable to the Corporation in 1914: $221,276.00.
4. Average rate of interest per annum paid by the Corporation during 1913: On deposits, 3%; on debentures, 4¾%; on debenture stock, none.
5. Average rate of interest per annum received by the Corporation during 1913: (a) On mortgages of realty; (b) on other securities.
   (i) Owned beneficially by the Corporation: (a) 6¼%; (b) 6¼%.
   (ii) Not owned beneficially: (a) All securities are owned beneficially.
6. Of the mortgages owned beneficially by the Corporation, all excepting $1,000.00 is on realty situate in Ontario, and $1,000.00 is on realty situate elsewhere.
7. Of the mortgages not owned beneficially by the Corporation,   is on realty situate in Ontario, and   is on realty situate elsewhere.
8. Loans written off or transferred to real estate account during 1913, viz.:
   (i) Funds or securities owned beneficially, none.
   (ii) Not so owned, none.
9. Number and aggregate amount of mortgages upon which compulsory proceedings have been taken by the Corporation in 1913, viz.:
   (i) Owned beneficially, none.
   (ii) Not so owned, none.
10. Aggregate market value of land mortgaged to the Corporation:
    (i) Mortgages owned beneficially, $1,200,000.00.
    (ii) Not so owned, none.
11. How often are the securities held by the Corporation valued? At time loan is made.

12. (a) Specify the officers of the Corporation who are under bond and for what sum
respectively: Manager for $10,000.00, and solicitor for $4,000.00.

(b) Are the said bonds executed by private sureties or by Guarantee Companies?
Private sureties.

13. Date when the accounts of the Corporation were last audited: To December 31, 1913.

14. Names and addresses of the auditors respectively for 1913 and for 1914 (if
appointed):

For 1913: A. F. Armstrong and H. H. Burgess.

For 1914: A. F. Armstrong and H. H. Burgess.

15. What were the dividend-days of the Corporation in 1913, and what rate or rates of
dividend were paid on those days respectively? January 1st and July 1st,
at 6 per cent. per annum.

16. What is the date appointed for the Annual Meeting? First Wednesday in February.
Date of last Annual Meeting? February 5th, 1913.

17. Special General Meetings held in 1913: None.

THE HAMILTON PROVIDENT AND LOAN SOCIETY.

Head Office, Hamilton, Ont.

———

CONSTATING INSTRUMENTS.

1871. Declaration of Incorporation under Building Societies' Act (Consol. Stat. U.C., c. 53) filed with the Clerk of the Peace for the County of Wentworth, 6th June, 1871.

1885. Special Act, 48.9 V. c. 30 (D), confirming Provincial incorporation, limiting share capital and the amount to be borrowed by way of deposits, debentures, etc.

1893. Special Act, 56 V. (D.), limiting total liabilities of Society (sec. 2), and extending its operations (sec. 3).

1895. Special Act, 58.9 V. c. 85 (D.), repealed sec. 6 of 56 V. c. 85 (D.), and provided for the registration and cancellation of debenture stock.

———

ANNUAL STATEMENT

Of the condition and affairs of the Hamilton Provident and Loan Society of Hamilton, Ont., at the 31st December, 1913, and for the year ending on that day, made to the Registrar of Loan Corporations for the Province of Ontario, pursuant to the laws of the said Province.

The head office of the Corporation is at No. 46 King Street East, in the City of Hamilton, in the Province of Ontario.

The Board is constituted of six directors, holding office for one year.

The directors and chief executive officers of the Corporation at 31st December, 1913, were as follows: All are elected at yearly meeting, first Monday in March each year:

George Rutherford, President, Hamilton.
John T. Glassco, Vice-President, Hamilton.
Hon. William Gibson, Director, Beamsville.
Henry L. Roberts, Director, Grimsby.
Joseph J. Greene, Director, Hamilton.
George Hope, Director, Hamilton.
C. Ferrie, Manager and Secretary, Hamilton.

All elected at yearly meeting on the first Monday of March, each year.

A. Permanent capital stock: Total amount authorized, $3,000,000; total amount subscribed, $2,000,000, as more particularly set out in Schedule A hereto.

SCHEDULE A.

Class 1.—Fixed and permanent capital stock created by virtue of Building Society Acts.

Description.	Total amount issued and subsisting 31st December, 1913.		Total amount of actual payments thereon.	Total amount unpaid and constituting an asset of the Corporation.
	No. of shares.	Par value of shares.		
		$	$	$
1. Fully called stock	10,000	100	1,000,000	1,000,000	....
2. Partly called stock	10,000	100	1,000,000	200,000	800,000
Totals.............	20,000	....	2,000,000	1,200,000	800,000

LIST OF SHAREHOLDERS AS AT 31ST DECEMBER, 1913.

(Not printed.)

BALANCE SHEET AS AT 31st DECEMBER, 1913.

Dr.   Capital and Liabilities.

Capital (Liabilities to Stockholders or Shareholders).

A.—Permanent Capital Stock or Shares.

1. (a) Ordinary joint stock capital, fully called; total called, $1,000,000; total paid thereon ....·..$1,000,000 00	
2. (b) Ordinary joint stock capital, 20 per cent. called; total called, $200,000; total paid thereon	200,000 00
4. (d) Dividends declared in respect of (1), (2), but not yet paid	47,822 01
6. (f) Reserve fund in respect of (1), (2)..................	866,000 00
7. (g) Contingent fund in respect of (1), (2) ....,.	21,144 12

$2,134,966 13

Liabilities to the Public.

27. Deposits, right reserved to require 30 days' notice of any withdrawal $753,844 39	
28. Interest on deposits, due or accrued or capitalized $26,827 19	
29. Debentures issued in Canada ....·.....	539,782 00
30. Interest due and accrued on (29)	8,700 00
31. Debentures issued elsewhere than in Canada	993,577 94
32. Interest due and accrued on (31) ....·...............	6,600 00
35. Debenture stock issued elsewhere than in Canada	372,786 66
36. Interest due and accrued on (35)	2,485 25
39. Due on loans in process of completion or to pay assumed mortgages. . . ..·...	18,433 59

$2,696,209 83

Total liabilities $4,831,175 96

Cr.   Assets.

I.—Assets of which the Corporation is the Beneficial Owner.

A.—Immovable Property Owned Beneficially by Corporation.

1. (a) Office premises situate as follows:	
2. (i) At Hamilton, Ont., held in freehold............$ 80,000 00	
3. (ii) At Brandon, Man., held in freehold	13,000 00

$ 93,000 00

B.—Debts secured by Mortgages of Land.

9. (a) Debts (other than item 10) secured by mortgages of land $4,309,961 97	
10. (b) Debts secured by mortgaged land held for sale ..	9,325 00

4,319,286 97

C.—Debts not above enumerated for which the Corporation holds securities as follows:

14. (b) Municipal bonds or debentures owned by Society ....$ 165,955 70	
15. (c) Public School debentures owned by Society	298 40
20. (h) Debts secured only by permanent stock or shares of the Corporation ....·..................	14,465 20
24. (l) Debts secured by Chartered Banks and Loan Companies stock	8,456 88

189,176 18

BALANCE SHEET.—Continued.

E.—Cash.

31. (a) On hand .... $ 6,287 54		
33. (i) In bank (England) 7,663 22		
34. (ii) In banks (Canada) 215,762 05		$ 229,712 81

Total assets $4,831,175 96

CASH ACCOUNT.

Receipts for the year ending 31st December, 1913.

I.—Received by the Corporation for Its Own Use.

A.—Balance from 31st December, 1912.

Total (Col. 4).

(b) Cash (not already shown under (1)):

2.   (i) On hand $3,701 03
3.   (ii) In bank 193,185 24

$196,886 27

B.—Sums received wholly or partly on Capital Stock.

4. (a) Calls on joint stock permanent capital 40,000 00
5. (b) Premiums on (4) 8,000 00

C.—Receipts on account of Investments, Loans or Debts.

(a) On mortgages of realty:

10.   (i) Principal 553,123 90
11.   (ii) Interest 219,776 74
(b) On other securities:
12.   (i) Principal (debentures) 8,329 08
13.   (ii) Interest 5,589 52
15.   (ii) Interest received from bank, etc. 10,764 66

D.—Receipts from Real Estate Owned Beneficially by Corporation.

17. (b) Rents, head office building 4,643 02

F.—Borrowed Money.

26. (b) Borrowed by taking deposits 924,878 74
27. (c) Borrowed on debentures 216,049 92

G.—Receipts from other sources, viz.:

30. (a) Sundry accounts 67,056 81

Total. $2,255,098 66

CASH ACCOUNT.

Expenditure for the year ending 31st December, 1913.

I.—Expended on Corporation Account.

A.—Sums Loaned or Invested on Capital Account.

		Total (Col. 4.)
1. (a) Loaned on mortgages of realty		$ 521,742 98
(b) Loaned or invested in other securities, viz.:		
3. (ii) Loaned on Society's stock		4,717 40
5. (iv) Municipal debentures purchased		44,412 00

B.—Expended on Stock Account.

8. Dividends paid on permanent stock	$ 81,200 00

C.—Borrowed Money (other than foregoing)or interest thereon paid, viz.:

19. (b) Deposits: Principal, $952,424.18; interest, $451.01	952,875 19
20. (c) Debentures issued in Canada: Principal, $119,878.00; interest, $21,818.20	141,696 20
21. (d) Debentures issued elsewhere: Principal, $49,493.98; interest, $40,788.58	90,282 56
23. (f) Debenture stock issued elsewhere: Principal, $48,666.67; interest, $15,167.32	63,833 99
24. (g) General interest	3,198 31

D.—Management Expenses (other than foregoing).

25. (a) Salaries, wages and fees, including directors	17,496 70
26. (b) Commission on brokerage	4,530 95
28. (d) Stationery, postage, printing and advertising	1,487 82
30. (f) Taxes, Government and business	2,169 41
31. (g) Travelling expenses, inspection of land, and Inspectors' salaries	5,520 89
32. (h) Registration fees	225 00
33. (i) Sundry accounts	79,099 22

E.—Other Expenditure, viz.:

34. (a) Manitoba branch expenses	7,873 35
35. (b) Debenture expenses	3,023 88

F.—Balance.

37. (a) Cash on hand and in banks	229,712 81
Total	$2,255,098 66

MISCELLANEOUS STATEMENT FOR THE YEAR ENDING 31ST DECEMBER, 1913.

1. Amount of debentures maturing in 1914: Issued in Canada, $207,127.00; issued elsewhere, $174,859.33.
2. Amount of other existing obligations which will mature in 1914: None.
3. Amount of securities held by the Corporation which will mature and become payable to the Corporation in 1914: $501,604.10.
4. Average rate of interest per annum paid by the Corporation during 1913: On deposits, 3.53; on debentures, 4.22. Average rate on all mortgage investments outstanding on December 31st, 1913: 6.84.
5. Average rate of interest per annum received by the Corporation on investments made during 1913: (a) On mortgages of realty; (b) on other securities.
   (i) Owned beneficially by the Corporation: (a) 7.25; (b) 5.27.
   (ii) Not owned beneficially: (a) None; (b) none.

6. Of the mortgages owned beneficially by the Corporation, $2,024,109.97 is on realty situate in Ontario, and $2,295,177.00 is on realty situate elsewhere.

7. Of the mortgages not owned beneficially by the Corporation, none is on realty situate in Ontario, and none is on realty situate elsewhere.

8. Loans written off or transferred to real estate account during 1913, viz.:
   (i) Funds or securities owned beneficially, $102.35.
   (ii) Not so owned, none.

9. Number and aggregate amount of mortgages upon which compulsory proceedings have been taken by the Corporation in 1913, viz.:
   (i) Owned beneficially: No. 15; amount, $27,467,00.
   (ii) Not so owned: None; amount, none.

10. Aggregate market value of land mortgaged to the Corporation:
    (i) Mortgaged owned beneficially, $10,922,725.00.

11. How often are the securities held by the Corporation valued? Yearly or oftener.

12. (a) Specify the officers of the Corporation who are under bond and for what sum respectively. All, from $5,000 down.
    (b) Are the said bonds executed by private sureties or by Guarantee Companies? Both.

13. Date when the accounts of the Corporation were last audited: 31st December, 1913; audited monthly.

14. Names and addresses of the auditors respectively for 1913 and for 1914 (if appointed):
    For 1913: Ralph E. Young, Toronto; G. E. F. Smith, Hamilton; H. M. Cherry, Brandon, Man.
    For 1914: Not yet appointed.

15. What were the dividend-days of the Corporation in 1912, and what rate or rates of dividend were paid on those days respectively? 2nd January, 2nd July; 7% for first half and 8% for second.

16. What is the date appointed for the Annual Meeting? First Monday in March   Date of last Annual Meeting? 3rd March, 1913.

17. Special General Meetings held in 1913: None.

THE HURON AND ERIE LOAN AND SAVINGS COMPANY.

Head Office, London, Ontario.

CONSTATING INSTRUMENTS.

This Company was, under the provisions of the Loan Corporations Act (R.S.O. 1897, c. 205), formed by the amalgamation of The Huron and Erie Loan and Savings Company with the Canadian Savings and Loan Company of London, Canada. See also 6 Edw. VII. (1906), c. 110 (D).

Of the above mentioned constituent Companies The Huron and Erie Loan and Savings Company was incorporated by declaration filed under the Building Societies Act (Consol. Stat. U. C., c. 53) with the Clerk of the Peace for the County of Middlesex, 18th March, 1864 (Decl. Book, p. 65). The original corporate name was The Huron and Erie Savings and Loan Society. The corporate name was changed to The Huron and Erie Loan and Savings Company by the Act of Ontario, 39 Vict., c. 95. The lending and borrowing powers of the Company were governed by 59 Vict. (1896), c. 49 (D), as amended by 62.3 Vict. (1899), c. 115 (D), and by 4.5 Edw. VII. (1905), c. 105 (D).

The Canadian Savings and Loan Company of London, Canada, was incorporated under the Building Societies Act (Consol. Stat. U.C., c. 53) by declaration filed with the Clerk of the Peace for the County of Middlesex on the 2nd of September, 1875 (Decl. Book I., p. 67). This Company's lending and borrowing powers were governed by the Loan Corporations Act, R.S.O. 1897, c. 205, and amending Acts.

The agreement for the amalgamation of these Companies under the corporate name of The Huron and Erie Loan and Savings Company was executed by both Companies on the 24th October, 1905; was ratified by the shareholders of the respective Companies on the 7th December, 1905; and was assented to by the Lieutenant-Governor of the Province of Ontario by Order-in-Council dated 29th day of December, 1905; and was further ratified and confirmed by the Act of the Legislature of the Province of Ontario, 6 Edw. VII., Chapter 130. See also Special Act of Dominion of Canada, 6 Edw. VII. (1906), c. 110 (D).

ANNUAL STATEMENT

Of the condition and affairs of The Huron and Erie Loan and Savings Company, of London, Ontario, at 31st December, 1913, and for the year ending on that day, made to the Registrar of Loan Corporations for the Province of Ontario, pursuant to the laws of the said Province.

The head office of the Corporation is at No. 442 Richmond Street, in the City of London, in the Province of Ontario.

The Board is constituted of nine Directors, holding office for one year.

The directors and chief executive officers of the Corporation at the 31st December, 1913, were as follows, together with their respective terms of office:

T. G. Meredith, K.C., President, London;   February, 1913; February, 1914.
Hume Cronyn, 1st Vice-President, London;   "   "
F. E. Leonard, 2nd Vice-President, London;   "   "
John Labatt, Director, London;
H. E. Gates, Director, London;
F. R. Eccles, M.D., Director, London;
Prof. Wm. Bowman, C.M.G., Director, London;
George T. Brown, Director, London;
Robt. Fox, Director, London;
M. Aylsworth, Secretary, London.

A. Permanent capital stock: Total amount authorized, $5,000,000 (6 Edw. VII., c. 130): total amount subscribed, $4,100,000, as more particularly set out in Schedule A hereto.

SCHEDULE A.

Class 1.—Fixed and permanent capital stock created by virtue of Building Society Acts.

Description.	Total amount issued and subsisting at 31st December, 1913.			Total amount of actual payments thereon.	Total amount unpaid and constituting an asset of the Corporation.
	No. of shares	Par value.	—		
		$	$	$	$
1. Fully called stock	32,000	50	1,600,000	1,600,000	....
2. Partly called stock	50,000	50	2,500,000	500,000	2,000,000
Totals.............	82,000	....	4,100,000	2,100,000	2,000,000

LIST OF SHAREHOLDERS AS AT 31st DECEMBER, 1913.

(Not printed.)

BALANCE SHEET AS AT 31st DECEMBER, 1913.

Dr.   Capital and Liabilities.

Capital (Liabilities to Stockholders or Shareholders).

A.—Permanent Capital Stock or Shares.

1. (a) Ordinary joint stock capital fully called; total called,
          ; total paid there $1,600,000 00
2. (b) Ordinary joint stock capital, 20 per cent. called; total
        called   ; total paid thereon............   500,000 00
4. (d) Dividend declared in respect of (1), (2), but not yet
        paid 63,000 00
5. (e) Unappropriated profits in respect of (1), (2)........   70,796 02
6. (f) Reserve fund in respect of (1), (2) 2,310,000 00
9. (i) Branch Office Extension Fund 10,000 00
10. (j) Officers' Pension Fund 10,000 00
                                                          ———————— $4,563,796 02

Liabilities to the Public.

27. Deposited, right reserved to require 30 days' notice of any
        withdrawal $1,986,706 79
28. Interest on deposits capitalized or paid in 1913..$56,676.93
29. Debentures payable in Canada 3,325,675 14
30. Interest due and accrued on (29) 50,675 54
31. Debentures payable elsewhere than in Canada 5,302,686 93
32. Interest due and accrued on (31) 31,526 03
                                                          ————————   10,697,270 43

        Total liabilities $15,261,066 45

Cr.   Assets.

I.—Assets of which the Corporation is the Beneficial Owner.

A.—Immovable Property Owned Beneficially by Corporation.

1. (a) Office premises situate at follows:
2.   (1) At 440-442-444 Richmond Street, London, Ont., ...
                held in freehold $28,000 00

        6 L.C.

BALANCE SHEET.—Continued.

B.—Debts secured by Mortgages of Land.

9. (a) Debts (other than item 10) secured by mortgages
of land, $12,157,517.71; less amount retained to
pay prior mortgages, $100,369.23 .... $12,957,148 48

C.—Debts not above enumerated for which the Corporation
holds securities as follows:

14. (b) Municipal bonds or debentures owned by Company..	$335,896 00	
15. (c) Public School debentures owned by Company	1,047,262 00	
16. (d) Bonds of other Corporations owned by Company ..	103,772 00	
22. (f) Debts secured by Life Insurance Policies	5,809 00	
23. (k) Debts secured by bank stocks	865 00	
24. (l) Debts secured by Municipal Debentures (demand loans)	244,985 00	
		1,738,589 00

E.—Cash.

31. (a) On hand	$38,207 83	
32. (b) In bank as follows:		
33. (i) In England	55,373 45	
34. (ii) In Canada	535,387 69	
		628,968 97

F.—Assets not hereinbefore mentioned.

37. (a) Permanent stock of other Corporations fully paid up 808,360 00

Total assets $15,261,066 45

CASH ACCOUNT.

Receipts for the year ending 31st December, 1913.

I.—Received by the Corporation for its Own Use.

A.—Balance from 31st December, 1912.

	(Col. 1.)	(Col. 4.)
1. (a) Cash (not already shown under (1):		
2. (i) On hand	$28,807 61	
3. (ii) In bank	490,867 82	
		$519,675 43

C.—Receipts on account of Investments, Loans or Debts.

(a) On mortgages of realty:

10. (i) Principal	$2,057,660 33	
11. (ii) Interest	777,088 81	

(b) On other securities:

12. (i) Principal	866,171 34	
13. (ii) Interest or dividends	109,502 33	
14. Retained to pay assumed mortgages	82,697 69	
		3,893,120 50

CASH ACCOUNT.—Continued.

Receipts for the year ending 31st December, 1913.

D.—Receipts from Real Estate Owned Beneficially by Corporation.

17. (b) Rents 660 00

F.—Borrowed Money.

26. (b) Borrowed by taking deposits $5,941,529 05
27. (c) Borrowed on debentures 1,480,933 18

7,422,462 23

G.—Receipts from other sources, viz.:

30. (a) Interest on bank accounts 10,588 32

Total $11,846,506 48

CASH ACCOUNT.

Expenditure for the year ending 31st December, 1913.

I.—Expended on Corporation Account.

A.—Sums Loaned or Invested on Capital Account.

	(Col. 1.)	(Col. 4.)
1. (a) Loaned on mortgages of realty, $1,810,898.11) including assumed mortgages, $116,021.75) $1,926,919 86		
(b) Loaned or invested in other securities:.		
3. (ii) Loaned on bonds 736,656.80		
4. (iii) Debentures and other securities purchased.. 865,147 00		
		$3,528,723 66

B.—Expended on Stock Account.

8. Dividends paid on permanent stock 246,657 69

C.—Borrowed Money (other than foregoing) or interest thereon paid, viz.:

19.(b) Deposits: Principal, $5,982,451.62; interest, $2,149.19..$5,984,600 81
20. (c) Debentures payable in Canada: Principal, $790,644.81; interest, $140,512.17 .... 931,156 98
21. (d) Debentures payable elsewhere: Principal, $173,759.41; interest, $207,672.55 .... 381,431 96

7,297,189 75

D.—Management Expenses (other than foregoing).

25. (a) Salaries, wages and fees	$61,174 48	
26. (b) Commission or brokerage	28,499 74	
27. (c) Insurance and guarantee premiums	279 49	
28. (d) Stationery, postage, printing and advertising.......	9,274 77	
29. (e) Law costs	1,684 08	
30. (f) Fuel, rent, taxes (other than in 7 and 32) and rates	8,094 23	
31. (g) Travelling expenses	8,761 48	
32. (h) Registration fees	489 02	
33. (i) Other management expenditure ..,.................	3,628 83	
		121,886 12

CASH ACCOUNT.—Continued.

Expenditure for the year ending 31st December, 1913.

E.—Other Expenditures, viz.:

34. (a) Building $23,080 29

F.—Balance.

37. (a) Cash on hand and in banks $628,968 97

Total $11,846,506 48

MISCELLANEOUS STATEMENT FOR THE YEAR ENDING 31ST DECEMBER, 1913.

1. Amount of debentures maturing in 1914: Payable in Canada, $824,110.90, including $30,599.14 overdue and not presented for payment; payable elsewhere, $1,004,285.33.
2. Amount of other existing obligations which will mature in 1914: Exclusive of deposit, none.
3. Amount of securities held by the Corporation which will mature and become payable to the Corporation in 1914, $2,062,707.45.
4. Average rate of interest per annum paid by the Corporation during 1913: On deposits, 3%; on debentures, 4.208%; on debenture stock, none.
5. Average rate of interest per annum received by the Corporation during 1913: (a) On mortgages of realty; (b) on other securities.
   (i) Owned beneficially by the Corporation: (a) 6.5121%; (b) 4.887%.
   (ii) Not owned beneficially: (a)   (b)   .
6. Of the mortgages owned beneficially by the Corporation, $8,715,970.71 is on realty situate in Ontario, and $3,441,547.00 is on realty situate elsewhere.
7. Of the mortgages not owned beneficially by the Corporation, none is on realty situate in Ontario, and   is on realty situate elsewhere.
8. Loans written off or transferred to real estate account during 1913, viz.:
   (i) Funds or securities owned beneficially, none.
   (ii) Not so owned, none.
9. Number and aggregate amount of mortgages upon which compulsory proceedings have been taken by the Corporation in 1913, viz.:
   (i) Owned beneficially, No. 46; amount, $87,523.76.
   (ii) Not so owned, none.
10. Aggregate market value of land mortgaged to the Corporation:
    (i) Mortgages owned beneficially, $26,172,379.
    (ii) Not so owned, none.
11. How often are the securities held by the Corporation valued? Annually.
12. (a) Specify the officers of the Corporation who are under bond and for what sum respectively: General Manager, $10,000.00; other officers, $123,000.00; total, $133,000.00
    (b) Are the said bonds executed by private sureties or by Guarantee Companies? Guarantee Company.
13. Date when the accounts of the Corporation were last audited: As at December 31st, 1913.
14. Names and addresses of the auditors respectively for 1913 and for 1914 (if appointed):
    For 1913: M. H. Rowland and F. G. Jewell, C.A.
    For 1914: M. H. Rowland and F. G. Jewell, C.A.
15. What were the dividend days of the Corporation in 1913 and what rate or rates of dividend were paid on those days respectively? 2nd January, 1913, 2½% and ¼ of 1% bonus. 1st April, 1913, 1st July and 1st October, each 2¾% and ¼ of 1% bonus.
16. What is the date appointed for the Annual Meeting? 11th February, 1914. Date of last Annual Meeting? 12th February, 1913.
17. Special General Meetings held in 1913: None.

THE INDUSTRIAL MORTGAGE AND SAVINGS COMPANY.

Head Office, Sarnia.

CONSTATING INSTRUMENTS.

Incorporated under the Building Societies Act, R.S.O. 1887, c. 169, by declaration filed with the Clerk of the Peace for the County of Lambton, 20th August, 1889.

The lending and the borrowing powers are governed by the Loan and Trust Corporations Act, R.S.O. 1914, chap. 184.

ANNUAL STATEMENT

Of the condition and affairs of the Industrial Mortgage and Savings Company, of Sarnia, Ontario, at the 31st December, 1913, and for the year ending on that day, made to the Registrar of Loan Corporations for the Province of Ontario, pursuant to the laws of the said Province.

The head office of the Corporation is at No. 181 Front Street, in the Town of Sarnia, in the Province of Ontario.

The Board is constituted of ten directors, holding office for two years.

The directors and chief executive officers of the Corporation at the 31st December, 1913, were as follows, together with their respective terms of office:

John Cowan, K.C., President, Sarnia, Ont.;	January, 1912.	January, 1914.
W. G. Willoughby, 1st Vice-Pres., Walnut, Ont.;	" 1912.	" 1914.
John McFarlane, 2nd Vice-Pres., Sarnia;	" 1912.	" 1914.
William McDonald, Director, Brigden, Ont.;	" 1913.	" 1915.
Malcolm McGugan, Director, Strathroy, Ont.;	" 1913.	" 1915.
Wm. G. Hall, Director, Arkona;	" 1913.	" 1915.
Peter Grant, Director, Avonroy, Ont.;	" 1912.	" 1914.
Byron Stephens, Director, Bridgen, Ont.;	" 1913.	" 1915.
William Armstrong, Director, Wyoming, Ont.;	" 1912.	" 1914.
Donald Sutherland, Director, Forest;	" 1913.	" 1915.
D. N. Sinclair, Managing-Secretary, Sarnia, Ont.		

A. Permanent capital stock: Total amount authorized, $1,000,000; total amount subscribed, $565,000, as more particularly set out in Schedule A hereto.

SCHEDULE A.

Class I.—Fixed and permanent capital stock created by virtue of Building Society Acts.

Description.	Total amount issued and subsisting at 31st December, 1913.			Total amount of actual payments thereon.	Total amount unpaid and constituting an asset of the Corporation.
	No. of shares.	Par value of shares.			
1. Fully called stock	11,300	$ 50 .	$ 565,000	$ c. 563,089 00	$ c. 1,911 00

LIST OF SHAREHOLDERS AS AT 31st DECEMBER, 1913.

(Not printed.)

BALANCE SHEET AS AT 31st DECEMBER, 1913.

Dr.   Capital and Liabilities.

Capital (Liabilities to Stockholders or Shareholders).

A.—Permanent Capital Stock or Shares.

1. (a) Ordinary joint stock fully called; total called, $565,000; total paid thereon....................	$563,089 00	
4. (d) Dividends declared in respect of (1) but not yet paid..............	19,674 44	
6. (f) Reserve fund in respect of (1)....................	254,766 65	
		$837,530 09

Liabilities to the Public.

27. Deposits (right reserved to require 30 days' notice of any withdrawal)	$633,862 07	
28. Interest on deposits, due, or accrued, or capitalized......	20,574 16	
29. Debentures issued in Canada.........................,.....	510,209 66	
30. Interest due and accrued on (29).....................	9,744 13	
		1,174,391 02
Total liabilities		$2,011,921 11

Cr.   Assets.

I.—Assets of which the Corporation is the Beneficial Owner.

B.—Debts secured by Mortgages of Land.

9. (a) Debts (other than item 10) secured by mortgages of land	$1,776,815 82	
11. (o) Interest due and accrued in item 9 and not included therein	1,763 35	
		$1,778,579 17

C.—Debts not above enumerated for which the Corporation holds securities, as follows:

14. (b) Debts secured by municipal bonds or debentures....	$150,935 97	
20. (h) Debts secured only by permanent stock or shares of the Corporation	14,577 14	
		165,513 11

E.—Cash.

31. (a) On hand	$17,595 96	
33. (b) In bank	49,732 87	
		67,328 83

F.—Assets not hereinbefore mentioned.

37. (a) Office furniture		500 00
Total assets		$2,011,921 11

CASH ACCOUNT.

Receipts for the year ending 31st December, 1913.

		(Col. 1.)	Total (Col. 4.)
	I.—Received by the Corporation for its Own Use. A.—Balance from 31st December, 1912.		
2.	(i) On hand	$5,232 28	
3.	(ii) In bank	31,578 34	$36,810 62
	B.—Sums received Wholly or Partly on Capital Stock.		
4.	(a) Call on joint stock permanent capital..............	$25,542 70	
5.	(b) Premiums on (4)	10,000 00	35,542 70
	C.—Receipts on account of Investments, Loans or Debts.		
	(a) On mortgages of realty:		
10.	(i) Principal.................................	$242,356 06	
11.	(ii) Interest.............	93,795 20	
	(b) On other securities:		
12.	(i) Principal...........	36,298 03	
13.	(ii) Interest or dividends	8,008 69	380,457 98
	F.—Borrowed Money.		
26.	(b) Borrowed by taking deposits	$963,903 13	
27.	(c) Borrowed on debentures	291,888 96	1,255,792 09
	Receipts from other sources, viz.:		
30.	(a) General interest (on bank balances)...........................		1,134 46
	Totals.........		$1,709,737 85

CASH ACCOUNT.

Expenditure for the year ending 31st December, 1913.

		(Col. 1.)	Total (Col.4.)
	I.—Expended on Corporation Account.		
	A.—Sums loaned or Invested on Capital Account.		
1.	(a) Loaned on mortgages or realty......................	$286,694 56	
	Loaned or invested in other securities, viz.:		
2.	(i) Municipal debentures	28,105 20	
3.	(ii) Permanent stock	16,755 00	$331,554 76
	B.—Expended on Stock Account.		
8.	Dividends paid on permanent stock......................		36,756 82

CASH ACCOUNT.—Continued.

Expenditure for the year ending 31st December, 1913.

C.—Borrowed money (other than foregoing) or interest thereon paid, viz.:

	(Col. 1.)	Total (Col.4.)
19. (b) Deposits: Principal, $990,953.60; interest, $369.04....	$991,322 64	
20. (c) Debentures issued in Canada: Principal, $253,597.31; interest, $20,188.67	273,785 98	
		$1,265,108 62

D.—Management Expenses (other than foregoing).

25. (a) Salaries, wages and fees	$5,727 00	
26. (b) Commission or brokerage	965 42	
28. (d) Stationery, postage, printing and advertising........	791 34	
29. (e) Law costs	6 00	
30. (f) Fuel rent, taxes (other than in 7 and 32) and rates..	1,113 16	
31. (g) Travelling expenses	238 75	
32. (h) Registration fee	130 00	
		8,971 67

E.—Other Expenditures, viz.:

34. (a) General interest (overdrafts) 17 15

F.—Balance.

37. (a) Cash on hand and in bank.................................... 67,328 83

Total................. .. .. $1,709,737 85

1. Amount of debentures maturing in 1914: Issued in Canada, $133,011.38; Issued elsewhere, none.

2. Amount of other existing obligations which will mature in 1914, none.

3. Amount of securities held by the Corporation which will mature and become payable to the Corporation in 1914, estimated, $250,000.

4. Average rate of interest per annum paid by the Corporation during 1913: On deposits, 3.18%; On debentures, 4.29%; On debenture stock, none.

5. Average rate of interest per annum received by the Corporation during 1913:
     (a) On mortgages of realty; (b) On other securities.
     (i) Owned beneficially by the Corporation: (a) 6%; (b) 5%.
     (ii) Not owned beneficially: (a) none; (b) none.

6. Of the mortgages owned beneficially by the Corporation, $1,624,979.17 is on realty situate in Ontario, and $153,600 is on realty situate elsewhere.

7. Of the mortgages not owned beneficially by the Corporation, none is on realty situate in Ontario, and none is on realty situate elsewhere .

8. Loans written off or transferred to real estate account during 1913, viz.:
     (i) Funds or securities owned beneficially, none.
     (ii) Not so owned, none.

9. Number and aggregate amount of mortgages upon which compulsory proceedings have been taken by the Corporation in 1913, viz.:
     (i) Owned beneficially, No., 1; Amount, $3,781.90.
     (ii) Not so owned, none; Amount, none.

10. Aggregate market value of land mortgaged to the Corporation:
    (i) Mortgages owned beneficially, $3,000,000.
    (ii) Not so owned, none.

11. How often are the securities held by the Corporation valued? Annually.

12. (a) Specify the officers of the Corporation who are under bond and for what sum respectively: Manager, $12,000; Accountant, $6,000; Assistant, $2,000.
    (b) Are the said bonds executed by private sureties or by Guarantee Companies? Manager and Accountant, private; Assistant, Guarantee Company.

13. Date when the accounts of the Corporation were last audited. Audited monthly.

14. Names and addresses of the auditors respectively for 1913 and for 1914 (if appointed):
    For 1913: Henry Ingram and A. B. Telfer.
    For 1914: Henry Ingram and A. B. Telfer.

15. What were the dividend days of the Corporation in 1913 and what rate or rates of dividend were paid on those days respectively? January 2nd and July 2nd; January 2nd, 1913, at rate of 6½%; July 2nd, 1913, at 7%.

16. What is the date appointed for the Annual Meeting? No fixed date. Date of last Annual Meet? January, 1913.

17. Special General Meetings held in 1913: Dates, none.

LANDED BANKING AND LOAN COMPANY.

Head Office, Hamilton, Ontario.

———

CONSTATING INSTRUMENTS.

Incorporated under the Building Societies Acts Consol. Stat. U. C., chap. 53, by declaration filed with the Clerk of the Peace for the County of Wentworth, 16th December, 1876.

The lending and the borrowing powers are governed by the Loan and Trust Corporations Act, R.S.O. 1914, chap. 184.

———

ANNUAL STATEMENT

Of the condition and affairs of the Landed Banking and Loan Company of Hamilton, Ont., at the 31st December, 1913, and for the year ending on that day, made to the Registrar of Loan Corporations for the Province of Ontario, pursuant to the laws of the said Province.

The Head Office of the Corporation is at No. 47 James Street South, in the City of Hamilton, in the Province of Ontario.

The Board is constituted of six directors, holding office for one year.

The directors and chief executive officers of the Corporation at 31st December, 1913, were as follows, together with their respective terms of office:

Hon. Thomas Bain, President, Dundas: 3rd, February, 1913. 2nd February, 1914.
C. S. Scott, Vice-President, Hamilton: "   "
Hon. Samuel Barker, M.P., Director, Hamilton: "   "
Robert Hobson, Director, Hamilton: "
S. F. Lazier, K.C., Director, Hamilton: "
Charles Mills, Director, Hamilton
C. W. Cartwright, Manager, Hamilton:

A. Permanent capital stock: Total amount authorized, $1,050,000.00; total amount subscribed, $1,000,000.00, as more particularly set out in Schedule A hereto.

SCHEDULE A.

Class 1.—Fixed and Permanent Capital Stock created by virtue of Building Society Acts.

Description.	Total amount issued and subsisting at 31st December, 1913.			Total amount of actual payments thereon.	Total amount unpaid and constituting an asset of the Corporation.
	No. of shares.	Par value of shares.	—		
1. Fully paid stock	7,000	$ 100	$ 700,000	$ c. 700,000 00	....
3. Instalment Stock......	3,000	100	300,000	229,125 95	70,874 05
Totals............	10,000	....	1,000,000	929,125 95	70,874 05

LIST OF SHAREHOLDERS AS AT 31st DECEMBER, 1913.

(Not printed.)

BALANCE SHEET AS AT 31st DECEMBER, 1913.

Capital and Liabilities.

Capital (Liabilities to Stockholders or Shareholders.)

A.—Permanent Capital Stock or Shares.

1. (a) Ordinary joint stock capital fully called; total called, $700,000; total paid thereon	$700,000 00	
2. (b) Ordinary Joint Stock capital, 50% called. Total called, $150,000. Total paid thereon	150,000 00	
(cc) Joint Stock capital paid in advance of calls	79,125 95	
4. (d) Dividends declared in respect of (1) (2) (3), but not yet paid	36,127 93	
5. (e) Unappropriated profits in respect of (1), (2), (3)....	1,959 93	
6. (f) Reserve fund in respect of (1) (2) (3)	620,000 00	
		$1,587,213 81

Liabilities to the Public.

27. Deposits (right reserved to require 30 days' notice of any withdrawal)	$868,996 83	
29. Debentures issued in Canada	438,545 34	
30. Interest due and accrued on (29)	6,190 19	
31. Debentures issued elsewhere than in Canada	524,735 88	
32. Interest due and accrued on (31)	3,045 02	
40. Other liabilities to the public, viz.:		
41. (a) Directors, auditors, valuators, etc.	· 782 82	
		1,842,296 08

Total liabilities 3,429,509 89

Cr.   Assets.

I.—Assets of which the Corporation is the Beneficial Owner.

A.—Immovable Property owned Beneficially by the Corporation.

1. (a) Office premises situate as follows:		
At Hamilton, held in freehold	$65,000 00	
5. (b) Freehold land (including buildings), other than foregoing	850 00	
		$65,850 00

B.—Debts secured by Mortgages of Land.

9. (a) Debts other than (10) secured by mortgages of land..	$3,172,742 24	
10. (b) Debts secured by mortgaged land held for sale	3,113 97	
		3,175,856 21

C.—Debts, not above enumerated, for which the Corporation holds securities as follows:

14. (b) Debts secured by municipal bonds or debentures	$42,956 61	
20. (h) Debts secured only by Permanent Stock or Shares of the Corporation	11,809 79	
22. (j) Debts secured by advances on Stocks and Bonds not owned by Company	68,730 53	
		123,496 93

BALANCE SHEET.—Continued.

E.—Cash.

31. (a) On hand	$5,279 27		
32. (b) In banks	52,712 24		
		57,991 51	

F.—Assets not hereinbefore mentioned.

37. (a) Bell Telephone Company Bonds	6,315 24	
Total assets	$3,429,509 89	

CASH ACCOUNT.

Receipts for the year ending 31st December, 1913.

1.—Received by the Corporation for Its Own Use.

A.—Balance from 31st December, 1912.

(Total Col. 4.)

1. (a) Cash (not already shown under (1)):		
2. (i) On hand	$2,883 70	
3. (ii) In bank	129,304 96	

B.—Sums Received Wholly or Partly on Capital Stock.

4. (a) Calls on Joint Stock Permanent Capital	150,000 00	
(aa) Joint Stock capital received in advance of calls	79,125 95	
5. (b) Premiums on (4)	45,915 00	

C.—Receipts on account of Investments, Loans or Debts.

(a) On mortgages of realty:		
10. (i) Principal		
11. (ii) Interest		
(b) On other securities:		
12. (i) Principal	572,078 36	
13. (ii) Interest or dividends		
(c) Unsecured debts:		
14. (i) Principal		
15. (ii) Interest		

D.—Receipts from Real Estate owned Beneficially by Corporation.

17. (b) Rents	74 85	

F.—Borrowed Money.

26. (b) Borrowed by taking deposits	2,034,547 73	
27. (c) Borrowed on debentures	52,604 66	

G.—Receipts from other sources, viz.:

30. (a) Bank interest, rents, etc.	7,216 54	
Totals	$3,073,751 75	

CASH ACCOUNT.

Expenditure for the year ending 31st December, 1913.

I.—Expended on Corporation Account.

A.—Sums Loaned or Invested on Capital Account.

(Col. 1.) (Total Col. 4.)

1. (a) Loaned on mortgages of realty and other securities.............;..... $661,517 40

B.—Expended on Stock Account.

8. Dividends paid on permanent stock 51,626 58

C.—Borrowed money (other than foregoing) or interest thereon paid.

19. (b) Deposits: Principal, $2,027,916.76; interest, $444.72..$2,028,361 48
20. (c) Debentures issued in Canada: Principal, $181,360.00; interest, $23,371.13 .... 204,731 13
21. (d) Debentures issued elsewhere: Principal, -$13,870.00; interest, $21,686.45 .... 35,556 45

2,268,649 06

D.—Management Expenses (other than the foregoing).

25. (a) Salaries, wages and fees $16,181 38
28. (d) Stationery, postage, printing and advertising 1,686 84
30. (f) Fuel, rent, taxes (other than 7 and 32) and rates.... 300 00
31. (g) Travelling expenses .... •5,631 80
32. (h) Registration fees 1,859 35

25,659 37

E.—Other Expenditures, viz.:

34. (a) Debenture expenses 1,026 77
35. (b) Head Office expenses 3,270 36
36. (c) Valuators' commission 4,010 70

F.—Balance.

37. (a) Cash on hand and in banks 57,991 51

Total $3,073,751 75

MISCELLANEOUS STATEMENT FOR THE YEAR ENDING 31ST DECEMBER, 1913.

---

1. Amount of debentures maturing in 1914: Issued in Canada, $147,250.45; issued elsewhere, $134,806.66.
2. Amount of other existing obligations which will mature in 1914: $868,996.83.
3. Amount of securities held by the Corporation which will mature and become payable to the Corporation in 1914: Approximately $300,000.
4. Average rate of interest per annum paid by the Corporation during 1913: On deposits, 3.634%; on debentures, 4.26%; on debenture stock, none.
5. Average rate of interest per annum received by the Corporation during 1913:
   (a) On mortgages of realty; (b) on other securities.
   (i) Owned beneficially by the Corporation: (a) 6.73%; (b) 5.61%.
   (ii) Not owned beneficially: (a) none; (b) none.
6. Of the mortgages owned beneficially by the Corporation, $1,574,033.97 is on realty situate in Ontario, and $1,598,708.27 is on realty situate elsewhere.

7. Of the mortgages not owned beneficially by the Corporation, none is on realty situate in Ontario, and none is on realty situate elsewhere.

8. Loans written off or transferred to real estate account during 1913, viz.:
   (i) Funds or securities owned beneficially, $1,449.94.
   (ii) Not so owned, none.

9. Number and aggregate amount of mortgages upon which compulsory proceedings have been taken by the Corporation in 1913, viz.:
   (i) Owned beneficially, No. 3; amount, $4,461.54.
   (ii) Not so owned, none; amount, none.

10. Aggregate market value of land mortgaged to the Corporation:
   (i) Mortgages owned beneficially, $6,906,000.
   (ii) Not so owned, none.

11. How often are the securities held by the Corporation valued? Yearly or oftener.

12. (a) Specify the officers of the Corporation who are under bond and for what sum respectively: Manager, $10,000; Accountant and Teller, $5,000 each; Ledger Keeper and Inspector, $2,000 each.
   (b) Are the said bonds executed by private sureties or by Guarantee Companies? Guarantee Company.

13. Date when the accounts of the Corporation were last audited. December, 1913.

14. Names and addresses of the auditors respectively for 1913 and for 1914 (if appointed):
   For 1913: Ralph E. Young and Charles Stiff, Hamilton.
   For 1914: Same.

15. What were the dividend days of the Corporation in 1913 and what rate or rates of dividend were paid on those days respectively? 2nd January, 1913, 3½%. 2nd July, 1913, 3½%.

16. What is the date appointed for the Annual Meeting? 1st Monday in February. Date of last Annual Meeting? 3rd February, 1913.

17. Special General Meetings held in 1913: Dates, 3rd February, 1913.

THE BRITISH MORTGAGE LOAN COMPANY OF ONTARIO.

Head Office, Stratford, Ontario.

CONSTATING INSTRUMENTS.

Incorporated by Letters Patent of Ontario, dated October 5th, 1877 (Lib. 5, No. 52), issued under R.S.O. 1877, c. 150, which Act was continued by R.S.O. 1887, c. 157, and was as to Loan Corporations superseded by 60 V. c. 38 (O), now R.S.O. 1914, c. 184.

The lending and the borrowing powers of the company are derived from its Letters Patent and the above public general Statute.

ANNUAL STATEMENT

Of the condition and affairs of The British Mortgage Loan Company of Ontario at the 31st December, 1913, and for the year ending on that day, made to the Registrar of Loan Corporations for the Province of Ontario, pursuant to the laws of the said Province.

The head office of the Corporation is No. 27 Downie Street, in the City of Stratford, in the Province of Ontario.

The Board is constituted of eight directors, holding office for one year.

The directors and chief executive officers of the Corporation at the 31st December, 1913, were as follows, together with their respective terms of office:—

John McMillan, President, Stratford;   January 23, 1913; January 22, 1914.
John Brown, Vice-President, Stratford;   "   "
John Waldron Scott, Director, Listowel;   "   "
Herbert M. Johnson, Director, Stratford;
James Trow, Director, Stratford;
James P. Morton, Director, Hamilton;
Hon. Nelson Monteith, Director, Stratford;
Thomas Ballantyne, Director, Stratford;   "   "
William Buckingham, Manager and Secretary, Stratford; 26th December, 1877, undetermined.

A. Permanent capital stock: Total amount authorized, $5,000,000; total amount subscribed, $450,000, as more particularly set out in Schedule A hereto.

SCHEDULE A.

Class 2.—Fixed and Permanent Capital Stock created by virtue of Joint Stock Companies' Act or Private Acts.

Last call made: Date, 2nd June, 1902. Rate—Balance due and unpaid.

Description.	No. of shares.	Par value.	Total amount held.	Total amount paid thereon.	Total remaining unpaid on calls.
		$	$	$ c.	$ c.
1. Fully called	4,500	100	450,000	449,450 00	550 00
Totals.......... ..	4,500	100	450,000	449,450 00	550 00

LIST OF SHAREHOLDERS AS AT 31ST DECEMBER, 1913.

(Not printed.)

BALANCE SHEET AS AT 31st DECEMBER, 1913.

Dr.   Capital and Liabilities.

Capital (Liabilities to Stockholders or Shareholders).

A.—Permanent Capital Stock or Shares.

1. (*a*) Ordinary joint stock capital fully called; total called, $450,000; total paid thereon	$449,450 00	
4. (*d*) Dividends declared in respect of (1), but not yet paid	17,978 00	
5. (*e*) Unappropriated profits in respect of (1)	15,343 67	
6. (*f*) Reserve fund in respect of (1)	270,000 00	
		$752,771 67

Liabilities to the Public.

27. Deposits (including all interest to 31st December, 1913, capitalized), right reserved to require 30 days' notice of any withdrawal	$588,371 78	
29. Debentures issued in Canada	323,213 00	
30. Interest due and accrued on (29)	11,899 10	
		923,483 88
Total liabilities		$1,676,255 55

Cr.   Assets.

I.—Assets of which the Corporation is Beneficial Owner.

A.—Immovable Property Owned Beneficially by Corporation.

1. (*a*) Office premises situate as follows:	
2. (i) At Stratford, held in freehold	$7,000 00

B.—Debts Secured by Mortgages of Land.

9. (*a*) Debts secured by mortgages of land	1,645,291 00

E.—Cash.

32. In bank	23,964 55
Total assets	$1,676,255 55

CASH ACCOUNT.

Receipts for the year ending 31st December, 1913.

I.—Received by the Corporation for its Own Use.

A.—Balance from 31st December, 1912.

1. (*b*) Cash (not already shown under (1)):	(Col. 1.) Total (Col. 4.)	
3. (ii) In bank		$994 85

B.—Sums Received Wholly or Partly on Capital Stock.

4. (*a*) Calls on Joint Stock Permanent Capital	1,020 00

CASH ACCOUNT.—Continued.

Receipts for the year ending 31st December, 1913.

C.—Receipts on account of Investments, Loans or Debts.

(a) On mortgages of realty:—
10.   (i) Principal and interest $342,126 32
11.   (ii) General interest and interest on bank balances   1,062 66
                                                                          $343,188 98

F.—Borrowed Money.

26. (b) Borrowed by taking deposits $665,661 56
27. (c) Borrowed on debentures 122,064 10
                                                                          787,725 66

        Total $1,132,929 49

CASH ACCOUNT.

Expenditure for the year ending 31st December, 1913.

I.—Expended on Corporation Account.

A.—Sums Loaned or Invested on Capital Account.

	(Col. 1.)	(Col. 4.)
1. (a) Loaned on mortgage of realty (including item 7)..	$198,240 28	$198,240 28

B.—Expended on Stock Account.

8. Dividends paid on permanent stock $35,883 81
                                                                          35,883 81

C.—Borrowed money (other than foregoing) or interest
            thereon paid, viz.:—
19. (b) Deposits: Principal, $700,974.71; interest, $21,382.85 $722,357 56
20. (c) Debentures issued in Canada: Principal, $128,318.32
            interest, $14,126.77 .... 142,445 09
                                                                          864,802 65

D.—Management Expenses (other than foregoing).

25. (a) Salaries, wages and fees $7,692 15
26. (b) Commission or brokerage 708 70
28. (d) Stationery, postage, printing and advertising 296 78
29. (e) Law costs 32 50
30. (f) Fuel, rent, taxes (other than 7 and 32) and rates 586 39
31. (g) Travelling expenses 6 50
32. (h) Registration fees and fyling fees 140 00
33. (i) Other management expenditure 225 18
                                                                          9,688 20

E.—Other Expenditure, viz.:

34. (a) Vote of shareholders to President, $200.00; Vice-
            President, $150.00 .... 350 00

F.—Balance.

37. (b) Cash in bank 23,964 55

        Totals $1,132,929 49
        7 L.C.

1. Amount of debentures maturing in 1914: Issued in Canada, $141,520.00; Issued elsewhere, none.
2. Amount of other existing obligations which will mature in 1914. Deposits payable on 30 days' notice.
3. Amount of securities held by the Corporation which will mature and become payable to the Corporation in 1914, $257,092.45.
4. Average rate of interest per annum paid by the Corporation during 1913 on deposits, 3.55%; On debentures, 4.32%; On debenture stock, none.
5. Average rate of interest per annum received by the Corporation during 1913:
      (a) On Mortgages of realty; (b) On other securities.
      (i) Owned beneficially by the Corporation: (a) 5.8%; (b) none.
      (ii) Not owned beneficially (a) none; (b) none.
6. Of the mortgages owned beneficially by the Corporation, $1,645,291.00 is on realty situate in Ontario, and ——— is on realty situate elsewhere.
7. Of the mortgages not owned beneficially by the Corporation, none is on realty situate in Ontario, and none is on realty situate elsewhere.
8. Loans written off or transferred to real estate account during 1913, viz:
      (i) Funds or securities owned beneficially, none.
      (ii) Not so owned, none.
9. Number and aggregate amount of mortgages upon which compulsory proceedings have been taken by the Corporation in 1913, viz.:
      (i) Owned beneficially, No. six; Amount, $15,793.61.
      (ii) Not so owned, No., none; Amount, none.
10. Aggregate market value of land mortgaged to the Corporation:
      (i) Mortgages owned beneficially, $2,478,595.00.
      (ii) Not so owned, none.
11. How often are the securities held by the Corporation valued? Always yearly, sometimes oftener.
12. (a) Specify the officers of the Corporation who are under bond and for what sum respectively: Manager for $10,000.00; Assistant Manager for $5,000.00; Accountant for $2,000.00.
      (b) Are the said bonds executed by private sureties or by Guarantee Companies? Managers' Bond, private sureties; Assistant Manager and Accountant, Guarantee Company.
13. Date when the accounts of the Corporation were last audited, January 7, 1914.
14. Names and addresses of the auditors respectively for 1913 and for 1914 (if appointed):
      For 1913: Geo. Hamilton and William Irwin, M.A., Stratford.
      For 1914: Geo. Hamilton and William Irwin, M.A., Stratford.
15. What were the dividend days of the Corporation in 1913, and what rate or rates of dividend were paid on these days respectively: January 2nd, 1913, 8%; July 2nd, 1913, 8%.
16. What is the date appointed for the Annual Meeting? 4th Thursday in January; Date of last Annual Meeting? January 23rd, 1913.
17. Special General Meetings held in 1913: Dates, none held.

CANADA INVESTMENT CORPORATION.

(FORMERLY THE STRATFORD BUILDING AND SAVINGS SOCIETY.)

Head Office, Toronto, Ontario.

Incorporated under the Building Societies Act (R.S.O. 1887, c. 169) by declaration filed with the Clerk of the Peace for the County of Perth on the 23rd August, 1889, (Decl. Book I., 19).

The lending and the borrowing powers are governed by the Loan and Trust Corporations Act, R.S.O., chap. 184.

ANNUAL STATEMENT

Of the conditions of affairs of The Canada Investment Corporation of Toronto, Ontario, at the 31st December, 1913, and for the year ending on that day, made to the Registrar of Loan Corporations for the Province of Ontario, pursuant to the laws of the said Province.

The head office of the Corporation is at No. 15 Wellington Street West, in the City of Toronto, in the Province of Ontario.

The Board is constituted of five directors, holding office for one year.

The directors and chief executive officers of the Corporation at the 31st December, 1913, were as follows, together with their respective terms of office:

Harry Symons, K.C., President, Toronto;   1st February, 1913; February, 1914.
H. Pollman Evans, Vice-President, Toronto;   "   "
E. H. Wainwright, Director, London, Eng.;   "   "
F. G. Hughes, L.D.S., Director, Galt;
G. E. Millichamp, M.B., Director, Toronto;
Harry Symons, K.C., Managing Director, Toronto;   "
William H. Carrie, Secretary, Toronto;

A. Permanent capital stock: Total amount authorized, $500,000; total amount subscribed, $260,900, as more particularly set out in Schedule A hereto.

*SCHEDULE A.

Class 1.—Fixed and permanent capital stock created by virtue of Building Society Acts.

Description.	Total amount issued and subsisting at 31st December, 1913.			Total amount of actual payments thereon.	Total amount unpaid and constituting an asset of the Corporation.
	No. of shares.	Par value of shares.	—		
2. Partly called stock	2,609	$ 100	$ 260,900	$ 184,853 19	$ 126,546 81

LIST OF SHAREHOLDERS AS AT 31st DECEMBER, 1913.

(Not printed.)

---

*By Order-in-Council dated 28th day of October, 1911, the Corporation converted all Terminating Stock or Shares into Permanent Stock or Shares.

BALANCE SHEET AS AT 31st DECEMBER, 1913.

Dr.   Capital and Liabilities.

Capital (Liabilities to Stockholders or Shareholders).

A.—Permanent Capital Stock or Shares.

2. (b) Ordinary joint stock capital, 40 per cent. called; total
       called, ...; total paid thereon $99,046 51
3. (cc) Joint stock capital paid in advance of calls*......   35,306 68
                                                                           $134,353 19

Liabilities to the Public.

27. Deposits: (including unclaimed deposits), right reserved to require ⎫
            30 days' notice of any withdrawal .... ⎬   472 07
28. Interest on deposits, due, or accrued or capitalized................. ⎭
29. Debentures issued in Canada ....⎫
30. Interest due and accrued on (29) .....⎬ 241,686 64
Profit and Loss 4 75

          Total liabilities $376,516 65

Cr.   Assets.

I.—Assets of which the Corporation is the Beneficial Owner.

5. (b) Freehold land (including buildings) other than foregoing $9,636 22

      B.—Debts secured by Mortgages on Land.

9. (a) Debts (other than item 10) secured by mortgages of land......   24,749 01

C.—Debts not above enumerated for which the Corporation
           holds securities as follows:

24. (i) Debts secured by debentures and stocks.** 341,971 69

                      E.—Cash.

32. (b) In bank 159 73

      Total assets $376,516 65

CASH ACCOUNT.

Receipts for the year ending 31st December, 1913.

I.—Received by the Corporation for its Own Use.

      A.—Balances from 31st December, 1912.
                                                    (Col. 1.)   (Col. 4.)
3.   (ii) In bank $1,270 81

N.B.
    *No special terms.   **Securities and stock at book, not actual value.

CASH ACCOUNT.—Continued.

Receipts for the year ending 31st December, 1913.

C.—Receipts on account of Investments, Loans or Debts.

   (a) On mortgages of realty:
10.	(i) Principal	$5,525 75	
11.	(ii) Interest	1,381 66	
			6,907 41

   (b) On other securities:
13.	(ii) Interest on dividends	133 00

D.—Receipts from Real Estate Owned Beneficially by Corporation.

17. (b) Rents		335 04

G.—Receipts from other sources.

Interest on bank accounts, etc.	6 36
Total	$8,652 62

CASH ACCOUNT.

Expenditure for the year ending 31st December, 1913.

I.—Expended on Corporation Account.

                                                        (Col. 1.)   (Total Col. 4.)

C.—Borrowed Money (other than foregoing) or interest
                thereon paid, viz.:

19. (b) Deposits: Principal, $550.00; interest, $7,041.73.....	$7,591 73

   D.—Management Expenses (other than foregoing).

25. (a) Salaries, wages and fees	901 16

F.—Balances.

37. (b) Cash in bank	159 78
Total	$8,652 62

MISCELLANEOUS STATEMENT FOR THE YEAR ENDING 31ST DECEMBER, 1913.

1. Amount of debentures maturing in 1914: Issued in Canada, none; issued elsewhere, none.
2. Amount of other existing obligations which will mature in 1914: None.
3. Amount of securities held by the Corporation which will mature and become payable to the Corporation in 1914: About $10,000.00.
4. Average rate of interest per annum paid by the Corporation during 1913: On deposits, none, on debentures, 4½ and 6%; on debenture stock, none.

5. Average rate of interest per annum received by the Corporation during 1913: (a) On mortgages of realty; (b) on other securities.
   (i) Owned beneficially by the Corporation: (a) 5 to 8%; (b) 5 and 6%.
   (ii) Not owned beneficially: (a) None; (b) none.
6. Of the mortgages owned beneficially by the Corporation, $22,244.76 is on realty situate in Ontario, and $1,850 is on realty situate elsewhere.
7. Of the mortgages not owned beneficially by the Corporation, none is on realty situate in Ontario, and none is on realty situate elsewhere.
8. Loans written off or transferred to real estate account during 1913, viz.:
   (i) Funds or securities owned beneficially, none.
   (ii) Not so owned, none.
9. Number and aggregate amount of mortgages upon which compulsory proceedings have been taken by the Corporation in 1913, viz.:
   (i) Owned beneficially: No., none; amount, none.
   (ii) Not so owned: No., none; amount, none.
10. Aggregate market value of land mortgaged to the Corporation:
    (i) Mortgages owned beneficially, $50,000.
    (ii) Not so owned, none.
11. How often are the securities held by the Corporation valued? Yearly.
12. (a) Specify the officers of the Corporation who are under bond and for what sum respectively: None.
    (b) Are the said bonds executed by private sureties or by Guarantee Companies? None.
13. Date when the accounts of the Corporation were last audited: 26 January, 1914.
14. Names and addresses of the auditors respectively for 1913 and for 1914 (if appointed):
    For 1913: William Fahey, Robert Rae.
    For 1914: William Fahey, Robert Rae.
15. What were the dividend days of the Corporation in 1913 and what rate or rates of dividend were paid on those days respectively? None.
16. What is the date appointed for the Annual Meeting? 1st Saturday in February. Date of last Annual Meeting? Special 17th February, 1914.
17. Special General Meetings held in 1913: Dates, none.

COLONIAL INVESTMENT AND LOAN COMPANY.

Head Office, Toronto.

Incorporated under special Act of Canada, 63.4 V., c. 95.

ANNUAL STATEMENT

Of the condition and affairs of the Colonial Investment and Loan Company, of Toronto, Ont., at the 31st December, 1913, and for the year ending on that day, made to the Registrar of Loan Corporations for the Province of Ontario, pursuant to the laws of the said Province.

The head office of the Corporation is No. 15 Richmond Street West, in the City of Toronto, in the Province of Ontario.

The Board is constituted of five directors holding office for one year.

The directors and chief executive officers of the Corporation at the 31st December, 1913, were as follows, together with their respective terms of office:

A. J. Jackson, President, Toronto: March 18, 1913; March 17, 1914.
J. H. Mitchell, Vice-President, Toronto, Ont.;   "   "
Henry O'Hara, Vice-President, Toronto, Ont.;
W. H. Cross, Director, Toronto, Ont.;
W. R. White, K.C., Director, Pembroke, Ont.;   "   "
A. J. Jackson, Manager, Toronto, Ont.;   February 28, 1913; February 28, 1914.
J. H. Mitchell, Secretary, Toronto, Ont.;   "   "

A.—Permanent capital stock: Total amount authorized, $5,000,000; permanent preference, $4,900,000; ordinary permanent, $100,000; total amount subscribed, permanent preference, $2,455,010.00; ordinary permanent, $100,000, as more particularly set out in Schedule A hereto.

SCHEDULE A.

Class 2.—Fixed and permanent capital stock created by virtue of Joint Stock Companies' Acts or Private Acts.

Last call made: Permanent preferred, May 12th, 1902; gross amount, $113,570.09; amount paid thereon, $87,000.65. Ordinary permanent, December 13th, 1910; rate per cent., ten per cent.; gross amount, $10,000.00; amount paid thereon, $10,000.00.

Description.	No. of shares.	Par value.	Total amount held.	Total amount paid thereon.	Total remaining unpaid on calls.
		$	$ c.	$ c.	$ c.
1. Fully called permanent preference..............	245,501	10	2,455,010 00	2,428,440 56	26,569 44
2. 20 per cent. called, ordinary permanent	10,000	10	100 000 00	20,000 00	None
Total	255,501	....	2,555,010 00	2,448,440 56	26,569 44

LIST OF SHAREHOLDERS AS AT 31st DECEMBER, 1913.

(Not printed.)

BALANCE SHEET AS AT 31st DECEMBER, 1913.

Dr.   Capital and Liabilities.

A.—Permanent Capital Stock or Shares.

1. (a) Permanent preference stock capital fully called: Total called, $2,455,010; total paid thereon.....$2,428,440 56		
2. (b) Ordinary joint stock capital 20 per cent. called: Total called, $20,000; total paid thereon	20,000 00	
4. (d) Dividends declared in respect of (1) and (2), but not yet paid: Permanent preference, $72,844.68; ordinary permanent, $600.00	73,444 68	
5 (e) Unappropriated profits in respect of (1) and (2) (profit and loss)	38,905 50	
6. (f) Reserve fund in respect of (1) and (2)	255,000 00	
Real Estate Reserve Fund	30,000 00	
Unclaimed dividends and balances	5,235 52	
		$2,851,026 26

Liabilities to the Public

29. Debentures issued in Canada	$200,850 00	
30. Interest due or accrued on (29)	4,519 65	
31. Debentures issued elsewhere than in Canada, sterling ...	605,447 42	
32. Interest due or accrued on (31)	3,749 06	
41. Other liabilities to the public, viz.:		
42. (a) Sundry accounts	1,000 00	
43. (b) Mortgages assumed with accrued interest	17,532 46	
		833,098 59

Total liabilities $3,684,124 85

Cr.   Assets.

I.—Assets of which the Corporation is the Beneficial Owner.

A.—Immovable Property Owned Beneficially by Corporation.

5. (b) Freehold land (including buildings)	$163,962 24	
		$163,962 24

B.—Debts secured by Mortgages of Land.

9. (a) *Debts (other than item 10) secured by mortgages of land: Loans, $3,332,363.42, less payment, $829,958.98 . . ..$2,502,404 44		
10. (b) Debts secured by mortgaged lands held for sale.......	9,886 79	
Interest current for month of December, 1913...	2,850 54	
11. (c) Interest due or accrued on item 9 and not included therein	84,014 58	
12. (d) Of the debts mentioned in item 13 the sum of $22,150.00 is due by directors or officers of the Corporation (not extended), Insurance premiums, taxes, loan expense	28,860 73	
		2,628,017 08

* Mortgages and other authorized securities to the value of $125.00 for each $100.00 of the aggregate value of outstanding debentures of the Company are deposited with The Imperial Trusts Company of Canada as trustee as security for the debenture holders.

Cr. Assets.

C.—Debts not above enumerated, for which the Corporation holds security as follows:

13. (a) Mortgages and agreements for sale purchased, net cost with accrued charges	$114,226 58	
19. (g) Debts secured by debentures	256 55	
20. (h) †Debts secured only by permanent stock or shares of the Corporation	170,124 98	
22. (j) Stocks owned by the Company	260,346 12	
23. (k) CaH loans	163,976 71	
26. (n) Interest due or accrued on item 22 and not included therein	5,942 50	
		714,873 44

E.—Cash.

32. (b) In banks and trust company	171,304 72

F. Assets not hereinbefore mentioned.

41 (e) Office furniture	$2,928 84	
42 (f) Sundry accounts	3,038 53	
		5,967 37

Total assets	$3,684,124 85

Note.—Assets reported in 1912, but written off in 1913 (not extended), $19,171.93.

CASH ACCOUNT.

Receipts for the year ending 31st December, 1913.

	(Col. 1.)	(Col. 2.)	(Col. 3.)	(Total, Col. 4.)
I.—Received by the Corporation its Own Use.				
A.—Balance at 31st December, 1912.				
1. Balance on hand and in bank		$235,672 27		
B. Sums received Wholly or Partly on Capital Stock.				
4. (a) Calls on permanent preference stock	....	....	$1,654 45	
C.—Receipts on account of Investments, Loans or Debts.				
(a) On Mortgages of realty:				
10. (i) Principal, loans repaid— including transfers to real estate......	....	459,734 64		
11. (ii) Interest, including December, 1913, accretions	$209,833 99			

†Of the debts mentioned in item 20 the sum of $33,500.00 is due by directors or officers of the Corporation.

CASH ACCOUNT.—Continued.

Receipts for the year ending 31st December, 1913.

	(Col. 1.)	(Col. 2.)	(Col. 3.)	(Total, Col. 4.)
(*b*) On other securities:				
Debenture loans ..	....	8 01		
12. (i) Principal call loans	....	1,354,602 75		
13. (ii) Share loans	....	40,067 69		
Mortgages and agreements for sale purchased.	....	132 612 92		
Mortgages assumed	....	8,589 27		
14. Principal new loaning plans.	....	221,826 14		
15. Repayment in arrears	....	13,351 02		
Accrued interest	....	90,864 77		
Sales of stocks and bonds..	4,347 40	15,942 85		
D.—Receipts from Real Estate Owned Beneficially by Corporation.				
16. (*a*) Sales (not included in any of the foregoing items)	....	23,539 01		
17. (*b*) Rents	3,720 95			
Profits in Properties Sold..	3,012 69			
E.—Miscellaneous.				
19. (*b*) Discharge of mortgage fees	617 50			
21. (*d*) Fines, transfer fees, etc	59 50			
22. (*e*) Interest on arrears....,	3,341 30			
23. (*f*) Interest on sundry bank deposits	3,614 78			
Sterling Exchange ...	84 81			
Commission on Sale of Deposits	1,762 70			
F.—Borrowed Money.				
27. (*c*) Borrowed on debentures sterling	....	$172,547 65		
28. (*d*) Borrowed on debentures, currency	....	51,200 00		
G.—Received from other sources, viz.:				
30. (*a*) Unclaimed dividends and balances	....	601 12		
(*b*)Sundry accounts	....	400 00		
(*c*) Sundry profits	$1,202 04			
Totals	$231,597 66	$2,821,560 11	$1,654 45	$3,054,812 22

CASH ACCOUNT.

Expenditure for the year ending 31st December, 1912.

A.—Sums Loaned or Invested on Capital Account.

	(Col. 1.)	(Col. 2.)	(Total, Col. 4.)
1. (a) Loaned on mortgages or realty	....	$838,539 76	
(b) Loaned or invested in other securities:			
2. (i) Share loans	....	108,860 00	
3. (ii) Call loans	....	992,684 00	
4. (iii) Agreements for sale and mortgages purchased	....	23,300 90	
5. (iv) Mortgages assumed	....	1,406 66	
6. (c) Real estate purchased, loans transferred	....	166,365 74	
7. (d) Stocks purchased	....	32,327 00	

B.—Expended on Stock Account.

8. Dividends on permanent preference stock.	$133,525 95		
Dividends on ordinary permanent stock..	1,100 00		

C.—Borrowed Money (other than foregoing) or interest thereon paid, viz.:

20. (c) Debentures issued in Canada: (Principal and interest)	9,046 34	54,900 00	
21. (d) Debentures issued elsewhere: Principal, interest	25,908 63	106,263 67	

D.—Management Expenses (other than foregoing).

25. (a) Salaries, wages and fees—directors, auditors, office assistants, etc ..	30,954 15		
26. (b) Commission on collections	2,099 24		
27. (c) Agents' commission on debentures and loans	10,587 99		
28. (d) Stationery, postage, printing and advertising	4,013 03		
29. (e) Law costs	209 26		
30. (f) Office rent	4,358 26		
31. (g) Travelling expenses	1,270 85		
32. (h) Registration fees (Ontario)	200 00		
33. (i) Other management expenditure:			
Head office and agency charges	1,680 66		
Stamp duty, etc	205 98		

E.—Other Expenditures, etc.

34. (a) Transfer fees, sterling debenture holders.....................	783 78		
35. (b) Registrar and transfer fees	400 00		
36. (c) Expenditure real estate	4,355 94		
Special audits and valuation fees	262 50		
Local Government tax	3,864 75		
Sundry losses	509 06		
Expenditure office premises			
Office furniture	....	352 43	
Agents' balances	....	1,026 27	
Accrued interest portion of repayment	....	324,089 21	
Loan expense, taxes and insurance premiums	....	7,556 53	

F.—Balance.

37. (b) Cash on hand and in banks.........	....	171,304 72	
Totals	$235,836 36	$2,818,975 86	$3,054,812 22

MISCELLANEOUS STATEMENT FOR THE YEAR ENDING 31ST DECEMBER, 1913.

1. Amount of Debentures maturing in 1914: Issued in Canada, $62,300.00; issued elsewhere, $163,481.11.
2. Amount of other existing obligations which will mature in 1914, none.
3. Amount of securities held by the Corporation which will mature and become payable to the Corporation in 1914, none.
4. Average rate of interest per annum paid by the Corporation during 1913: On deposits, none; on debentures, 4, 4½ and 5%; on debenture stock, none.
5. Average rate of interest per annum received by the Corporation during 1913:
    (a) On mortgages of realty; (b) on other securities.
    (i) Owned beneficially by the Corporation: (a) 8.374%; (b) 6.283%.
    (ii) Not owned beneficially: (a) 8.374%; (b) 5.384%.
6. Of the mortgages owned beneficially by the Corporation, $125,876.81 is on realty situate in Ontario, and $1,260,015.16 is on realty situate elsewhere.
7. Of the mortgages not owned beneficially by the Corporation, $22,500.00 is on realty situate in Ontario, and $1,094,022.47 is on realty situate elsewhere.
8. Loans and agreements for sale purchased written off or transferred to real estate account during 1913, viz.:
    (i) Funds or securities owned beneficially, $133,608.56.
    (ii) Not so owned, none.
9. Number and aggregate amount of mortgages upon which compulsory proceedings have been taken by the Corporation in 1913, viz.:
    (i) Owned beneficially: Number, 2; amount, $1,860.00.
    (ii) Not so owned: Number, none; amount, none.
10. Aggregate market value of land mortgaged to the Corporation:
    (i) Mortgages owned beneficially, $9,303,174.50.
11. How often are the securities held by the Corporation valued? As occasion may require.
12. (a) Specify the officers of the Corporation who are under bond, and for what sum respectively: Secretary, $10,000.00; General Manager, $10,000.00; Cashier, $10,000.00.
    (b) Are the said bonds executed by private sureties or by Guarantee Companies? Guarantee Companies.
13. Date when the accounts of the Corporation were last audited? December 31st, 1913.
14. Names and addresses of the auditors respectively for 1913 and for 1914 (if appointed):
    For 1913: W. H. Cross, F.C.A., Toronto, Ont.; G. T. Clarkson, F.C.A., Toronto, Ont.; Jas. Hardy, F.C.A., Toronto, Ont.
15. What were the dividend days of the Corporation in 1913, and what rate or rates of dividend were paid on those days respectively? January 2nd, 1913, 2½%; July 2nd, 1913, 3%.
16. What is the date appointed for the Annual Meeting? March 17th, 1914. Date of last Annual Meeting? March 18th, 1913.
17. Special General Meetings held in 1913: Dates, none.

THE LAMBTON LOAN AND INVESTMENT COMPANY.

Head Office, Sarnia, Ontario.

CONSTATING INSTRUMENTS.

Incorporated under the Building Societies Act, 9 Vict., c. 90 (Province of Canada) by declaration filed on 27th March, 1847, with the Clerk of the Peace for the Western District. The original corporate name was "The Port Sarnia Building Society." The Society was reorganized as "The Lambton Permanent Building and Investment Society" under the said Act and other Acts all of which became consolidated as chapter 53 of the Consolidated Statutes of Upper Canada, by declaration filed 19th June, 1855, with the Clerk of the Peace for the County of Lambton. This latter corporate name was changed by Order-in-Council, 4th June, 1880 to The Lambton Loan and Investment Company.

The lending and the borrowing powers are governed by the Loan and Trust Corporations Act, 2 Geo. V. chap. 34.

ANNUAL STATEMENT

Of the condition and affairs of The Lambton Loan and Investment Company, of Sarnia, Ontario, at the 31st of December, 1913, and for the year ending on that day, made to the Registrar of Loan Corporations for the Province of Ontario, pursuant to the laws of the said Province.

The Head Office of the Corporation is at No. 191 Front Street, in the Town of Sarnia, in the Province of Ontario.

The Board is constituted of eight directors holding office for two years.

The directors and chief executive officers of the Corporation at the 31st December, 1913, were as follows, together with their respective terms of office:

Isaac Unsworth, President, Florence;	1st January, 1914; 1st January, 1916.
Norman S. Gurd, Vice-President, Sarnia;	" " " "
David Milne, Director, Sarnia;	" " " "
W. J. Hanna, Director, Sarnia;	" " " "
F. F. Pardee, Director, Sarnia;	1st January, 1913; 1st January, 1915.
Robert Mackenzie, Director, Sarnia;	" " " "
Thomas Boulton, Director, Mooretown;	" " " "
John Scott, Director, Wallaceburg;	
J. H. Kittermaster, Manager, Sarnia.	

A. Permanent capital stock: Total amount authorized, $1,000,000; total amount subscribed, $789,750, as more particularly set out in Schedule A hereto.

SCHEDULE A.

Class 1.—Fixed and permanent capital stock created by virtue of Buildings Society Acts.

Description.	Total amount issued and subsisting at 31st December, 1913.		Total amount of actual payments thereon.	Total amount unpaid and constituting an asset of the Corporation.
	No. of shares.	Par value of shares	—	
1. Fully called stock.....	15,795	$50	$789,750	$789,750	....

LIST OF SHAREHOLDERS AS AT 31st DECEMBER, 1913.

(Not printed.)

BALANCE SHEET AS AT 31st DECEMBER, 1913.

Dr. . Capital and Liabilities.

Capital (Liabilities to Stockholders or Shareholders).

A.—Permanent Capital Stock or Shares

1. (a) Ordinary joint stock fully called; total called, $789,750.00; total paid thereon..................	$789,750 00	
4. (d) Dividends declared in respect of (1).................	39,487 50	
6. (f) Reserve fund in respect of (1)	620,000 00	
7. (g) Contingent fund in respect of (1).................	14,259 94	
		$1,463,497 44

Liabilities to the Public.

27. Deposits (right reserved to require 30 days' notice of any withdrawal).....................	$925,571 67	
28. Interest on deposits due, or accrued or capitalized.......	33,246 41	
29. Debentures issued in Canada...........................	457,763 74	
30. Interest due and accrued on (29)......................	9,210 71	
		1,425,792 53
Total liabilities		$2,889,289 97

Cr. Assets.

I.—Assets of which the Corporation is the Beneficial Owner.

A.—Immovable Property owned Beneficially by Corporation.

1. (a) Office premises situate as follows:		
2. (1) At Town of Sarnia; held in freehold..........		$4,500 00

B.—Debts secured by Mortgages of Land.

9. (a) Debts (other than item 10) secured by mortgages of land............................$2,601,282 90	$2,601,282 90	
10. (b) Debts secured by mortgaged land held for sale.....	50,750 50	
		2,652,033 40

C.—Debts not above enumerated for which the Corporation holds securities as follows:

14. (b) Debts secured by municipal bonds or debentures....	$144,347 68	
20. (h) Debts secured only by permanent stock or shares of the Corporation	51,459 73	
		195,807 41

E.—Cash.

31. (a) On hand	$6,616 19	
32. (b) In bank	30,332 97	
		36,949 16
Total assets		$2,889,289 97

CASH ACCOUNT,

Receipts for the year ending 31st December 1913.

I.—Received by the Corporation for its Own Use.

A.—Balance for 31st December, 1912.

1. Cash:		
2.	(i) On hand $23,588 33	
3.	(ii) In bank 85,889 59	$109,477 92

C.—Receipts on account of Investments, Loans or Debts.

(a) On mortgages of realty:
10.   (i) Principal $337,617 94
11.   (ii) Interest.................. .... 143,950 89
(b) On other securities:
12.   (i) Principal................................ . . .. 35,391 57
13.   (ii) Interest or dividends........................ 9,399 82   526,360 22

F.—Borrowed Money.

26. (b) Borrowed by taking deposits $1,076,208 19
27. (c) Borrowed on debentures........................... 222,317 13   1,298,525 32

G.—Receipts from other sources:

30. (a) General interest 2,025 19

Total...... .... $1,986,388 65

CASH ACCOUNT.

Expenditure for the year ending 31st December, 1913.

I.—Expended on Corporation Account.

A.—Sums Loaned or Invested on Capital Account.

1. (a) Loaned on mortgages of realty $358,300 51

(b) Loaned or invested in other securities:—
3.   (ii) Municipal debentures 19,595 35
5.   (iv) Shareholders' stock 17,542 50
7. (e) Insurances or taxes advanced on property mortgaged
      to Corporation 2,458 48 $397,896 84

B.—Expended on Stock Account.

8. Dividends paid on permanent stock 71,077 50

C.—Borrowed money (other than foregoing) or interest thereon
paid.

19. (b) Deposits: Principal, $1,127,629.83; interest, $503.24...$1,128,133 07
20. (c) Debentures issued in Canada; Principal, $271,726.27;
      interest, $19,142.59 .... 290,868 86   1,419,001 93

CASH ACCOUNT.—Continued.

Expenditure for the year ending 31st December, 1913.

D.—Management Expenses (other than foregoing).

25. (a) Salaries, wages and fees	$7,351 04	
26. (b) Commission	176 50	
28. (d) Stationery, postage, printing and advertising	894 61	
30. (f) Fuel, rent, taxes (other than in 7 and 32) and rates	957 15	
31. (g) Travelling expenses	28 95	
32. (h) Registration fees	180 00	
33. (i) Other management expenditure	422 04	
		10,010 29

E.—Other Expenditures, viz.:

34. (a) General interest	1,452 93

F.—Balance.

37 (a) Cash on hand and in bank	36,949 16
Total	$1,936,388 65

MISCELLANEOUS STATEMENT FOR THE YEAR ENDING 31ST DECEMBER, 1913.

1. Amount of debentures maturing in 1914: Issued in Canada, $213,317.25; issued elsewhere, none.
2. Amount of other existing obligations which will mature in 1914, none.
3. Amount of securities held by the Corporation which will mature and become payable to the Corporation in 1914. Estimate, $350,000.00.
4. Average rate of interest per annum paid by the Corporation during 1913 on deposits: On deposits, 3.46%; On debentures, 4%; On debenture stock, none.
5. Average rate of interest, per annum received by the Corporation during 1913:
    (a) On mortgages of realty; (b) On other securities:
      (i) Owned beneficially by the Corporation: (a) 5½%; (b) 4 4-5%.
      (ii) Not owned beneficially (a) none; (b) none.
6. Of the mortgages owned beneficially by the Corporation, $2,771,689.32 is on realty situate in Ontario, and $76,151.49 is on realty situate elsewhere.
7. Of the mortgages not owned beneficially by the Corporation, none is on realty situate in Ontario, and none is on realty situate elsewhere.
8. Loans written off or transferred to real estate account during 1913, viz.:
      (i) Funds or securities owned beneficially, none.
      (ii) Not so owned, all owned beneficially.
9. Number and aggregate amount of mortgages upon which compulsory proceedings have been taken by the Corporation in 1913, viz:
      (i) Owned beneficially, No., 1; Amount, $2,821.54.
      (ii) Not so owned, No., none; Amount none.
10. Aggregate market value of land mortgaged to the Corporation:
      (i) Mortgages owned beneficially, $4,271,760.00.
      (ii) Not so owned, none.
11. How often are the securities held by the Corporation valued: Yearly.
12. (a) Specify the officers of the Corporation who are under bond and for what sum respectively: Manager, $10,000.00; Accountant, $5,000.00; Cashier, $5,000.00.
    .(b) Are the said bonds executed by private sureties or by Guarantee Companies? Guarantee Company
13. Date when the accounts of the Corporation were last audited: Daily audit.
14. Names and addresses of the auditors respectively for 1913 and for 1914 (if appointed):
      For 1913: A. F. Wade, Alex. Saunders.
      For 1914: A. F. Wade, Alex. Saunders.
15. What were the dividend days of the Corporation in 1913, and what rate or rates of dividend were paid on those days respectively: January 1st and July 1st: 5% and 4%.
16. What is the date appointed for the Annual Meeting? Fourth Wednesday in January. Date of last Annual Meeting? January 28th.
17. Special General Meetings held in 1913: Dates, none.

THE SOUTHERN LOAN AND SAVINGS COMPANY.

Head Office, St. Thomas, Ontario.

This Company was, under the provisions of The Loan Corporations Act, formed by the amalgamation of The Southern Loan and Savings Company, The South-Western Farmers' and Mechanics' Savings and Loan Society and The Star Loan Company.

The agreement for the amalgamation of these Companies under the name of The Southern Loan and Savings Company was duly executed by the said several Corporations on the twenty-third day of September, A.D. 1903, and duly ratified by the shareholders of the said respective Corporations on the seventeenth day of November, A.D. 1903, and was assented to by the Lieutenant-Governor of the Province of Ontario by Order-in-Council, dated twenty-fifth day of November, A.D. 1903.

The lending and the borrowing powers are governed by the Loan and Trust Corporations Act, R.S.O. 1914, chap. 184.

ANNUAL STATEMENT

Of the condition and affairs of the Southern Loan and Savings Company, of St. Thomas, Ont., as at the 31st December, 1913, and for the year ending on that day, made to the Registrar of Loan Corporations for the Province of Ontario, pursuant to the laws of said Province.

The head office of the Corporation is at No. 390 Talbot Street, in the City of St. Thomas, in the Province of Ontario.

The Board is constituted of seven directors, holding office for the term of one year.

The directors and chief executive officers of the Corporation at the 31st December, 1913, were as follows, together with their respective terms of office:

Wm. Mickleborough, President, St. Thomas;	February, 1913; 23rd February, 1914.
Geo. K. Crocker, Vice-President, St. Thomas;	" "
Robert Kains, M.D., Director, St. Thomas;	" "
James A. Bell, Director, St. Thomas;	
D. McColl, Director, St. Thomas;	
C. W. Marlatt, M.D., Director, St. Thomas;	
W. L. Wickett, B.A., Director, St. Thomas;	
J. W. Stewart, Secretary, Manager, St. Thomas.	

A. Permanent capital stock: Total amount authorized, $908,950; total amount subscribed, $908,950, as more particularly set out in Schedule A hereto.

SCHEDULE A.

Class 1.—Fixed and permanent capital stock created by virtue of Building Society Acts.

Description.	Total amount issued and subsisting at 31st December, 1913.			Total amount of actual payments thereon.	Total amount unpaid and constituting an asset of the Corporation.
	No. of shares.	Par value of shares.	—		
1. Fully called stock	8,179	$ 50	$ 908,950	907,500 00	$ 1,450 00

LIST OF SHAREHOLDERS AS AT 31st DECEMBER, 1913.

(Not printed.)

8 L.C.

BALANCE SHEET AS AT 31st DECEMBER, 1913.

Dr. Capital and Liabilities.

A.—Permanent Capital Stock or Shares.

1. (a) Ordinary joint stock capital fully called; total called, $907,950; total paid thereon	$907,500 00
4. (d) Dividends declared in respect of (1), but not yet paid..........	27,121 50
5. (e) Unappropriated profits in respect of (1)........................	3,215 03
6. (f) Reserve fund in respect of (1)..............................	170,000 00

Liabilities to the Public.

27. Deposits (including unclaimed deposits), right reserved to require 30 days' notice of any withdrawal	416,498 21
29. Debentures issued in Canada	658,050 00
30. Interest due and accrued on (29)...............................	12,874 90
Total liabilities	$2,195,259 64

Cr. Assets.

I.—Assets of which the Corporation is the Beneficial Owner.

A.—Immovable Property Owned Beneficially by Corporation.

1. (a) Office premises at St. Thomas, Ontario, held in freehold........	$26,000 00

B.—Debts secured by Mortgages of Land.

9. (a) Debts (other than item 10) secured by mortgages of land........	2,130,310 03

C.—Debts, not above enumerated, for which the Corporation holds securities, as follows:

10. (b) Debts secured by mortgaged land held for sale..................	3,556 21
16. (d) Debts secured by Loan Corporation debentures	15,558 50

E.—Cash.

33. Cash on hand and in bank	19,834 90
Total assets	$2,195,259 64

CASH ACCOUNT.

Receipts for the year ending 31st December, 1913.

I.—Received by the Corporation for Its Own Use.

B.—Sums received Wholly or Partly on Capital Stock.

(Total Col. 4.)

4. (a) Calls on joint stock permanent capital	$159 30

CASH ACCOUNT.—Continued.

Receipts for the year ending 31st December, 1913.

C.—Receipts on account of Investments, Loans or Debts.

(a) On mortgages of realty:

10.	(i) Principal	$350,479 01
11.	(ii) Interest	118,894 17

(b) On other securities:

12.	(i) Principal	4,435 30
13.	(ii) Interest	106 36

E.—Miscellaneous.

19. (b) Premiums or bonus on loans	779 11

F.—Borrowed Money.

26. (b) Borrowed by taking deposits	714,610 63
27. (c) Borrowed on debentures	156,600 00

G.—Receipts from other sources, viz.:

30. (a) Rents, office building	2,525 60
(b) Bank interest	273 85
(c) Sundries	19 65
Totals	$1,348,882 98

CASH ACCOUNT.

Expenditure for the year ending 31st December, 1913.

I.—Expended on Corporation Account.

A.—Sums Loaned or Invested on Capital Account.

1. (a) Loaned on mortgages of realty	$344,429 75
(b) Loaned or invested in other securities, viz.:	
(i) Loan Company debentures	21,148 63

B.—Expended on Stock Account.

8. Dividends paid on permanent stock	54,243 00

C.—Borrowed Money (other than foregoing) or interest thereon paid, viz.:

18. (a) Bank account (principal and interest)	2,434 34
19. (b) Deposits: Principal, $729,881.05; interest, $215.28	730,096 33
20. (c) Debentures issued in Canada: Principal, $132,550.00; interest, $29,244.18	161,794 18

D.—Management Expenses (other than foregoing):

25. (a) Salaries, wages and fees	8,116 38
26. (b) Commission or brokerage	2,826 85
28. (d) Stationery, postage, printing and advertising	810 30
30. (f) Fuel, rent, taxes (other than 7 and 32)	761 57
31. (g) Travelling expenses	274 25
32. (h) Registration fees	150 00
33. (i) Other management expenditure	153 60

CASH ACCOUNT.—Continued.

Expenditure for the year ending 31st December, 1913.

E.—Other Expenditures, viz.:

34. (a) Maintenance of Company's building 1,809 00

F.—Balance.

37. (a) Cash on hand and in banks 19,834 90

Total $1,348,882 98

MISCELLANEOUS STATEMENT FOR THE YEAR ENDING 31ST DECEMBER, 1913.

1. Amount of Debentures maturing in 1914: Issued in Canada, $300,050.00; issued elsewhere, none.
2. Amount of other existing obligations which will mature in 1914, none.
3. Amount of securities held by the Corporation which will mature and become payable to the Corporation in 1914: Approximately, $500,000.00.
4. Average rate of interest per annum paid by the Corporation during 1913: On deposits, 3.10%; on debentures, 4.42%; on debenture stock, none.
5. Average rate of interest per annum received by the Corporation during 1913:
   (a) On mortgages of realty; (b) on other securities.
   (i) Owned beneficially by the Corporation: (a) 5.89%; (b) 5.50%.
   (ii) Not owned beneficially: (a) None; (b) none.
6. Of the mortgages owned beneficially by the Corporation, $2,133,866.24 is on realty situate in Ontario, and none is on realty situate elsewhere.
7. Of the mortgages not owned beneficially by the Corporation, none is on realty situate in Ontario, and none is on realty situate elsewhere.
8. Loans written off or transferred to real estate account during 1913, viz.:
   (i) Funds or securities owned beneficialy, $3,556.21.
   (ii) Not so owned, none.
9. Number and aggregate amount of mortgages upon which compulsory proceedings have been taken by the Corporation in 1913, viz.:
   (i) Owned beneficially: Number, 7; amount, $11,378.54.
   (ii) Not so owned: Number, none; amount, none.
10. Aggregate market value of land mortgaged to the Corporation:
   (i) Mortgages owned beneficially, $2,133,866.24.
   (ii) Not so owned, none.
11. How often are the securities held by the Corporation valued? Continually under revision.
12. (a) Specify the officers of the Corporation who are under bond, and for what sum respectively: Manager, $8,000; Accountant, $5,000; Book-keeper, $5,000; Inspector, $1,000.
   (b) Are the said bonds executed by private sureties or by Guarantee Companies? Guarantee Companies.
13. Date when the accounts of the Corporation were last audited? 31st December, 1913.
14. Names and addresses of the auditors respectively for 1913 and for 1914 (if appointed):
   For 1913: R. Graham, C. H. Caughell, St. Thomas, Ont.
   For 1914:
15. What were the dividend days of the Corporation in 1913, and what rate or rates of dividend were paid on those days respéctively? 2nd January, 2nd July, 3% (6% per annum).
16. What is the date appointed for the Annual Meeting? 23rd February, 1914. Date of last Annual Meeting? 18th February, 1913.
17. Special General Meetings held in 1913: Dates, none.

THE ONTARIO LOAN AND DEBENTURE COMPANY.*

Head Office, London, Ontario.

CONSTATING INSTRUMENTS.

Incorporated under Building Societies Act. Con. Statutes of Upper Canada, c. 53, by declaration filed in the office of the Clerk of the Peace for the County of Middlesex, 26th September, 1870. The original corporate name was The Ontario Savings and Investment Society.

By Order-in-Council of Ontario, dated 4th October, 1879, and also by Order-in-Council of Canada dated 29th October, 1879, the corporate name was changed to The Ontario Loan and Debenture Company.

The lending and borrowing powers are governed by 52 Vict. (1889), c. 94 (D.); 57-58 Vict. (1894), c. 116 (D.), and by the Loan and Trust Corporations Act, R.S.O. 1914, chap. 184.

ANNUAL STATEMENT

Of the condition and affairs of The Ontario Loan and Debenture Company, of London, Ontario, at the 31st December, 1913, and for the year ending on that day, made to the Registrar of Loan Corporations for the Province of Ontario, pursuant to the laws of the said Province.

The head office of the Corporation is at No. 139 Dundas Street, in the City of London, in the Province of Ontario.

The Board is constituted of nine directors, holding office for one year.

The directors and chief executive officers of the Corporation at the 31st December, 1913, were as follows, together with their respective terms of office:

John McClary, President, London;	12th February, 1913; 11th February, 1914.
Wm. J. Reid, First Vice-Pres., London;	" "
Alfred M. Smart, Second Vice-Pres., London;	" "
Thos. H. Smallman, Director, London;	
Lieut.-Col. Wm. M. Gartshore, Director, London;	"
John M. Dillon, Director, London;	
Major Thomas Beattie, M.P., Director, London;	"
Moses Masuret, Director, London;	
Thomas P. McCormick, Director, London;	" "
Alfred M. Smart, Manager and Secretary-Treasurer, London; 1st August, 1906.	

A. Permanent capital stock: Total amount authorized, $5,000,000; total amount subscribed, $2,550,000, as more particularly set out in Schedule A hereto.

SCHEDULE A.

Class 1.—Fixed and permanent capital stock created by virtue of Building Society Acts.

Description.	Total amount issued and subsisting at 31st December, 1913.			Total amount of actual payments thereon.	Total amount unpaid and constituting an asset of the Corporation.
	No. of shares.	Par value of shares.			
		$	$	$	$
1. Fully called stock	31,000	50	1,550,000	1,550,000 00	....
2. Partly "	20,000	50	1,000,000	200,000 00	800,000 00
Total	51,000	....	2,550,000	1,750,000 00	800,000 00

LIST OF SHAREHOLDERS AS AT 31st DECEMBER, 1913.
(Not printed.)

---

*The Agricultural Savings and Loan Company of London was amalgamated with this company by Order-in-Council dated 10th November, 1911.

BALANCE SHEET AS AT 31st DECEMBER, 1913.

Dr.   Capital and Liabilities.

Capital (Liabilities to Stockholders or Shareholders).

A.—Permanent Capital Stock or Shares.

1. (a) Ordinary joint stock capital fully called; total called,
        $1,550,000; total paid thereon $1,550,000 00
2. (b) Ordinary joint stock capital, 20 per cent. called;
        total called, $200,000.00; total paid thereon....   200,000 00
4. (d) Dividends declared in respect of (1) and (2), but not
        yet paid 43,750 00
5. (e) Unappropriated profits in respect of (1) and (2) ...   45,859 36
6. (f) Reserve fund in respect of (1) and (2) 1,550,000 00
                                                                        $3,389,609 36

                    Liabilities to the Public.

27. Deposits (including unclaimed deposits): Right reserved
        to require 30 to 60 days' notice of any with-
        drawal* $1,069,127 26
28. Interest on deposits capitalized during the
        year........................ $33,929.13
29. Debentures issued and payable in Canada 1,231,594 72
30. Interest due and accrued on (29) 18,990 03
31. Debentures issued in Canada but payable elsewhere..... 2,051,724 11
32. Interest due and accrued on (31) 19,458 60
                                                                        4,890,894 72

        Total liabilities $7,780,504 08

Cr.   Assets.

I.—Assets of which the Corporation is the Beneficial Owner.

A.—Immovable Property Owned Beneficially by Corporation.

1. (a) Office premises situate as follows:—
2.   (1) At London, Ont., held in freehold $69,000 00

        B.—Debts secured by Mortgages of Land.

9. (a) Debts (other than item 10) secured by mortgages of
        land less amount retained to pay prior mort-
        gages, $5,042.74 ....$7,253,075 62
10. (b) Debts secured by mortgaged land held for sale....   675 00
                                                                        7,253,750 62

C.—Debts not above enumerated for which the Corporation
        holds securities as follows:—

14. (b) Debts secured by municipal bonds or debentures.. $119,154 20
15. (c) Debts secured by Public School debentures........   19,448 37
16. (d) Debts secured by Loan Corporations' debentures..   5,938 24
20. (h) Debts secured only by permanent stock or shares of
        the Corporation 986 70
22. (j) Debts secured by Bank stock 20,160 04
                                                                        165,687 55

*On amounts of $1,000 and under, 30 days' notice; over $1,000, 60 days' notice.

BALANCE SHEET.—Continued.

E.—Cash.

32. (b) In banks in London, England $7,081 26
      In banks in Canada 280,584 65
                                       $ 287,665 91

    F.—Assets not hereinbefore mentioned.

37. (a) Stocks (owned) 4,400 00

          Total assets $7,780,504 08

CASH ACCOUNT.

Receipts for the year ending 31st December, 1913.

   I.—Received by the Corporation for its Own Use.

     A.—Balance from 31st December, 1912.

3.   (ii) Cash in bank .... $ 116,838 04

C.—Receipts on account of Investments, Loans or Debts.

   (a) On mortgages of realty:—
10.   (i) Principal $1,146,679 08
11.   (ii) Interest 481,220 29
   (b) On other securities:—
12.   (i) Principal 5,213 21
13.   (ii) Interest or dividends 7,378 77
                                        1,640,491 35

D.—Receipts from Real Estate Owned Beneficially by Corporation.

17. (b) Rents 3,554 83

       F.—Borrowed Money.

26. (b) Borrowed by taking deposits $2,219,286 41
27. (c) Borrowed on debentures 687,233 70
                                      2,906,522 11

      G.—Receipts from other sources, viz.: ....

30. (a) Interest on bank accounts, etc. 1,544 65

        Total $4,668,950 98

CASH ACCOUNT.

Expenditure for the year ending 31st December, 1913.

   A.—Sums loaned or invested on Capital Account.

1. (a) Loaned on mortgages of realty, less amount retained
            to pay prior mortgages $932,798 17
   (b) Loaned or invested in other securities, viz.:—
2.   (i) Invested in municipal and school debentures.. 10,320 96
3.   (ii) This Corporation's debentures 5,870 45
4.   (iii) Loaned on bank stock 400 00
                                        $ 949,389 58

CASH ACCOUNT.—Continued.

Expenditure for the year ending 31st December, 1913.

	(Col. 1.)	(Col. 2.)	(Total, Col. 4.)
B.—Expended on Stock Account.			
8. Dividends paid on permanent stock ....$		140,000 00	
			$ 140,000 00
C.—Borrowed Money (other than foregoing) or interest.			
19. (b) Deposits: Principal, $2,387,750.90; interest, $2,038.94.	$2,389,789 84		
20. (c) Debentures issued and payable in Canada: Principal, $471,975.52; interest, 56,899.00		528,874 52	
21. (d) Debentures issued in Canada and payable elsewhere: Principal, $223,623.30; interest, $82,004.17		305,627 47	
			3,224,291 83
D.—Management Expenses (other than foregoing).			
25. (a) Salaries, wages and fees ....$		29,639 17	
26. (b) Commission or brokerage ....·.................		26,928 19	
28. (d) Stationery, postage, printing, advertising, etc......		4,256 82	
30. (f) Taxes (other than in 7 and 32) and rates		5,084 28	
31. (g) Travelling expenses		1,445 20	
32. (h) Registration fee ·.................................		250 00	
			67,603 66
F.—Balance.			
37. (b) Cash in banks			287,665 91
Total			$4,668,950 98

MISCELLANEOUS STATEMENT FOR THE YEAR ENDING 31ST DECEMBER, 1913.

---

1. Amount of debentures maturing in 1914: Issued and payable in Canada, $315,143.72; issued in Canada but payable elsewhere, $312,702.80.
2. Amount of other existing obligations which will mature in 1914: None.
3. Amount of securities held by the Corporation which will mature and become payable to the Corporation in 1914: $1,227,464.00.
4. Average rate of interest per annum paid by the Corporation during 1913: On deposits, 3.3678%; on debentures, 4.2328%; on debentures stock, none.
5. Average rate of interest per annum received by the Corporation during 1913:
   (a) On mortgages of realty; (b) on other securities.
   (i) Owned beneficially by the Corporation: (a) 6.5973%; (b) 4.9431%.
   (ii) Not owned beneficially: (a) None; (b) none.
6. Of the mortgages owned beneficially by the Corporation, $4,546,956.79 is on realty situate in Ontario, and $2,706,793.83 is on realty situate elsewhere.
7. Of the mortgages not owned beneficially by the Corporation, none is on realty situate in Ontario, and none is on realty situate elsewhere.
8. Loans written off or transferred to real estate account during 1913, viz.:
   (i) Funds or securities owned beneficially, $5,147.97.
   (ii) Not so owned, none.
9. Number and aggregate amount of mortgages upon which compulsory proceedings have been taken by the Corporation in 1913, viz.:
   (i) Owned beneficially, No. 3; amount, $3,176.36.
   (ii) Not so owned, No., none; amount, none.

10. Aggregate market value of land mortgaged to the Corporation:
    (i) Mortgages owned beneficially, $17,062,234.
    (ii) Not so owned, none.

11. How often are the securities held by the Corporation valued? Annually.

12. (a) Specify the officers of the Corporation who are under bond and for what sum respectively: Manager, $5,000; Accountant, $5,000; Teller, $5,000; Inspector, $6,000; other office clerks; $20,000; total, $41,000.
    (b) Are the said bonds executed by private sureties or by Guarantee Companies? Guarantee Company.

13. Date when the accounts of the Corporation were last audited: 26th January, 1914.

14. Names and addresses of the auditors respectively for 1913 and for 1914 (if appointed):
    For 1913: F. C. Jewell, C.A., J. F. Kern, both of London.
    For 1914: F. C. Jewell, C.A., J. F. Kern, both of London.

15. What were the dividend days of the Corporation in 1913 and what rate or rates of dividend were paid on those days respectively? 2nd January, 1st April, 2nd July, and 1st October. 2% each time.

16. What is the date appointed for the Annual Meeting? Second Wednesday in each February. Date of last Annual Meeting? 12th February, 1913.

17. Special General Meetings held in 1913: Dates, none.

THE VICTORIA LOAN AND SAVINGS COMPANY.

Head Office, Lindsay, Ontario.

———

Incorporated under the Building Societies Act, 1887, c. 169, as amended by 56 V. c. 31 (O.), by declaration filed with the Clerk of the Peace for the County of Victoria, on the 4th September, 1897.

The operations of the Company were for a time by law restricted to the County of Victoria (56 V. c. 31), continued by R.S.O. 1897, c. 205, s. 8 (4) ; but the Company having fulfilled the statutory requirements, was by Letters Patent of Ontario, bearing date 11th November, 1898, relieved from the above restriction of its operations.

The lending and borrowing powers are governed by the Loan and Trust Corporations Act, R.S.O. 1914, chap. 184.

———

ANNUAL STATEMENT

Of the conditions and affairs of the Victoria Loan and Savings Company, of Lindsay, Ontario, at the 31st December, 1913, and for the year ending on that day, made to the Registrar of Loan Corporations for the Province of Ontario, pursuant to the laws of the said Province.

The head office of the Corporation is at No. 71 Kent Street, in the Town of Lindsay, in the Province of Ontario.

The Board is constituted of seven directors, holding office for one year.

The directors and chief executive officers of the Corporation at the 31st December, 1913, were as follows, together with their respective terms of office:

W. Flavelle, President, Lindsay: February 3rd, 1913.   February 2nd, 1914.
R. J. McLaughlin, K.C., Vice-President, Toronto: "   "
W. H. Clarke, M.D., Vice-President, Lindsay: "   "
W. H. Stevens, B.A., Director, Lindsay:
C. Chittick, Director, Lindsay:
H. J. Lytle, Director, Lindsay:
F. C. Taylor, Director, Lindsay:
C. E. Weeks, Manager, Lindsay, Ont.

A permanent capital stock; total amount authorized, $500,000; total amount subscribed, $400,000, as more particularly set out in Schedule A hereto.

Amount paid in, $396,953.92.

SCHEDULE A.

Class I.—Fixed and permanent capital stock created by virtue of Building Society Acts.

Description.	Total amount issued and subsisting 31st December, 1913			Total amount of actual payments thereon.	Total amount unpaid and constituting an asset of the Corporation.
	No. of shares.	Par value.	—		
		$	$	$	$
1. Fully called stock	3,969	100	396,900	396,900 00	....
2. Partly called stock ...	31	100	3,100	53 92	3,046 08
Total..............	4,000	....	400,000	396,953 92	3,046 08

LIST OF SHAREHOLDERS AS AT 31st DECEMBER, 1913.

(Not printed.)

BALANCE SHEET AS AT 31st DECEMBER, 1913.

Dr. Capital and Liabilities.

Capital (Liabilities to Stockholders or Shareholders).

A.—Permanent Capital Stock or Shares.

1.	(a) Ordinary joint stock capital fully called; total called, ———; total paid thereon	$396,953 92	
4.	(d) Dividends declared in respect of (1) but not yet paid	6,445 00	
5.	(e) Unappropriated profits in respect of (1)	2,753 51	
6.	(f) Reserve fund in respect of (1)	125,000 00	
			$531,152 43

Liabilities to the Public.

27.	Deposits (including accrued interest), right reserved to require 30 days' notice on any withdrawal	$243,633 49	
29.	Debentures issued in Canada	280,174 81	
30.	Interest due and accrued on (29)	7,182 85	
31.	Debentures issued elsewhere than in Canada	11,679 99	
32.	Interest due and accrued on (31)	71 20	
38.	Due on bills payable other than (37) including interest due or accrued	27,000 00	
39.	Due on loans in process of completion or to pay assumed mortgages	12,241 21	
40.	Unclaimed dividends	28 00	
41.	Other liabilities to public, viz.:		
42.	(a) Owing to agents	147 96	
			582,109 51

Total liabilities $1,113,261 94

Cr. Assets.

I.—Assets of which the Corporation is the Beneficial Owner.

A.—Immovable Property Owned Beneficially by Corporation.

1.	(a) Office premises situate as follows:		
3.	(ii) At Lindsay, held in leasehold		$2,618 48

B.—Debts secured by Mortgages of Land.

9.	Debts (other than item 10) secured by mortgages of land	$894,608 76	
11.	(c) Interest due or accrued on item (9) and not included therein	45,389 52	
			939,998 28

C.—Debts not above enumerated for which the Corporation holds securities as follows:

14.	(b) Debts secured by Municipal bonds or debentures	$32,965 73	
15.	(c) Debts secured by Public School debentures	23,608 16	
16.	(d) Debts secured by Loan Corporation debentures	3,750 00	
21.	(i) Debts secured only by terminating stock or shares of the Corporation	25,774 20	
22.	(j) Debts secured by mortgage bonds	31,192 72	
26.	(n) Interest due and accrued on items 14 to 22, and not included therein	2,697 95	
			119,988 76

BALANCE SHEET.—Continued.

E.—Cash.

31. (a) On hand	$13,576 82	
32. (b) In bank	27,917 10	
		$41,493 92

F.—Assets not hereinbefore mentioned.

38. (b) Bank stock and accrued interest 9,162 50

Total assets $1,113,261 94

CASH ACCOUNT.

Receipts for the year ending 31st December, 1913.

I.—Received by the Corporation for its Own Use.

A.—Balance from 31st December, 1912.

(Col. 1.)   (Col. 2.)   (Total Col. 4.)

(a) Cash (not already shown under (1) :
2.   (i) On hand $5,869 04

B.—Sums received wholly or partly on Capital
            Stock.

4. (a) Calls on joint stock permanent capital.. $71,480 59
5. (b) Premiums on (4) 17,870 15
                                                               89,350 74

C.—Receipts on account of Investments, Loans
            or Debts.

(a) On mortgages of realty:
10.   (i) Principal $133,072 72
11.   (ii) Interest 60,278 17
    (b) On other securities:
12.   (i) Principal 25,184 36
13.   (ii) Interest or dividends 4,977 92
                                                               223,513 17

E.—Miscellaneous.

18. (a) Commission, brokerage $551 29
19. (b) Premiums or bonuses on loans 7,114 75
                                                               7,666 04

F.—Borrowed Money.

25. (a) Bank or other advances, discounts or
            overdrafts $27,000 00
26. (b) Borrowed by taking deposits 497,609 95
27. (c) Borrowed on debentures 197,012 90
                                                               721,622 85

G.—Receipts from other sources.

30. (a) Sundry accounts $1,146 84
    (c) 20% refund on Double Liability On-
            tario Bank stock 960 00
                                                               2,106 84

Totals $1,050,128 68

CASH ACCOUNT.

Expenditure for the year ending 31st December, 1913

I.—Expended on Corporation Account.

A.—Sums Loaned or Invested on Capital Account.

1. (a) Loaned on mortgages of realty	$237,705 61	
(b) Loaned or invested in other securities:		
2. (1) Bonds, etc.	92,144 73	
		$329,850 34

B.—Expended on Stock Account.

3. Dividends paid on permanent stock	23,476 60

C.—Borrowed Money (other than foregoing) or interest thereon paid, viz.:

18. (a) Bank account (principal and interest) overdraft December 31st, 1912	$6,744 84	
19. (b) Deposits: Principal, $505,674.10; and interest, $9,321.53	514,995 63	
20. (c) Debentures issued in Canada: Principal, $109,623.00; interest, $10,124.20	119,747 20	
		641,487 67

D.—Management Expenses (other than foregoing).

25. (a) Salaries, wages and fees	$8,741 35	
26. (b) Commission or brokerage	1,878 97	
28. (d) Stationery, postage, printing and advertising	897 32	
30. (f) Fuel, rent, taxes (other than in 7 and 32) and rates	476 18	
31. (g) Travelling expenses	344 60	
33. (i) Other management expenditure	230 10	
		12,568 52

E.—Other Expenditure.

34. (a) Sundry accounts	$1,161 15	
36. (c) Office furniture	118 48	
		1,279 63

F.—Balance.

37. (b) Cash on hand and in banks	41,465 92
Totals	$1,050,128 68

MISCELLANEOUS STATEMENT FOR THE YEAR ENDING 31ST DECEMBER, 1913.

1. Amount of debentures maturing in 1914: Issued in Canada, $36,861.27. Issued elsewhere, none.
2. Amount of other existing obligations which will mature in 1914, none.
3. Amount of securities held by the Corporation which will mature and become payable to the Corporation in 1914, $168,190.00.
4. Average rate of interest per annum paid by the Corporation during 1913: On deposits, 3.54 per cent.; on debentures, 4.72 per cent.; on debenture stock, none.

5. Average rate of interest per annum received by the Corporation during 1913: (a) On mortgages of realty; (b) On other securities.
    (i) Owned beneficially by the Corporation: (a) 7.33 per cent; (b) 6.51 per cent.
    (ii) Not owned beneficially: (a) None; (b) none.
6. Of the mortgages owned beneficially by the Corporation, $339,678.00 is on realty situate in Ontario, and $554,930.76 is on realty situate elsewhere.
7. Of the mortgages not owned beneficially by the Corporation, none is on realty situate in Ontario, and none is on realty situate elsewhere.
8. Loans written off or transferred to real estate account during 1913, viz.:
    (i) Funds or securities owned beneficially, none.
    (ii) Not so owned, none.
9. Number and aggregate amount of mortgages upon which compulsory proceedings have been taken by the Corporation in 1913, viz.:
    (i) Owned beneficially, none.
    (ii) Not so owned, none.
10. Aggregate market value of land mortgaged to the Corporation:
    (i) Mortgages owned beneficially, $2,762,754.15.
    (ii) Not so owned, none.
11. How often are the securities held by the Corporation valued? When placed, renewed, or when mortgage gets in arrears.
12. (a) Specify the officers of the Corporation who are under bond and for what sum respectively. Manager, $5,000; assistant, $5,000; accountant, $4,000; teller, $4,000.
    (b) Are the said bonds executed by private sureties or by Guarantee Companies? Guarantee Company.
13. Date when the accounts of the Corporation were last audited. January, 1914.
14. Names and addresses of the auditors respectively for 1913 and for 1914 (if appointed):
    For 1913: R. Williamson, C.A., G. A. Peters, Toronto.
    For 1914: R. Williamson, C.A., G. A. Peters, Toronto.
15. What were the dividend-days of the Corporation in 1913, and what rate or rates of dividend were paid on those days respectively? January 2nd, 1913; April 1st, 1913; July 1st, 1913, and October 1st, 1913; rate, seven per cent.
16. What is the date appointed for the Annual Meeting? First Monday in February. Date of last Annual Meeting? February 2nd, 1914.
17. Special General Meetings held in 1913: None.

THE TORONTO MORTGAGE COMPANY.

Head Office, Toronto Street, Toronto.

———

This Company was, under the provisions of the Loan Corporations Act, formed by the amalgamation of the Building and Loan Association with the Union Loan and Savings Company.

The agreement for the amalgamation of these Companies under the new Corporate name of The Toronto Mortgage Company was executed by both Companies on the 27th September, 1899; was ratified by the shareholders of the respective Companies on the 15th November, 1899, and was assented to by the Lieutenant-Governor of the Province of Ontario by Order-in-Council dated 15th December, 1909.

———

ANNUAL STATEMENT

Of the condition and affairs of The Toronto Mortgage Company, of Toronto, at the 31st December, 1913, and for the year ending on that day, made to the Registrar of Loan Corporations for the Province of Ontario, pursuant to the laws of the said Province.

The head office of the Corporation is at No. 13 Toronto Street, in the City of Toronto, in the Province of Ontario.

The Board is constituted of seven directors, holding office for one year.

The directors and chief executive officers of the Corporation at 31st December, 1913, were as follows, together with their respective terms of office:

Hon. Sir Wm. Mortimer Clark, Pres.,   Feb. 12th, 1913; Feb. 11th, 1914.
Wellington Francis, K.C., Vice-Pres., Toronto;   "   "   "
Casimir S. Gzowski, Director, Toronto;   "   "
Thomas Gilmour, Director, Toronto;
Herbert Langlois, Director, Toronto;
Geo. Martin Rae, Director, Toronto;
Henry B. Yates, M.D., Director, Montreal;
Walter Gillespie, Managing-Secretary, Toronto.

A. Permanent capital stock: Total amount authorized, $1,445,860; total amount subscribed, $724,550, as more particularly set out in Schedule A hereto.

SCHEDULE A.

Class I.—Fixed and permanent capital stock created by virtue of Building Society Acts.

Description.	Total amount issued and subsisting at 31st December, 1913.			Total amount of actual payments thereon.	Total amount unpaid and constituting an asset of the Corporation.
	No. of shares.	Par value of shares.	——		
1. Fully called stock	14,491	$ 50	$ 724,550	$ 724,550	$ ....

LIST OF SHAREHOLDERS AS AT 31st DECEMBER, 1913.

(Not printed.)

BALANCE SHEET AS AT 31st DECEMBER, 1913.

Dr.   Capital and Liabilities.

Capital (Liabilities to Stockholders or Shareholders).

A.—Permanent Capital Stock or Shares.

1. (a) Ordinary joint stock capital fully called; total called, $724,550.00; total paid thereon	$724,550 00	
4. (d) Dividends declared in respect of (1), but not yet paid	14,491 00	
5. (e) Unappropriated profits in respect of (1)	38 25	
6. (f) Reserve fund in respect of (1)	465,000 00	
7. (g) Contingent fund in respect of (1)	25,287 75	
		$1,229,367 00

Liabilities to the Public.

27. Deposits (including unclaimed deposits), right reserved to require 30 days' notice of any withdrawal..	$147,405 70	
29. Debentures issued in Canada	333,228 33	
30. Interest due and accrued on (29)	5,426 91	
31. Debentures issued elsewhere than in Canada	1,537,946 35	
32. Interest due and accrued on (31)	10,723 28	
		2,034,730 57
Total liabilities		$3,264,097 57

Cr.   Assets.

I.—Assets of which the Corporation is the Beneficial Owner.

A.—Immovable Property Owned Beneficially by the Corporation.

1. (a) Office premises situate as follows:	
2. (1) At 13 and 15 Toronto Street, Toronto, held in freehold..	$ 45,000 00

B.—Debts secured by Mortgages of Land.

9. (a) Debts (other than item 10) secured by mortgages of land	2,625,481 94
12. (d) Of the debts mentioned in item 9, the sum of $5,000.00 is due by directors or officers of the Corporation.	

C.—Debts, not above enumerated, for which the Corporation holds Securities as follows:

22. (j) Call loans on bank stocks	171,672 23

E.—Cash.

31. (a) On hand	$ 554 63	
32. (b) In banks in Canada	53,529 56	
In banks in England	2,056 69	
		56,140 88

F.—Assets not hereinbefore mentioned.

37. (a) Bonds and stocks owned by the Company	365,802 52
Total assets	$3,264,097 57

CASH ACCOUNT.

Receipts for the year ending 31st December, 1913.

I.—Received by the Corporation for Its Own Use.

A.—Balance from 31st December, 1912.

Cash (not already shown under (1)):

		(Col. 4.) Total.
2.	(i) On hand	$ 893 26
3.	(ii) In banks	59,621 36

C.—Receipts on account of Investments, Loans or Debts.

	(a) On mortgages of realty:	
10.	(i) Principal	316,906 06
11.	(ii) Interest	158,941 68
	(b) On other securities:	
12.	(i) Principal	135,079 60
13.	(ii) Interest or dividends	31,562 10

D.—Receipts from Real Estate Owned Beneficially by Corporation.

17. (b) Rent, net, from Company's office building	3,949 36

F.—Borrowed Money.

26. (b) Borrowed by taking deposits	163,472 55
27. (c) Borrowed on debentures	440,180 99
Totals	$1,310,606 96

CASH ACCOUNT.

Expenditure for the year ending 31st December, 1913.

I.—Expended on Corporation Account.

1. (a) Loaned on mortgages of realty	$ 357,112 73
	(b) Loaned on other securities:	
2.	(i) Call loans on bank stocks	167,483 15

B.—Expended on Stock Account.

8. Dividends paid on permanent stock	56,152 63

C.—Borrowed Money (other than foregoing) or interest thereon paid, viz.:

19. (b) Deposits (including interest)	176,408 64
20. (c) Debentures issued in Canada: Principal, $134,550.00; interest, $13,303.25	147,853 25
21. (d) Debentures issued elsewhere: Principal, $223,598.98; interest, $61,482.73	285,081 71

D.—Management Expenses (other than foregoing).

25. (a) Salaries, wages and fees	18,712 35
26. (b) Commission or brokerage	5,227 32
28. (d) Stationery, postage, printing and advertising	1,169 56
30. (f) Fuel, rent, taxes (other than in 7 and 32), and rates	1,975 69
32. (h) Registration fees	200 00

9 L.C.

CASH ACCOUNT.—Continued.

Expenditure for the year ending 31st December, 1913.

E.—Other Expenditure, viz.:

(Col. 4.) Total.
34. (a) Municipal and School debentures purchased .... $ 37,089 05

F.—Balance.

37. (a) Cash on hand and in various banks 56,140 88

Total $1,310,606 96

MISCELLANEOUS STATEMENT FOR THE YEAR ENDING 31ST DECEMBER, 1913.

1. Amount of debentures maturing in 1914: Issued in Canada, $37,575. Issued else-
   where, $322,806.
2. Amount of other existing obligations which will mature in 1914 exclusive of deposits, none.
3. Amount of securities held by the Corporation which will mature and become payable to the Corporation in 1914, $667,276.
4. Average rate of interest per annum paid by the Corporation during 1913: On deposits, 3.455 per cent.; on debentures, 4.198 per cent.; on debenture stock,
   nil.
5. Average rate of interest per annum received by the Corporation during 1913:
   (a) On mortgages of realty; (b) on other securities:
   (i) Owned beneficially by the Corporation: (a) 5.95 per cent; (b) nil.
   (ii) Not owned beneficially: (a) Nil; (b) nil.
6. Of the mortgages owned beneficially by the Corporation, $2,625,481.94 is on realty
   situate in Ontario, and nil is on realty situate elsewhere.
7. Of the mortgages not owned beneficially by the Corporation, nil is on realty situate
   in Ontario, and nil is on realty situate elsewhere.
8. Loans written off or transferred to real estate account during 1913, viz.:
   (i) Funds or securities owned beneficially, $2,000.
   (ii) Not so owned, nil.
9. Number and aggregate amount of mortgages upon which compulsory proceedings
   have been taken by the Corporation in 1913, viz.:
   (i) Owned beneficially, No. 1; amount, $2,050.00.
   (ii) Not so owned, nil; amount, nil.
10. Aggregate market value of land mortgaged to the Corporation:
    (i) Mortgages owned beneficially, $6,100,000..
    (ii) Not so owned, nil.
11. How often are the securities held by the Corporation valued? Mortgages yearly;
    property as occasion requires.
12. (a) Specify the officers of the Corporation who are under bond and for what sum
    respectively: All in sums of $1,000 to $5,000.
    (b) Are the said bonds executed by private sureties or by Guarantee Companies?
    Guarantee Company.
13. Date when the accounts of the Corporation were last audited. December 31st, 1913.
14. Names and addresses of the auditors respectively for 1913 and for 1914 (if
    appointed):
    For 1913: E. R. C. Clarkson, F.C.A., and Jas. Hardy, F.C.A.
    For 1914: E. R. C. Clarkson, F.C.A., and Jas. Hardy, F.C.A.
15. What were the dividend-days of the Corporation in 1913, and what rate or rates
    of dividend were paid on those days respectively? 8 per cent. per annum,
    January 2nd, April 1st, July 2nd and October 1st.
16. What is the date appointed for the Annual Meeting? 11th February, 1914. Date of
    last Annual Meeting? 12th February, 1913.
17. Special General Meetings held in 1913: Dates, nil.

THE ONTARIO LOAN AND SAVINGS COMPANY.

Head Office, Oshawa.

CONSTATING INSTRUMENTS.

Incorporated under the Building Societies-Acts, Consol. Stat. U. C., chap. 53, by declaration filed with the Clerk of the Peace for the County of Ontario on 12th February, 1873.

The lending and the borrowing powers are governed by the Loan and Trust Corporations Act, R.S.O. 1914, chap. 184.

ANNUAL STATEMENT

Of the condition and affairs of the Ontario Loan and Savings Company, of Oshawa, Ontario, at the 31st December, 1913, and for the year ending on that day, made to the Registrar of Loan Corporations for the Province of Ontario, pursuant to the laws of the said Province.

The head office of the Corporation is in the Town of Oshawa, in the Province of Ontario.

The Board is constituted of seven directors holding office for one year:

The directors and chief executive officers of the Corporation at the 31st December, 1913, were as follows, together with their respective terms of office:

W. F. Cowan, President, Oshawa: February 20th, 1913; February 19th, 1914
W. F. Allen, Vice-President, Bowmanville;   "   "
John Cowan, Director, Oshawa;   "   "
F. W. Cowan, Director, Oshawa;
T. H. McMillan, Director, Oshawa;
Charles Larke, Director, Colborne;
Wm. Brien, Director, Trillick, Ireland;
T. H. McMillan, Manager-Secretary, Oshawa.

A.—Permanent capital stock: Total amount authorized, $300,000; total amount subscribed, $300,000, as more particularly set out in Schedule A hereto.

SCHEDULE A.

Class I.—Fixed and permanent capital stock created by virtue of Building Societies Act.

Description.	Total amount issued and subsisting at 31st December, 1913.			Total amount of actual payments thereon.	Total amount unpaid and constituting an asset of the Corporation.
	No. of shares.	Par value.	—		
Fully called	6,000	$ 50	$ 300,000	$ 300,000	$ ....

LIST OF SHAREHOLDERS AS AT 31st DECEMBER, 1913.

(Not printed.)

BALANCE SHEET AS AT 31st DECEMBER, 1913.

Dr.   Capital and Liabilities.

Capital (Liabilities to Stockholders or Shareholders).

A.—Permanent Capital Stock or Shares.

1. (a) Ordinary capital stock, fully called; total called,
       $300,000.00; total paid thereon ....$ 300,000 00.
6. (f) Reserve fund in respect of (1) 72,304 48
7. (g) Contingent fund in respect of (1)..................   384 15   .

Liabilities to the Public.

27. Deposits, right reserved to require 30 days' notice of any
       withdrawal 240,333 36
29. Debentures issued in Canada 53,000 00

            Total liabilities ....$ 666,021 99

Cr.   Assets.

I.—Assets of which the Corporation is the Beneficial Owner.

    B.—Debts secured by Mortgages of Land.
9. (a) Debts (other than item 10) secured by mortgages of
       land . . . .$ 533,474 27
10. (b) Debts secured by mortgaged land held for sale, about   15,000 00
    (bb) Debts secured by land held by the Company as mort-
        gagee in possession or secured by land for the
        rents and profits, of which the Company is
        accountable, about 20,000 00
                                                          ————————— $ 568,474 27
C.—Debts not above enumerated for which the Corporation
            holds securities as follows:
20. (h) Debts secured only by permanent stock of shares of
       Corporation 24,190 00

            E.—Cash.
31. (a) On hand ....$ 1,057 79
32. (b) In banks 71,899 93
                                                          —————————
    F.—Assets not hereinbefore mentioned.   72,957 72
39. (c) Office furniture 400 00

            Total assets . . . . $ 666,021 99

CASH ACCOUNT.

Receipts for the year ending 31st December, 1913.

I.—Received by the Corporation for its Own Use.

      A.—Balances from 31st December, 1912.   (Col. 1.)   Total (Col. 4.)
    (b) Cash (not already shown under (1)):—
2.   (i) On hand . . . .$ 791 33
3.   (ii) In bank 192,185 54
                                                                    $ 192,976 87

CASH ACCOUNT.—Continued.

Receipts for the year ending 31st December, 1913.

C.—Receipts on account of Investments, Loans or Debts.

(a) On mortgages of realty:—

10.	(i) Principal	$129,173 51	
11.	(ii) Interest	34,238 78	
	(b) On other securities:—		
13.	(ii) Interest	1,451 40	
	Bank interest	2,633 24	
			167,496 93

F.—Borrowed Money.

26.	(b) Borrowed by taking deposits	$ 134,204 19	
27.	(c) Borrowed on debentures	2,000 00	
			136,204 19

Total .... $ 496,677 99

CASH ACCOUNT.

Expenditure for the year ending 31st December, 1913.

I.—Expended on Corporation Account.

A.—Sums Loaned or Invested on Capital Account.

	Col. 1.	Total Col. 4.
1. (a) Loaned on mortgages of realty		$ 15,355 44

B.—Expended on Stock Account.

8. Dividends paid on permanent stock		18,000 00

C.—Borrowed money (other than foregoing) or interest thereon paid, viz.:

19. (b) Deposits: Principal, $180,946.94; interest, $10,767.97.	$ 191,714 91	
20. (c) Debentures issued in Canada: Principal, $192,100.00; interest, $2,990.55	195,090 55	
		386,805 46

D.—Management Expenses (other than foregoing).

25. (a) Salaries, wages and fees	$2,500 00	
28. (d) Stationery, postage, printing and advertising	271 00	
29. (e) Law costs	20 00	
30 (f) Fuel, rent, taxes (other than in 7 and 32) and rates, including Government taxes	550 60	
31. (g) Travelling expenses	25 00	
32. (h) Registration fees, etc.	80 00	
33. (i) Other management expenditure	112 77	
		$ 3,559 37

F.—Balance.

37. (a) Cash on hand and in banks		72,957 72

Total .... $ 496,677 99

1. Amount of debentures maturing in 1914: Issued in Canada, $2,000. Issued elsewhere, nil.
2. Amount of other existing obligations which will mature in 1914: Cannot say when depositors will call for money.
3. Amount of securities held by the Corporation which will mature and become payable to the Corporation in 1914, about $100,000.
4. Average rate of interest per annum paid by the Corporation during 1913: On deposits, about 3¾ per cent; on debentures, 4¼ per cent; on debenture stock, nil.
5. Average rate of interest per annum received by the Corporation during 1913:
   (a) On mortgages of realty; (b) on other securities.
   (i) Owned beneficially by the Corporation: (a) About 5¾ per cent.; (b) about 5 per cent.
   (ii) Not owned beneficially: (a) None; (b) None.
6. Of the mortgages owned beneficially by the Corporation, $568,474.27 is on realty situate in Ontario, and nil is on realty situate elsewhere.
7. Of the mortgages not owned beneficially by the Corporation, ———— is on realty situate in Ontario, and ———— is on realty situate elsewhere.
8. Loans written off or transferred to real estate account during 1913, viz.:
   (i) Funds or securities owned beneficially, $12,208.00.
   (ii) Not so owned ————.
9. Number and aggregate amount of mortgages upon which compulsory proceedings have been taken by the Corporation in 1913, viz.:
   (i) Owned beneficially, No. four; amount, $13,300.00.
   (ii) Not so owned, nil; amount, nil.
10. Aggregate market value of land mortgaged to the Corporation:
    (i) Mortgages owned beneficially, say one million.
    (ii) Not so owned, nil.
11. How often are the securities held by the Corporation valued? Once a year.
12. (a) Specify the officers of the Corporation who are under bond and for what sum respectively: Teller and Accountant, $2,500 each.
    (b) Are the said bonds executed by private sureties or by Guarantee Companies? Guarantee Companies.
13. Date when the accounts of the Corporation were last audited. Up to December 31st, 1913 (inclusive).
14. Names and addresses of the auditors respectively for 1913 and for 1914 (if appointed):
    For 1913: C. W. Owens and W. B. Puckett, both of Oshawa.
    For 1914: Same appointed for 1914.
15. What were the dividend-days of the Corporation in 1913, and what rate or rates of dividend were paid on those days respectively? January 2nd and July 2nd, at 6 per cent. per annum.
16. What is the date appointed for the Annual Meeting? Third Thursday in February. Date of last Annual Meeting? February 20th, 1913.
17. Special General Meetings held in 1913: Dates, none.

DYMENT SECURITIES LOAN AND SAVINGS COMPANY.

Head Office, Barrie, Ontario.

———

CONSTATING INSTRUMENTS.

Incorporated on 15th May, 1902, by Special Act of the Dominion of Canada, 2 Edward VII., c. 60.

———

ANNUAL STATEMENT

Of the condition and affairs of the Dyment Securities Loan and Savings Company, Barrie, Ont., at 31st December, 1913, and for the year ending on that day, made to the Registrar of Loan Corporations for the Province of Ontario, pursuant to the laws of the said Province.

The head office of the Corporation is at No. 93 Dunlop Street, in the Town of Barrie, in the Province of Ontario.

The Board is constituted of five directors holding office for the term of one year.

The directors and chief executive officers of the Corporation at 31st December, 1913, were as follows, together with their respective term of office:

A. E. Dyment, President, Toronto, Ont.;   February 11th, 1913.   February 9th, 1914.
Thos. W. Baker, Vice-President, London;   "   "
A. E. H. Creswicke, Director, Barrie;   "   "
W. E. Wismer, Director, London;
S. Dyment, Director, Barrie;
S. Dyment, Manager-Secretary, Barrie;

A.—Permanent capital stock; total amount authorized, $2,000,000; total amount subscribed, $652,200, as more particularly set out in Schedule A hereto.

SCHEDULE A.

Class 2—Fixed and Permanent Capital Stock created by virtue of Private Act.

Description.	No of shares.	Par value of shares.	Total amount held.	Total amount paid thereon.	Total remaining uncalled.
		$	$	$	
1. Fully called	6,522	100	652,200	652,200	....

LIST OF SHAREHOLDERS AS AT 31st DECEMBER, 1913.

(Not printed.)

BALANCE SHEET AS AT 31st DECEMBER, 1913.

Dr.   Capital and Liabilities.

Capital (Liabilities to Stockholders or Shareholders).

A.—Permanent Capital Stock or Shares.

1. Ordinary joint stock capital fully called; total called, $652,200; total paid thereon	$652,200 00
4. (d) Dividend declared in respect of (1), not yet paid	16,305 00
5. (e) Unappropriated profits in respect of (1)	74,205 55

Liabilities to the Public.

27. Deposits (right reserved to require 30 days' notice of any withdrawal)	87,069 88
41. Other liabilities to the public:	
42. (a) Solicitors	34 40
Total liabilities	$829,814 83

Cr.   Assets.

I.—Assets of which the Corporation is the Beneficial Owner.

B.—Debts secured by Mortgages of Land.

(Col. 4.)

9. (a) Debts (other than item 10) secured by mortgages of land	$395,863 94	
C.—Debts not above enumerated for which the Corporation holds securities as follows:		
23. (j) Debts secured by stocks and bonds	426,057 43	

E.—Cash.

31. (a) On hand and in bank	7,893 46	
Total assets		$829,814 83

CASH ACCOUNT.

Receipts for the year ending 31st December, 1913.

I.—Received by the Corporation for its Own Use.

A.—Balance from 31st December, 1912.

2.	(i) On hand	$2,073 02
	(ii) In bank	1,330 38

C.—Receipts on account of Investments, Loans or Debts.

	(a) On mortgages of realty:	
10.	(i) Principal	
11.	(ii) Interest	54,461 39
	(b) On other securities:	9,706 01
12.	(i) Principal	
13.	(ii) Interest	43,749 82
		22,088 72

CASH ACCOUNT.—Continued.

Receipts for the year ending 31st December, 1913.

F.—Borrowed Money.

26. (b) Borrowed by taking deposits 57,506 45

G.—Receipts from other sources.

30. (a) Solicitor's fees 6 00

Totals $190,923 79

CASH ACCOUNT.

Expenditure for the year ending 31st December, 1913.

I.—Expended on Corporation Account.

A.—Sums Loaned or Invested on Capital Account.

1. (a) Loaned on mortgages of realty $46,067 27
   (b) Loaned or invested in other securities 53,677 04

B.—Expended on Stock Account.

8. Dividends paid on permanent stock 32,610 00

C.—Borrowed Money (other than foregoing) or interest thereon paid, viz.:

19. (b) Deposits: Principal, $48,571.32; interest, $69.56 .... 48,640 88

D.—Management Expenses (other than foregoing).

25. (a) Salaries, wages and fees 1,274 00
28. (d) Stationery, postage, printing and advertising 7 59
30. (f) Fuel, rent and taxes (other than in 7 and 32) and rates 245 10
32. (h) Registration fees 504 45

E.—Other Expenditure.

35. (b) Solicitors' fees 4 00

F.—Balance.

37. (a) Cash on hand and in bank 7,893 46

Totals $190,923 79

MISCELLANEOUS STATEMENT FOR THE YEAR ENDING 31ST DECEMBER, 1913.

1. Amount of debentures maturing in 1914: Issued in Canada, none.
2. Amount of other existing obligations which will mature in 1914: None.
3. Amount of securities held by the Corporation which will mature and become payable in 1914: None.
4. Average rate of interest per annum paid by the Corporation during 1913: On deposits, 4%; on debentures, none; on debenture stock, none.

5. Average rate of interest per annum received by the Corporation during 1913: (a) On mortgages of realty; (b) on other securities.
   (i) Owned beneficially by the Corporation: (a) None; (b) none.
   (ii) Not owned beneficially: (a) All securities owned beneficially by Corporation.
6. Of the mortgages owned beneficially by the Corporation, $395,863.94 is on realty situate in Ontario, and none is on realty situate elsewhere.
7. Of the mortgages not owned beneficially by the Corporation, none is on realty situate in Ontario, and none is on realty situate elsewhere.
8. Loans written off or transferred to real estate account during 1913, viz.:
   (i) Funds or securities owned beneficially, none.
   (ii) Not so owned, none.
9. Number and aggregate amount of mortgages upon which compulsory proceedings have been taken by the Corporation in 1913, viz.:
   (i) Owned beneficially, No., amount, none.
   (ii) Not so owned, No., amount, none.
10. Aggregate market value of land mortgaged to the Corporation:
    (i) Mortgages owned beneficially, none.
    (ii) Not so owned, none.
11. How often are the securities held by the Corporation valued? No stated period.
12. (a) Specify the officers of the Corporation who are under bond and for what sum respectively. Manager, $5,000.
    (b) Are the said bonds executed by private sureties or by Guarantee Companies? Private.
13. Date when the accounts of the Corporation were last audited. February 8th, 1913.
14. Names and addresses of the auditors respectively for 1913 and for 1914 (if appointed):
    For 1913: Wm. R. King and John B. Barr.
    For 1914: Wm. R. King and John B. Barr.
15. What were the dividend days of the Corporation in 1913 and what rate or rates of dividend were paid on those days respectively? January 2nd and July 2nd. 5% per annum.
16. What is the date appointed for the Annual Meeting? February 9th, 1914. Date of last Annual Meeting? February 10th, 1913.
17. Special General Meetings held in 1913. Dates: None.

THE STANDARD RELIANCE MORTGAGE CORPORATION.

Head Office, Toronto, Ontario.

CONSTATING INSTRUMENTS.

Incorporated under the Building Societies Act (Consol. Stat. U. C., chap. 53), by declaration filed with the Clerk of the Peace for the County of Wellington, on 14th February, 1873 (Decl. Book II., 133). The original corporate name was " The Orangeville Building and Loan Association." which name was by Order-in-Council of Ontario, dated 19th May, 1898, changed to The Standard Loan Company. By the same Order-in-Council the head office was changed from Orangeville to Toronto.

By Order-in-Council, dated 21st April, 1913, The Standard Loan Company was amalgamated with The Reliance Loan and Savings Company of Ontario, and by the same Order-in-Council, the name was changed to The Standard Reliance Mortgage Corporation.

The lending and the borrowing powers are governed by the Loan and Trust Corporations Act, R.S.O. 1914, chap. 184.

ANNUAL STATEMENT

Of the conditions of affairs of the Standard Reliance Mortgage Corporation at 31st December, 1913, and for the year ending on that day, made to the Registrar of Loan Corporations for the Province of Ontario, pursuant to the laws of the said Province.

The head office of the Corporation is at No. 84 King Street East, in the City of Toronto.

The Board is constituted of sixteen directors, holding office for one year.

The directors and chief executive officers of the Corporation at the 31st December, 1913, were as follows, together with their respective terms of office:

Nathan H. Stevens, President, Chatham, Ont.:   May 9th, 1913. March 2nd, 1914.
Wilfrid S. Dinnick, Vice-President, Toronto, Ont.:   "   "
Hugh S. Brennen, Vice-President, Hamilton, Ont.:   "   "
John Firstbrook, Vice-President, Toronto, Ont.:   "
E. F. B. Johnston, K.C., Director, Toronto, Ont.:   "
Lord Hyde, Director, Pickering, Ont.:   "
E. Jessop, M.D., M.L.A., Director, St. Catharines, Ont.: "
J. A. McEvoy, Director, Toronto, Ont.:   "
David Ratz, Director, New Hamburg. Ont.:   "
James Gunn, Director, Toronto, Ont.:
David Kemp, Director, Toronto, Ont.:
E. C. McNally, Director, Niagara Falls, Ont.:
W. L. Horton. Director, Goderich, Ont.:
Rev. G. I. Taylor, M.A., Director, Toronto, Ont.:   "
R. H. Greene, Director, Toronto, Ont.:   "
Herbert Waddington. Managing Director, Toronto, Ont.: "
Edward E. Lawson, Asst. Gen. Manager, Toronto, Ont.: "
Charles Bauckham, Secretary, Toronto, Ont.: "
Chas. R. Hill, Treasurer, Toronto, Ont.:

A.—Permanent capital stock: Total amount authorized, $5,000,000; total amount subscribed, $2,070,810, more particularly described in Schedule A hereto.

SCHEDULE A.

Class 1.—Fixed and permanent capital stock created by virtue of Building Society Acts.

Description.	Total amount issued and subsisting at 31st December, 1913.			Total amount of actual payments thereon.	Total amount unpaid and constituting an asset of the Corporation.
	No. of shares,	Par value of shares.	—		
		$	$	$ c.	$ c.
1. Fully called stock.....	38,154-1/5	50	1,907,710	1,907,710 00	....
2. Partly called stock (35% called)...............	1,738	50	86,900	26,348 08	43,700 74
3. Partly called stock (no uniform call).........	1,524	50	76,200	34,195 02	42,004 98
4. Paid in advance of calls	....	....	....	16,851 18	....
Totals	41,416-1/5	....	2,070,810	1,985,104 28	85,705 72

LIST OF SHAREHOLDERS AS AT 31ST DECEMBER, 1913.

(Not printed.)

BALANCE SHEET AS AT 31ST DECEMBER, 1913.

Capital and Liabilities.

Capital (Liabilities to Stockholders or Shareholders).

A.—Permanent Capital Stock or Shares.

1. (a) Ordinary joint stock capital, fully called; total called, $1,907,710 total paid thereon	$1,907,710 00	
2. (b) Ordinary joint stock capital, 35% called; total called, $31,415; paid thereon	26,348 08	
3. (c) Ordinary joint stock capital: No uniform call made; total called, $34,195.02; total paid thereon	34,195 02	
(cc) Joint stock capital paid in advance of calls	16,851 18	
4. (d) Dividends declared in respect of (1), (2) and (3), but not yet paid	63,913 63	
5. (e) Unappropriated profits in respect of (1), (2) or (3)	14,035 25	
6. (f) Reserve fund in respect of (1), (2) and (3)	400,000 00	
		$2,463,053 16

Liabilities to the Public.

27. Deposits, right reserved to require 30 days' notice of any withdrawal (including unclaimed deposits)	$512,877 58	
29. Debentures issued in Canada	2,088,602 33	
30. Interest due and accrued on (29)	31,386 72	
40. Other liabilities to the public:		
41. (a) Mortgages payable	13,195 58	
42. (b) Accounts payable	1,217 49	
		2,647,279 65
Total liabilities		$5,110,332 81

Cr. Assets.

I. Assets of which the Corporation is a Beneficial owner.

A.—Immovable Property Owned Beneficially by Corporation.

1. (a) Office premises situate as follows:

2.	(i) At Chatham, held in freehold ....$	10,000 00	
3.	(ii) At Toronto, held in freehold	162,195 53	
4.	(iii) At New Hamburg, held in freehold	2,365 00	
			$ 174,560 53

B.—Debts secured by Mortgages of Land.

9.	(a) Debts (other than item 10) secured by mortgages of land ....$	4,226,078 62	
10.	(b) Debts secured by mortgaged land held for sale....	88,162 85	
11.	(c) Interest due and accrued on items 9 and 10 and not included therein.	29,141 81	
			4,343,383 28

C.—Debts not above enumerated for which the Corporation holds securities as follows:

16.	(d) Debts secured by Loan Corporations debentures....$	1,327 91	
20.	(h) Debts secured only by permanent stock or shares of the Corporation	20,105 63	
22.	(j) Debts secured by stocks	8,624 73	
26.	(n) Interest due or accrued items (16 and 20)........	621 50	
			30,679 77

D.—Unsecured Debts.

27.	(a) Due from agents ....$	3,357 97	
28.	(b) Rents accrued	548 84	
			$ 3,906 81

E.—Cash.

31.	(a) Cash on hand ....$	7,096 98	
32.	(b) Cash in banks	99,688 08	
			106,785 06

F.—Assets not hereinbefore mentioned.

37.	(a) Office furniture ....$	5,000 00	
38.	(b) Stocks and bonds	445,320 51	
39.	(c) Personal accounts	696 85	
			451,017 36

	Total assets	$5,110,332 81

CASH ACCOUNT.

Receipts for the period ending 31st December, 1913.

I.—Received by the Corporation for its Own Use.

A.—Balance from 9th May, 1913.

1. Cash:

		(Col. 1.)	(Col. 3.)	(Col. 4.)
2.	(i) On hand	....	....	$ 2,655 70
3.	(ii) In bank	....	....	44,663 74

CASH ACCOUNT.—Continued.

Receipts for the period ending 31st December, 1913.

B.—Sums received wholly or partly on
    Capital Stock.

4. (*a*) Calls on joint stock permanent capital. 57,987 77

C.—Receipts on account of Investments,
    Loans or Debts.

    (*a*) On mortgages of realty:
10.   (i) Principal ..../. 708,311 58
11.   (ii) Interest . . . .$ 211,099 73
    (*b*) On other securities:
12.   (i) Principal . .: 398,086 43
13.   (ii) Interest or dividends 16,814 04

D.—Receipts from Real Estate Owned
    Beneficially by Corporation.

16. (*a*) Sales 14,543 38
17. (*b*) Rents 12,139 89
               E.—Miscellaneous.

18. (*a*) Commission, brokerage, etc. 1,590 95

          F.—Borrowed Money.

25. (*a*) Bank or other advances, discounts or
        overdrafts $2,273,797 92
26. (*b*) Borrowed by taking deposits 751,903 37

G.—Receipts from other sources, viz.:

30. (*a*) Decrease in amounts due from agencies 4,807 63

        Totals . . . . $256,187 99 .... $4,242,204 14

CASH ACCOUNT.

Expenditure for the period ending 31st December, 1913.

I.—Expended on Corporation Account.

A.—Sums Loaned or Invested on Capital
    Account.

                             (Col. 1.)   (Col. 3.) (Total, Col. 4.)
1. (*a*) Loaned on mortgages of realty $1,184,224 62
    (*b*) Loaned on or invested in other securi-
        ties 263,820 21
6. (*c*) Real estate purchased 19,376 15
7. (*d*) Incumbrances on realty paid off.......$ 292 50
    (*e*) Insurance or taxes advanced on pro-
        perty mortgaged to the Corporation 2,177 75

B.—Expended on Stock Account.

8. Dividends paid on permanent stock 55,234 19

CASH ACCOUNT.—Continued.

Expenditure for the period ending 31st December, 1913.

C.—Borrowed Money other than foregoing,
interest paid thereon, viz.:

18. (a) Bank account: Principal and interest..	7,705 90	....	132,287 02
19. (b) Deposits: Principal and interest	13,893 32	....	2,236,286 78
20. (c) Debentures: Principal and interest...	54,676 52	....	349,929 61

D.—Management Expenses (other than
foregoing):

25. (a) Salaries, wages and fees	24,069 31
26. (b) Commission or brokerage	6,617 82
28. (d) Stationery, postage, printing, advertising.	5,255 25
29. (e) Law costs	503 39
30. (f) Fuel, rent,, taxes (other than 7 and 32), and rates	8,967 16
31. (g) Travelling expenses	2,559 62
32. (h) Registration fees, expense of agencies.	3,019 38
33. (i) Other management expenses	1,932 87

E.—Other expenditures, viz.:

34. (a) Office furniture	....	....	398 20
35. (b) Loss on real estate sold previously held under foreclosure	5,667 00		
36. (c) Amalgamation expense, including amount especially voted of $10,000 to retiring officers of previous companies	12,712 50		

F.—Balance.

37. (a) Cash on hand and in banks	....	....	106,785 06
Totals	$203,106 73	....	$4,295,285 40

MISCELLANEOUS STATEMENT FOR THE YEAR ENDING 31ST DECEMBER, 1913.

---

1. Amount of debentures maturing in 1914: Issued in Canada, $304,341.09. Issued elsewhere, nil.
2. Amount of other existing obligations which will mature in 1914, nil.
3. Amount of securities held by the Corporation which will mature and become payable to the Corporation in 1914, $271,263.66.
4. Average rate of interest per annum paid by the Corporation during 1913: On deposits, 4 per cent.; on debentures, 5 per cent.; on debenture stock, nil.
5. Average rate of interest per annum received by the Corporation during 1913:
    (a) On mortgages of realty; (b) on other securities.
    (i) Owned beneficially by the Corporation: (a) 7¾%; (b) 6½%.
    (ii) Not owned beneficially: (a) nil; (b) nil. '
6. Of the mortgages owned beneficially by the Corporation, $3,267,132.53 is on realty situate in Ontario, and $958,946.09 is on realty situate elsewhere.
7. Of the mortgages not owned beneficially by the Corporation, nil is on realty situate in Ontario, and nil is on realty situate elsewhere.
8. Loans written off or transferred to real estate account during 1913, viz.:
    (i) Funds or securities owned beneficially, $20,617.09.
    (ii) Not so owned, nil.

9. Number and aggregate amount of mortgages upon which compulsory proceedings have been taken by the Corporation in 1913, viz.:
  (i) Owned beneficially, No. 64; amount, $80,387.15.
  (ii) Not so owned, nil; amount, nil.
10. Aggregate market value of land mortgaged to the Corporation:
  (i) Mortgages owned beneficially, $7,939,794.87.
11. How often are the securities held by the Corporation valued? Once a year.
12. (a) Specify the officers of the Corporation who are under bond and for what sum respectively: Man. Dir., $5,000; Asst. Gen. Manager, Secretary and Treasurer, $2,500 each.
  (b) Are the said bonds executed by private sureties or by Guarantee Companies? Guarantee Companies.
13. Date when the accounts of the Corporation were last audited. Monthly during year.
14. Names and addresses of the auditors respectively for 1913 and for 1914 (if appointed):
  For 1913: A. C. Neff and G. T. Clarkson.
  For 1914:
15. What were the dividend-days of the Corporation in 1913, and what rate or rates of dividend were paid on those days respectively? January 1st and July 1st. Rates, 6% and 7%.
16. What is the date appointed for the Annual Meeting? March 2nd, 1914. Date of last Annual Meeting?
17. Special General Meetings held in 1913: Dates, ———.

THE SECURITY LOAN AND SAVINGS COMPANY.

Head Office, St. Catharines, Ont.

Incorporated under the Building Societies Act (Consol. Stat. U. C., c. 53) by declaration filed with the Clerk of the Peace for the County of Lincoln on the 12th March, 1870. The original corporate name was The Security Permanent Building and Savings Society.

The Corporate name was changed to The Security Loan and Savings Company in 1876 by 39 V. c. 64 (D); and also by Order-in-Council of Ontario, dated 18th August, 1876.

The lending and the borrowing powers of the Company are governed by the Loan and Trust Corporations Act, R.S.O. 1914, chap. 184.

ANNUAL STATEMENT

Of the condition and affairs of The Security Loan and Savings Company, of St. Catharines, at the 31st December, 1913, and for the year ending on that day, made to the Registrar of Loan Corporations for the Province of Ontario, pursuant to the laws of the said Province.

The head office of the Corporation is at No. 26 James Street, in the City of St. Catharines, in the Province of Ontario.

The Board is constituted of seven directors, holding office for one year.

The directors and chief executive officers of the Corporation at the 31st December, 1913, were as follows, together with their respective terms of office:

Henry J. Taylor, President, St. Catharines;   5th February, 1913; 4th February, 1914.
J. H. Ingersoll, K.C., Vice-Pres., St. Catharines;   "   "
M. Y. Keating, Director, St. Catharines;   "
Dr. W. H. Merritt, Director, St. Catharines;   "
Jabes Newman, Director, St. Catharines;
A. W. Moore, Director, St. Catharines;
E. F. Dwyer, Director and Secretary-Treasurer,   "
     St. Catharines.

A.—Permanent capital stock: Total amount authorized, $500,000; total amount subscribed, $458,100.00, as more particularly set out in Schedule A hereto.

SCHEDULE A.

Class 1.—Fixed and permanent capital stock created by virtue of Building Society Acts.

Description.	Total amount issued and subsisting at 31st December, 1913.			Total amount actual payments thereon.	Total amount unpaid and constituting an asset of the Corporation.
	Number of shares.	Per value of shares.	—		
		$	$	$	$
1. Fully called stock...	4,000	100	400,000	400,000	none
2. Partly called stock (subscribed)	581	100	58,100	50,250	7,850
	4,581	....	458,100	450,250	7,850

LIST OF SHAREHOLDERS AS AT 31ST DECEMBER, 1913.

(Not printed.)

10 L.C.

BALANCE SHEET AS AT 31st DECEMBER, 1913.

Dr.   Capital and Liabilities.

Capital (Liabilities to Stockholders or Shareholders).

A.—Permanent Capital Stock or Shares.

1. (a) Ordinary joint stock capital fully called; total called, $458,100; total paid thereon..............	$450,250 00	
4. (d) Dividends declared in respect of (1), but not yet paid...	11,135 39	
6. (f) Reserve fund in respect of (1).....................	75,000 00	
7. (g) Contingent fund in respect of (1).................	895 45	
		$537,280 84

Liabilities to the Public.

27. Deposits (including unclaimed deposits), right reserved to require 30 days' notice of any withdrawal.......	$246,391 45	
28. Interest on deposits, due or accrued or capitalized......	1,845 56	
29. Debentures issued in Canada	186,388 50	
30. Interest due or accrued on (29).......................	3,492 02	
		438,117 53
Total liabilities		$975,398 37

Cr.   Assets.

I.—Assets of which the Corporation is the Beneficial Owner.

A.—Immovable Property Owned Beneficially by the Corporation.

1. (a) Office premises situate as follows:		
2. (i) At 26 James Street, St. Catharines, held in freehold..................................	$19,000 00	

B.—Debts secured by Mortgages of Land.

9. (a) Debts (other than item 10) secured by mortgages of land...........	901,891 46	
10. (b) Debts secured by mortgaged land held for sale......	2,462 62	

C.—Debts not above enumerated for which the Corporation holds securities, as follows:

20. (h) Debts secured only by permanent stock or shares of the Corporation	16,250 27	
23. (k) Debts secured by life insurance policies............	9,510 05	

E.—Cash.

32. (b) In bank	26,027 97	

F.—Assets not hereinbefore mentioned.

37. (a) Furniture	256 00	
Total assets		$975,398 37

CASH ACCOUNT.

Receipts for the year ending 31st December, 1913.

I.—Received by the Corporation for its Own Use.

A.—Balance from 31st December, 1912.

(Col. 1.)

3.	(ii) In bank	$34,144 23

B.—Sums Received Wholly or Partly on Capital Stock.

4. (a) Calls on joint stock permanent capital (subscribed and paid)	50,250 00

C.—Receipts on account of Investments, Loans or Debts.

(a) On mortgages of realty:

10.	(i) Principal.........	174,672 35
11.	(ii) Interest.......	54,682 93

(b) On other securities:

12.	(i) Principal......	7,565 15
13.	(ii) Interest or dividends	595 53

D.—Receipts from Real Estate Owned Beneficially by Corporation.

17. (b) Rents...........	348 00

F.—Borrowed Money.

26. (b) Borrowed by taking deposits	730,982 37
27. (c) Borrowed on debentures	77,360 26

G.—Receipts from other sources, viz.:

30. (a) Interest, Imperial Bank of Canada..................	744 95
Total...............	$1,131,345 77

CASH ACCOUNT.

Expenditure for the year ending 31st December, 1913.

I.—Expended on Corporation Account.

A.—Sums Loaned or Invested on Capital Account.

(Col. 1.)

1.	(a) Loaned on mortgages of realty, including item (7) ..	$224,724 19
	(b) Loaned or invested in other securities, viz.:	
4.	(iii) Permanent stock of this Company...........	13,600 00
7.	(e) Insurance or taxes advanced on property mortgaged to the Corporation, included in item 1 (a).	

B.—Expended on Stock Account.

8. Dividends paid on permanent stock	19,832 86

C.—Borrowed Money (other than foregoing) or interest thereon paid, viz.:

18.	(a) Bank Account: Interest	6 19
19.	(b) Deposits: Principal, $738,101.42; interest, $7,969.10..	746,070 52
20.	(c) Debentures issued in Canada: Principal, $85,335.08; interest, $8,664.26	93,999 34

CASH ACCOUNT.—Continued.

Expenditure for the year ending 31st December, 1913.

D.—Management Expenses (other than foregoing).
25. (a) Salaries, wages and fees	$5,076	96
28. (d) Stationery, postage, printing and advertising	526	80
29. (e) Law costs	7	80
30. (f) Fuel, rent, taxes (other than 7 and 33), and rates	752	43
31. (g) Travelling expenses	24	40
32. (h) Registration fees	340	00
33. (i) Other management expenditure	228	29

E.—Other Expenditure, viz.:
34. (a) Life insurance premiums	110	52
35. (b) Insurance premium on office building	17	50

F.—Balance.
39. (ii) Cash in bank	26,027	97
Totals	$1,131,345	77

MISCELLANEOUS STATEMENT FOR THE YEAR ENDING 31ST DECEMBER, 1913.

1. Amount of debentures maturing in 1914: Issued in Canada, $54,462.00; Issued elsewhere, none.
2. Amount of other existing obligations which will mature in 1914, none.
3. Amount of securities held by the Corporation which will mature and become payable to the Corporation in 1914, $162,605.07.
4. Average rate of interest per annum paid by the Corporation during 1913: On deposits, 3.03%; On debentures, 4.51%; On debenture stock, none.
5. Average rate of interest per annum received by the Corporation during 1913:
   (a) On mortgages of realty; (b) On other securities.
   (i) Owned beneficially by the Corporation: (a) 6½%; (b) 5%.
   (ii) Not owned beneficially: (a) None; (b) None.
6. Of the mortgages owned beneficially by the Corporation, $901,891.46 is on realty situate in Ontario, and none is on realty situate elsewhere.
7. Of the mortgages not owned beneficially by the Corporation, none is on realty situate in Ontario, and none is on realty situate elsewhere.
8. Loans written off or transferred to real estate account during 1913, viz.:
   (i) Funds or securities owned beneficially, $2,462.62.
   (ii) Not so owned, none.
9. Number and aggregate amount of mortgages upon which compulsory proceedings have been taken by the Corporation in 1913, viz.:
   (i) Owned beneficially: No., none; Amount, none.
   (ii) Not so owned: No., none; Amount, none.
10. Aggregate market value of land mortgaged to the Corporation:
    (i) Mortgages owned beneficially, $2,125,136.00.
    (ii) Not so owned, none.
11. How often are the securities held by the Corporation valued? Yearly.
12. (a) Specify the officers of the Corporation who are under bonds and for what sum respectively: Secretary-Treasurer, $10,000; private bond and mortgage; Accountant-Teller, Guarantee Company bond, $5,000; Assistant, private bond ($2,000 in real estate),
    (b) Are the said bonds executed by private sureties or by Guarantee Companies As above.
13. Date when the accounts of the Corporation were last audited? 15th January, 1914.
14. Names and addresses of the auditors respectively for 1913 and for 1914 (if appointed):
    For 1913: R. Fowlie, J. Albert Pay, St. Catharines.
    For 1914: R. Fowlie, J. Albert Pay, St. Catharines.
15. What were the dividend-days of the Corporation in 1913, and what rate or rates of dividend were paid on those days respectively? January 2nd, 1913; July 2nd 1913; 2½%.
16. What is the date appointed for the Annual Meeting? First Wednesday in February. Date of last Annual Meeting? February 5th, 1913.
17. Special General Meetings held in 1913: Dates, none.

THE GREAT WEST PERMANENT LOAN COMPANY.

Head Office, Winnipeg, Manitoba.

CONSTATING INSTRUMENTS.

Incorporated on 19th May, 1909, by Special Act of the Parliament of Canada (9 Edward VII. chap. 89 D), which Act was, on the 16th March, 1910, validated and confirmed by a Special Act of the Legislature of Manitoba [File page 457]. For the lending and borrowing powers see the above cited Acts.

For Ontario, see The Loan and Trust Corporations Act, R.S.O. 1914, chap. 184.

ANNUAL STATEMENT

Of the condition and affairs of The Great West Permanent Loan Company, of Winnipeg, Manitoba, at the 31st December, 1913, and for the year ending on that day, made to the Registrar of Loan Corporations for the Province of Ontario, pursuant to the laws of the said Province.

The head office of the Corporation is at No. 436 Main Street, in the City of Winnipeg, in the Province of Manitoba.

The Chief Agency for Ontario is situate at No. 20 King Street West, City of Toronto, Ontario.

The Chief Agent and Attorney for Ontario is William McLeish, and his address is 20 King Street W., Toronto, in the Province of Ontario.

The Board is constituted of eleven directors holding office for one year.

The directors and chief executive officers of the Corporation at 31st December, 1913, were as follows, together with their respective terms of office:

W. T. Alexander, President, Winnipeg;	February 18, 1914; February 17, 1915.
E. S. Popham, 1st Vice-Pres., Winnipeg;	" "
N. Bawlf, 2nd Vice-Pres., Winnipeg;	" "
Wm. Robinson, Director, Winnipeg;	
E. D. Martin, Director, Winnipeg;	
Sir Gilbert Parker, Bart., Director, London, Eng;	"
E. L. Taylor, Director, Winnipeg;	
S. D. Lazier, Director, London, Eng.;	"
D. E. Sprague, Director, Winnipeg;	"
F. H. Alexander, Director, Winnipeg;	"
E. F. Hutchings, Director, Winnipeg;	
W. T. Alexander, Manager, Winnipeg;	
F. H. Alexander, Secretary, Winnipeg;	

A.—Permanent capital stock: Total amount authorized, $5,000,000; total amount subscribed, $2,426,750, as more particularly set out in Schedule A hereto.

SCHEDULE A.

Class 2.—Fixed and permanent capital stock created by virtue of Joint Stock Companies' Acts or Private Acts.

Description.	No. of shares.	Par value.	Total amount held.	Total amount paid thereon.	Total remaining unpaid on calls.
		$	$	$ c.	$ c.
1. Fully called ..	23,451½	100	2,345,150	2,345,150 00	....
2. Partly called	816	100	81,600	10,875 88	70,724 12
Totals......	24,267½	....	2,426,750	2,356,025 88	70,724 12

LIST OF SHAREHOLDERS AS AT 31st DECEMBER, 1913.

(Not printed.)

BALANCE SHEET AS AT 31st DECEMBER, 1913.

Dr.   Capital and Liabilities.

Capital (Liabilities to Stockholders or Shareholders).

A.—Permanent Capital Stock or Shares.

1. (a) Ordinary joint stock capital fully called; total called, total paid thereon $2,345,150 00		
4. (d) Dividends declared in respect of (1), but not yet paid	104,498	55
6. (f) Reserve fund	652,749	54
8. (h) Instalment permanent stock (payable by fixed periodical payments): Total subscribed, $81,600.00 on which has been paid	10,875	88
Accrued interest on (8)	693	40
9. (i) Dividends declared on (8), but not yet paid	665	07
26. Unclaimed dividends	1,402	35
		$3,116,034 79

Liabilities to the Public.

27. Deposits, right reserved to require 30 days' notice of any withdrawal....................................$1,348,104 48		
28. Interest on deposits due or accrued or capitalized........	46,104	85
29. Debentures issued in Canada	488,052	00
30. Interest due and accrued on (29) and (31)...............	9,620	05
31. Debentures issued elsewhere than in Canada...........	499,466	04
39. Due on loans in process of completion or to pay assumed mortgages..........	595,986	62
41. Other liabilities to public:		
Accounts payable	71	02
42. (a) Loan repayments	1,376,899	55
		4,364,304 61

         Total liabilities $7,480,339 40

Cr.   Assets.

I.—Assets of which the Corporation is the Beneficial Owner.

A.—Immovable Property Owned Beneficially by the Corporation.

1. (a) Office premises situate as follows:		
3. (ii) At Winnipeg for H. O. site..................	$498,924	62
5. (b) Freehold land (including buildings) other than foregoing..	15,248	87
		$514,173 49

B.—Debts secured by Mortgages of Land.

9. (a) Debts (other than item 10) secured by mortgages of land $6,470,732 56		
11. (c) Interest accrued on item 9 not included therein:		
Not due $21,063 04		
Past due ....: 1,567 92		
	22,630	96
		6,493,363 52

C.—Debts not above enumerated for which the Corporation holds securities, as follows:

20. (h) Debts secured only by permanent stock or shares of the Corporation	$1,770	85
22. (j) Debts secured by bank and trust company stocks...	121,643	50
26. (n) Interest due or accrued on items 20, 22, and not included therein	2,137	65
		125,552 00

BALANCE SHEET.—Continued.

E.—Cash.

31. (a) On hand in head office and branches	$27,787 88		
33. (i) In the bank	237,421 88		
			$265,209 76

F.—Assets not hereinbefore mentioned.

37. (a) Sundry accounts due Company	$4,713 05	
38. (b) Commission suspense account	20,782 28	
39. (c) Due by Company's agents	5,116 88	
40. (d) Charter and license account	6,452 92	
41. (e) Office furniture and fixtures	44,975 50	
		82,040 63

Total assets $7,480,339 40

CASH ACCOUNT.

Receipts for the year ending 31st December, 1913.

I.—Received by the Corporation for its Own Use.

A.—Balance from 31st December, 1912.

		(Col. 1.)	(Col. 3.)	(Col. 4,)
2.	(i) Cash on hand	....	....	$110,606 16
	(ii) In Bank	....	....	93,934 59
B.—Sums received wholly or partly on Capital Stock.				
4. (a) Calls on permanent capital		....	$109,573 58	
5. (b) Premiums on (4)		....	10,960 37	
				$120,533 95
C.—Receipts on account of Investments, Loans or Debts.				
(a) On mortgages of realty:				
10.	(i) Principal	....	....	898,590 70
11.	(ii) Interest	$445,833 00	....	445,833 00
(b) On other securities, stocks and bonds:				
13.	(ii) Interest or dividends	5,118 35	....	5,118 55
(c) Stock loans:				
14.	(i) Principal	....	....	2,040 00
15.	(ii) Interest	63 27	....	63 27
D.—Receipts from Real Estate Owned Beneficially by Corporation.				
16. (a) Sales		....	....	3,556 25
17. (b) Rents		531 40	....	531 40
F.—Borrowed Money.				
26. (b) Borrowed by taking deposits		....	....	7,732,226 98
27. (c) Borrowed on debentures		....	....	471,833 01
G.—Receipts from other sources.				
30. (a) Unclaimed dividends		....	....	850 94
(b) Bank and Trust Company interest		....	....	21,626 63

Total $9,907,345 43

CASH ACCOUNT.—Continued.

Expenditure for the year ending 31st December, 1913.

I.—Expended on Corporation Account.

A.—Sums Loaned or Invested on Capital Account.

1. Loaned on mortgages of realty ....,........		$1,061,003 60
(b) Loaned or invested in other securities:		
2. (i) Loan on H. O. premises		375,866 94
3. (ii) Bank and trust company stocks		1,931 25
4. (iii) Loans on company's stock		2,520 00
6. (c) Real estate purchased		11,798 12
7. (d) Incumbrances on realty paid off		783 95
(e) Insurance or taxes, repairs, advanced on property mortgaged to the Corporation		32,682 91

B.—Expended on Stock Account.

8. Dividends on permanent stock	$197,065 63	
(a) Interest on partly paid stock paid up	3,544 77	
		200,610 40

C.—Borrowed Money (other than foregoing) or interest thereon paid, viz.:

19. (b) Deposits: Principal, $7,574,025.55; interest, $46,104.85	$46,104 85	7,574,025 55
20. (c) Debentures payable in Canada: Principal, $32,200.00..	....	32,200 00
21. (d) Debentures issued elsewhere: Principal, $18,201.33..	....	18,201 33
Interest on (20) and (21)	33,629 10	
		79,733 95

D.—Management Expenses (other than foregoing).

25. (a) Salaries, wages and fees	$75,710 41	
26. (b) Commission or brokerage	10,869 01	
27. (c) Advances to agents	3,957 14	
28. (d) Stationery, postage, printing and advertising	28,605 33	
29. (e) Law costs	730 70	
30. (f) Fuel, rent, taxes (other than in 7 and 32) and rates	19,295 69	
31. (g) Travelling expenses	2,273 95	
32. (h) Registration fees	2,739 24	
33. (i) Other management expenditure	19,316 08	
		163,497 50

E.—Other Expenditures, viz.:

Transient, fire losses, etc.	$1,209 69	
34. (a) Branch clearances	23,101 20	
35. (b) Furniture and fixtures	17,053 58	
36. (c) Charter and license expenses	676 10	
(d) Organization expenses	45,239 60	
		$87,280 17

F.—Balance.

37. (a) Cash on hand and in banks		265,209 76
Totals $9,907,345 43		

MISCELLANEOUS STATEMENT FOR THE YEAR ENDING 31ST DECEMBER, 1913.

1. **Amount** of debentures maturing in 1914: Issued in Canada, $32,200.00; Issued elsewhere, $26,280.00.
2. **Amount** of other existing obligations, which will mature in 1914, excluding deposits, none.
3. **Amount** of securities held by the Corporation which will mature and become payable to the Corporation in 1914, excluding loans, none.
4. **Average** rate of interest per annum paid by the Corporation during 1913 on deposits, 4%; on debentures, 4¾%; on debenture stock, none.
5. **Average** rate of interest per annum received by the Corporation during 1913 (a) On mortgages of realty; (b) On other securities; (i) Owned beneficially by the Corporation; (a) 9.8%; (b) 6%; (ii) Not owned beneficially (a) none.; (b) none.
6. **Of** the mortgages owned beneficially by the Corporation,, $150,333.96 is on realty situate in Ontario, and $4,966,130.01 is on realty situate elsewhere.
7. **Of** the mortgages not owned beneficially by the Corporation, none is on realty situate in Ontario, and none is on realty situate elsewhere.
8. **Loans** written off or transferred to real estate account during 1913, viz.: (i funds or securities owned beneficially, $11,798.12; (ii) not so owned, none.
9. **Number** and aggregate amount of mortgages upon which compulsory proceedings have been taken by the Corporation in 1913, viz.: (i) owned beneficially, No., 15; Amount, $15,134.21; (ii) not so owned, No., none; Amount, none.
10. **Aggregate** market value of land mortgaged to the Corporation: (i) Mortgages owned beneficially, $16,074,352; (ii) Not so owned, none.
11. **How** often are the securities held by the Corporation valued? When loan is made and at such times as Directors deem advisable.
12. **(a)** Specify the officers of the Corporation who are under bond, and for what sum respectively. Person holding responsible position in Company—from $1,000 to $10,000.
    (b) Are the said bonds executed by private sureties or by Guarantee Companies? Guarantee Companies.
13. **Date** when the accounts of the Corporation were last audited, as at December 31st, 1913.
14. **Names** and addresses of the auditors respectively for 1913 and for 1914 (if appointed): For 1913: D. A. Pender, Winnipeg; and Riddell, Stead, Graham & Hutchison. For 1914: Same as 1913.
15. **What** were the dividend days of the Corporation in 1913, and what rate or rates of dividend were paid on those days respectively, January 1st and July 1st, 9% per annum.
16. **What** is the date appointed for the Annual Meeting: February 18th, 1914. Date of last Annual Meeting, February 19th, 1913.
17. **Special** General Meetings held in 1913: Date, February 19th, 1913.

THE LONDON LOAN AND SAVINGS COMPANY OF CANADA.

Head Office, London, Ont.

Incorporated under the Building Societies Act (Consol. Stat. U.C., chap. 53), by declaration filed with the Clerk of the Peace for the County of Middlesex, 2nd May, 1877.

The lending and the borrowing powers are governed by the Loan and Trust Corporations Act, R.S.O. 1914, chap. 184.

ANNUAL STATEMENT

Of the condition and affairs of the London Loan and Savings Company of Canada, of London, Ontario, at the 31st December, 1913, and for the year ending on that day, made to the Registrar of Loan Corporations for the Province of Ontario, pursuant to the laws of the said Province.

The head office of the Corporation is at No. 220 Dundas Street, in the City of London, in the Province of Ontario.

The Board is constituted of five directors, holding office for one year.

The directors and chief executive officers of the Corporation at the 31st December, 1913, were as follows, together with their respective terms of office:

R. W. Puddicombe, President, London; February 13, 1913; February 12, 1914.
G. G. McCormick, 1st Vice-President, London; " "
Thomas Baker, 2nd Vice-President, London; " "
W. E. Robinson, Director, London;
M. J. Kent, Director, London; " "
M. J. Kent, Manager, London; 1st May, 1877, at discretion of Directors.

A.—Permanent capital stock: Total amount authorized, $1,000,000; total amount subscribed, $1,000,000, as more particularly set out in Schedule A hereto.

SCHEDULE A.

Class 1.—Fixed and permanent Capital Stock created by virtue of Building Society Acts.

Description.	Total amount issued and subsisting at 31st December, 1913.			Total amount of actual payments thereon.	Total amount unpaid.
	No. of shares.	Par value.	—		
		$	$	$ c.	$ c.
1. Fully called stock........	16,784	50	839,200	839,200 00	....
2. Partly called stock........	None	....	....	....	....
3. Instalment stock	3,216	50	160,800	27 78	160,772 27
(Payable by fixed periodical payments and still in process of payment.)					
	20,000	....	1,000,000	839,227 78	160,772 27

LIST OF SHAREHOLDERS AS AT 31st DECEMBER, 1913.

(Not printed.)

BALANCE SHEET AS AT 31st DECEMBER, 1913..

Dr.   Capital and Liabilities.

Capital (Liabilities to Stockholders or Shareholders).

A.—Permanent Capital Stock or Shares.

1. (*a*) Ordinary joint stock capital fully called; total called, $839,200 total paid thereon	$839,200 00	
4. (*d*) Dividends declared in respect of (1)	12,513 57	
5. (*e*) Unappropriated profits in respect of (1)	3,625 60	
6. (*f*) Reserve fund in respect of (1).....................	260,000 00	
8. (*h*) Instalment Permanent Stock (payable by fixed periodical payments): Total subscribed, $160,800; on which has been paid	27 73	
		$1,115,366 90

Liabilities to the Public.

27. Deposits, right reserved to require 30 or more days' notice on any withdrawal	$470,430 94	
29. Debentures issued in Canada	477,443 24	
30. Interest due and accrued on (29)	9,939 14	
31. Debentures issued elsewhere than in Canada	617,755 19	
32. Interest due and accrued on (31)	4,896 69	
		1,580,465 20

Total liabilities $2,695,832 10

Cr.   Assets.

I.—Assets of which the Corporation is the Beneficial Owner.

A.—Immovable Property Owned Beneficially by Corporation.

1. (*a*) Office premises situate as follows:	
2. (i) At London, Ont., held in freehold	$63,000 00

B.—Debts secured by Mortgages of Land.

9. (*a*) Debts secured by mortgages of land	2,175,618 00

12. (*d*) Of the debts mentioned in items 9, the sum of $33,078.00 is due by directors or officers of the Corporation (not extended).

C.—Debts not above enumerated for the which the Corporation holds securities, as follows:

14. (*b*) Debts secured by municipal bonds or debentures ..	$6,566 00	
15. (*c*) Debts secured by Public School debentures, included in 14		
16. (*d*) Debts secured by Loan Corporation debentures.....	1,111 00	
20. (*h*) Debts secured only by permanent stock or shares of the Corporation	78,811 00	
22. (*j*) Debts secured by other stocks	3,844 00	
		90,332 00

D.—Unsecured Debts.

27. (*a*) Rents due and accrued	572 83

BALANCE SHEET.—Continued.

E.—Cash.

31. (a) On hand	$10,943 83		
32. (b) In banks	119,208 44		
		$130,152 27	

F.—Assets not hereinbefore mentioned.

37. (a) Loan companies' stocks	$234,823 00		
40. (d) Sundries, and steel deposit boxes, office furniture, etc., not valued	1,334 00		
		236,157 00	
Total Assets		$2,695,832 10	

CASH ACCOUNT.

Receipts for the year ending 31st December, 1913.

I.—Received by the Corporation for its Own Use.

A.—Balance from 31st December, 1912.

(b) Cash (not already shown under (1)):			
2. (i) On hand	$7,427 04		
3. (ii) In bank	12,148 41		
		$19,575 45	

B.—Sums received wholly or partly on Capital Stock.

4. (a) Calls on joint stock capital		98,361 98

C.—Receipts on account of Investments, Loans or Debts.

(a) Mortgages of realty:			
10. (i) Principal	$308,511 38		
11. (ii) Interest	171,042 92		
		479,554 30	

D.—Receipts from Real Estate Owned Beneficially by Corporation.

17. (b) Rents		7,020 18

F.—Borrowed Money.

26. (b) Borrowed by taking deposits	$1,664,398 34		
27. (c) Borrowed on debentures	277,179 25		
		1,941,577 59	

G.—Receipts from other sources, viz.:

30. (a) Sundry cash items	$218 20		
(b) Safety deposit vault rents	193 73		
		411 93	
Total		$2,546,501 88	

CASH ACCOUNT.

Expenditure for the year ending 31st December, 1913.

I.—Expended on Corporation Account.

A.—Sums Loaned or Invested on Capital Account.

		(Col. 1.)	
1. (a) Loaned on mortgages of realty		$338,868 73	
(b) Loaned or invested in other securities. Included in (1).			
7. (d) Incumbrances on realty paid off (taxes on Company's block)		1,360 75	$340,229 48

B.—Expended on Stock Account.

8. Dividends paid on permanent stock	$45,777 34	
(a) Bonus paid on joint stock capital	19,496 00	65,273 34

C.—Borrowed Money (other than foregoing) or interest thereon paid.

19. (b) Deposits: Principal, $1,707,201.52; Interest, $15,781.03	$1,722,982 55	
20. (c) Debentures issued in Canada: Principal, $158,189.41; Interest, $17,446.23	175,635 64	
21. (d) Debentures issued elsewhere: Principal, $61,319.86; Interest, $26,714.13	88,033 99	1,986,652 18

D.—Management Expenses (other than foregoing).

25. (a) Salaries, wages and fees	$11,479 56	
26. (b) Commission or brokerage	3,000 15	
28. (d) Stationery, postage, printing and advertising	1,469 16	
29. (e) Law costs	672 88	
30. (f) Fuel, rent, taxes (other than in 7 and 32) and rates.	3,501 59	
31. (g) Travelling expenses	163 50	
32. (h) Registration fees	180 00	
33. (i) Other management expenditure	1,004 68	21,471 52

E.—Other Expenditures, viz.:

34. (a) Interest	$1,312 56	
35. (b) Insurance	507 16	
36. (c) Janitor's fees, repairs	902 87	2,722 59

F.—Balance.

37. (b) Cash on hand and in banks	130,152 27
Total	$2,546,501 38

MISCELLANEOUS STATEMENT FOR THE YEAR ENDING 31ST DECEMBER, 1913.

1. Amount of debentures maturing in 1914: Issued in Canada, $116,133.70; Issued elsewhere, $112,765.52.
2. Amount of other existing obligations which will mature in 1914: None, save deposits and rent.
3. Amount of securities held by the Corporation which will mature and become payable to the Corporation in 1914: Estimated at $200,000.
4. Average rate of interest per annum paid by the Corporation during 1913: On deposits, 3.206%; On debentures, 4.89%; On debenture stock, none.

5. Average rate of interest per annum received by the Corporation during 1913:
    (a) On mortgages of realty; (b) On other securities.
    (i) Owned beneficially by the Corporation: (a) 7.15%; (b) 6 to 10%.
    (ii) Not owned beneficially: (a) None; · (b) None.
6. Of the mortgages owned beneficially by the Corporation, $2,175,618 is on realty situate in Ontario, and none is on realty situate elsewhere.
7. Of the mortgages not owned beneficially by the Corporation, none is on realty situate in Ontario, and none is on realty situate elsewhere.
8. Loans written off or transferred to real estate account during 1913, viz.:
    (i) Funds or securities owned beneficially none.
    (ii) Not so owned, none.
9. Number and aggregate amount of mortgages upon which compulsory proceedings have been taken by the Corporation in 1913, viz.:
    (i) Owned beneficially: None; Amount, none.
    (ii) Not so owned, none.
10. Aggregate market value of land mortgaged to the Corporation:
    (i) Mortgages owned beneficially, $4,934,268.00.
    (ii) Not so owned, none.
11. How often are the securities held by the Corporation valued? Lands when loans made, and mortgages yearly.
12. (a) Specify the officers of the Corporation who are under bond and for what sum respectively: Manager, $10,000; Teller, $10,000; other officers, $13.000; in all, $33,000.
    (b) Are the said bonds executed by private sureties or by Guarantee Companies? Partly private, principally Guarantee Companies.
13. Date when the accounts of the Corporation were last audited. 31st December, 1913.
14. Names and addresses of the auditors respectively for 1913 and for 1914 (if appointed):
    For 1913: Francis B. Ware and A. Screaton.
    For 1914: Not yet appointed.
15. What were the dividend days of the Corporation in 1913 and what rate er rates of dividend were paid on those days respectively? January 2nd, April 1st, July 2nd, October 1st; 1½% each quarter at rate of 6% per annum.
16. What is the date appointed for the Annual Meeting? 2nd Thursday in February. Date of last Annual Meeting? February 13th, 1913.
17. Special General Meetings held in 1913: Dates, none.

THE MIDLAND LOAN AND SAVINGS COMPANY.

Head Office, Port Hope, Ontario.

CONSTATING INSTRUMENTS.

Incorporated under the Building Societies Act, Consol. Stat. U.C., Chap. 53, by declaration filed with the Clerk of the Peace for the United Counties of Northumberland and Durham, 5th July, 1872. (Decl. Book II., 127.)

The corporate name was, by Order-in-Council of Ontario, 21st June, 1876 (*Ibid*), changed to the Midland Loan and Savings Company.

A by-law altering the amount of the capital stock and par value of the share was, pursuant to the Loan Corporations Act, approved by Order-in-Council of Ontario, 3rd October, 1900.

The borrowing and lending powers are governed by the Loan and Trust Corporations Act, R.S.O. 1914, chap. 184.

ANNUAL STATEMENT

Of the condition of affairs of the Midland Loan and Savings Company, of Port Houe, Ont., at the 31st December, 1913, and for the year ending on that day, made to the Registrar of Loan Corporations for the Province of Ontario, pursuant to the laws of the said Province.

The head office of the Corporation is on Walton Street, in the Town of Port Hope, in the Province of Ontario.

The Board is constituted of seven directors, holding office for one year.

The directors and chief executive officers of the Corporation at the 31st December, 1913, were as folowls, together with their respective terms of office.

William Henwood, President, Welcome, Ont, 2nd August, 1912; February 3rd, 1914.
John Wickett, Vice-Pres., Port Hope, Ont., 2nd August, 1912, "
Henry Mulligan, Director, Millbrook, Ont., 20th Nov., 1908, "
Thomas Wickett, Director, Port Hope, Ont., 1st February, 1910,
Thomas Roberts, Director, Welcome, Ont., 1st February, 1910,
R. A. Mulholland, Director, Port Hope, Ont., 2nd August, 1912,
J. H. Helm, Manager, Port Hope, Ont., 1st January, 1905.

A.—Permanent capital stock: Total amount authorized, unlimited; total amount subscribed, $360,000, as more particularly set out in Schedule A hereto.

SCHEDULE A.

Class I.—Fixed and permanent capital stock created by virtue of Building Societies Acts.

Description.	Total amount issued and sub-sisting at 31st December, 1913.			Total amount of actual payments thereon.	Total amount unpaid and constituting an asset of the Corporation.
	No. of shares.	Par value.			
1. Fully called...........	36,000	$ 10	$ 360,000	$ c. 360,000 00	....

LIST OF SHAREHOLDERS AS AT 31st DECEMBER, 1913.

(Not printed.)

BALANCE SHEET AS AT 31st DECEMBER, 1913.

Dr.   Capital and Liabilities.

Capital (Liabilities to Stockholders or Shareholders).

A.—Permanent Capital Stock or Shares.

1. (a) Ordinary joint stock capital fully called; total called,
       $360,000; total paid thereon $360,000 00
4. (d) Dividends declared in respect of (1), but not yet paid   14,430 00
5. (e) Unappropriated profits in respect of (1) 6,484 13
6. (f) Reserve fund 'n respect of (1) 225,000 00
                                                         ─────────── $605,914 13

Liabilities to the Public.

27. Deposits (including Unclaimed Deposits): Right reserved
       to require 30 days' notice of any withdrawal... $319,223 60
28. Interest on deposits, due or accrued or capitalized.......   13,032 33
29. Debentures issued in Canada 486,424 72
30. Interest due and accrued on (29) 12,728 06
                                                         ───────────   831,408 71

       Total liabilities $1,437,322 84

Cr.   Assets.

I.—Assets of which the Corporation is the Beneficial Owner.

A.—Immovable Property Owned Beneficially by Corporation.

1. (a) Office premises situate as follows:

2.   (i) At Port Hope, held as freehold 5,000 00

B.—Debts secured by Mortgages of Land.

9. (a) Debts (other than item 10) secured by mortgages
       of land $1,226,943 82

10. (b) Debts secured by mortgaged land held for sale 671 23
11. (c) Interest due and accrued on items 9 and 10 and not
        included therein 31,864 40
                                                         ───────────   1,259,479 45

C.—Debts not above enumerated for which the Corporation
       holds securities as follows:

14. (b) Debts secured by Municipal Bonds or Debentures .. $42,150 00
20. (h) Debts secured only by permanent stock or shares of
        the Corporation 5,953 20
22. (j) Bonds and Debentures of Ontario Municipalities owned
        by the Company 49,531 04
26. (n) Interest due or accrued on items 14 to 25 and not
        included therein 1,517 48
                                                         ───────────   99,151 72

D.—Unsecured Debts.

27. (a) Rents due or accrued on Company's properties 86 65

BALANCE SHEET.—Continued.

E.—Cash.

31. (a) On hand	$1,323 56	
32. (b) In banks	71,547 89	72,871 45

F.—Assets not hereinbefore mentioned:

37. (a) Contingent Fund		733 57
Total assets		$1,437,322 84

CASH ACCOUNT.

Receipts for the year ending 31st December, 1913.

I.—Received by the Corporation for its Own Use.

(Total, Col. 4.)

A.—Balances from 31st December, 1912.

1. (b) Cash not already shown under (1):		
2.　　　(i) On hand	$1,681 08	
3.　　　(ii) In bank	65,738 41	67,419 49

C.—Receipts on account of Investments, Loans or Debts.

(a) On mortgages of realty:		
10.　　　(i) Principal	215,955 36	
11.　　　(ii) Interest	79,866 04	
(b) On loans on shares of the Corporation:		
12.　　　(i) Principal	4,672 40	
13.　　　(ii) Interest	129 83	
(c) Loans on Municipal Debentures:		
14.　　　(i) Principal	72,580 32	
15.　　　(ii) Interest	3,080 32	
(d) Bonds and debentures owned by the Corporation:		
15½.　　　(i) Principal	16,649 16	
16.　　　(ii) Interest	2,750 34	395,683 77

D.—Receipts from Real Estate Owned Beneficially by Corporation

16. (a) Sales (not included in any of the foregoing items) ..	$2,021 88	
17. (b) Rents	140 00	2,161 88

F.—Borrowed Money.

26. (b) Borrowed by taking deposits	$556,707 14	
27. (c) Borrowed on debentures	241,000 40	797,707 54

11 L.C.

CASH ACCOUNT.—Continued.

Receipts for the year ending 31st December, 1913.

G.—Receipts from other Sources.

80. (a) Interest reserved for one month on Savings Deposits	$1,000 00	
(b) Sundry receipts and inspection fees	1,425 00	
(c) Bank Interest	1,536 66	
		3,961 66

Total $1,266,934 34

CASH ACCOUNT.

Expenditure for the year ending 31st December, 1913.

I.—Expended on Corporation Account

A.—Sums Loaned or Invested on Capital Account.

1. (a) Loaned on mortgages of realty	$185,051 34	
(b) Loaned or invested in other securities, viz.:		
2. (i) On municipal debentures	98,880 32	
3. (ii) Bonds and debentures owned by the Company..	11,550 34	
4. (iii) Real estate on hand	801 93	
5 (iv) Shares of the Corporation	7,208 90	
6. (c) Contingent account	733 57	
		$304,226 40

B.—Expended on Stock Account.

8. Dividends paid on permanent stock		23,821 00

C. Borrowed Money (other than foregoing) or interest thereon paid, viz.:

19. (b) Deposits: Principal, $546,709.57, interest $13,032.33...	$559,741 90	
20. (c) Debentures issued in Canada: Interest, $20,738.13; principal, $267,609.36	288,347 49	
		848,089 39

D.—Management expenses (other than foregoing):

25. (a) Salaries, wages and fees	8,951 61	
26. (b) Commission and brokerage	1,172 70	
28. (d) Stationery, postage, printing and advertising	475 67	
30 (f) Fuel, taxes (other than in 7 and 32), rates and light..	121 68	
31. (g) Travelling expenses	173 05	
32. (h) Registration fees	105 00	
33. (i) Other management expenditure	274 13	
		11,273 84

E.—Other Expenditure, viz.:

34. (a) Ontario Government tax	$234 00	
35. (b) Municipal tax	174 14	
36. (c) Sundry unrealizable amounts written off	656 82	
36½ Company's Office Building	587 30	
		1,652 26

F. Balance.

37. (a) Cash on hand and in bank		72,871 45

Total $1,266,934 34

MISCELLANEOUS STATEMENT FOR THE YEAR ENDING 31ST DECEMBER, 1913.

1. Amount of Debentures maturing in 1914: Issued in Canada, $143,192.00; Issued elsewhere, none.
2. Amount of other existing obligations, which will mature in 1914: None.
3. Amount of securities held by the Corporation, which will mature and become payable to the Corporation in 1914; $212,536.90.
4. Average rate of interest per annum paid by the Corporation during 1913 on deposits: 3.52%; On debentures, 4.34%; On debenture stock, none; on both, 3.99%.
5. Average rate of interest per annum received by the Corporation during 1913:—
    (a) On mortgages of realty; (b) on other securities.
    (i) Owned beneficially by the Corporation: (a) 6.45%; (b) 5.72%.
    (ii) Not owned beneficially: (a) None; (b) 6%.
6. Of the mortgages owned beneficially by the Corporation, $1,226,943.82 is on realty situate in Ontario, and none is on realty situate elsewhere.
7. Of the mortgages not owned beneficially by the Corporation, none is on realty situate situate in Ontario, and none is on realty situate elsewhere.
8. Loans written off or transferred to real estate account during 1913, viz.:—
    (i) Funds or securities owned beneficially, $656.82 written off; $801.93 transferred to real estate on hand.
9. Number and aggregate amount of mortgages upon which compulsory proceedings have been taken by the Corporation in 1913, viz.:
    (i) Owned beneficially, No. 5; amount, $7,086.69.
    (ii) Not so owned, No., none; amount, none.
10. Aggregate market value of land mortgaged to the Corporation:—
    (i) Mortgages owned beneficially, $3,183,000.00.
    (ii) Not so owned, none.
11. How often are the securities held by the Corporation valued? Once each year.
12. (a) Specify the officers of the Corporation who are under bond and for what sum respectively. Manager, $6,000; Assistant Manager, $3,000; Teller and Accountant, $3,000; Mortgage Clerk, $2,000; Ledger Keeper, $2,000.
    (b) Are the said bonds executed by private sureties or by Guarantee Companies? First three named, Guarantee Companies; last two, private sureties.
13. Date when the accounts of the Corporation were last audited? December 10th, 1913.
14. Names and addresses of the auditors respectively for 1913 and for 1914 (if appointed):
    For 1913: Henry White and John D. Smith. After latter's death in September, Norman S. Choate was appointed.
    For 1914: Not appointed until Annual Meeting.
15. What were the dividend days of the Corporation in 1913, and what rate or rates of dividend were paid on those days respectively? January 2nd, 1913, 3½% and bonus of ½%; July 2nd, 1913, 3½% and bonus of ½%.
16. What is the date appointed for the Annual Meeting? First Tuesday in February. Date of last Annual Meeting? February 4th, 1913.
17. Special General Meetings held in 1913. Dates: None.

THE OXFORD PERMANENT LOAN AND SAVINGS SOCIETY.

Head Office, Woodstock, Ontario.

CONSTATING INSTRUMENTS.

Incorporated under the Buildings Societies Act, Consol. Stat. U.C., chapter 53, by declaration filed with the Clerk of the Peace for the County of Oxford, on the 27th October, 1865. (Decl. Book I., 25.) The original corporate name was "The Oxford Permanent Building and Savings Society."

By Order in Council of Ontario, dated 23rd September, 1878, the corporate name was changed to the Oxford Permanent Loan and Savings Society.

A by-law altering the amount of the capital stock was, pursuant to the Loan Corporations Act, approved by Order-in-Council, 27th May, 1905.

The borrowing and the lending powers are governed by the Loan and Trust Corporations Act, R.S.O. 1914, chap. 184.

ANNUAL STATEMENT

Of the condition and affairs of the Oxford Permanent Loan and Savings Society, of Woodstock, at the 31st December, 1913, and for the year ending on that day, made to the Registrar of Loan Corporations for the Province of Ontario, pursuant to the laws of the said Province.

The head office of the Corporation is at No. 388 Dundas Street, in the City of Woodstock, in the Province of Ontario.

The Board is constituted of six directors, holding office for two years.

The directors and chief executive officers of the Corporation at the 31st December, 1913 were as follows, together with their respective terms of office:

Dr. W. T. Parke, President, Woodstock;	February 22nd, 1912; February 26th, 1914
Jas. S. Scarff, Vice-Pres., Woodstock;	" "
Lieut.-Col. John White, Director, Woodstock;	" "
James White, Director, Woodstock;	February 27th, 1913; February 25th, 1915
Henry J. Finkle, Director, Woodstock;	" "
Malcolm Douglas, Managing Director,	February 22nd, 1900; February 25th, 1915

A.—Permanent capital stock: Total amount authorized, $500,000; total amount subscribed, $300,000, as more particularly set out in Schedule A hereto.

SCHEDULE A.

Class 1.—Fixed and permanent capital stock created by virtue of Building Societies Acts

Description.	Total amount issued and subsisting at 31st December, 1913.			Total amount of actual payments thereon	Total amount unpaid and constituting an asset of the Corporation.
	No. of shares.	Par value.	—		
		$	$	$	$
1. Fully called stock.....	5,466	50	273,300	273,300	....
2. Partly " "	534	50	26,700	5,340	9,550
3. Paid in advance of calls	....	....	....	11,800	....
Totals..............	6,000	....	300,000	290,440	9,550

LIST OF SHAREHOLDERS AS AT 31st DECEMBER, 1913.

(Not printed.)

BALANCE SHEET AS AT 31st DECEMBER, 1913.

Dr.   Capital and Liabilities.

Capital (Liabilities to Stockholders or Shareholders).

A.—Permanent Capital Stock or Shares.

1.	(a) Ordinary joint stock capital fully called; total called, $273,300; total paid thereon	$273,300 00	
2.	(b) Ordinary joint stock capital, 20 per cent. called; total called, $5,340; total paid thereon	5,340 00	
3.	(cc) Joint stock capital paid in advance of calls	11,800 00	
4.	(d) Dividends declared in respect of (1), (2) and (3), but not yet paid	10,361 42	
6.	(f) Reserve fund in respect of (1), (2) and (3)	111,200 00	
7.	(g) Contingent fund in respect of (1), (2) and (3)	1,000 00	$413,001 42

Liabilities to the Public.

27.	Deposits (including unclaimed deposits): Right reserved to require 30 days' notice of any withdrawal	$265,263 01	
29.	Debentures issued in Canada	245,600 15	
30.	Interest due and accrued on (29)	5,900 18	
40.	Other liabilities to the public, viz.:		
41.	(a) Sundry accounts	135 71	516,899 05
	Total liabilities		$929,900 47

Cr.   Assets.

I.—Assets of which the Corporation is the Beneficial Holder.

A.—Immovable Property owned Beneficially by Corporation.

1.	(a) Office premises situate as follows:		
2.	(i) At Woodstock, held in freehold.		$6,500 00

B.—Debts secured by Mortgages of Land.

9.	(a) Debts (other than item 10) secured by mortgages of land	$770,925 97	
10.	(b) Debts secured by mortgage land held for sale	525 11	771,451 08

C.—Debts not above enumerated for which the Corporation holds securities as follows:

14.	(b) Debts secured by municipal bonds or debentures	$18,850 34	
16.	(d) Debts secured by Loan Corporation's debentures	3,349 90	
20.	(h) Debts secured only by permanent stock or shares of the Corporation	29,282 82	
22.	(j) Debts secured by stock of other corporations	1,154 10	
23.	(k) Debts secured by debentures of other corporations	6,180 00	58,817 16

D.—Unsecured Debts.

27.	(a) Rents, office building		209 08

BALANCE SHEET.—Continued.

E.—Cash.

31. (a) On hand	$1,895 43	
32. (b) In banks	58,031 09	
		$59,926 52

F.—Assets not hereinbefore mentioned.

37. (a) Permanent stock of other corporations		32,996 63
Total assets		$929,900 47

CASH ACCOUNT.

Receipts for the year ending 31st December, 1913.

I.—Received by the Corporation for its Own Use.

A.—Balance from 31st December, 1912.

	(Col. 1.)	(Total Col. 4.)
(a) Cash (not already shown under (1)):		
2. (i) On hand	$2,525 03	
3. (ii) In bank	55,487 74	
		$58,012 77

C.—Receipts on account of Investments, Loans or Debts.

(a) On mortgages of realty:		
10. (i) Principal	$80,372 36	
11. (ii) Interest	43,374 91	
(b) On other securities:		
12. (i) Principal	6,191 69	
13. (ii) Interest or dividends	4,461 19	
		134,400 15

D.—Receipts from Real Estate Owned Beneficially by Corporation.

17. (b) Rents		431 00

F.—Borrowed Money.

26. (b) Borrowed by taking deposits	$308,976 00	
27. (c) Borrowed on debentures	90,832 03	
		399,808 03

G.—Receipts from Other Sources

30. (a) Bank interest	$1,697 05	
(b) Transfer fees	1 14	
		1,698 19
Totals		$594,350 14

CASH ACCOUNT.

Expenditure for the year ending 31st December, 1913.

I.—Expended on Corporation Account.

A.—Sums Loaned or Invested on Capital Account.

		(Col. 1.)	(Total, Col. 4.)
1. (a) Loaned on mortgages of realty......................		$67,580 80	
(b) Loaned on or invested in other securities, viz.:			
2. (i) On capital stock of this Corporation..........		8,096 87	
3. (ii) On debentures of this Corporation...........		2,339 98	
4. (iii) Stocks purchased		9,519 00	
5. (iv) Loans on other stocks and debentures........		6,002 25	
7. (e) Insurance or taxes advanced on property mortgaged to the Corporation		215 05	
			$93,753 95

B.—Expended on Stock Account.

8. Dividends paid on permanent stock		17,454 90

C.—Borrowed Money (other than foregoing) or interest thereon paid, viz.:

18. (a) Bank account, interest		$4 95	
19. (b) Deposits: Principal, $318,928.13; interest, $84.64....		319,012 77	
20. (c) Debentures issued in Canada: Principal, $88,176.55; interest, $9,772.50		97,949 05	
			416,966 77

D.—Management Expenses (other than the foregoing).

25. (a) Salaries, wages and fees		$4,912 50	
27. (c) Commission..		49 25	
28. (d) Stationery, postage, printing and advertising.......		342 74	
29. (e) Law costs		10 00	
30. (f) Fuel, rent, taxes (other than in 7 and 32) and rates.		701 65	
32. (h) Registration fees		205 00	
33. (i) Other management expenditure		26 02	
			6,247 16

E.—Other Expenditures, viz.:

34. (a) Transfer fees		84

F.—Balance.

37. (a) Cash on hand and in bank....................................		59,926 52
Total..		$594,350 14

MISCELLANEOUS STATEMENT FOR THE YEAR ENDING 31ST DECEMBER, 1913.

1. Amount of debentures maturing in 1914: Issued in Canada, $90,481.62; Issued elsewhere? None.
2. Amount of other existing obligations which will mature in 1914. None.
3. Amount of securities held by the Corporation which will mature and become payable to the Corporation in 1914. $97,253.25.
4. Average rate of interest per annum received by the Corporation during 1913: On deposits, 3.50; On debentures, 4.0661; On debenture stock, none.
5. Average rate of interest per annum received by the Corporation during 1913:
    (a) On mortgages of realty; (b) On other securities.
    (i) Owned beneficially by the Corporation: (a) 5.706%; (b) 5.87%.
    (ii) Not owned beneficially: (a) None; (b) None.

6. Of the mortgages owned beneficially by the Corporation, $771,451.08 is on realty situate in Ontario, and none is on reatly situate elsewhere.

7. Of the mortgages not owned beneficially by the Corporation, none is on realty situate in Ontario, and none is on realty situate elsewhere.

8. Loans written off or transferred to real estate account during 1913, viz.:
   (i) Funds or securities owned beneficially: None.
   (ii) Not so owned: None.

9. Number and aggregate amount of mortgages upon which compulsory proceedings have been taken by the Corporation in 1913, viz.:
   (i) Owned beneficially, No. 1; amount $2,986.33.
   (ii) Not so owned, No., none; amount, none.

10. Aggregate market value of land mortgaged to the Corporation:
   (i) Mortgages owned beneficially, $1,022,825.00.
   (ii) Not so owned, none.

11. How often are the securities owned by the Corporation valued? Half-yearly by the Manager; yearly by the Directors.

12. (a) Specify the officers of the Corporation who are under bond and for what sum respectively. Treasurer for $10,000 and Book Keeper for $2,000.
   (b) Are the said bonds executed by private sureties or by Guarantee Companies? By Guarantee Company.

13. Date when the accounts of the Corporation were last audited? As at 31st December, 1913.

14. Names and addresses of the auditors respectively for 1913 and for 1914 (if appointed):
   For 1913: W. H. Ingram and James Campbell.
   For 1914: Not yet appointed.

15. What were the dividend days of the Corporation in 1913, and what rate or rates of dividend were paid on those days respectively? Second days of January and July. Six per cent. per annum.

16. What is the date appointed for the Annual Meeting? Fourth Thursday in February. Date of last Annual Meeting? February 27th, 1913.

17. Special General Meetings held in 1913. Dates: None.

THE LONDON AND CANADIAN LOAN AND AGENCY COMPANY.

Head Office, Toronto, Ontario.

CONSTATING INSTRUMENTS.

1863. The Company was incorporated in 1863 by Special Act of the Province of Canada, 27 V., c. 50, which has from time to time been amended by six special Acts of the Dominion of Canada, viz.:

1872. 35 V., c. 108 (D).
1873. 36 V., c. 107 (D).
1876. 39 V., c. 60 (D).
1879. 42 V., c. 75 (D).
1889. 52 V., c. 93 (D).
1891. 54-5 V., c. 114 (D).

For the lending powers of the Company see 27 V. (1863), c. 50 (Province of Canada), secs. 3 and 4; 35 V. (1872), c. 108 (D), sec. 5; also sec. 6 as amended by 36 V. (1873), c. 107 (D), sec. 8; 36 V. (1873), c. 107 (D), sec. 9, and 35 V. (1872), c. 108 (D), sec. 7 as amended by 36 V. (1873), c. 107 (D), s. 10. See Statutes of Canada, 1899, 62 V., c. 117.

For the borrowing powers of the Company see 27 V. (1863), c. 50, (Province of Canada), s. 5, as amended by 36 V. (1873), c. 107 (D), sec. 1; 35 V. (1872), c. 108 (D), s. 8, as amended by 39 V. (1873), c. 50 (D), sec. 1; 54-5 V. (1891), c. 114 (D), s. 2. (Issue of debenture stock.)

ANNUAL STATEMENT

Of the condition and affairs of The London and Canadian Loan and Agency Company (Ltd.), of Toronto, Ont., at the 31st December, 1913, and for the year ending on that day, made to the Registrar of Loan Corporations for the Province of Ontario, pursuant to the laws of the said Province.

The head office of the Corporation is at No. 51 Yonge Street, in the City of Toronto, in the Province of Ontario.

The Board is constituted of eight directors, holding office for one year.

The directors and chief executive officers of the Corporation as at the 31st December, 1913, were as follows, together with their respective terms of office:

Thomas Long, President, Toronto; 5th February, 1913; 11th February, 1914.
Casimir S. Gzowski, Vice-President, Toronto; " "
Rt. Hon. Lord Strathcona and Mount Royal,
 G.C.M.G., Director, Montreal;
A. H. Campbell, Director, Toronto;
Charles C. Dalton, Director, Toronto;
David B. Hanna, Director, Toronto;
Goldwin Larrat Smith, Director, Toronto;
Vernon B. Wadsworth, Manager, Toronto.
William Wedd, Jr., Secretary, Toronto.

A.—Permanent Capital Stock: Total amount authorized, $2,000,000; total amount subscribed, $1,250,000, as more particularly set out in Schedule A hereto.

Class 2.—Fixed and permanent capital stock created by virtue of Private Acts.
Last call made: Date, 2nd January, 1914; rate per cent., 20 per cent.; gross amount.
$50,000; amount paid thereon, all paid at end of year except $6,240, which was paid
in full when instalment matured, January, 1914.

Description.	No. of shares.	Par value.	Total amount held.	Total amount paid thereon.	Total remaining unpaid on calls.
		$	$	$	
Fully called	25,000	50	1,250,000	1,243,760	6,240 00 as of 31st Dec., 1913

LIST OF SHAREHOLDERS AS AT 31st DECEMBER, 1913.

(Not printed.)

BALANCE SHEET AS AT 31st DECEMBER, 1913.

Dr.   Capital and Liabilities.

Capital (Liabilities to Stockholders or Shareholders).

A.—Permanent Capital Stock or Shares.

1. (a) Ordinary joint stock capital fully called; total called, $1,250,000; total paid thereon	$1,243,760 00	
4. (d) Dividends declared in respect of (1)................	24,857 60	
5. (e) Unappropriated profits in respect of (1)	17,828 84	
6. (f) Reserve fund in respect of (1)	565,000 00	
		$1,851,446 44

Liabilities to the Public.

29. Debentures issued and payable in Canada.............	$5,533 33	
30. Interest due or accrued on (29)......................	118 35	
31. Debentures issued in Canada, payable elsewhere........	2,571,011 33	
32. Interest due or accrued on (31)......................	48,626 00	
35. Debenture stock issued in Canada, payable elsewhere....	440,482 02	
36. Interest due and accrued on (35)....................	2,343 00	
37. Owing to banks (including interest due or accrued).....	17,845 70	
40. Other liabilities to the public, viz.:		
41. (a) Sterling-certificates, payable at fixed dates.........	93,841 84	
42. (b) Interest due and accrued on 41 (a)	1,953 00	
43. (c) Currency certificates: Payable at fixed dates; interest due and accrued on same.....................	15,190 00	
Sundry creditors	6,398 61	
		3,203,343 18

Contingent liabilities (not extended), $75,295.11.

Total actual liabilities $5,054,789 62

Cr.   Assets.

I.—Assets of which the Corporation is the Beneficial Holder.

A.—Immovable Property Owned Beneficially by Corporation.

BALANCE SHEET.—Continued.

B.—Debts secured by Mortgages of Land.

9. (a) Debts (other than item 10) secured by mortgages on land $4,580,087 59		
10. (b) Debts secured by mortgaged land held for sale....	4,398 99	
(bb) Debts secured by land held by the Company as mortgagee in possession, or secured by land for the rents and profits of which the Company is accountable	7,312 82	
11. (c) Interest due and accrued on items 9 and 10 and not included therein	177,472 79	
		$4,769,272 19

C.—Debts not above enumerated for which the Corporation holds securities as follows:

22. (j) Municipal bonds or debentures owned by Company..	$174,101 39	
23. (k) School debentures owned by Company	16,918 67	
25. (m) Debts secured by hypothecation of stocks, etc......	2,984 90	
26. (n) Interest due or accrued on items 22 to 25 and not included therein	5,276 69	
		199,281 65

E.—Cash.

32. (b) In banks in Canada	86,235 78
Contingent assets (not extended), $75,295.11.	
Total assets	$5,054,789 62

CASH ACCOUNT.

Receipts for the year ending 31st December, 1913.

I.—Received by the Corporation for Its Own Use.

A.—Balances from 31st December, 1912.

2. (b) Cash (not already shown under (1)):—	(Total, Col. 4.)
3. (ii) In banks	$8,932 28

B.—Sums Received Wholly or Partly on Capital Stock.

4. (a) Calls on Joint Stock Permanent Capital: Payments on new stock allotted	243,760 00
5. (b) Profits on unallotted stock subsequently sold.....................	4,253 62

C.—Receipts on account of Investments, Loans or Debts.

(a) On mortgages of realty:—

10. (i) Principal	555,808 72
11. (ii) Interest	342,774 01

(b) On other securities:—

12. (i) Principal	66,272 70
13. (ii) Interest or dividends	8,270 91

F.—Borrowed Money.

27. (c) Borrowed on debentures or certificates at fixed dates............	$381,103 00

CASH ACCOUNT.—Continued.

Receipts for the year ending 31st December, 1913.

G.—Receipts from other sources.

30. (a) Sundry accounts 4,981 94

Total **$1,616,157 18**

II.—Received as a Corporate Trustee Representative Guardian or Agent in Trust.

A.—Balance from 31st December, 1912.

32.   (i) On hand 1,651 83
34. (a) On mortgages: Principal, $5,357.69; Interest, $6,029.35.......... 11,387 04

Totals **$13,038 87**

CASH ACCOUNT.

Expenditure for the year ending 31st December, 1913.

I.—Expended on Corporation Account.

A.—Sums Loaned or Invested on Capital Account.

(Total Col. 4.)

1. (a) Loaned on mortgages of realty $683,246 57
   (b) Loaned or invested in other securities, viz.:
2.   (i) Loans on stocks, bonds, etc. 59,118 50

B.—Expended on Stock Account.

8. Dividends paid on permanent stock (including amount reserved in 1912) 79,721 52

C.—Borrowed Money (other than foregoing) or interest thereon paid, viz.:

18. (a) Bank account (interest) 21,107 54
20. (c) Debentures, etc., issued and payable in Canada: Principal...... 143,385 50
21. (d) Debentures, etc., issued in Canada, payable elsewhere: Principal, $333,246.74; Interest on debentures, debenture stock, etc., $136,348.65 . . . . 469,595 39
23. (f) Debenture stock issued in Canada and payable elsewhere: Principal 26,766 66

D.—Management Expenses (other than foregoing).

25. (a) Salaries, directors' fees, etc., Ontario, Manitoba and Saskatchewan $26,636 96
26. (b) Commission on debentures issued and renewed, and loans made and renewed, etc. 5,034 53
27. (c) Agency charges, British directors' fees, etc.......... 2,144 83
28. (d) Stationery, postage, printing, advertising, etc...... 4,373 99
29. (e) Law costs 275 26
30. (f) Fuel, rent, taxes (other than on 7 and 32), rates, etc. 5,736 63
31. (g) Travelling expenses, inspection, etc. 624 35
32. (h) Registration fees Loan Corporations Act, Ontario... 205 00
33. (i) Other management expenditure, Auditors' fees...... 1,050 00

46,081 55

E.—Other Expenditures, viz.:

34. (a) Tax on capital (Ontario) and business tax (Toronto).......... 898 17

CASH ACCOUNT.—Continued.

Expenditure for the year ending 31st December, 1913.

F.—Balance.

37. Cash in various banks in Canada 86,235 78

   Total $1,616,157 18

II.—Expended on Trust or Agency Account.

B.—Other Expenditures.

50. (a) Commission or remuneration paid for management of estate,
       trust or agency (including item 26)......................... $675 25
53. (d) Remitted or paid over to various estates 6,597 01

C.—Balance.

54. (a) Cash on hand 5,766 61

   Total $13,038 87

MISCELLANEOUS STATEMENT FOR THE YEAR ENDING 31ST DECEMBER, 1913.

1. Amount of Debentures, etc., maturing in 1914: Issued and payable in Canada,
   $17,623; Issued in Canada, payable elsewhere, $520,918.
2. Amount of other existing obligations which will mature in 1914, none.
3. Amount of securities held by the Corporation which will mature and become payable
   to the Corporation in 1914, $697,025.
4. Average rate of interest per annum paid by the Corporation during 1913: On
   deposits, no deposits taken; on debentures, 4¼%; on debenture stock, 4%.
5. Average rate of interest per annum received by the Corporation during 1913:
   (a) On mortgages of realty; (b) On other securities.
   (i) Owned beneficially by the Corporation: (a) About 7½%; (b) About 5%.
   (ii) Not owned beneficially: (a) About 7½%; (b) None.
6. Of the mortgages owned beneficially by the Corporation, $1,163,172 is on realty
   situate in Ontario, and $3,428,627 is on realty situate elsewhere.
7. Of the mortgages not owned beneficially by the Corporation, $11,111 is on realty
   situate in Ontario, and $63,184 is on realty situate elsewhere.
8. Loans written off or transferred to real estate account during 1913, viz.: (i) Funds
   or securities owned beneficially, none; (ii) Not so owned, none.
9. Number and aggregate amount of mortgages upon which compulsory proceedings
   have been taken by the Corporation in 1913 ,viz.:
   (i) Owned beneficially: Number, 1; Amount, $500.
   (ii) Not so owned: Number, none; Amount, none.
10. Aggregate market value of land mortgaged to the Corporation:
   (i) Mortgages owned beneficially, about $9,000,000.
   (ii) Not so owned, about $160,000.
11. How often are the securities held by the Corporation valued? Yearly or oftener, as
   required.
12. (a) Specify the officers of the Corporation who are under bond and for what sum
       respectively: All officers of the Company and solicitors and inspectors in
       the Northwest, $61,000.
   (b) Are the said bonds executed by private sureties or by Guarantee Companies?
       Guarantee Companies.
13. Date when the accounts of the Corporation were last audited? Accounts audited
   monthly. Last full yearly audit, 31st December, 1913.
14. Names and addresses of the auditors respectively for 1913 and for 1914 (if
   appointed):
   For 1913: G. H. G. McVity, Toronto; James George, F.C.A., Toronto, Canada.
   For 1914: Not yet appointed.
15. What were the dividend days of the Corporation in 1913, and what rate or rates of
   dividend were paid on those days respectively? January 2nd, April 1st,
July 2nd and October 1st; 1¾% per quarter.
16. What is the date appointed for the Annual Meeting? 11th February, 1914. Date of
   last Annual Meeting? 5th February, 1913.
17. Special General Meetings held in 1913: Dates, none.

THE PEOPLE'S LOAN AND SAVINGS CORPORATION.

Head Office, London, Ont.

Incorporated under The Building Societies Act, R.S.O., 1887, c. 169, by declaration filed with the Clerk of the Peace for the County of Middlesex, on 22nd June, 1892. (Decl. Book I., 75.)

The lending and borrowing powers are governed by The Loan and Trust Corporations Act, R.S.O. 1914, chap. 184.

ANNUAL STATEMENT

Of the condition and affairs of The People's Loan and Savings Corporation, at 31st December, 1913, and for the year ending on that day, made to the Registrar of Loan Corporations for the Province of Ontario, pursuant to the laws of the said Province.

The head office of the Corporation is at 428 Richmond Street, in the City of London, in the Province of Ontario.

The Board is constituted of seven directors, holding office for one year.

The directors and chief executive officers of the Corporation at the 31st December, 1913, were as follows, together with their respective terms of office:

W. F. Roome, M.D., President, London, Ont.;   March 5th, 1913; March 4th, 1914.
A. A. Campbell, Vice-President, London, Ont.;
W. H. Moorehouse, M.D., Director, London, Ont.;   "   "
Wm. Spittal, Director, London, Ont.;
Malcolm McGugan, Director, Hendrick, Ont.;
Fred G. Rumball, Director, London;
A. W. Pune, Director, Hamilton;
A. A. Campbell, Managing-Director, London, Ont.;   "
Wm. Spittal, Secretary-Treasurer, London, Ont.;

A.—Capital stock: Total amount authorised, $5,000,000; total amount subscribed permanent stock, $500,000.00, as more particularly set out in Schedule A hereto.

SCHEDULE A.

Class 1.—Fixed and Permanent Capital Stock created by virtue of Building Society Acts.

Description.	Total amount issued and subsisting at 31st December, 1913.			Total amount of actual payments thereon.	Total amount unpaid and constituting an asset of the Corporation.
	No. of shares.	Par value of shares.	—		
		$	$	$ c.	$ c.
1. Fully called..................	4,136	100	413,600	413,600 00	....
3. Instalment stock (payable by fixed periodical payments and still in process of payment)	864	100	86,400	24,637 63	61,762 37
Totals..............	5,000	....	500,000	438,237 63	61,762 37

BALANCE SHEET AS AT 31st DECEMBER, 1913.

Dr.   Capital and Liabilities.

Capital (Liabilities to Stockholders or Shareholders).

A.—Permanent Capital Stock or Shares.

1. (a) Ordinary joint stock capital fully called: Total called, $500,000.00; total paid thereon	$438,237 63	
6. (f) Reserve fund in respect of (1)	41,000 00	
		$479,237 63

Liabilities to the Public.

27. Deposits (right reserved to require 30 days' notice of any withdrawal)	$198,824 57	
29. Debentures issued in Canada	61,382 87	
		260,207 44
Total liabilities		$739,445 07

Cr.   Assets.

I.—Assets of which the Corporation is the Beneficial Owner.

A.—Immovable Property Owned Beneficially by Corporation.

1. (a) Office premises situate as follows:		
2. (1) London, held in freehold		$34,000 00

B.—Debts secured by Mortgages of Land.

9. (a) Debts (other than item 10) secured by mortgages of land	....	$669,970 77

C.—Debts not above enumerated for which the Corporation holds securities as follows:

22. (j) Debts secured by Trust Company's stock...........	$2,450 00	
24. (l) Agents' balances	398 41	
		2,848 41

D.—Unsecured Debts and other Assets.

27. (a) Office furniture	$1,700 00	
28. (b) Accrued rent	136 00	
29. (c) Auxiliary safes	208 00	
		2,044 00

E.—Cash.

32. (b) In bank in Canada .. .:	$30,392 10	
35. In bank in London, England	189 79	
		30,581 89
Total assets		$739,445 07

CASH ACCOUNT.

Receipts for the year ending 31st December, 1913.

	(Col. 1.)	(Col. 2.)	(Col. 3.)	(Total Col. 4.)
I.—Received by the Corporation for its Own Use.				
A.—Balance from 31st December, 1912.				
3. (ii) In bank	....	....	....	$11,960 90
B.—Sums received wholly or partly on Capital Stock.				
4. (a) Calls on joint stock permanent capital	....	....	$19,956 06	
5. (b) Premiums on (4)	....	....	257 00	
				20,213 06
C.—Receipts on account of Investments, Loans or Debts.				
(a) On Mortgages of realty:—				
10. .(i) Principal	....	....	146,625 50	
11. (ii) Interest	....	....	46,663 06	
(b) On other securities:—				
12. (i) P r i n c i p a l (School Bonds)	....	....	200 00	
13. Suspense account	....	....	60 00	
(c) Unsecured Debts.				
14. (i) P r i n c i p a l (Real Estate)	....	....	1,900 00	
				195,448 56
D.—Receipts from Real Estate owned beneficially by Corporation.				
17. (b) Rent of head office building.	....	....	....	1,832 00
E.—Miscellaneous.				
19. (b) Premiums or bonus on loans	....	....	....	1,155 95
F.—Borrowed Money.				
26. (b) Borrowed by taking deposits	$640,966 28			
27. (c) Borrowed on debentures....	15,112 06			
				656,078 34
Total				$886,688 81

CASH ACCOUNT.

Expenditure for the year ending 31st December, 1913.

	(Col. 1.)	(Col. 2.)	(Col. 3.)	(Total Col. 4.)
I.—Expended on Corporation Account.				
A.—Sums Loaned or Invested on Capital Account.				
1. (a) Loaned on mortgages of realty	....	....	$145,132 00	
3. (ii) Trust company	....	....	1,000 00	
6. (c) Real estate purchased, written off real estate........	....	....	650 00	
				$146,782 00

CASH ACCOUNT.—Continued.

Expenditure for the year ending 31st December, 1913.

B.—Expended on Stock Account.

8. Dividends paid on permanent stock	....	....	....	$25,887 72

C.—Borrowed Money.

18. (a) Bank account (interest)...	$4,304 70	....	....	4,304 70
19. (b) Deposits: Principal, $642,-347.55; interest, $6,369.71	....	....	....	648,717 26
20. (c) Debentures issued in Canada; Principal, $15,268.30; interest, $2,795.57	....	....	....	18,063 87

D.—Management Expenses (other than foregoing).

25. (a) Salaries, wages, and fees...	4,901 90			
26. (b) Commission or brokerage..	4,400 72			
28 (d) Stationery, postage, printing and advertising	956 74			
29. (e) Law costs	136 45			
30. (f) Fuel, rent, taxes (other than in 7 and 32) and rates	1,024 99			
31. (g) Travelling expenses	21 95			
32. (h) Registration fees	352 35			
Other management expenses: Accrued rent, $81.00; Office furniture, $50.00	131 00	....	....	11,926 10

E.—Other Expenditures, viz.:

34. (a) Insurance	$274 50			
35. (b) Office expenses	86 48			
36. (c) Bank Commission	64 29	....	....	425 27

F.—Balance.

37. (a) Cash on hand and in banks.	....	....	....	30,581 89
Total	....	....	....	$886,688 81

MISCELLANEOUS STATEMENT FOR THE YEAR ENDING 31ST DECEMBER, 1913.

1. Amount of debentures maturing in 1914: Issued in Canada, $7,900.00; Issued elsewhere, none.
2. Amount of other existing obligations which will mature in 1914: None.
3. Amount of securities held by the Corporation which will mature and become payable to the Corporation in 1914, $117,900.00.
4. Average rate of interest per annum paid by the Corporation during 1913: On deposits, 3.72%; on debentures, 4.70%; on debenture stock, none.
5. Average rate of interest per annum received by the Corporation during 1913:
   (a) On mortgages of realty; (b) On other securities.
   (i) Owned beneficially by the Corporation: (a) 7.73%; (b) 7.25%.
   (ii) Not owned beneficially: (a) None; (b) None.

12 L.C.

6. Of the mortgages owned beneficially by the Corporation, all owned is on realty situate in Ontario, and none is on realty situate elsewhere.

7. Of the mortgages not owned beneficially by the Corporation, none is on realty in Ontario, and none is on realty situate elsewhere.

8. Loans written off or transferred to real estate account during 1913, viz.:
    (i) Funds or securities owned beneficially, none.
    (ii) Not so owned, none.

9. Number and aggregate amount of mortgages upon which compulsory proceedings have been taken by the Corporation in 1913, viz.:
    (i) Owned beneficially: No, none; Amount, none.
    (ii) Not so owned: No, none; Amount, none.

10. Aggregate market value of land mortgaged to the Corporation:
    (i) Mortgages owned beneficially, $1,473,900.00.
    (ii) Not so owned, none.

11. How often are the securities held by the Corporation valued? Yearly.

12. (a) Specify the officers of the Corporation who are under bond and for what sum respectively: Secretary-Treasurer, $5,000.00; Managing Director, $5,000.00; Accountant, $2,000.00.
    (b) Are the said bonds executed by private sureties or by Guarantee Companies? Guarantee Companies.

13. Date when the accounts of the Corporation were last audited: January 31st, 1914.

14. Names and addresses of the auditors respectively for 1913 and for 1914 (if appointed):
    For 1913: Major Geo. W. Hayes and O. H. Talbot.
    For 1914: To be appointed.

15. What were the dividend days of the Corporation in 1913, and what rate or rates of dividend were paid on those days respectively? June 30th and Dec. 31st; rate, 6% per annum.

16. What is the date appointed for the Annual Meeting? March 4th, 1914. Date of last Annual Meeting? March 5th, 1913.

17. Special General Meetings held in 1913: Dates, none.

THE REAL ESTATE LOAN COMPANY OF CANADA, LIMITED.

Head Office, Toronto, Ontario.

CONSTATING INSTRUMENTS

Incorporated under the Building Society's Act (R.S.O. 1877, c. 164), by declaration filed with the Clerk of the Peace for the County of York, 17th September, 1879, with the corporate name of the Real Estate Loan and Debenture Company.—Decl. Book II, p. 57.

Letters Patent of Canada (6th April, 1883) incorporating the Company under the Canada Joint Stock Companies Act, 1877, with the corporate name of the Real Estate Loan Company of Canada, Limited.—Lib. 85, folio 282, Office of the Registrar-General of Canada. The capital authorized by this instrument was $2,000,000, being the capital of the said the Real Estate Loan and Debenture Company, with the same powers throughout Canada as now possessed by the said the Real Estate Loan and Debenture Company, and for the same purposes and objects, subject always to the provisions of the said last mentioned Act (Canada J. S. Co.'s Act, 1877), and with all such further powers, purposes and objects as are conferred upon Loan Companies incorporated under the provisions of the said last mentioned Act.

1884. Act of the Dominion of Canada, 47 V., c. 101 (D), respecting sales of assets. Supplementary Letters Patent of Canada, 20th June, 1892, reciting By-law No. 62 of the Company, and (as therein provided), reducing the capital stock from $2,000,000 to $1,600,000.

1913. Act of the Dominion of Canada, 3-4 George V c. 184, increasing capital stock to $2,000,000 in shares of $100 each par value.

ANNUAL STATEMENT

Of the condition and affairs of the Real Estate Loan Company of Canada (Limited), at the 31st December, 1913, and for the year ending on that day, made to the Registrar of Loan Corporations for the Province of Ontario, pursuant to the laws of the said Province.

The head office of the Corporation is at No. 2 Toronto Street, in the City of Toronto, in the Province of Ontario.

The Board is constituted of five directors, holding office for one year.

The directors and chief executive officers of the Corporation at the 31st December, 1913, were as follows, together with their respective terms of office:

M. H. Aikens, M.P., Pres., Burnhamthorpe;   5th Feb., 1913; 11th Feb., 1914.
E. Douglas Armour, K.C., Vice-Pres., Toronto;   "   "
G. M. Rae, Director, Toronto;   "   "
Edmund Wragge, Director, Toronto;   "   "
Wm. A. Cooke, Director, Toronto;
E. L. Morton, Manager, Toronto.

A.—Permanent capital stock: Total amount authorized, $2,000,000; total amount subscribed, $500,000, as more particularly set out in Schedule A hereto.

Schedule A.

Schedule A.

Class 2.—Fixed and permanent capital stock created by virtue of Joint Stock Companies Act or Private Acts.

Description.	No. of shares.	Par value.	Total amount held.	Total amount of actual payments thereon.	Total amount unpaid and constituting an asset of the Corporation.
		$	$	$ c.	$ c.
1. Fully called stock......	5,000	100	500,000	500,000 00	....
Totals ...:	5,000	....	500,000	500,000 00	....

LIST OF SHAREHOLDERS AS AT 31st DECEMBER, 1913.

(Not printed.)

BALANCE SHEET AS AT 31st DECEMBER, 1913.

Capital and Liabilities.

Capital (Liabilities to Stockholders or Shareholders).

A.—Permanent Capital Stock or Shares.

1. (a) Ordinary joint stock capital fully called; total called, $500,000; total paid thereon	$500,000 00	
4. (d) Dividends declared in respect of (1), but not yet paid	17,536 60	
5. (e) Unappropriated profits in respect of (1)	4,492 01	
6. (f) Reserve fund in respect of (1)	170,000 00	
7. (g) Contingent fund in respect of (1).................	10,000 00	
		702,028 61

Liabilities to the Public

27. Unclaimed deposits	$257 33	
29. Debentures issued in Canada	39,933 50	
30. Interest due and accrued on (29)	472 00	
31. Debentures issued elsewhere than in Canada	607,867 76	
32. Interest due and accrued on (31)	3,834 45	
		652,365 04

Total liabilities **$1,354,393 65**

Cr.   Assets.

I.—Assets of which the Corporation is the Beneficial Owner.

B.—Debts secured by Mortgages of Land.

9. (a) Debts (other than item 10) secured by mortgages of land $1,307,961 18		
10. (b) Debts secured by mortgaged land held for sale	978 06	
		$1,308,939 24

BALANCE SHEET.—Continued.

C.—Debts not above enumerated for which the Corporation holds securities as follows:

15. (c) Public School debentures owned by Company	$20,150 90	
20. (h) Debts secured only by permanent stock or shares of the Corporation	636 84	
21. (j) Debts secured only by stock loans................	900 00	
		$21,687 74

B.—Unsecured Debts.

27. (a) Agents' balances	....	22 73

E.—Cash.

32. (b) In banks	....	23,743 94
Total assets		$1,354,393 65

CASH ACCOUNT.

Receipts for the year ending 31st December, 1913.

I.—Received by the Corporation for its Own Use.

A.—Balance from 31st December, 1912.

	(Col. 1.)	(Col. 3.)	(Total Col. 4.)
(b) Cash not already shown under (1):			
3. (ii) In bank	....	....	$46,444 65

C.—Receipts on account of Investments, Loans, or Debts.

	(Col. 1.)	(Col. 3.)	(Total Col. 4.)
(a) Mortgages of realty:			
10. (i) Principal	....	....	119,790 39
11. (ii) Interest	$93,920 55	....	93,920 55
(b) On other Securities:			
12. (i) Principal	....	....	15,410 00
13. (ii) Interest or Dividends	1,784 14	....	1,784 14

F.—Borrowed Money.

	(Col. 1.)	(Col. 3.)	(Total Col. 4.)
27. (c) Borrowed on debentures	....	....	71,035 24

G.—Receipts from other sources, viz.:

	(Col. 1.)	(Col. 3.)	(Total Col. 4.)
30. (a) Unclaimed dividends outstanding	....	....	32 76
(b) Bank interest	116 31	....	116 31
Total			$348,534 04

CASH ACCOUNT.

Expenditure for the year ending 31st December, 1913.

	(Col. 1.)	(Col. 3.)	(Total Col. 4.)
I.—Expended on Corporation Account.			
1. (a) Loaned on mortgages of realty	....	....	$190,660 11

CASH ACCOUNT.—Continued.

Expenditure for the year ending 31st December, 1913.

B.—Expended on Stock Account.

8. Dividends paid on permanent stock........	$35,183 53	....	35,183 53

C.—Borrowed Money (other than foregoing) or interest thereon paid, viz.:

18. (a) Bank account (principal and interest) ..	....	....	12,888 15
20. (c) Debentures issued in Canada: Principal, $15,525.00; interest, $1,867.59......	....	....	17,392 59
21. (d) Debentures issued elsewhere: Principal, $27,561.56; interest, $26,576.15	....	....	54,137 71

D.—Management Expenses (other than foregoing):

25. (a) Salaries, wages and fees	$7,757 49	....	....
26. (b) Commission or brokerage	1,546 71	....	....
27. (c) Advances to Agents	22 73	....	....
28. (d) Stationery, postage, printing and advertising, telegrams and telephone	367 04	....	....
29. (e) Law costs	53 34	....	....
30. (f) Fuel, rent, taxes (other than in 7 and 32) and rates	702 20	....	....
32. (h) Registration fees	938 81	....	....
33. (i) Other management expenditure	600 32	....	....
		....	11,987 64

E.—Other Expenditures, viz.:

34. (a) Paid on Stock Expenses of conversion..	$60 00	....	....
35 (b) Expenses of Legislation	1,280 37	....	....
36. (c) Vote at Annual Meeting to President and Vice-President	1,200 00	....	....
		....	2,540 37

F.—Balance.

37. (a) Cash in banks	....	....	23,743 94
Total	....	....	$348,534 04

MISCELLANEOUS STATEMENT FOR THE YEAR ENDING 31ST DECEMBER, 1913.

---

1. Amount of debentures maturing in 1914: Issued in Canada, $14,283.50; Issued elsewhere, $71,671.85.
2. Amount of other existing obligations which will mature in 1914, none.
3. Amount of securities held by the Corporation which will mature and become payable to the Corporation in 1914, $106,085.00.
4. Average rate of interest per annum paid by the Corporation during 1913: On deposits, none; on debentures, 4.53%; on debenture stock, none.
5. Average rate of interest per annum received by the Corporation during 1913:
    (a) On mortgages of realty; (b) On other securities;
    (i) Owned beneficially by the Corporation: (a) 7.88%; (b) 5.96%.
    (ii) Not owned beneficially: (a) None; (b) None.
6. Of the mortgages owned beneficially by the Corporation, $165,696 is on realty situate in Ontario, and $1,142,265 is on realty situate elsewhere.
7. Of the mortgages not owned beneficially by the Corporation, none is on realty situate in Ontario, and none is on realty situate elsewhere.

8. Loans written off or transferred to real estate account during 1913, viz.:
    (i) Funds or securities owned beneficially, $978.06;
    (ii) Not so owned, none.
9. Number and aggregate amount of mortgages upon which compulsory proceedings
    . have been taken by the Corporation in 1913, viz.:
    (i) Owned beneficially, No., 1; amount, $978.06;
    (ii) Not so owned, No., none; amount, none.
10. Aggregate market value of land mortgaged to the Corporation:
    (i) Mortgages owned beneficially, $2,500,000 at least;
    (ii) Not so owned, none.
11. How often are the securities held by the Corporation valued? Each year.
12. (a) Specify the officers of the Corporation who are under bond and for what sum
            respectively: Manager and Agents at Winnipeg and Edmonton, $5,000 each;
    (b) Are the said bonds executed by private sureties or by Guarantee Companies?
            Guarantee Company.
13. Date when the accounts of the Corporation were last audited? 22nd January, 1914.
14. Names and addresses of the auditors respectively for 1913, and for 1914 (if ap-
        pointed):
        For 1913: S. W. Black and H. D. Lockhart Gordon (elected).
        For 1914: S. W. Black and H. D. Lockhart Gordon (elected).
15. What were the dividend days of the Corporation in 1913, and what rate or rates of
        dividend were paid on those days respectively? 2nd January and 2nd July,
        1913; 3½% each.
16. What is the date appointed for the Annual Meeting? 11th February, 1914. Date of
        last Annual Meeting? 5th February, 1913.
17. Special General Meetings held in 1913: Dates, none.

THE ROYAL LOAN AND SAVINGS COMPANY.

Head Office Brantford, Ontario.

CONSTATING INSTRUMENTS.

Incorporated under the Building Societies Act (Consol. Stat. U. C., chap. 53), by declaration filed with the Clerk of the Peace for the County of Brant, on the 24th March, 1876 (Decl. Book 1, 3.)

The lending and the borrowing powers are governed by the Loan and Trust Corporations Act, R.S.O., 1914, Chap. 184.

ANNUAL STATEMENT

Of the condition and affairs of the Royal Loan and Savings Company of Brantford, Ontario, at the 31st December, 1913, and for the year ending on that day, made to the Registrar of Loan Corporations for the Province of Ontario, pursuant to the laws of the said Province.

The head office of the Corporation is at 38.40 Market Street, in the City of Brantford, in the Province of Ontario.

The Board is constituted of six directors holding office for one year.

The directors and chief executive officers of the Corporation at the 31st December, 1913 were as follows, together with their respective terms of office:

Christopher Cook, President, Brantford;   February, 1913.   February, 1914.
Charles B. Heyd, Vice-President, Brantford;   "   "
John Mann, Director, Brantford;   "   "
A. J. Wilkes, K.C., Director, Brantford;
A. K. Bunnell, C.A., Director, Brantford;
Franklin Grobb, Director, Brantford;
W. G. Helliker, Manager, Brantford;

A. Permanent capital stock; total amount authorized, $1,000,000.00; total amount subscribed, $581,700.00, as more particularly set out in Schedule A hereto.

SCHEDULE A.

Class 1.—Fixed and permanent capital stock created by virtue of Building Society Acts.

Description.	Total amount issued and subsisting at 31st December, 1913.			Total amount of actual payments thereon.	Total amount unpaid and constituting an asset of the Corporation.
	No. of shares.	Par value of shares.			
1. Fully called stock.....	11,634	$ 50	$ 581,700	$ c. 581,700 00	$ c. ....

LIST OF SHAREHOLDERS AS AT 31st DECEMBER, 1913.

(Not printed.)

BALANCE SHEET AS AT 31st DECEMBER, 1913.

Dr.   Capital and Liabilities.

Capital (Liabilities to Stock holders or Shareholders).

A.—Permanent Capital Stock or Shares.

1. (a) Ordinary joint stock capital fully called; total called, $581,700; total paid thereon	$581,700 00	
4. (d) Dividends declared in respect of (1), but not yet paid	10,180 03	
6. (f) Reserve fund in respect of (1)	350,000 00	
		$941,880 03

Liabilities to the Public.

27. Deposits, right reserved to require 30 days' notice of any withdrawal	$368,470 27	
28. Interest on deposits, due or accrued or capitalized	1,060 42	
29. Debentures issued in Canada	1,016,769 62	
30. Interest due and accrued on (29)	17,990 45	
41. Other liabilities to the public:		
42. (a) Sundry accounts	280 74	
43. (b) Balance carried to Profit and Loss	834 06	
		1,405,405 56
Total liabilities		$2,347,285 59

Cr.   Assets.

I. Assets of which the Corporation is the Beneficial Owner.

A.—Immovable Property Owned Beneficially by Corporation.

1. (a) Office premises situate as follows: (1) At Brantford (held in freehold)		$55,000 00

B.—Debts secured by Mortgages of Land.

9. (a) Debts (other than item 10) secured by mortgages of land	$1,635,918 77	
10. (b) Debts secured by mortgaged land held for sale	6,540 45	
11. (c) Interest due or accrued on items (9) and (10) and not included therein	70,446 48	
		1,712 905 70

C.—Debts not above enumerated for which the Corporation holds securities, as follows:

14. (b) Debts secured by municipal bonds or debentures	$75,750 00	
20. (h) Debts secured only by permanent stock or shares of the Corporation	30,699 23	
23. (k) Loans on stocks and debentures	88,947 40	
25. (m) Stocks owned by company	319,013 50	
		514,410 13

D.—Unsecured Debts.

27. (a) Rents accrued		127 77

E.—Cash.

31. (a) On hand	$4,212 28	
32. (b) In banks	60,629 71	
		64,841 99
Total assets		$2,347,285 59

CASH ACCOUNT.

Receipts for the year ending 31st December, 1913.

I.—Received by the Corporation for its Own Use.

A.—Balance from 31st December, 1912.

		(Total, Col. 4.)
2.	(i) on Hand	$4,886 02
3	(ii) In bank	42,521 95

B. Sums Received Wholly or Partly on Capital Stock.

4.	(a) Calls on joint stock permanent capital	1,100 00
5.	(b) Premiums on (4)	275 00

C.—Receipts on account of Investments, Loans or Debts.

	(a) On mortgages of realty:	
10.	(i) Principal	212,739 19
11.	(ii) Interest	115,189 84
	(b) On other securities:	
12.	(i) Principal	83,910 00
13.	(ii) Interest or dividends	26,623 27

D.—Receipts from Real Estate Owned Beneficially by Corporation.

17.	(b) Rents	540 75

F.—Borrowed Money.

26.	(b) Borrowed by taking deposits	904,195 86
27.	(c) Borrowed on debentures	202,420.81

G.—Receipts from other sources, viz.:

30.	(a) Rent of office premises	1,806 25
	(b) Sundry accounts	263 24
	Total	$1,596,472 18

CASH ACCOUNT.

Expenditure for the year ending 31st December, 1913. ......

I.—Expended on Corporation Account.

A.—Sums Loaned or Invested on Capital Account.

		Total (Col. 4.)
1.	(a) Loaned on mortgages of realty	$209,233 92
	(b) Loaned or invested on other securities:—	
2.	(i) Stocks owned by company	2,960 00
4.	(ii) Loans on stocks or debentures	142,260 00
6.	(c) Property held for sale (repairs and insurance)	2,614 66
7.	(d) Sundry accounts	2 60

B.—Expended on Stock Account.

8. Dividends paid on permanent stock	40,661 72

C.—Borrowed Money (other than foregoing) or interest.

19.	(b) Deposits: Principal, $925,668.53; interest, $10,071.94	935,740 47
20.	(c) Debentures issued in Canada: Principal, $135,376.00; interest, $45,243.69	180,619 69

CASH ACCOUNT.—Continued.

Expenditure for the year ending 31st December, 1913.

D.—Management Expenses (other than foregoing).

25. (a) Salaries, wages and fees	6,726 66
26. (b) Commission or brokerage and exchange	2,445 91
28. (d) Stationery, postage, printing and advertising	1,107 96
29. (e) Law costs and solicitor's salary	412 00
30. (f) Fuel, rent, taxes (other than 7 and 32) and rates...............	3,283 33
32. (h) Registration fees	559 09
33. (i) Other management expenditure, telegram, telephone, repairs......	395 48

E.—Other Expenditure, viz.:

35. (b) Auditors, $700; directors, $2.735	3,435 00
36. (c) Valuator's costs, $103.45; Guarantee Company, $68.25	171 70

F.—Balance.

37. (a) Cash on hand and in banks....................................	64,841 99
Total	$1,596,472 18

MISCELLANEOUS STATEMENT FOR THE YEAR ENDING 31ST DECEMBER, 1913.

1. Amount of debentures maturing in 1914: Issued in Canada, $195,089.00; Issued elsewhere, none.
2. Amount of other existing obligations which will mature in 1914, none.
3. Amount of securities held by the Corporation which will mature and become payable to the Corporation in 1914, $202,860.
4. Average rate of interest per annum paid by the Corporation during 1913: On deposits, 3.05%; On debentures, 4.38%; On debenture stock, none.
5. Average rate of interest per annum received by the Corporation during 1913:
    (a) On mortgages of realty; (b) On other securities.
    (i) Owned beneficially by the Corporation: (a) 6.94%; (b) 5.02%.
    (ii) Not owned beneficially: (a) All owned beneficially; (b) All owned beneficially.
6. Of the mortgages owned beneficially by the Corporation, $765,084.93 is on realty situate in Ontario, and $870,833.84 is on realty situate elsewhere.
7. Of the mortgages not owned beneficially by the Corporation: All owned beneficially.
8. Loans written off or transferred to real estate account during 1913, viz.:
    (i) Funds or securities owned beneficially, $2,134.60;
    (ii) Not so owned; All owned beneficially.
9. Number and aggregate amount of mortgage upon which compulsory proceedings have been taken by the Corporation in 1913, viz.:
    (i) Owned beneficially, No. 46; Amount, $46,493.31;
    (ii) Not so owned, No., none; Amount none.
10. Aggregate market value of land mortgaged to the Corporation:
    (i) Mortgages owned beneficially, $4,856.716.
11. How often are the securities held by the Corporation valued? Yearly.
12. (a) Specify the officers of the Corporation who are under bond and for what sum respectively: Manager, $10,000; Accountant, $5,000; Teller, $2,500; Ledgerkeeper, $1,000.
    (b) Are the said bonds executed by private sureties or by Guarantee Companies? Guarantee Company.
13. Date when the accounts of the Corporation were last audited? December 31st, 1913.
14. Names and addresses of the auditors respectively for 1913 and for 1914 (if appointed):
    For 1913: F. W. Frank and C. J. Parker, C.A., Brantford.
    For 1914: F. W. Frank and C. J. Parker, C.A., Brantford.
15. What were the dividend days of the Corporation in 1913 and what rate or rates of dividend were paid on those days respectively: 1¾%, Jan. 2, 1913; 1¾% April 1, 1913; 1¾%, July 2, 1913; 1¾%, Oct. 1, 1913.
16. What is the date appointed for the Annual Meeting? Second Wednesday in February. Date of last Annual Meeting? 11th February, 1914.
17. Special General Meetings held in 1913: Dates ———

THE EDINBURGH CANADIAN MORTGAGE COMPANY, LIMITED.

Head Office, Edinburgh, Scotland.

CONSTATING INSTRUMENTS.

Certificate of Incorporation (24th February, 1912), issued by Registrar of Joint Stock Companies for Scotland, under the Companies' (Consolidation) Act, 1908.

Memorandum of Association and Articles of Association under the above Act.

For the lending and borrowing powers, see Loan and Trust Corporations Act, R.S.O. 1914, chap. 184.

ANNUAL STATEMENT

Of the condition and affairs of The Edinburgh Canadian Mortgage Company, Limited, at the 31st December, 1913, and for period ending on that day, made to the Registrar of Loan Corporations for the Province of Ontario, pursuant to the laws of the said Province.

The Head Office of the Corporation is at No. 4 Melville Street, in the City of Edinburgh, Scotland.

The chief agency for Ontario is situate at C. P. R. Building, in the City of Toronto, in the Province of Ontario.

The chief agents and attorneys for Ontario are Messrs. Wood, Gundy & Co., and their address is C. P. R. Building, Toronto, in the Province of Onario.

The Board is constituted of eight directors, holding office for the term of one, two and three years.

The directors and chief executive officers of the Corporation at the 31st December, 1913, were as follows:

Sir Andrew H. L. Fraser, President, Edinburgh;   *24th February, 1912.
Sir David Paulin, Director, Edinburgh;   "
Thomas Jackson, Director, Glasgow;   "
James Macdonald, Director, Edinburgh;
William Gauden, Director, Uttershill, Penicuik;
Samuel John Moore, Director, Toronto;
Newton Wesley Rowell, Toronto;
George Herbert Wood, Toronto;
Wood, Gundy & Co., Managers, Toronto.
W. G. C. Hanna, Secretary, 4 Melville Street, Edinburgh.

A. Permanent capital stock: Total amount authorized, $1,216,625; total amount subscribed, $973,300, as more particularly set out in Schedule A hereto.

SCHEDULE A.

Class 2.—Fixed and Permanent Capital Stock created by virtue of Joint Stock Companies' Acts or private Acts.

Description.	No. of shares.	Par value of shares.	Total amount held.	Total amount paid thereon.	Total remaining unpaid on calls.
1. Fully called			$ c.	$ c.	
Preference shares	100,000	£1	486,650 00	486,650 00	Nil
Ordinary shares	100,000	each	486,650 00	486,650 00	
Totals	200,000	....	973,300 00	973,300 00	....

LIST OF SHAREHOLDERS AS AT 31st DECEMBER, 1913.
(Not printed.)

---

*Retire at general meetings in rotation.

BALANCE-SHEET AS AT 31st DECEMBER, 1913.

Dr. **Capital and Liabilities.**

I.—Capital (Liabilities to Stockholders or Shareholders).

A.—Permanent Capital Stock or Shares.

Preference shares fully paid	$486,650 00	
1. (a) Ordinary shares fully paid	486,650 00	
5. (e) Unappropriated profits, profit and loss	27,953 45	
		$1,001,253 45

Liabilities to the Public.

27. Deposits	8,163 43	
28. Interest on deposits, due, or accrued or capitalized	840 52	
31. Debentures issued elsewhere than in Canada	200,463 13	
32. Interest due and accrued or (31)	5,229 54	
37. Owing to banks	52,453 64	
39. Due on loans in process of completion or to pay assumed mortgages	66,186 06	
41. Other liabilities to the public, viz.:		
42. (a) Income tax	1,272 50	
43. (b) Charges recoverable	301 02	
Total actual liabilities	$1,336,163 29	

Cr. **Assets.**

B.—Debts secured by Mortgages of Land.

9. (a) Debts secured by mortgages of land	$1,118,290 34	
11. (c) Interest due and accrued on item (9)	31,941 45	

C.—Debts not above enumerated for which the Corporation holds securities, as follows:

14. (b) Debts secured by municipal bonds or debentures	148,550 00	
26. (n) Interest due or accrued on item (14)	736 30	

E.—Cash

31. (a) On hand	706 36	
32. (b) In banks	14,635 51	

F.—Assets not hereinbefore mentioned.

37. (a) Preliminary expenses and brokerage	$11,777 72	
38. (b) Suspense	9 85	
39. (c) Furniture	2,381 41	
40. (d) Commission on mortgages	7,134 35	
		21,303 33
Total assets		$1,336,163 29

CASH ACCOUNT.

Receipts for the year ending 31st December, 1913.

I.—Received by the Corporation for its Own Use.

A.—Balance as at 31st December, 1912.

(*i*)	On hand	$3,937 65

B.—Sums received wholly or partly on Capital Stock.

4. (*a*)	Calls on preference and ordinary shares........................	28,108 91
	(*a*) On mortgages of realty:	
10.	(i) Principal..	63,148 22
11.	(ii) Interest on mortgages	41,863 46
	(*b*) On other securities:	
12.	(i) Principal, Corporation bonds	1,201,330 00
13.	(ii) Interest or dividends, on (12)........................	21,591 14

E.—Miscellaneous.

19. (*b*)	Premiums or bonus on loans	2,174 97

F.—Borrowed Money.

25. (*a*)	Bank or other advances	42,720 64
26. (*b*)	Borrowed by taking deposits	8,163 43
27. (*c*)	Borrowed on debentures ....:...............................	200,463 13
29. (*e*)	Borrowed otherwise, viz.:	
	Loans..	9,733 00

G.—Receipts from other sources.

30. (*a*)	Gain on exchange	215 27
(*b*)	Transfer fees	27 37
(*c*)	Appraisers fee, etc.	1,188 06
	Totals......................	**$1,624,665 25**

CASH ACCOUNT.

Expenditure for the year ending 31st December, 1913.

I.—Expended on Corporation Account.

A.—Sums loaned or invested on Capital Account.

1. (*a*)	Loaned on mortgages of realty	$847,242 20
	(*b*) Loaned or invested on other securities, viz.:	
2.	(i) Corporation bonds	696,900 00
7. (*e*)	Insurances or taxes advanced on property mortgaged to the Corporation.................................	91 67

B.—Expended on Stock Account.

8.	Dividends paid on preference shares................................	23,052 53

C.—Borrowed Money (Other than Foregoing) or Interest Paid
Thereon, viz.:

18. (*a*)	Bank account, interest on overdraft...........................	756 90
21. (*d*)	Debentures issued elsewhere than in Canada....................	4,107 20
24. (*g*)	Interest on loans	968 92

CASH ACCOUNT.—Continued.

Expenditure for the year ending 31st December, 1913.

D.—Management Expenses.

25. (a) Salaries, wages and fees	14,384 93
26. (b) Commission or brokerage, capital charge	351 35
28. (d) Stationery, postage, printing and advertising	2,391 69
30. (f) Fuel, rent, taxes	2,268 23
31. (g) Travelling expenses	2,095 70
32. (h) Registration fees	126 50

E.—Other Expenditures, viz.:

34. (a) Commission on debentures	$1,705 25
35. (b) Commission on mortgages	9,157 70
36. (c) Interest on assumed mortgages	3,722 61

F.—Balance.

37. (a) Cash on hand	$706 36	
(b) Cash in banks	14,635 51	
		15,341 87
Total		$1,624,665 25

Miscellaneous Statement for the Year Ending 31st December, 1913.

1. Amount of debentures maturing in 1914: Issued in Canada, nil; Issued elsewhere, nil.
2. Amount of other existing obligations which will mature in 1914, nil.
3. Amount of securities held by the Corporation which will mature and become payable to the Corporation in 1914, nil.
4. Average rate of interest per annum paid by the Corporation during 1913: On deposits, 4¼%; on debentures, 4½%; on debenture stock, nil.
5. Average rate of interest per annum received by the Corporation during 1913: (a) On mortgages of realty; (b) on other securities:
    (i) Owned beneficially by the Corporation: (a) 7¾%; (b) 6¼%.
    (ii) Not owned beneficially: (a) nil; (b) nil.
6. Of the mortgages owned beneficially by the Corporation, $99,625 is on realty situate in Ontario, and $1,018,565.34 is on realty situate elsewhere.
7. Of the mortgages not owned beneficially by the Corporation, nil is on realty situate in Ontario, and nil is on realty situate elsewhere.
8. Loans written off or transferred to real estate account during 1913, viz.:
    (1) Funds or securities owned beneficially, nil.
    (ii) Not so owned, nil.
9. Number and aggregate amount of mortgages upon which compulsory proceedings have been taken by the Corporation in 1913, viz.:
    (i) Owned beneficially, No., nil; Amount, nil.
    (ii) Not so owned, No., nil; Amount, nil.
10. Aggregate market value of land mortgaged to the Corporation:
    (1) Mortgages owned beneficially, $3,167,760.
    (ii) Not so owned, nil.

11. How often are the securities held by the Corporation valued?　Quarterly.
12. (a) Specify the officers of the Corporation who are under bond and for what sum
　　　　respectively.　Total, $11,000.
　　(b) Are the said bonds executed by private sureties or by Guarantee Companies?
　　　　Guarantee Company.
13. Date when the accounts of the Corporation were last audited?　31st May, 1913.
14. Names and addresses of the auditors respectively for 1913 and for 1914 (if
　　　　appointed):
　　　For 1913: Messrs. Martin Currie & Co.
　　　For 1914: Messrs. Martin Currie & Co.
15. What were the dividend days of the Corporation in 1913, and what rate or rates
　　　　of dividend were paid on those days respectively?　Five per cent. paid on 15th
　　　　April and 15th October, 1913, on preference shares.
16. What is the date apointed for the Annual Meeting.　Not fixed.　Date of last Annual
　　　　Meeting?　21st August, 1913.
17. Special General Meetings held in 1913.　Dates: Nil.

THE WATERLOO COUNTY LOAN & SAVINGS COMPANY.

Head Office, Waterloo, Ontario.

CONSTATING INSTRUMENTS.

Incorporated by Letters Patent under the Loan and Trust Corporation Act, 2 George V, 1912, chap 34, dated 7th April, 1913.

The lending and borrowing powers are governed by the Loan and Trust Corporations Act, R.S.O. 1914, chapter 184.

ANNUAL STATEMENT

Of the condition and affairs of the Waterloo County Loan & Savings Company of Waterloo, Ontario, at the 31st December, 1913, and for the year ending on that day, made to the Registrar of Loan Corporations for the Province of Ontario, pursuant to the laws of the said Province.

The head office of the Corporation is at Erb Street, in the Town of Waterloo, in the Province of Ontario.

The Board is constituted of ten directors, holding office for one year.

The directors and chief executive officers of the Corporation at the 31st December, 1913, were as follows, together with their respective terms of office:

Thos. Hilliard, President, Waterloo, Ont.;   May 20th, 1913; February 12th, 1914.
Edward F. Seagram, Vice-President, Waterloo, Ont.;   "   "
S. B. Bricker, Director, Waterloo, Ont.;
F. S. Kumpf, Director, Waterloo, Ont.;
Fred. Halstead, Director, Waterloo, Ont.;
Dr. W. G. Hilliard, Director, Waterloo, Ont.;
P. H. Sims, Director, Toronto, Ont.;
Geo. D. Forbes, Director, Hespeler, Ont.;
Thos. Trow, Director, Stratford, Ont.;
M. M. Bricker, Director, Berlin, Ont.;   "
P. V. Wilson, Manager and Secretary, Waterloo, Ont., March 1st, 1913.

A.—Permanent capital stock: Total amount authorized, $2,000,000; total amount subscribed, $355,700, as more particularly set out in Schedule A hereto.

SCHEDULE A.

Class 1.—Fixed and permanent Capital Stock created by virtue of Building Society Acts, and other Acts.

Description.	Total amount issued and subsisting at 31st Dec., 1913.		Total amount of actual payments thereon.	Total amount unpaid and constituting an asset of the Corporation.	Remarks.
	Par value of shares.	No. of shares.	—		Stock sold at a premium of $10 a share.
			$ c.	$ c.	$ c.	Total premium: $35,570 Paid; 30,625
2; Partly called stock.	3,557	100	355,700 00	167,436 00	188,264 90	$4,945 still to be paid on premium account.

LIST OF SHAREHOLDERS AS AT 31st DECEMBER, 1913.

(Not printed.)

15 L.C.

BALANCE SHEET AS AT 31st DECEMBER, 1913.

Dr. Capital and Liabilities.

1.—Capital (Liabilities to Stockholders or Shareholders).

A.—Permanent Capital Stock or Shares.

2. (b) Ordinary joint stock capital, 40 per cent. called; total called, $142,280; total paid thereon............	$116,085 00	
3. (cc) Joint stock capital paid in advance of calls......	51,351 00	
4. (d) Dividends declared in respect of (2) not yet paid..	5,117 62	
5. (e) Unappropriated profits in respect of (2)	2,501 83	
6. (f) Reserve fund in respect of (2)	30,625 00	
		$205,680 45

Liabilities to the Public.

27. Deposits (including unclaimed deposits), right reserved to require 30 days' notice on any withdrawal....	$131,982 74	
28. Interest on deposits, due, or accrued or capitalized......	1,342 83	
		133,325 57
Total actual liabilities		$339,006 02

Cr. Assets.

I.—Assets of which the Corporation is the Beneficial Owner.

A.—Immovable Property Owned Beneficially by Corporation.

1. (a) Office premises situate as follows:		
2. (i) At Waterloo, Ont.; held in freehold.......................		$10,500 00

B.—Debts Secured by Mortgages of Land.

9. (a) Debts (other than item 10) secured by mortgages of land	$211,225 00	
11. (c) Interest due or accrued on item 9 not included therein	4,332 38	
		215,557 38

C.—Debts not above enumerated for which the Corporation holds Securities as follows:

14. (b) Debts secured by municipal bonds or debentures....	$16,061 54	
15. (c) Debts secured by public school debentures..........	11,866 05	
22. (j) Debts secured by stocks	6,100 00	
26. (n) Interest due or accrued ....·.......	700 83	
		34,728 42

E.—Cash.

31. (a) On hand		4,067 16
32. (b) In banks		74,153 06
Total assets		$339,006 02

CASH ACCOUNT.

Receipts for the year ending December 31st, 1913.

I.—Received by the Corporation for Its Own Use.

B.—Sums Received Wholly or Partly on Capital Stock.

		Col. 1.	Col. 3.	Col. 4.
4. (a) Calls on joint stock permanent capital..		....	$116,085 00	
(aa) Joint stock capital received in advance of calls		....	51,351 00	
5. (b) Premiums on (4)		....	30,625 00	
				$198,061 00

C.—Receipts on account of Investments Loans or Debts.

(a) On mortgages of realty:				
10.	(i) Principal	$8,350 00		
11.	(ii) Interest	8,492 63		
(b) On other securities:				
12.	(i) Principal	270 92		
	(ii) Interest	896 53		

D.—Receipts from Real Estate Owned Beneficially by Corporation.

17. (b) Rents	60 00	

F.—Borrowed Money.

26. (b) Borrowed by taking deposits.	172,889 54	

G.—Receipts from Other Sources.

30. (a) Interest from bank deposits.	70 75	
(b) Exchange	21 35	
		191,051 72

	Col. 1	Col. 3	Col. 4
Totals	$191,051 72	$198,061 00	$389,112 72

CASH ACCOUNT.

Expenditure for the year ending 31st December, 1913.

I.—Expended on Corporation Account.

A.—Sums Loaned or Invested on Capital Account.

		Col. 1.	Col. 3.	Col. 4.
1. (a) Loaned on mortgage of realty.		$219,575 00		
(b) Loaned or invested on other securities, viz.:				
2.	(i) Municipal debentures	16,332 46		
3.	(ii) School debentures	11,866 05		
4.	(iii) Other securities	6,100 00		
6. (c) Real estate purchased and office fixtures		10,836 43		

C.—Borrowed Money (other than foregoing or interest thereon paid,) viz.:

19. (b) Deposits: Principal, $39,563.97; Interest, $1,342.83	$40,906 80	

CASH ACCOUNT.—Continued.

Expenditure for the year ending 31st December, 1913.

D.—Management Expenses (other than foregoing:)

25. (a) Salaries, wages and fees................	1,873 87	
26. (b) Commission or brokerage commissions on loans	1,330 97	
28. (d) Stationery, postage, printing, and advertising	767 38	
30. (f) Fuel, rent, taxes (other than 7 and 32) and rates	313 11	
31. (g) Travelling expenses	49 90	
33. (i) Other management expenditure	86 97	

E.—Other Expenditures, viz.:

34. (a) Transportation expenses charters and Provincial licenses	853 56	

F.—Balance.

37. (a) Cash on hand	4,067 16	
38. (i) In banks	74,153 06	
Total	$389,112 72	.... $389,112 72

MISCELLANEOUS STATEMENT FOR THE YEAR ENDING 31ST DECEMBER, 1913.

1. Amount of debentures maturing in 1914: Issued in Canada, none; Issued elsewhere, none.
2. Amount of other existing obligations which will mature in 1914. None.
3. Amount of securities held by the Corporation which will mature and become payable to the Corporation in 1914. $61,305.00.
4. Average rate of interest per annum paid by the Corporation during 1912: On deposits, 4%; On debentures, none; On debenture stock, none.
5. Average rate of interest per annum received by the Corporation during 1913: (a) On mortgages of realty; (b) On other securities.
   (i) Owned beneficially by the Corporation: (a) 8%; (b) About 7½%.
   (ii) Not owned beneficially: (a) None; (b) None.
6. Of the mortgages owned beneficially by the Corporation, $55,000 is on realty situate in Ontario, and $156,225 is on realty situate elsewhere.
7. Of the mortgages not owned beneficially by the Corporation, none is on realty situate in Ontario, and none is on realty situate elsewhere.
8. Loans written off or transferred to real estate account during 1913, viz.:
   (i) Funds or securities owned beneficially: None.
   (ii) Not so owned: None.
9. Number and aggregate amount of mortgages upon which compulsory proceedings have been taken by the Corporation in 1913, viz.:
   (i) Owned beneficially, No., none; Amount, none.
   (ii) Not so owned, No., none; Amount, none.
10. Aggregate market value of land mortgaged to the Corporation:
    (i) Mortgages owned beneficially, $456,900.
    (ii) Not so owned, none.
11. How often are the securities held by the Corporation valued? Will be yearly.

12. (*a*) Specify the officers of the Corporation who are under bond and for what sum respectively? Manager, $5,000; Clerk, $2,000.

(*b*) Are the said bonds executed by private sureties or by Guarantee Companies? Guarantee Company.

13. Date when the accounts of the Corporation were last audited? January 16, 1914.

14. Names and addresses of the auditors respectively for 1913, and for 1914 (if appointed):

For 1913: J. M. Scully, F.C.A., Berlin.

For 1914: Jeremiah Scully, Berlin.

15. What were the dividend days of the Corporation in 1913, and what rate or rates of dividend were paid on those days respectively? Dividend declared at end of year, 6%.

16. What is the date appointed for the Annual Meeting? February 12th, 1914. Date of Statutory Meeting? May 20th, 1913.

17. Special General Meetings held in 1913. Dates: Special General Meeting April 25th, and Statutory Meeting May 20th.

II. LOAN COMPANIES.

B. COMPANIES HAVING TERMINATING AS WELL AS PERMANENT STOCK OR HAVING TERMINATING STOCK ONLY.

(SEE 4 EDW. VII. (1904) CHAPTER 17, SECTION 6).

DETAILED REPORTS OF THE SEVERAL COMPANIES.

[199]

DOMINION PERMANENT LOAN COMPANY.

Head Office, Toronto, Ontario.

Constating Instruments.

1890.—Declaration under R.S.O. 1887, c. 169; filed with the Clerk of the Peace for the County of York, 7th May, 1890. The original corporate name was The Dominion Building and Loan Association.

1897.—Act of the Dominion of Canada, 60-61 V., c. 85, extending the business of the Company to the whole Dominion; defining the borrowing powers of the Company; regulating its issue of debentures and debenture stock; providing for the prohibition of loans upon the Company's own stock; continuing the Company under the control of the Loan Corporation Act of Ontario.

1898.—Order in Council of Ontario (29th January, 1898), changing the corporate name to the Dominion Permanent Loan Company, to take effect from and after 1st August, 1898.

1898.—Act of Dominion of Canada, confirming the said change of corporate name.

See Statutes of Canada, 1899.

Annual Statement

Of the condition and affairs of the Dominion Permanent Loan Company of Toronto, Ontario, at the 31st December, 1913, and for the year ending on that day, made to the Registrar of Loan Corporations for the Province of Ontario, pursuant to the laws of the said Province.

The head office of the Corporation is at No. 12 King Street West, in the City of Toronto, in the Province of Ontario.

The Board is constituted of six directors, holding office for one year.

The directors and chief executive officers of the Corporation at the 31st December, 1913, were as follows, together with their respective terms of office:

Hon. J. R. Stratton, Pres., Peterborough;   Feb. 5th, 1914. Feb. 4th, 1915.
D. W. Karn, Vice-President, Woodstock;   "   "
A. C. Macdonell, Director, Toronto;   "   "
Thomas H. Johnson, Winnipeg;
Geo. H. Cowan, K.C., Director, Vancouver, B.C.; "
F. M. Holland, Man.-Director and Secretary, Toronto; "   —

A. Permanent capital stock: Total amount authorized, $10,000,000; total amount subscribed $1,402,500.00 as more particularly set out in Schedule A hereto.

Schedule A.

Class 1.—Fixed and permanent capital stock, created by virtue of Building Society Acts.

Description.	Total amount issued and subsisting at 31st December, 1913.		Total amount of actual payments thereon.	Total amount unpaid and constituting an asset of the Corporation.
	Number of shares.	Par value of shares.		
		$	$	$ c.	$ c.
1. Fully called stock.....	8,806	100	880,600	880,600 00	....
2. Partly called stock	5,219	100	521,900	243,581 49	278,318 51
Totals............	14,025	..........| 1,402,500	1,124,181 49	278,318 51

LIST OF SHAREHOLDERS AS AT 31st DECEMBER, 1913.

(Not printed.)

SCHEDULE B.

Terminating or Withdrawable Stock.

Shares of Terminating or Withdrawable Stock.			Fully paid.		Prepaid.		Instalment.		Total.
			No.	Amount.	No.	Amount.	No.	Amount.	
				$		$		$	$
Number and amount in force at 31st December, 1912			3½	350	1,631	163,100	......	....	163,450
Gross total in force at any time in 1913			3½	350	1,631	163,100	......	....	163,450
Deduct as follows :	No. of shares	Amount							
Converted into perma-nent stock during 1913..............	157	$ 15,700	.....	....	157	15,700	......	....	15,700
Forfeited and lapsed during 1913........	153	15,300	.....	....	153	15,300	......	....	15,300
Total deduction ...	310	31,000	.....	....	310	31,000	......	....	31,000
Net total remaining in force at 31st December, 1913			3½	350	1,321	132,100	......	....	132,450

Summary of Terminating Withdrawable Stock in force at 31st December, 1913:

3½ shares fully paid stock at $100 per share, $350, on which 1 shareholder
has paid in (credit to loan fund) $350 00

1321 shares prepaid stock (other than above) at $100 per share, $132,100,
on which 135 shareholders have paid in (credit to loan fund).. 66,050 00

Total $66,400 00

Total amount distributed or credited in 1913:

(1) As interest:
Rate of such interest, per cent. per annum, 10.80 per cent. (2.80 per cent.)

(2) As dividends out of profits, $21 and $4,842.00.
Rate or rates per cent. of such dividends, 6 per cent. per annum.

BALANCE SHEET AS AT 31st DECEMBER, 1913.

Dr. Capital and Liabilities.

Capital (Liabilities to Stockholders or Shareholders).

A.—Permanent Capital Stock or Shares.

1, (a) Ordinary joint stock capital fully called; total called, $880,600.00,
total paid thereon $880,600 00

2. (b) Ordinary joint stock capital; total called, $243.581.49; total paid
thereon. 243,581 49

4. (d) Dividends declared in respect of (1) and (2) but not yet paid.. 33,724 34

BALANCE SHEET.—Continued.

5. (e) Unappropriated profits in respect of (1) and (2)..	$53,290 86	
6. (f) Reserve fund in respect of (1) and (2)	438,000 00	
7. (g) Contingent fund in respect of (1) and (2)	5,964 68	
		$1,655,161 37

B.—Terminating Capital Stock or Shares.

14. (a) Fully paid stock, less shown in (24); total in force, 3½ shares at $100 per share, on which has been paid into loan fund	350 00	
15. (b) Profits or accrued interest on (14), less shown in (25) and credited or appropriated, but not yet paid	10 50	
17. (d) Prepaid stock, less shown in (24); total in force, 1321 shares at $100 per share, on which has been paid into loan fund	66,050 00	
18. (e) Profits or accrued interest on (17), less shown in (25) and credited or appropriated, but not yet paid	12,202 18	
25. Interest, profits or dividends due by Corporation, unclaimed dividends	45 00	
		78,657 68
		$1,733,819 05

Liabilities to the Public.

27. Deposits, right reserved to require 30 days' notice of any withdrawal	$233,864 81	
28. Interest on deposits due, or accrued or capitalised	11,348 10	
29. Debentures issued in Canada	2,111,080 47	
30. Interest due and accrued on (29)	36,945 07	
40. Other liabilities to the public, viz.:—		
41. (a) Sundry accounts	613 39	
		2,393,851 84
Total liabilities		$4,127,670·89

Cr.   Assets.

I.—Assets of which the Corporation is the Beneficial Owner.

A.—Immovable Property Owned Beneficially by Corporation.

5. (b) Freehold land (including buildings) other than foregoing........................	$14,906 26

B.—Debts secured by Mortgages of Land.

9. (a) Debts (other than item 10) secured by mortgages of land........................	$3,901,967 82	
10. (b) Debts secured by mortgaged land held for sale......	33,391 47	
11. (c) Interest due or accrued on items (9) and (10), not included therein	11,159 98	
		3,946,519 27

Assets.—Continued.

C.—Debts not above enumerated for which the Corporation holds securities as follows:

16. (d) Debts secured by loan corporations debentures......	$202 95	
20. (h) Debts secured only by permanent stock or shares of the Corporation	1,055 96	
22. (j) Debts secured by stocks...........................	2,357 28	$3,616 19

E.—Cash.

31. (a) On hand	$25,238 12	
32. (b) In banks	5,961 53	31,199 65

F.—Assets not hereinbefore mentioned.

37. (a) Office fixtures and furniture	$5.006 80	
38. (b) Sundry accounts	3.126 96	
40. (d) Debenture stock and bonds.........................	123,295 76	131,429 52

Total assets **$4,137,670 89**

CASH ACCOUNT.

Receipts for the year ending 31st December, 1913.

I.—Received by the Corporation for its Own Use.

A.—Balance from 31st December, 1912.

(b) (Not already shown under (1)):

		(Col. 1.)	(Col. 3.)	(Col. 4.)
2.	(i) On hand	....	....	$33,509 27
3.	(ii) In bank	....	....	59,985 94

B.—Sums received wholly or partly on Capital Stock.

4. (a) Calls on joint stock permanent capital		....	....	5,009 13

C.—Receipts on account of Investments, Loans or Debts.

(a) On mortgages of realty:

10.	(i) Principal........	$92,082 32		
11.	(ii) Interest......................			

(b) On other securities:

12.	(i) Investment stock and call loans	51,693 97	....	143,776 29

D.—Receipts from Real Estate Owned Beneficially by Corporation.

16. (a) Sales	$125 00		
17. (b) Rents	563 42		688 42

CASH ACCOUNT.—Continued.

Receipts for the year ending 31st December, 1913.

E.—Miscellaneous.

	(Col. 1.)	(Col. 3.)	(Col. 4.)
19. (b) Premiums or bonus on loans..........	$ 83 62		
22. (e) Forfeiture- on lapses	2,145 46		
24. (g) Conversion of terminating into permanent stock	....	$15,668 67	
			$17,897 75

F.—Borrowed Money.

26. (b) Borrowed by taking deposits.........	$965,949 87		
27. (c) Borrowed on debentures	797,496 03		
		....	1,763,445 90

G.—Receipts from other sources, viz.:

30. (a) Interest on deposits in bank..........	$231 55		
(b) Sundry accounts	614 96		
		....	846 51
Total			$2,025,159 21

CASH ACCOUNT.

Expenditure for the year ending 31st December. 1913.

	(Col. 1.)	(Col. 2.)	(Col. 4.)
I.—Expended on Corporation Account.			
A.—Sums Loaned or Invested on Capital Account.			
1. (a) Loaned on mortgages of realty	$80,531 62		
(b) Loaned or invested in other securities:			
2. (i) Real estate, repairs, insurance, etc.	303 57		
3. (ii) Bonds and stock purchased........	600 00		
4. (iii) Loans on stocks	43,806 66		
		....	$125,241 85
B.—Expended on Stock Account.			
8. Dividends paid on permanent stock........	$66,262 78		
9. Interest paid on terminating stock........	4,863 00		
15. Terminating stock forfeited or lapsed......	....	$2,145 46	
16. Terminating stock converted into permanent	....	15,668 67	
			88,939 91
C.—Borrowed Money (other than foregoing) or interest thereon paid.			
18. (a) Bank account	$38,513 79		
19. (b) Deposits: Principal, $902,689.06; interest, $11,333.55	914,022 61		
20. (c) Debentures issued in Canada: Principal, $683,388.84; interest, $95,879.92....	779,268 76		
		....	1.731,805 16

CASH ACCOUNT.—Continued.

Expenditure for the year ending 31st December, 1913.

D.—Management Expenses (other than fore going):

25. (a) Salaries, wages and fees	$25,728 90	
26. (b) Commisson or brokerage	6,212 69	
28. (d) Stationery, postage, printing and advertising..........	3,130 81	
29. (e) Law costs	3 35	
30. (f) Fuel, rent, taxes (other than in 7 and 32) and rates	4,795 00	
31. (g) Travelling expenses	3,983 25	
32. (h) Registration fees	687 14	
33. (i) Other management expenses	2.773 94	
	....	$47,315 08

E.—Other Expenditure, viz.:

34. (o) Interest on bank overdraft	657 56

F.—Balance.

37. (a) Cash on hand and in banks...................................	31,199 65
Total................	$2,025,159 21

MISCELLANEOUS STATEMENT FOR THE YEAR ENDING 31ST DECEMBER, 1913.

1. Amount of debentures maturing in 1914: Issued in Canada, $631,977.56; Issued elsewhere, none.
2. Amount of other existing obligations which will mature in 1914, none.
3. Amount of securities held by the Corporation which will mature and become payable to the Corporation in 1914, none.
4. Average rate of interest per annum paid by the Corporation during 1913: On deposits, 4%; On debentures, 5%; On debenture stock, none.
5. Average rate of interest per annum received by the Corporation during 1913:
    (a) On mortgages of realty; (b) On other securities.
    (i) Owned beneficially by the Corporation: (a) 7½%; (b) 6%.
    (ii) Not owned beneficially: (a) None; (b) None.
6. Of the mortgages owned beneficially by the Corporation. $22,645.72 is on realty situate in Ontario, and $3,879,322.10 is on realty situate elsewhere.
7. Of the mortgages not owned beneficially by the Corporation, none is on realty situate in Ontario, and none is on realty situate elsewhere.
8. Loans written off or transferred to real estate account during 1913, viz.:
    (i) Funds or securities owned beneficially, none.
    (ii) Not so owned, none.
9. Number and aggregate amount of mortgages upon which compulsory proceedings have been taken by the Corporation in 1913, viz.:
    (i) Owned beneficially: No. 2; Amount, $677.75.
    (ii) Not so owned: No., none; Amount, none.
10. Aggregate market value of land mortgaged to the Corporation:
    (i) Mortgages owned beneficially, $6,700,000.
    (ii) Not so owned, none.
11. How often are the securities held by the Corporation valued? Yearly.

12. (a) Specify the officers of the Corporation who are under bond and for what sum
        respectively: Manager, $5,000; Accountant, $1,000; Branch Manager, $5,000;
        Teller. $2,500; Assistant Branch Manager, $1,000.

   (b) Are the said bonds executed by private-sureties or by Guarantee Companies?
        Guarantee Company.

13. Date when the accounts of the Corporation were last audited: December 31st, 1913.

14. Names and addresses of the auditors respectively for 1913 and for 1914 (if
        appointed):

        For 1913: H. Vigeon, Bryan Pontifex.

        For 1914: H. Vigeon, Bryan Pontifex.

16. What is the date appointed for the Annual Meeting? February 5th, 1914. Date of
        of dividend were paid on those days respectively? January 2nd, 1913, July
        2nd, 1913; 6% per annum.

16.) What is the date appointed for the Annual Meeting? February 5th, 1914. Date of
        last Annual Meeting? February 6th, 1913.

17. Special General Meetings held in 1913: Dates, none.

THE HOME BUILDING AND SAVINGS ASSOCIATION, OF OTTAWA

Head Office, Ottawa, Ontario.

Incorporated under the Building Societies' Act (R.S.O. 1887, c. 169), by declaration filed with the Clerk of the Peace for the County of Carleton, on the 24th June. 1890. (Decl. Book II., 119.) The Company, for purposes of distinction, ordinarily uses the words "of Ottawa" as part of its corporate name, but those words do not appear in the declaration of incorporation.

The lending and the borrowing powers are governed by the Loan and Trust Corporations Act, R.S.O. 1914, chap. 184.

ANNUAL STATEMENT

Of the condition and affairs of the Home Building and Savings Association, of Ottawa, Ontario, at the 31st December, 1913, and for the year ending on that day, made to the Registrar of Loan Corporations for the Province of Ontario, pursuant to the laws of the said Province.

The head office of the Corporation is at No. 95 Sparks Street, in the City of Ottawa, in the Province of Ontario.

The Board is constituted of seven directors, holding office for two years.

The directors and chief executive officers of the Corporation at the 31st December, 1913, were as follows, together with their respective terms of office:

John R. Armstrong, President, Ottawa;	January, 1913;	January, 1915.
M. Kavanagh, Vice-President, Ottawa;	" 1913;	" 1915.
E. B. Butterworth, Director, Ottawa;	" 1912;	" 1914.
J. H. Thompson, Director, Ottawa;	" 1913;	" 1915.
D. O'Connor, Jr., Director, Ottawa;	" 1913;	" 1915.
F. H. Chrysler, K.C., Director, Ottawa;	" 1912;	" 1914.
D. M. Finnie, Director, Ottawa;	" 1912;	" 1914.
C. A. Douglas, Manager, Ottawa.		

SCHEDULE B.

Terminating or Withdrawable Stock.

Shares of Terminating or Withdrawable Stock.	Instalment.	
	No.	Amount.
		$
Number and amount in force at 31st December, 1912	1,803	360,600
" " issued during 1913......................	180	36,000
Gross total in force at any time during 1913	1,983	396,600

	No.	Amount.		
		$		
Deduct as follows:				
Withdrawn and paid off during 1913	117	23,400		
Retired by Corporation during 1913..........	232	46,400		
Total deductions....................	349	69,800	349	69,800
Net total remaining in force 31st December. 1913 ....|..........			1,634	326,800

Summary of Terminating or Withdrawable stock in force at 31st December, 1913.

1634 shares of instalment stock (payable by fixed periodical payments) at $1.00 and $1.20 per share of $200, on which shareholders have paid in $123,076 00

BALANCE SHEET AS AT 31st DECEMBER, 1913.

Dr. Capital and Liabilities.

Capital (Liabilities to Stockholders or Shareholders).

B.—Terminating Capital Stock or Shares.

20. (g) Instalment stock, less shown in (24) total issue now in force, 1,634 shares at $200 per share, $326,800, on which has been paid in all of which sum there has been paid into Loan Fund..	$123,031 60	
21. (h) Profits or accrued interest on (20), less shown in (25) and credited' or appropriated 'but not yet paid . .	41,113 47	
22. ((i) Profits or accrued interest on (20), less shown in (25) and not accredited or appropriated	3,500 00	
23. (j) Instalments or premiums paid on (20) in advance	44 40	
26. Instalments due	1,196 60	
		$168,886 07

Liabilities to the Public.

41. Other liabilities to the public:

42. (a) Toronto General Trust Corporation (including interest due and accrued)	$25,474 65	
43. (b) Mortgage account	4,749 77	
		$30,224 42
Total liabilities		$199,110 49

Cr. Assets.

I.—Assets of which the Corporation is the Beneficial Owner.

A.—Immovable Property Owned Beneficially by the Corporation.

B.—Debts secured by Mortgages of Land.

9. (a) Debts (other than item 10) secured by mortgages of land......		$158,069 72

C.—Debts not above enumerated for which the Corporation holds securities as follows:

21. (i) Debts secured only by terminating stock or shares of the Corporation	$15,950 00	
22. (j) Debts secured by terminating stock, being arrears of instalments	2,142 56	
		18,092 56

E.—Cash

33. (b) In bank		22,948 21
Total assets		$199,110 49

CASH ACCOUNT.

Receipts for the year ending 31st December, 1913.

I.—Received by the Corporation for its Own Use.

A.—Balance from 31st December, 1912.

3.	(ii) Cash in bank	$2,087 58

B.—Sums received wholly or partly on Capital Stock.

8. e)	Dues on instalment building society stock	24,318 80

C.—Receipts on account of Investments, Loans or Debts.

(a) On mortgages of realty:

10.	(i) Principal	18,893 73
11.	(ii) Interest	12,832 33

(b) On other securities:

12.	(i) Principal loans on stock	5,240 00
13.	(ii) Interest on deposits	355 50

E.—Miscellaneous.

19. (b)	Premiums or bonus on loans	269 40
20. (c)	Membership or entry fee (being income of Corporation)	52 50
21. (d)	Fines	458 17
	Transfer fees	18 75

F.—Borrowed Money.

29. (e)	Borrowed otherwise, viz.: Toronto General Trusts Corporation	20,000 00

G.—Receipts from Other Sources.

30. (a)	Insurances paid	130 00
	Total	**$84,656 76**

CASH ACCOUNT.

Expenditure for the year ending 31st December, 1913.

I.—Expended on Corporation Account.

A.—Sums Loaned or Invested on Capital Account.

(Col. 2.)

1. (a)	Loaned on Mortgages of realty	$4,200 00
2.	(b) Loaned or invested in other securities: (i) Stock	7,845 00
7. (e)	Insurance or taxes advanced on property mortgaged to the Corporation	169 90

14 L.C.

CASH ACCOUNT.—Continued.

Expenditure for the year ending 31st December, 1913.

B.—Expended on Stock Account.

11. Paid for terminating stock withdrawn	$216 00
12. Paid for terminating stock matured	30,553 00
13. Profits paid on (11) and (12)	15,356 20

D.—Management Expenses (other than foregoing).

25. (a) Salaries, wages and fees	1,898 00
28. (d) Stationery, postage printing and advertising	18 20
29. (e) Law costs	149 03
30. (f) Fuel, rent, taxes (other than in 7 and 32) and rates	142 68
32. (h) Registration fee	30 00

E.—Other Expenditure, viz.:

34. (a) Interest on advances	1,130 54

F. Balance.

37. (b) Cash in bank	22,948 21
Total	$84,656 76

MISCELLANEOUS STATEMENT FOR THE YEAR ENDING 31ST DECEMBER, 1913.

1. Amount of debentures maturing in 1914: Issued in Canada, None; issued elsewhere, none.
2. Amount of other existing obligations which will mature in 1914: Estimated at $60,600.00.
3. Amount of securities held by the Corporation which will mature and become payable to the Corporation in 1914.
4. Average rate of interest per annum paid by the Corporation during 1913: On stock matured, 8 4-5%; on debentures, none; on debenture stock, none; 4% on stock withdrawn.
5 Average rate of interest per annum received by the Corporation during 1913:
    (a) On mortgages of realty; (b) On other securities.
    (i) Owned beneficially by the Corporation, (a) 7 1-5%, (b) 7 1-5%.
    (ii) Not owned beneficially, (a) 7 1-5%, (b)
6. Of the mortgages owned beneficially by the Corporation $44,969.72 is on realty situate in Ontario, and none is on realty situate elsewhere.
7. Of the mortgages not owned beneficially by the Corporation $113,100.00 is on realty situate in Ontario, and none is on realty situate elsewhere.
8. Loans written off or transferred to real estate account during 1913, viz.:
    (i) Funds or securities owned beneficially, none.
    (ii) Not so owned, none.
9. Number and aggregate amount of mortgages upon which compulsory proceedings have been taken by the Corporation in 1913, viz.:
    (i) Owned beneficially. No. none; Amount, none.
    (ii) Not so owned, none; Amount, none.

10. Aggregate market value of land mortgaged to the Corporation:
    (i) Mortgages owned beneficially, $80,000.00.
    (ii) Not so owned, $164,500.00.

11. How often are the securities held by the Corporation valued? At time loan is effected.

12. (a) Specify the officers of the Corporation who are under bond and for what sum respectively: Manager, for $2,000.00.
    (b) Are the said bonds executed by private sureties of by Guarantee Companies? Private sureties.

13. Date when the accounts of the Corporation were last audited; 9th January, 1914.

14. Names and addresses of the auditors respectively for 1913 and for 1914 (if appointed):
    For 1913; T. E. Clendennen and J. T. Hammill.
    For 1914: T. E. Clendennen and J. T. Hammill.

15. What were the dividend days of the Corporation in 1913 and what rate or rates of dividend were paid on those days respectively? None.

16. What is the date appointed for the Annual Meeting? 3rd Friday of January. Date of last Annual Meeting? 17th January, 1913.

17. Special General Meetings held in 1913: Dates, none.

THE NIAGARA FALLS BUILDING, SAVINGS AND LOAN ASSOCIATION.

Declaration of Incorporation filed with the Clerk of the Peace for the County of Welland, on the 5th March, 1894. (Decl. Book I, 29.)

Incorporated under the Building Societies' Act, R.S.O., 1887, c. 169, s. 2, as amended by 56 V. c. 31, s. 1, which (continued by R.S.O. 1897, c. 205, s. 8 (4) has the effect of limiting the operations of the Association to the County of Welland.

The lending and the borrowing powers are governed by the Loan and Trust Corporations Act, R.S.O., 1914, chap, 184.

Annual Statement

On the condition and affairs of the Niagara Falls Building, Savings and Loan Association of Niagara Falls, Ontario, at the 31st December, 1913, and for the year ending on that day, made to the Registrar of Loan Corporations for the Province of Ontario, pursuant to the laws of the said Province.

The head office of the Corporation is at No. 39 Parks Street, in the City of Niagara Falls, in the Province of Ontario.

The Board is constituted of ten directors, holding office for two years.

The directors and chief executive officers of the Corporation at the 31st December, 1913, were as follows, together with their respective terms of office:

R. P. Slater, President, Niagara Falls, Ontario;	April, 1913; April, 1914.
R. F. Carter, Vice-President, Niagara Falls, Ontario;	April, 1912; April, 1914.
J. C. Rothery, Director, Toronto, Ontario;	" "
James Harriman, Director, Niagara Falls, Ontario;	" "
W. W. Robertson, Director, Niagara Falls (Centre);	
J. L. Harriman, Director, Niagara Falls, Ontario;	" "
J. H. McGarry, M.D., Director, Niagara Falls, Ontario;	April, 1913; April, 1915.
F. W. Swannell, Director, Niagara Falls, Ontario;	" "
F. LeBlond, Director, Niagara Falls, N.Y.;	" "
J. G. Cadham, Director, Niagara Falls (South), Ontario;	" "
J. L. Harriman, Secretary, Niagara Falls, Ontario;	April. 1913; Dec. 31, 1913.

Schedule B.

Terminating or Withdrawable Stock.

Subscribed Shares of Terminating or Withdrawable Stock.	Prepaid.		Instalment.		Total.	
	No.	Amount.	No.	Amount.		
		$ c.		$ c.	$ c	
Number and amount in force at 31st Dec., 1912	477	62,010 00	2321	77,413 31	139,423 31	
Number and amount issued during 1913	163	21,190 00	514	31,175 45	52,365 45	
Gross total in force at any time in 1913.	640	83,200 00	2835	108,588 76	191,788 76	
Deduct as follows: Withdrawn and paid off during 1913	202	26,260 00	172	17,418 90	43,678 90	
Net total remaining in force at 31st Dec., 1913	438	56,940 00	2663	91,169 86	148,109 86	

Summary of Terminating or Withdrawable Stock in force at 31st December:

438 shares prepaid stock at $130.00 per share, $56,940.00, on which 73
     shareholders have paid in $56,940 00
2,663 shares instalment stock at $130.00 per share, $346,190.00, on which
     226 shareholders have paid in 91,169 86
    Total amount distributed or credited into terminating or withdrawable stock in 1913:
(2) As dividends out of profits: On prepaid stock, 2,896.15; rate 5%, 5½% and 6%; on instalment stock, $6,784.96, per cent. 8%.

BALANCE SHEET AS AT 31st DECEMBER, 1913.

Dr. Capital and Liabilities.

Capital (Liabilities to Stockholders or Shareholders).

B.—Terminating Capital Stock or Shares.

17. (d) Prepaid stock, less shown in (24), total in force, 438 shares at $130 per share, on which has been paid into Loan Fund	$56,940 00	
20. (g) Instalment stock, less shown in (24), total issue now in force, 2,663 shares at $130 per share, $346,190, on which has been paid in all $91,169.86 into Loan Fund	91,169 86	
21. (h) Profits or accrued interest on (20), less shown in (25), and credited or appropriated but not paid	19,191 51	
22. (i) Profits or accrued interest on (20), less shown in (25) and not credited or appropriated	13,611 51	$180,912 88

Liabilities to the Public.

37. Owing to banks (including interest due or accrued)....	$2,112 47	
39. Due on loans in process of completion or to pay assumed mortgages	5,980 00	8,092 47
Total liabilities		$189,005 35

Cr. Assets.

I.—Assets of which the Corporation is the Beneficial Owner.

B.—Debts secured by Mortgages of Land.

9. (a) Debts (other than item 10) secured by mortgages of land	$188,890 00	

E.—Cash.

31. (a) On hand	65 35	

F.—Assets not hereinbefore mentioned.

37. (a) Office furniture	50 00	
Total assets		$189,005 35

CASH ACCOUNT.

Receipts for the year ending 31st December, 1913.

I.—Received by the Corporation for its Own Use.

A.—Balance from 31st December, 1912.

	(Col. 1.)	(Col. 2.)	(Total Col. 4.)
(a) Cash (not already shown under (1)....	....	....	$579 15

CASH ACCOUNT.—Continued.

Receipts for the year ending 31st December, 1913.

B.—Sums received wholly or partly on Capital Stock.

	(Col. 1)	(Col. 2)	(Total Col. 4)
7. (d) Sales of prepaid building stock.........	....	$21,190 00	
8. (e) Dues on instalment building society stock	......:..	14,394 46	
			$35,584 46

C.—Receipts on account of Investments, Loans or Debts.

(a) On mortgages of realty:

		(Col. 1)	(Col. 2)	(Total Col. 4)
10.	(i) Principal, $16,780.99 and $16,250.00	....	$33,030 99	
11.	(ii) Interest.....	....	10,143 65	
				43,174 64

E.—Miscellaneous.

	(Col. 1)	(Col. 2)	(Total Col. 4)
19. (b) Premium or bonus on loans............	$2,500 00		
20. (c) Membership or entry fees (being income of Corporation)	189 50		
21. (d) Fines....	114 92		
22. (e) Withdrawal profits....	32 33		
		....	2,836 75

F.—Borrowed Money.

	(Col. 1)	(Col. 2)	(Total Col. 4)
25. (a) Bank or other advances, discounts or over-drafts.....	....	....	2,112 47
Totals.....			$84,287 47

CASH ACCOUNT.

Expenditure for the year ending 31st December, 1913.

I.—Expended on Corporation Account.

A.—Sums Loaned or Invested on Capital Account.

	(Col. 1.)	(Col. 2.)	(Total Col. 4.)
1. (a) Loaned on mortgages of realty..........	....	....	$32,890 00

B.—Expended on Stock Account.

	(Col. 1.)	(Col. 2.)	(Total Col. 4.)
9. Dividends paid on terminating stock........	$2,896 15		
		....	2,896 15
11. Paid for terminating stock withdrawn......	....	$43,678 90	
13. Profits paid on (11)	....	3,533 37	
			47,212 27

CASH ACCOUNT.—Continued.

Expenditure for the year ending 31st December, 1913.

C.—Borrowed Money (other than foregoing) or
    interest thereon paid, viz.:

	(Col. 1.)	(Col. 2.)	(Total Col. 4.)
18. (a) Bank account (principal and interest)..	....	....	$7 '10

D.—Management Expenses (other than
    foregoing).

	(Col. 1.)	(Col. 2.)	(Total Col. 4.)
25. (a) Salaries, wages and fees	$960 50		
26. (b) Commission or Brokerage	35 40		
27. (c) Provincial tax	26 00		
28. (d) Stationery, postage, printing, advertising	32 25		
29. (e) Treasurer's bond....................	8 00		
30. (f) Taxes (other than 7 and 32), business tax...............................	2 70		
31. (g) Rent..........................	100 00		
32. (h) Registration fee....................	30 00		
33. (i) Other management expenditure: Auditor's fees; treasurer's bond; cleaning office, etc........................	21 75	....	1,216 60

F.—Balance.

	(Col. 1.)	(Col. 2.)	(Total Col. 4.)
37. (a) Cash on hand	....	....	65 35
Total..			$84,287 47

MISCELLANEOUS STATEMENT FOR THE YEAR ENDING 31ST DECEMBER, 1913.

1. Amount of debentures maturing in 1914: Issued in Canada, none; issued elsewhere, none.
2. Amount of other existing obligations which will mature in 1914: None.
3. Amount of securities held by the Corporation which will mature and become payable to the Corporation in 1914: None.
4. Average rate of interest per annum paid by the Corporation during 1913 on deposits: None; on debentures, none; on debenture stock, none.
5. Average rate of interest per annum received by the Corporation during 1913: (a) On mortgages of realty; (b) on other securities.
    (i) Owned beneficially by the Corporation: (a) Six;. (b) none.
    (ii) Not owned beneficially: (a) None; (b) none.
6. Of the mortgages owned beneficially by the Corporation, $188,890.00 is on realty situate in Ontario, and none is on realty situate elsewhere.
7. Of the mortgages not owned beneficially by the Corporation, none is on realty situate in Ontario, and none is on realty situate elsewhere.
8. Loans written off or transferred to real estate account during 1913, viz.:
    (i) Funds or securities owned beneficially: None. ....
    (ii) Not so owned: None.
9. Number and aggregate amount of mortgages upon which compulsory proceedings have been taken by the Corporation in 1913, viz.:
    (i) Owned beneficially: No., none; amount, none.
    (ii) Not so owned: No., none; amount, none.
10. Aggregate market value of land mortgaged to the Corporation:
    (i) Mortgages owned beneficially: $286,000.00.
    (ii) Not so owned; None.

11. How often are the securities held by the Corporation valued? Whenever deemed necessary.

12. (a) Specify the officers of the Corporation who are under bond and for what sum respectively: Treasurer, $2.000; solicitor, $1,000.

(b) Are the said bonds executed by private sureties or by Guarantee Companies? Both.

13. Date when the accounts of the Corporation were last audited: September 30th, 1913.

14. Names and addresses of the auditors respectively for 1913 and for 1914 (if appointed): For 1913: Miss E. Edmand and W. G. McMurray (Miss Hopkins replacing Miss Edmand).

15. What were the dividend days of the Corporation in 1913 and what rate or rates of dividend were paid on those days respectively: March 31st, 1913; September 30th, 1913. ————

16. What is the date appointed for the Annual Meeting? April 21st, 1914. Date of last Annual Meeting? April 15th, 1913.

17. Special General Meetings held in 1913. Dates: None.

THE OWEN SOUND LOAN AND SAVINGS COMPANY.

Head Office, Owen Sound, Ontario.

———

Incorporated under the Building Societies Act, R.S.O., 1887, c. 169, by declaration filed with the Clerk of the Peace for the County of Grey, on the 1st April, 1889.

The lending and borrowing powers are governed by the Loan and Trust Corporations Act, R.S.O. 1914, chap. 184.

———

ANNUAL STATEMENT.

Of the condition and affairs of The Owen Sound Loan and Savings Company, of Owen Sound, Ont., at the 31st December, 1913, and for the year ending on that day, made to the Registrar of Loan Corporations for the Province of Ontario, pursuant to the laws of the said Province.

The head office of the Corporation is at 823 Second Avenue E., in the Town of Owen Sound, in the Province of Ontario.

The Board is constituted of ten directors, holding office for two years.

The directors and chief executive officers of the Corporation at the 31st December, 1913, were as follows, together with their respective terms of office:—

W. A. Bishop, President, Owen Sound;	February, 1913;	February, 1915.
F. W. Harrison, Vice-President, Owen Sound;	" 1914;	" 1916.
C. A. Fleming, Director, Owen Sound;	" 1913;	" 1915.
W. G. McLauchlan, Director, Owen Sound;	" 1913;	" 1915.
M. Forhan, Director, Owen Sound;	" 1913;	" 1915.
N. P. Horton, Director, Owen Sound;	" 1914;	" 1916.
Chas. Julyan, Director, Owen Sound;	" 1914;	" 1916.
John S. Findlay, Director, Owen Sound;	" 1914;	" 1916.
John M. Kilbourn, Director, Owen Sound;	" 1913;	" 1915.
G. E. Sharpe, Director, Owen Sound;	" 1914;	" 1916.
C. A. Fleming, Manager and Secretary, Owen Sound.		

A.—Capital stock: Total amount authorized, $1,000,000; total amount subscribed, permanent stock, $143,100.00, as more particularly set out in Schedule A hereto.

SCHEDULE A.

Class 1.—Fixed and permanent capital stock created by virtue of Building Society Acts.

Description.	No. of shares.	Par value.	Total amount held.	Paid thereon.	Total amount unpaid.
		$	$	$ c.	$ c.
2. Partly called	1,431	100	143,100	117,444 84	25,655 16

Terminating or Withdrawable Stock.

		Instalment.	
		No.	Amount.
Subscribed Shares of Terminating or Withdrawable Stock.			
Number and amount in force at 31st December, 1912 ....:..........		103	$ 10,300
Number and amount issued during 1913		5	500
Gross total in force at any time in 1913.............................		·108	10,800

	No. of shares	Amount		
Deduct as follows:		$		
Withdrawn and paid off during 1913	7	700	7	700
Net total remaining in force 31st December, 1913		·	101	$10,100

Summary of Terminating or Withdrawable Stock in force at 31st December, 1913.

101 Shares Instalment Stock at $100 per share, $10,100, on which 17 shareholders have
        paid in $2,182.80.
Total amount of stock distributed or credited to Terminating or Withdrawable in 1913
        (2) As dividends out of profits, $119.57. .
Rate or rates per cent. of such dividends, 6% per annum.

BALANCE SHEET AS AT 31st_DECEMBER, ˙1913˙

Dr.   Capital and Liabilities.

Capital (Liabilities to Stockholders or Shareholders).

    A.—Permanent Capital Stock or Shares.

3. (c) Ordinary joint stock capital; no regular calls made;
        total paid thereon* $117,444 84
7. (g) Contingent fund in respect of (3)............... 5,461 88
                                    $122,906 72

    B.—Terminating Capital Stock or Shares.

20. (g) Instalment stock, less shown in (24): Total issue
        now in force, 101 shares at $100 per share,
                on which has been paid in all
        of which sum there has been paid into loan fund, 2,182 80 · · · ·
21. (h) Profits or accrued interest on (20), less shown in
        (25), and credited or appropriated, but not paid. 309 20
                                    2,492 00

---

*Shareholders are allowed to pay in as suits their convenience.

BALANCE SHEET.—Continued.

Dr.   Capital and Liabilities.

Liabilities to the Public.

27. Deposits, right reserved to require 30 days' notice of any withdrawal.	$62,156 29	
28. Interest on deposits due on accrued or capitalized	46 68	
29. Debentures issued in Canada	10,967 83	
30. Interest due and accrued on (29).	238 00	
37. Owing to Banks (including interest due or accrued). . . .	7,335 07	$80,743 87
Total liabilities.		$206,142 59

Assets.

I.—Assets of which the Corporation is the Beneficial Owner.

1. (a) Office premises situate		
2. (1) At Owen Sound, held in freehold.	. . . .	$15,174 35

B.—Debts secured by Mortgages of Land.

9. (a) Debts (other than item 10) secured by mortgages of land.	$167,619 32	
11. (c) Interest due and accrued on item (9) and not included therein.	8,630 90	176,250 22

C.—Debts not above enumerated for which the Corporation holds securities as follows:

15. (c) Debts secured by Public School Debentures	$2,400 00	
20. (h) Debts secured only by permanent stock of the Corporation.	8,565 84	
21. (i) Debts secured only by terminating Stock or Shares of the Corporation	900 00	
26. (n) Interest due or accrued on (14-25) and not included therein.	611 36	12,477 20

E.—Cash.

31. (a) On hand.	. . . .	1,485 45

F.—Assets not hereinbefore mentioned.

33. (b) Office furniture, etc.	. . . .	755 37
Total assets.		$206,142 59

CASH ACCOUNT.

Receipts for the year ending 31st December, 1913.

I.—Received by the Corporation for its Own Use.

A.—Balance from 31st December, 1912.

1. (b) Cash:		
2. (1) On hand	. . . .	$1,136 41

CASH ACCOUNT.—Continued.

Receipts for the year ending 31st December, 1913.

B.—Sums received wholly or partly on Capital Stock.

4. (a) Calls on Joint Stock permanent capital	$9,005 89		
8. (e) Dues on instalment building society stock........	780 25		
		9,786 14	

C.—Receipts on account of Investments, Loans or Debts.

(a) On mortgages of realty:

10.	(i) Principal.	$22,034 50	
11.	(ii) Interest	9,750 84	

(b) On other securities:

12.	(i) Principal Stock Loans	2,585 27	
13.	(ii) Interest or dividends	359 11	
		34,729 72	

D.—Receipts from Real Estate Owned Beneficially by Corporation.

17. (b) Rents 263 50

F.—Borrowed Money.

25 (a) Bank overdraft	$7,335 07		
26. (b) Borrowed by taking deposits	81,289 81		
27. (c) Borrowed on Debentures.	10,967 83		
		99,592 71	

G.—Receipts from other sources, viz.:

30. (a) Interest on Bank account, etc.	$17 97		
(b) Sundries.	3 00		
		20 97	

Total . . . .+.. $145,519 45

CASH ACCOUNT.

Expenditure for the year ending 31st December, 1913.

I.—Expended on Corporation Account.

A.—Sums Loaned or Invested on Capital Account.

1. (a) Loaned on mortgages of realty	$42,980 18		
(b) Loaned on other securities:			
2.	(i) Stock Loans.	4,624 15	
4.	(iii) School Debentures.	2,400 00	
5.	(iv) Accrued Interest on School Debentures......	65 00	
		$50,069 33	

B.—Expended on Stock Account.

8. Dividends paid on permanent stock....................	....	6,979 26	
12. Paid for terminating stock matured...................	....	700 00	

CASH ACCOUNT.—Continued.

Expenditure for the year ending 31st December, 1913.

C.—Borrowed Money (other than foregoing) or interest thereon paid, viz.:

18. (a) Bank acct., Principal, $3,824.90; interest, $168.60......	$3,993 50	
19. (b) Deposits: Principal, $69,403.22; interest, $2,093.75..	71,496 97	
		75,490 47

D.—Management Expenses (other than foregoing).

25. (a) Salaries, wages and fees	$746 00	
28. (d) Stationery, postage, printing, and advertising......	219 92	
30. (f) Fuel, Rent and Rates, Taxes (other than in 7 and 32)	297 19	
32. (h) Registration fees..............................	30 00	
33. (i) Other Management Expenditure:		
Furniture, etc....	147 37	
		1,440 48

E.—Other Expenditure.

34. (a) Real Estate (Head Office)	$3,174 35	
35. (b) Paid Mortgage on Office Premises	6,000 00	
36. (c) Interest on Mortgage on Head Office	180 11	
		9,354 46

F.—Balance.

37. (b) Cash on hand		1,485 45
Total.		$145,519 45

Miscellaneous Statement for the Year Ending 31st December, 1913.

1. Amount of debentures maturing in 1914: Issued in Canada, $500.00; issued elsewhere, none.
2. Amount of other existing obligations which will mature in 1914: None.
3. Amount of securities held by the Corporation whch will mature and become payable to the Corporation in 1914: $15,539.00.
4. Average rate of interest per annum paid by the Corporation during 1913: On deposits, 4%; on debentures, 4¾%; on debenture stock, none.
5. Average rate of interest per annum received by the Corporation during 1913: (a) On mortgages of realty; (b) on other securities:
   (i) Owned beneficially by the Corporation: (a) 6½%; (b) 6%.
   (ii) Not owned beneficially: (a) ——; (b) ——.
6. Of, the mortgages owned beneficially by the Corporation all is on realty situate in Ontario, and none is on realty situate elsewhere.
7. Of the mortgages not owned beneficially by the Corporation, none is on realty situate in Ontario, and none is on realty situate elsewhere.
8. Loans written off or transferred to real estate account during 1913, viz.:
   (i) Funds or securities owned beneficially: None.
   (ii) Not so owned: None.
9. Number and aggregate amount of mortgages upon which compulsory proceedings have been taken by the Corporation in 1913, viz.:
   (i) Owned beneficially: No., none; amount, none.
   (ii) Not so owned: No., none; amount, ——.

10. Aggregate market value of land mortgaged to the Corporation:
    (i) Mortgages owned beneficially:: $623,900.
    (ii) Not so owned: None.
11. How often are the securities held by the Corporation valued? When loan is made or when in arrears.
12. (a) Specify the officers of the Corporation who are under bond and for what sum respectively: The Manager for $1,000.
    (b) Are the said bonds executed by private sureties or by Guarantee Companies? Guarantee Company.
13. Date when the accounts of the Corporation were last audited: October 31st, 1913.
14. Names and addresses of the auditors respectively for 1913 and for 1914 (if appointed):
    For 1913: A. F. Armstrong, J. C. Kennedy.
    For 1914: A. F. Armstrong, J. C. Kennedy.
15. What were the dividend days of the Corporation in 1913 and what rate or rates of dividend were paid on those days respectively: June 30th and December 31st; six per cent. per annum.
16. What is the date appointed for the Annual Meeting? February 20th, 1914. Date of last Annual Meeting? February 24th, 1913.
17. Special General Meetings held in 1913. Dates: None.

THE PETERBOROUGH WORKINGMEN'S BUILDING AND SAVINGS SOCIETY.

Head Office, Peterborough, Ontario.

Incorporated under the Building Societies Act (R.S.O., 1887, c. 169) by declaration filed with the Clerk of the Peace for the County of Peterborough, on the 17th January, 1889. (Decl. Book L, 47.)

The lending and borrowing powers are governed by the Loan and Trust Corporations Act. R.S.O. 1914, chap. 184.

ANNUAL STATEMENT

Of the condition and affairs of the Peterborough Workingmen's Building and Savings Society, of Peterborough, at the 31st December, 1913, and for the year ending on that day, made to the Registrar of Loan Corporations for the Province of Ontario, pursuant to the laws of the said Province.

The head office of the Corporation is at George Street, in the City of Peterborough, in the Province of Ontario.

The Board is constituted of nine directors, holding office for one year.

The directors and chief executive officers of the Corporation at the 31st December, 1913, were as follows, together with their respective terms of office:

T. B. McGrath, President, Peterborough;   January 15th, 1913; one year.
James Lynch, Vice President, Peterborough;   "   "   "
R. Sheehy, Director, Peterborough;   "   "
A. Murty, Director, Peterborough;
A. E. Peek, Director, Peterborough;
James Garrow, Director, Peterborough;
S. W. English, Director, Peterborough;
Geo. Ball, Director, Peterborough;
Jas. Murty, Treasurer, Peterborough;
John Corkery, Secretary, Peterborough;

SCHEDULE B.

Terminating or Withdrawable Stock.

Shares of Terminating or Withdrawable Stock.		No.	Amount.
			$ c.
Number and amount in force at 31st December, 1912		787	42,684 87
Number and amount issued during 1913...............................		149	9,962 00
Gross total in force at any time in 1913......................		936	52,596 87

	No. of shares	Amount.		
		$ c.		
Deduct as follows:				
Withdrawn and paid off during 1913............	72	2,959 50		
Retired by Corporation during 1913	41	5,578 50		
Total deductions.........................	113	8,538 00	113	8,538 00
Net total remaining in force 31st December, 1913..			823	$44,058 87

Summary of Terminating or Withdrawable Stock in force at 31st December, 1913:
823 Shares Instalment stock (payable by fixed periodical payments) at $200 per share,
on which Shareholders have paid in $44,058.87.

Total amount distributed or credited in
    (1) As interest, $422.68.
        Rate of such interest per cent. per annum. 4%.
    (2) As dividends out of profits, $2,883.14.
        Rate per cent. of such dividends, .073747.

BALANCE SHEET AS AT 31st DECEMBER, 1913.

Dr.   Capital and Liabilities.

Capital (Liabilities to Stockholders or Shareholders).

B.—Terminating Capital Stock.

20. (g) Instalment stock, less shown in (24); Total issue now in force, 823 shares at $200 per share, on which has been paid in all of which sum there has been into loan fund......	$44,058 87	
21. (h) Profits or accrued interest on (20), less shown in (25), and credited or appropriated, but not yet paid..	10,857 25	
		$54,916 12

Liabilities to the Public.

37. Owing to banks (including interest due or accrued)....	$2,384 52	
38. Due on bills payable other than (37). including interest due and accrued	2,000 00	
		4,384 52
Total liabilities		$59,300 64

Cr.   Assets.

I.—Assets of which the Corporation is the Beneficial Owner.

B.—Debts secured by Mortgages of Land.

9. (a) Debts (other than item 10) secured by mortgages of land.........	$44,150 00	
11. (c) Interest due and accrued on (9) not included therein	795 20	
		44,945 20

C.—Debts not above enumerated for which the Corporation holds securities as follows:

21. (i) Debts secured by terminating stock or shares of the Corporation	$14,159 00	
26. (n) Interest due or accrued on item (21) and not included therein	165 29	
		14,324 29

E.—Cash.

31. (a) On hand		31 15
Total assets		$59,300 64

CASH ACCOUNT.

Receipts for the year ending 31st December, 1913.

I.—Received by the Corporation for its Own Use.

A.—Balances from 31st December, 1912.

		(Col. 2.)	(Col. 4.)
1. Cash:			
3.	(ii) In bank	$21 50	
			$21 50

B.—Sums received wholly or partly on Capital Stock.

7. (d) Sales of prepaid Building Society stock	$9,962 00	
		$9,962 00

C.—Receipts on account of Investments, Loans or Debts.

(a) On mortgages of realty:		
10.	(i) Principal...........................	$9,915 00	
11.	(ii) Interest	2,991 75	
(b) On other securities:			
12.	(i) Principal stock of Society	3,376 00	
13.	(ii) Interest or dividends	857 80	
(c) Unsecured debts:			
15.	(ii) Interest on bank balances	9 25	
			17,149 80

E.—Miscellaneous.

20. (c) Membership or entry fees (being income of Corporation)..	$36 00	
21. (d) Fines.......................................	78 95	
		114 95

F.—Borrowed Money.

25. (a) Bank or other advances, discounts or overdrafts................	2,384 52

G.—Receipts from Other Sources.

30. (a) Loan on promissory note	5,000 00
Total..	$34,632 77

CASH ACCOUNT.

Expenditure for the year ending 31st December, 1913.

I.—Expended on Corporation Account.

A.—Sums Loaned or Invested on Capital Account.

	(Col. 2)	(Col. 4)
1. (a) Loaned on mortgages of realty......................	$4,600 00	
2. (b) Loaned or invested in other securities:		
3.	(ii) Stock of the Society	2,300 00	
		$6,900 00

15 L.C.

CASH ACCOUNT.—Continued.

Expenditure for the year ending 31st December, 1913.

B.—Expended on Stock Account.

10. Interest paid on terminating stock......................	$2,959 50	
12. Paid for terminating stock matured....................	8,200 00	
13. Profits paid on (11) and (12)...........................	422 68	
		$11,582 18

C.—Borrowed Money (other than foregoing) or interest thereon paid. viz.:

18. (a) Bank account: Principal, $10,354.39; interest, $185.55...........	10,539 94

D.—Management Expenses (other than foregoing.)

25. (a) Salaries, wages and fees	$225 00	
28. (d) Stationery, postage. printing and advertising.......	8 25	
32. (h) Registration fees	30 00	
		263 25

E.—Other Expenditures, viz.:

34. (a) Promissory note paid	$5,000 00	
35. (b) Interest on loan (promissory note)	316 25	
		5,316 25

F.—Balance.

37. (a) Cash on hand	31 15
Total	$34,632 77

Miscellaneous Statement for the Year Ending 31st December, 1913.

1. Amount of debentures maturing in 1914: Issued in Canada, none; Issued elsewhere, none.
2. Amount of other existing obligations which will mature in 1914, $6,000.00.
3. Amount of securities held by the Corporation which will mature and become payable to the Corporation in 1914, none.
4. Average rate of interest per annum paid by the Corporation during 1913: On deposits, none; on debentures, none; on debenture stock, none.
5. Average rate of interest per annum received by the Corporation during 1913: (a) On mortgages of realty; (b) on other securities:
   (i) Owned beneficially by the Corporation: (a) 6%; (b) 6%.
   (ii) Not owned beneficially: (a) None; (b) none.
6. Of the mortgages owned beneficially by the Corporation, $44,150 is on realty situate in Ontario, and none is on realty situate elsewhere.
7. Of the mortgages not owned beneficially by the Corporation, none is on realty situate in Ontario, and none is on realty situate elsewhere.
8. Loans written off or transferred to real estate account during 1913, viz.:
   (i) Funds or securities owned beneficially, none.
   (ii) Not so owned, none.
9. Number and aggregate amount of mortgages upon which compulsory proceedings have been taken by the Corporation in 1913, viz.:
   (i) Owned beneficially: No., none; Amount, none.
   (ii) Not so owned: No., none; Amount, none.
10. Aggregate market value of land mortgaged to the Corporation:
    (i) Mortgages owned beneficially, $65,000.
    (ii) Not so owned, none.

11. How often are the securities held by the Corporation valued? When loan is effected.
12. (a) Specify the officers of the Corporation who are under bond and for what sum respectively: The Secretary. $1,000; The Treasurer, $1,000.
    (b) Are the said bonds executed by private sureties or by Guarantee Companies? Private sureties.
13. Date when the accounts of the Corporation were last audited. January 5th, 1914.
14. Names and addresses of the auditors respectively for 1913 and for 1914 (if appointed): appointed):
    For 1913: James Drain.
    For 1914: James Drain.
15. What were the dividend days of the Corporation in 1913, and what rate or rates of dividend were paid on those days respectively? No dividend day.
16. What is the date appointed for the Annual Meeting? January 14th, 1914. Date of last Annual Meeting January 15th, 1913.
17. Special General Meetings held in 1913: Dates, none.

THE SUN AND HASTINGS SAVINGS AND LOAN COMPANY OF ONTARIO

Head Office, Toronto, Ontario.

This Company was formed by the amalgamation of the two Provincial Companies described in the Report of the Registrar of Loan Corporations for 1901 under the respective titles: " The Sun Savings and Loan Company of Ontario " and " The Hastings Loan and Investment Society."

The deed of amalgamation, after ratification by the shareholders of the respective companies, was on the 27th day of August, A.D. 1902, assented to by the Lieutenant-Governor of Ontario in Council. (R.S.O., 1897, c. 205, s. 44.)

The lending and borrowing powers are governed by the Loan and Trust Corporations Act, R.S.O. 1914, chap. 184.

ANNUAL STATEMENT

Of the condition and affairs of The Sun and Hastings Savings and Loan Company of Ontario, at the 31st December, 1913, and for the year ending on that day, made to the Registrar of Loan Corporations for the Province of Ontario, pursuant to the laws of the said Province.

The head office of the Corporation is at No. 4 Richmond Street East, in the City of Toronto, in the Province of Ontario.

The Board is constituted of eight directors holding office for the term of one year.

The directors and chief executive officers of the Corporation at the 31st December, 1913, were as follows, together with their respective terms of office:

Whitford Vandusen, President, Toronto;   17th February, 1913; 16th February. 1914.
Ambrose Kent, Vice-President, Toronto;   "   "
Sir Mackenzie Bowell, K.C.M.G., P.C., Director,
      Belleville;
Rev. A. Campbell, Director, Belleville;
W. J. Fawcett, Director, Toronto;
J. T. Gilmour, M.D., Director, Toronto;   "
John Tolmie, Director, Kincardine;
W. Pemberton Page, Managing-Dir., Toronto;   "

A. Permanent capital stock: total amount authorized, $2,000,000.00; total amount subscribed, $609,050.00, as more particularly set out in Schedule A hereto.

SCHEDULE A.

Class 1.—Fixed and Permanent Capital Stock created by virtue of Building Society Acts.

Description.	No. of shares.	Par value of shares.	Total amount held	Total amount paid thereon.	Total remaining unpaid.
		$	$	$ c.	$ c.
1. Fully called.....................	5,930½	100	593,050	573,113 81	19,936 19
3. Instalment, stock (payable by fixed periodical payments and still in process of payment)	160	100	16,000	875 90	15,124 10
Totals	6,090½₁	....	609,050	573,989 71	35,060 29

LIST OF SHAREHOLDERS AS AT 31st DECEMBER, 1913.

(Not printed.)

SCHEDULE B.

Terminating or Withdrawable Stock.

Shares of Terminating or Withdrawable Stock.	Fully paid.		Prepaid.		Instalment.		Total.
	No.	Amount.	No.	Amount.	No.	Amount.	
Number and amount in force 31st December, 1912............................	22	$ 2,200	1,763	$ 176,300	999	$ 99,900	278,400
Number and amount issued during 1913	....	....	3	300	....	... .	300
Gross total in force at any time in 1913	22	2,200	1,766	176,600	999	99,900	278,700

	No. of shares	Amount.						
Deduct as follows: Withdrawn and paid off during 1913..........	541	$ 54,100	20	2,000	264	26,400	257	25,700	54,100
Total deductions.....	541	54,100	2	2,000	264	26,400	257	25,700	54,100
Net total remaining in force at 31st December, 1913.....	2	200	1,502	150,200	742	74,200	224,600

Summary of Terminating or Withdrawable stock in force 31st December, 1913:

2 shares fully paid up stock at $100 per share on which 1 shareholder has paid in.	$200 00	$200 00	$200 00
1,502 shares prepaid stock (other than above), at $100 per share .... on which 159 shareholders have paid in	$150,200 00	...... 89,950 00	91,142 49
742 shares instalment stock at $100 per share on which 105 shareholders have paid in	74,200 00	...... 54,172 49	45,962 16
2,246 Totals	$224,600 00	$144,322 49	$137,304 65
Paid up certificates			354 79
			$137,659 44

Total amount distributed or credited in 1913.
(1) As interest, $4,690.60; Rate, 5% and 6%.
(2) As dividends out of profits, $8,344.18.
Rates or rates per cent. of such dividends, 9 per cent. on instalment and $50 prepaid stock; and 2 per cent. on $60 prepaid stock.

BALANCE SHEET AS AT 31st DECEMBER, 1913

Dr.   Capital and Liabilities.

Capital (Liabilities to Stockholders or Shareholders).

A.—Permanent Capital Stock or Shares.

1. Ordinary joint stock capital: Fully called; total called, $593,050.00; total paid thereon.................. $573,113 81
4. (d) Dividends declared in respect of (1) and (8) but not yet paid 17,495 47
8. (h) Instalment permanent stock (payable by fixed periodical payments); total subscribed, $16,000.00, of which has been paid 875 90

                                                              $591,485 18

BALANCE SHEET.—Continued.

Dr. Capital and Liabilities.

B.—Terminating Capital Stock or Shares.

14. (*a*) Fully paid stock, less shown in (24): Total in force, 2 shares at $100 per share, carried to loan fund	$200 00
17. (*d*) Prepaid stock less shown in (24); Total in force, 1,502 shares at $100 per share. on which has been paid in loan fund	91,142 67
18. (*e*) Profits or accrued interest on (17), less shown in 25, credited or appropriated, but not yet paid	2,766 03
20. (*g*) Instalment stock less shown in (24). Total issue now in force, 742 shares at $100 per share, $74,200 on which has been paid in all, of which Which sums there has been paid into loan fund..	45,962 16
22. (*i*) Profits or accrued interest on 17 and 20, not credited or appropriated	16,200 37
	$156,271 23

C.—Liabilities to Stockholders or Shareholders other than as already shown under A or B. viz.:

26. Paid up certificates	$ 354 79
Reserve	220,000 00
	220,354 79

Liabilities to the Public.

$968,111 20

27. Deposits right reserved to require 30 days' notice of any withdrawal, including interest	$ 28,591 22
29. Debentures issued in Canada	100,445 00
30. Interest due or accrued on (29)	1,340 62
31. Debentures issued elsewhere than in Canada	85,896 67
32. Interest due or accrued on (31)	582 58
41. (*a*) Sundry accounts	910 18
	217 766 27

Total liabilities $1,185,877 47

Cr. Assets.

I.—Assets of which the Corporation is the Beneficial Owner.

A.—Immovable Property Owned Beneficially by Corporation.

5. (*b*) Freehold land (including buildings) other than fore-foing	$17,390 70

B.—Debts secured by Mortgages of Land.

9. (*a*) Debts (other than item 10) secured by mortgages of land	$1,121,668 67
11. (*c*) Interest due or accrued on item 9 and not included therein	8,587 14
	1,130,255 81

C.—Debts not above enumerated for which the Corporation holds securities as follows:

20. (*h*) Debts secured only by permanent stock or shares of the Corporation	$8,695 00
21. (*i*) Debts secured only by terminating stock or shares of the Corporation	600 00
	9,295 00

BALANCE SHEET.—Continued.

Cr.   Assets.

D.—Unsecured Debts.

27. (*a*) Sundry accounts $1,169 22

E.—Cash.

31. (*a*) On hand $2,286 91
32. (*b*) In banks 23,979 83
                                                          —————
                                                          26,266 74

F.—Assets not hereinbefore mentioned.

37. (*a*) Office furniture and supplies 1,500 00

Total assets $1,185,877 47

CASH ACCOUNT.

Receipts for the year ending 31st December, 1913.

I.—Received by the Corporation for its Own Use.

	(Col. 1.)	(Col. 2.)	(Col. 3.)	(Total Col. 4.)
A.—Balance from 31st December, 1912.				
1. (*b*) Cash (not already shown under (1)):				
2. (i) On hand }		$6,966 44	....	$6,966 44
3. (ii) In bank }				
B.—Sums Received Wholly or Partly on Capital Stock.				
4. (*a*) Calls on joint stock permanent capital			$713 61	
7. (*d*) Sales of prepaid building society stock		200 00	....	
8. (*e*) Dues on instalment building society stock	546 00	2,825 24		4,284 85
C.—Receipts on account of Investments, Loans or Debts.				
(*a*) On mortgages of realty:				
10. (i) Principal....		279,760 22		
11. (ii) Interest....		96,203 24		
(*b*) On other securities:				
12. (i) Principal, stock loans repaid		3,725 00	....	379,238 46
D.—Receipts from Real Estate Owned Beneficially by Corporation				
16. (*a*) Sales		7,812 71	....	7,812 71
E.—Miscellaneous.				
18. (*a*) Commission or brokerage ...$646 56				
19. (*b*) Premiums on bonus on loans		$4,960 95	....	5,730 51
21. (*d*) Fines or transfer fees...... 123 00		....	....	

CASH ACCOUNT.—Continued.

Receipts for the year ending 31st December, 1913.

F.—Borrowed Money

	(Col. 1.)	(Col. 2.)	(Col. 3.)	(Total Col. 4.)
26. (b) Borrowed by taking deposits		95,654 30		
27. (c) Borrowed on debentures		44,300 44	....	139,954 74

G.—Receipts from other sources.

30. (a) Gain on property sold.......		89 68		
On loans paid off		74 72		
(b) Bank interest, etc.		6,774 73		
(c) Sundry accounts		2,012 81		
Suspense		738 86		
Discharge mortgage		14 60		
Short remitted		30 68		
				9,736 08
Totals................$1,315 56		$551,694 62	$713 61	$553,723 79

CASH ACCOUNT.

Expenditure for the year ending 31st December, 1913.

I.—Expended on Corporation Account.

A.—Sums Loaned or Invested on Capital Account.

	(Col.1.)	(Col. 2.)	(Total Col. 4.)
1. (a) Loaned on mortgages of realty	....	$203,647 88	
(b) Loaned or invested in other securities:			
2. (1) Stock loans	....	4,620 00	
6. (c) Real estate written off sundry properties	....	1,191 36	
7. (d) Incumbrances on realty paid off	....	4,189 95	
7. (e) Insurance or taxes advanced on property mortgaged to the Corporation	....	942 17	$214,591 36

B.—Expended on Stock Account.

8. Dividends paid on permanent stock	$34,415 19		
9. Dividends paid on terminating stock	5,219 16		
11. Paid on terminating stock withdrawn	....	$36,266 16	
			$75,900 51

C.—Borrowed Money and Interest thereon paid.

18. (a) Bank account	....	$17,650 82	
19. (b) Deposits: Principal, $101,910.22; interest, $1,456.23	....	103,366 45	
20. (c) Debentures issued in Canada: Principal, $50,270.00; interest, $5,752.32	....	56,022 32	
21. (d) Debentures issued elsewhere: Principal, $28,065.67; interest, $4,552.77	....	32,618 44	
			209,658 03

CASH ACCOUNT.—Continued.

Expenditure for the year ending 31st December, 1913.

D.—Management Expenses (other than fore-going.)

25. (a) Salaries and fees	....	$11,466 63	
26. (b) Commission or brokerage...............	....	5,729 02	
28. (d) Stationery, postage, printing and adver-tising	....	1,182 72	
29. (e) Law costs	....	334 89	
30. (f) Rent	....	1,299 30	
31. (g) Travelling expenses	....	291 70	
32. (h) Registration fees	....	976 19	
33. (i) Other management expenditure, mis-cellaneous expenses	....	606 91	
			$21,887 36

E.—Other Expenditures, viz.:

34. (a) Loss on properties sold	....	$857 34	
On loans paid off	....	2,711 81	
35. (b) Sundry accounts written off	....	1,850 64	
			5,419 79

F.—Balance.

37. (a) Cash on hand and in banks	....	$26,266 74	26,266 74
Total	$39,634 35	$514,089 44	$553,723 79

MISCELLANEOUS STATEMENT FOR THE YEAR ENDING 31ST DECEMBER, 1913.

1. Amount of Debentures maturing in 1914: Issued in Canada, $19,190.00; Issued else-where, $13,140.00.
2. Amount of other existing obligations which will mature in 1914: none.
3. Amount of securities held by the Corporation which will mature and become pay-able to the Corporation in 1914: None, except mortgages.
4. Average rate of interest per annum paid by the Corporation during 1913, on deposits, 4 per cent.; on debentures, 5½ per cent.; on debenture stock, none.
5. Average rate of interest per annum received by the Corporation during 1913: (a) On mortgages of realty, (b) On other securities:
   (i) Owned beneficially by the Corporation: (a), 10 per cent.; (b), 12 per cent.
   (ii) Not owned beneficially: (a), All mortgages and other securities are owned beneficially.
6. Of the mortgages owned beneficially by the Corporation, $631,486.49 is on realty situate in Ontario, and $490,182.20 is on realty situate elsewhere.
7. Of the mortgages not owned beneficially by the Corporation, none is on realty situate in Ontario, and none is on realty situate elsewhere.
8. Loans written off or transferred to real estate account during 1913, viz.:
   (i) Funds or securities owned beneficially, $4,025.19.
   (ii) Not so owned: See 5 (ii).
9. Number and aggregate amount of mortgages upon which compulsory proceedings have been taken by the Corporation in 1913, viz.:
   (i) Owned beneficially, none; Amount, none.
   (ii) Not so owned, none; Amount, see 5, (ii).

10. Aggregate market value of land mortgaged to the Corporation:
    (i) Mortgages owned beneficially, $2,140,037.00.
    (ii) Not so owned, see 5, (ii).

11. How often are the securities held by the Corporation valued: Yearly.

12: (a) Specify the officers of the Corporation who are under bond and for what sum
    respectively: Manager, $5,000; Cashier, $2,000; Accountant, $2,000.
   (b) Are the said bonds executed by private sureties or by Guarantee Companies
    Guarantee Companies.

13. Date when the accounts of the Corporation were last audited: 31st December, 1913.

14. Names and addresses of the auditors, respectively, for 1913 and for 1914 (if appointed):
    For 1913: J. F. Lawson, C.A.; J. L. Atkinson, C.A.
    For 1914: None.

15. What were the dividend days of the Corporation in 1913, and what rate or rates
    of dividend were paid on those days respectively:
    1st January, and 1st July: 5 per cent. and 6 per cent.

16. What is the date appointed for the Annual Meeting 3rd Monday in February. Date
    of last Annual Meeting; 16th February, 1914.

17. Special General Meetings held in 1913: Dates, none.

III. LOANING LAND COMPANIES.

DETAILED REPORTS OF THE SEVERAL COMPANIES.

[235]

THE LAND SECURITY COMPANY.

Head Office, Toronto.

CONSTATING ACTS OR INSTRUMENTS.

1873. Special Act of Incorporation, 36 V. c. 128 (O), under the name of The Toronto House Building Association.

1882. 45 V. c. 80 (O), changing the corporate name to The Land Security Company; increasing capital stock and amending powers.

1885. 48 V. c. 82 (O), amending powers.

1889. 52 V. c. 86 (O), increasing capital stock; authorizing conversion of existing shares into new shares, and amending powers.

1890. 53 V. c. 132 (O), increasing capital stock to $5,000,000; defining rights of transferee on transmission of shares by death, etc.

1896. 59 V. c. 113 (O), changing ordinary shares into preference shares; dividing existing shares, etc.

For the lending powers see 48 V. c. 82 (O), ss. 1, 2; and 52 V. c. 86 (O), s. 5.

For the borrowing powers see 36 V. c. 128 (O), s. 5, as amended by 45 V. c. 80 (O), s. 5, and by 48 V. c. 82 (O), s. 2; and see 59 V. c. 113 (O), secs. 10 to 13.

ANNUAL STATEMENT

Of the condition and affairs of the Land Security Company, of Toronto, at the 31st December, 1913, and for the year ending on that day, made to the Registrar of Loan Corporations for the Province of Ontario, pursuant to the laws of the said Province.

The head office of the Corporation is at No. 36 Canada Life Building, in the City of Toronto, in the Province of Ontario.

The Board is constituted of seven directors holding office for one year.

The Directors and chief executive officers of the Corporation at the 31st December, 1913, were as follows, together with their respective terms of office:

Geo. F. Little, President, Toronto;   18th February, 1913; 17th March, 1914.
C. R. Acres, Vice-President, Toronto;   "   "
Senator Geo. A. Cox, Director, Toronto;   "   16th January, 1914.
J. H. Hunter, Director, Toronto;   17th March, 1914.
E. W. Cox, Director, Toronto;   "
H. C. Cox, Director, Toronto;   "
Alfred H. Cox, Managing Director, Toronto;
Richard G. Roberts, Secretary, Toronto.

A. Permanent capital stock; total amount authorized, $5,000,000; total amount subscribed,* $1,108,010.00, as more particularly set out in Schedule A hereto.

SCHEDULE A.

Class 2.—Fixed and permanent capital stock created by virtue of Joint Stock Companies' Acts or Private Acts.

Description.	No. of shares.	Par value of shares.	Total amount held.	Total amount paid thereon.	Total amount remaining unpaid on calls.	Amount paid back on stock.	Balance unpaid.
	$	$	$	$ c.	$ c.	$ c.	$ c.
Partly called 100	1,913	100	191,300	75,392 17	39,387 83	23,559 96	51,832 21
90	2,412	90	217,080	96,538 21	24,061 79	30,167 76	66,370 45
80	8,090	80	647,200	323,600 00	....	101,125 00	222,475 90
70	709	70	49,630	28,360 00	....	8,862 50	19,497 50
60	32	60	1,920	1,280 00	....	400 00	880 00
40	22	40	880	880 00	....	275 00	605 00
Totals..........	13,178	....	1,108,010	526,050 38	63,449 62	164,390 22	361,660 16

LIST OF SHAREHOLDERS AS AT 31st DECEMBER, 1913.
(Not printed.)

* The balance of preference stock was, during 1910, 1911 and 1912, repaid to shareholders, together with 3% in each year of amount paid up returned to holders of common stock.

BALANCE SHEET AS AT 31st DECEMBER, 1913.

Dr.   .   Capital and Liabilities.

Capital (Liabilities to Stockholders or Shareholders).

    . A.—Permanent Capital Stock or Shares.

2. (b) Ordinary joint stock capital, total called, ———; total paid
thereon. $361,660 16

Liabilities to the Public. None.

    Total Liabilities. $361,660 16

Cr.   Assets.

I.—Assets of which the Corporation is the Beneficial Owner.

    D.—Unsecured Debts.

27. (a) Profit and loss account $361,660 16

    Total. $361,660 16

MISCELLANEOUS STATEMENT FOR THE YEAR ENDING 31st DECEMBER, 1913.

---

13. Dates when the accounts of the Corporation were last audited; 31st December, 1912.
14. Names and addresses of the auditors respectively for 1913 and for 1914 (if appointed:
    For 1913: None.
    For 1914: None.
15. What were the dividend days of the Corporation in 1913 and what rate or rates of
    dividend were paid on those days respectively? ———.
16. What is the date appointed for the Annual Meeting? 17th March, 1914. Date of
    last Annual Meeting 18th February, 1913.
17. Special General Meetings held in 1913. Dates: None.

THE WALKERVILLE LAND AND BUILDING COMPANY, LIMITED.

Head Office, Walkerville, Ontario.

Incorporated by Letters Patent of Ontario (22nd October, 1890) issued under the Ontario Joint Stock Companies Letters Patent Act, R.S.O. 1887, c. 157.

For the lending and borrowing powers see the above instrument and Act, also R.S.O. 1914, chap. 184.

ANNUAL STATEMENT

Of the condition and affairs of the Walkerville Land and Building Company Limited), Walkerville, Ontario, at the 31st December, 1913, and for the year ending on that day, made to the Registrar of Loan Corporations for the Province of Ontario, pursuant to the laws of the said Province.

The head office of the Corporation is on Sandwich Street, in the Town of Walkerville, in the Province of Ontario.

The Board is constituted of five directors, holding office for one year.

The directors and chief executive officers of the Corporation at the 31st December, 1913, were as follows, together with their respective terms of office:

E. Chandler Walker, President, Walkerville, Ont.;   Feb. 8th, 1913.
F. H. Walker, Vice-President, Walkerville, Ont.;
J. Harrington Walker, Vice-President, Walkerville, Ont.;
Harrington E. Walker, Director, Walkerville, Ont.;   "
Hiram H. Walker, Director, Walkerville, Ont.;   "
Douglas F. Matthew, Secretary, Walkerville, Ont.

In one year, or when their successors are appointed.

A.—Permanent capital stock: Total amount authorized, $1,000,000; total amount subscribed, $1,000,000, as more particularly set out in Schedule A hereto.

SCHEDULE A.

Class 2.—Fixed and permanent capital stock created by virtue of Joint Stock Companies Acts or Private Acts.

Last call made: January 1st, 1891; rate per cent. 50 per cent.; gross amount, $500,000; amount paid thereon, $500,000.

Description.	No. of shares.	Par value of shares.	Total amount held.	Total amount paid thereon.
		$	$	$
1. 50 per cent. called	10,000	100	1,000,000	500,000

LIST OF SHAREHOLDERS AS AT 31st DECEMBER, 1913.

(Not printed.)

BALANCE SHEET AS AT 31st DECEMBER, 1913.

Dr.   Capital and Liabilities.

Capital (Liabilities to Stockholders or Shareholders).

A.—Permanent Capital Stock or Shares.

1. (b) Ordinary joint stock capital, 50 per cent. callel; total called, $500,000; total paid thereon........	$500,000 00	
5. (e) Unappropriated profits in respects of (2)	169,465 90	$669,465 90

Liabilities to the Public.

29. Debentures issued in Canada	$500,000 00	
38. Due on bills payable (including interest)	9,150 00	
41. Other liabilities to public:		
42. (a) Loan	13,000 00	
43. (b) Suspense	2,750 00	
44. (c) Accounts payable	12,429 29	537,329 29
Total		$1,206,795 19

Cr.   Assets.

I.—Assets of which the Corporation is the Beneficial Owner.

A.—Immovable Property Owned Beneficially by the Corporation.

5. (b) Freehold land (including buildings) other than foregoing......	$1,003,766 51

B.—Debts secured by Mortgages of Land.

9. (a) Debts (other than item 10) secured by mortgages of land........	56,775 85

C.—Debts not above enumerated.

22. (f) Debts secured by retaining titles, being amounts outstanding on sales and advances	132,735 42

E.—Cash.

31. (a) On hand and in bank..	3,942 71

F.—Assets not hereinbefore mentioned.

37. (a) Furniture	$699 39	
38. (b) Accounts receivable	4,178 61	
39. (c) Rents accrued	2,329 57	
40. (d) Insurance unearned	1,432 68	
41. (e) Tools and implements	314 29	
42. (f) National Trust Co., Ltd.	620 16	9,574 70
Total assets		$1,206,795 19

CASH ACCOUNT.

Receipts for the year ending 31st December, 1913.

I.—Received by the Corporation for its Own Use.

A.—Balances from 31st December, 1912.

(b) Cash (not already shown under (1)):

2.	(1) On hand	$425 93

D.—Receipts from Real Estate Owned Beneficially by Corporation.

17. (b)	Rents	61,363 22

G.—Receipts from Other Sources.

30. (a)	From sales and loans	86,297 44
(b)	From interest	7,629 22
(c)	From loan	13,000 00
	From debentures sold	192,200 00
	From accounts	8,732 72
	Totals	$369,648 53

CASH ACCOUNT.

Expenditure for the year ending 31st December, 1913.

I.—Expended on Corporation Account.

A.—Sums Loaned or Invested on Capital Account.

6. (c)	Real estate, built and improved	$251,742 60

C.—Borrowed Money (other than foregoing) or interest thereon paid.

18. (a)	Paid on account of loan	13,000 00
24. (g)	Interest on debentures	15,969 36
	Ordinary interest	2,039 78

B.—Management Expenses (other than foregoing).

25. (a)	Salaries and supplies	2,615 86
30. (f)	Fuel, water and light	2,949 34

E.—Other Expenditure, viz.:

	Expense	1,468 90
34. (a)	Government fees and taxes	417 00
35. (b)	Municipal taxes	12,572 47
36. (c)	Repairs and maintenance	17,961 73
	Money loaned	43,592 12
	Accounts paid	1,376 66

F.—Balance.

37. (b)	Cash on hand and in bank	3,942 71
	Total	$369,648 53

MISCELLANEOUS STATEMENT FOR THE YEAR ENDING 31ST DECEMBER, 1913.

1. Amount of debentures maturing in 1914: Issued in Canada, none; Issued elsewhere, none.
2. Amount of other existing obligations which will mature in 1914: $12,429.29.
3. Amount of securities held by the Corporation which will mature and become payable to the Corporation in 1914: $4,178.61.
4. Average rate of interest per annum paid by the Corporation during 1912: On deposits, None; on debentures, 4¼%; on debenture stock, none.
5. Average rate of interest per annum received by the Corporation during 1913: (a) On mortgages of realty; (b) on other securities:
    (i) Owned beneficially by the Corporation: (a) 6%; (b) 6%.
    (ii) Not owned beneficially: (a) None; (b) none.
6. Of the mortgages owned beneficially by the Corporation, $56,775.85 is on realty situate in Ontario, and none is on realty situate elsewhere.
7. Of the mortgages not owned beneficially by the Corporation, none is on realty situate in Ontario, and none is on realty situate elsewhere.
8. Loans written off or transferred to real estate account during 1913, viz.:
    (i) Funds or securities owned beneficially: None.
    (ii) Not so owned: None.
9. Number and aggregate amount of mortgages upon which compulsory proceedings have been taken by the Corporation in 1913, viz.:
    (i) Owned beneficially, No., none; amount, none.
    (ii) Not so owned, No., none; amount, none.
10. Aggregate market value of land, including buildings thereon, mortgaged to the Corporation:
    (i) Mortgages owned beneficially, $110,000.
    (ii) Not so owned, none.
11. How often are the securities held by the Corporation valued? At least annually.
12. (a) Specify the officers of the Corporation who are under bond and for what sum respectively. Treasurer, $5,000; Cashier, $5,000; Bookkeeper, $2,000.
    (b) Are the said bonds executed by private sureties or by Guarantee Companies? Private sureties.
13. Date when the accounts of the Corporation were last audited. January 27th, 1914.
14. Names and addresses of the auditors respectively for 1913 and for 1914 (if appointed):
    For 1913: R. L. Daniels and Alfred Miers.
    For 1914: R. L. Daniels and Alfred Miers.
15. What were the dividend days of the Corporation in 1913, and what rate or rates of dividend were paid on those days respectively?
16. What is the date appointed for the Annual Meeting? Second Tuesday in February. Date of last Annual Meeting? January 29th, 1914.
17. Special General Meetings held in 1913. Dates: None.

THE PROVIDENT INVESTMENT COMPANY.

Head Office, Toronto, Ontario.

Incorporated on 3rd November, 1893, by Letters Patent of Ontario, issued under the Ontario Joint Stock Companies Act (R.S.O. 1887, c. 157).

For the lending and borrowing powers see the Letters Patent (which contain special limitations).

By Letter Patent of Ontario, dated January 9th, 1912, the Company renounced its borrowing powers and accepted those provided in the Loan Corporation Act (R.S.O. 1897, c. 205), and amending Acts.

ANNUAL STATEMENT

Of the condition and affairs of The Provident Investment Company, at the 31st of December, 1913, and for the year ending on that day, made to the Registrar of Loan Corporations for the Province of Ontario, pursuant to the laws of the said Province.

The head office of the Corporation is at No. 44 King Street West, in the City of Toronto, in the Province of Ontario.

The Board is constituted of six directors holding office for one year.

The directors and chief executive officers of the Corporation at the 31st December, 1913, were as follows, together with their respective terms of office:

E. W. Cox, President, Toronto;   January 15th, 1913; January 21st, 1914.
H. C. Cox, Vice-President, Toronto;   "   "
G. A. Morrow, Director, Toronto;   "   "
E. R. Wood, Director, Toronto;
A. H. Cox, Director, Toronto;
A. H. Cox, Manager, Toronto;
R. G. Roberts, Secretary, Toronto;

A. Permanent capital stock: Total amount authorized, $1,800,000; total amount subscribed, $500,000, as more particularly set out in Schedule A hereto.

SCHEDULE A.

Class 2.—Fixed and permanent capital stock created by virtue of Joint Stock Companies' Acts or Private Acts.

Description.	No. of shares.	Par value of shares.	Total amount held.	Total amount paid thereon.	Total remaining unpaid on calls.
		$	$	$	$
1. Fully called	5,000	100	500,000	500,000	....

LIST OF SHAREHOLDERS AS AT 31st DECEMBER, 1913.

(Not printed.)

BALANCE SHEET AS AT 31st DECEMBER, 1913.

Dr. Capital and Liabilities.

Capital Liabilities to Stockholders or Shareholders.

A.—Permanent Capital Stock or Shares.

1. (a) Ordinary joint stock capital fully called; total called, $500,000; total paid theron	$500,000 00	
4. (d) Dividends declared in respect of (1) not yet paid ..	25,000 00	
5. (e) Unappropriated profits in respect of (1)	25,166 44	
6. (f) Reserve Fund in respect of (1)	375,000 00	
		$925,166 44

Liabilities to the Public.

37. Owing to banks, loans against security of bonds, stocks and debentures, including interest accrued to date		1,889,397 49
43. (b) Agency Account in Central Canada Loan & Savings Company..		1,149 54
Total liabilities		$2,315,713 47

Cr. Assets.

I.—Assets of which the Corporation is the Beneficial Owner.

A.—Immovable Property Owned Beneficially by Corporation.

5. (b) Freehold land (including buildings) other than foregoing	$607,217 77	
7. (d) Less amount to credit of tenants' account	192 00	
		$607,025 77

B.—Debts secured by mortgages of Land.

9. (b) Debts (other than item 10) secured by mortgages of land	$22,642 66	
11. (c) Interest due and accrued on item 9 and not included therein	783 11	
		$23,425 77

C.—Debts not above enumerated for which the Corporation holds securities as follows:

14. (b) Debts secured by bonds, stocks and debentures	$93,284 31	
26. (n) Interest due and accrued on item 14 and not included therein	1,955 10	
		95,239 41
27. (a) Bonds, stocks and debentures $1,561,548 56	$1,561,548 56	
28. (b) Accrued interest on bonds, stocks and debentures..	17,532 25	
		1,579,080 81

E.—Cash.

31. (a) Deposited in Loan Company and Bank		9,792 17

F.—Assets not Hereinbefore Mentioned.

37. (a) Amount due the Company on Agency Account		1,149 54
Total		$2,315,713 47

CASH ACCOUNT.

Receipts for the year ending 31st December, 1913.

I.—Received by the Corporation for its Own Use.

A.—Balances from 31st December, 1912.

(1) Cash (not already shown under (1):)
3.   (ii) In Bank $12,801 48

C.—Received on account of Investments, Loans or Debts.

(a) On Mortgages of realty:
10.   (i) Principal $19,423 54
11.   (ii) Interest 6,180 16

(b) Bonds, stocks and debentures owned by Company:

12.   (i) Principal 145,143 60
13.   (ii) Interest or dividends 108,481 63
14.   (i) Loans secured by bonds, stocks and debentures 42,247 70
15.   (iii) Interest (included in item 11).   321,476 63

D.—Receipts from Real Estate Owned Beneficially by Corporation.

16. (a) Sales not included in any of the foregoing items .. $51,980 34
17. (b) Rents 6,565 04   58,545 38

E.—Miscellaneous.

18. (a) Commission, brokerage (or remuneration as corporate Agent, Trustee, etc.) $586 00   586 00

F.—Borrowed Money.

25. (a) Bank or other advances, overdrafts $401,946 81   401,946 81

G.—Receipts From Other Sources.

30. (a) Syndicate for which we are agents 21,457 09
(c) Central Canada Loan & Savings Co., overdraft for Syndicate account 1,149 54

    Total $817,962 93

II.—Received as Corporate Trustee, Representative, Guardian or Agent in Trust.

A.—Balances from 31st December, 1912.

31. (a) Capital account:
33.   (ii) Cash in bank 809 27

CASH ACCOUNT.—Continued.

Receipts for the year ending 31st December, 1913.

C.—Receipts from Real Estate.

38. (b) Rents	$8,707 09	
		8,707 09

D.—Receipts from other Sources, viz.:

39. (a) Received from Syndicate	$12,750 00	
41. (c) Central Canada Loan & Savings Co., overdraft for Syndicate account	1,149 54	
		13,899 54
Totals		$23,415 90

CASH ACCOUNT.

Expenditure for the year ending 31st December, 1913.

I.—Expended on Corporation Account.

	(Col. 1.)	(Total Col. 4.)
1. (a) Loaned on mortgages of realty		$8,623 48
(b) Loaned or invested in other securities, viz.:		
2. (i) Loaned on security of bonds, stocks and debentures....		62,571 18
4. (iii) Purchase of bonds, stocks and debentures		28,062 60
6. (c) Real estate purchased		364,342 52

B.—Expended on Stock Account.

8. Dividends paid on Permanent Stock. (Extend into Column 1)	$50,000 00	50,000 00

C.—Borrowed Money (other than foregoing) or interest paid thereon, viz.:

18. (a) Repayment of bank advances { Principal	$197,514 20	
Interest	63,277 59	
		260,791 79

D.—Management Expenses (other than foregoing).

25. (a) Salaries, wages and fees	$5,546 00	
26. (b) Commission or brokerage	220 00	
28. (d) Stationery, postage, printing and advertising	385 96	
29. (e) Law costs	820 70	
30. (f) Fuel, rent, taxes (other than 7 and 32) and rates....	2,049 13	
31. (g) Travelling expenses	150 00	
32. (h) Registration fees	150 00	
33. (i) Other management expenditure	271 75	
		9,593 54

E.—Other Expenditures.

34. (a) Taxes and insurance	$726 83	
36. (c) Repairs and improvements	42 92	
		769 75
Paid out for syndicate for which we are agents		23,415 90

F.—Balance.

39. (ii) Cash in Loan and Savings Co. and bank		9,792 17
Total		$817,962 93

CASH ACCOUNT.—Continued.

Expenditure for the year ending 31st December, 1913.

II.—Expended on Trust or Agency Account.

B.—Other Expenditures.

50. (a) Commission or remuneration paid for management of estate, trust or agency	$586 00	
51. (b) Rent, taxes and rates	1,982 24	
52. (c) Debts or obligations wholly or partly paid: Principal, $10,000.00; interest, $5,625.00	15,625 00	
53. (d) Caretaking and repairs	5,222 66	
		$23,415 90
Totals		$23,415 90

MISCELLANEOUS STATEMENT FOR THE YEAR ENDING 31ST DECEMBER, 1913.

1. Amount of Debentures maturing in 1914: Issued in Canada, none; Issued elsewhere, none.
2. Amount of other existing obligations which will mature in 1914, none.
3. Amount of securities held by the Corporation which will mature and become payable to the Corporation in 1914, none.
4. Average rate of interest per annum paid by the Corporation during 1913: On deposits, none; on debentures, none; on debenture stock, none.
5. Average rate of interest per annum received by the Corporation during 1913:
     (a) On mortgages of realty; (b) On other securities.
     (i) Owned beneficially by the Corporation: (a) 5.12%; (b) Fluctuates.
     (ii) Not owned beneficially: (a) None; (b) None.
6. Of the mortgages owned beneficially by the Corporation, $20,423.27 is on realty situate in Ontario, and $3,002.50 is on realty situate elsewhere.
7. Of the mortgages not owned beneficially by the Corporation, none is on realty situate in Ontario, and none is on realty situate elsewhere.
8. Loans written off or transferred to real estate account during 1913, viz.:
     (i) Funds or securities owned beneficially, none.
     (ii) Not so owned, none.
9. Number and aggregate amount of mortgages upon which compulsory proceedings have been taken by the Corporation in 1913, viz.:
     (i) Owned beneficially: Number, none; Amount, none.
     (ii) Not so owned: Number, none; Amount, none.
10. Aggregate market value of land mortgaged to the Corporation:
     (i) Mortgages owned beneficially, $59,792,01; (ii) Not so owned, none.
11. How often are the securities held by the Corporation valued? Yearly.
12. (a) Specify the officers of the Corporation who are under bond and for what sum respectively, none.
     (b) Are the said bonds executed by private sureties or by Guarantee Companies.
13. Date when the ccounts of the corporation were last audited? December 31st, 1913.
14. Names and addresses of the auditors respectively for 1913 and for 1914 (if appointed):
     For 1913: A. B. Fisher, R. T. Thompson, both of Toronto.
     For 1914: A. B. Fisher, R. T. Thompon, both of Toronto.
15. What were the dividend days of the Corporation in 1913, and what rate or rates of dividend were paid on those days respectively? 5% January 2nd, 1913, and 5% July 2nd, 1913.
16. What is the date appointed for the Annual Meeting? January 24th, 1914. Date of last Annual Meeting? January 15th, 1913.
17. Special General Meetings held in 1913: Dates, none held.

THE TORONTO SAVINGS AND LOAN COMPANY.

Head Office, Peterborough, Ontario.

———

Incorporated as "The Toronto Real Estate Investment Company," by Letters Patent of Ontario (June 15th, 1885), issued under the Ontario Joint Stock Companies' Letters Patent Act, R.S.O. 1877, c. 150. Supplementary Letters Patent of Ontario (29th December, 1877), were issued under R.S.O. 1887, c. 157, defining the borrowing powers, etc. Further Supplementary Letters Patent of Ontario (25th September, 1889) were issued under the last mentioned Act, increasing the capital stock from $400,000 to $2,000,000. Further Supplementary Letters Patent of Ontario (30th March, 1891) were issued under the same Act, conferring agency powers on the Company. The Corporate name was by Order-in-Council (2nd April, 1891) changed to "The Toronto Savings and Loan Company."

For the lending and borrowing powers, see the Letters Patent and the Acts, R.S.O. 1877, c. 150; R.S.O. 1887, c. 157; R.S.O. 1914, chap. 184.

ANNUAL STATEMENT

Of the condition and affairs of the Toronto Savings and Loan Company, of Peterborough, Ontario, at the 31st December, 1913, and for the year ending on that day, made to the Registrar of Loan Corporations for the Province of Ontario, pursuant to the laws of the said Province.

The head office of the Corporation is at No. 437 George Street South, in the City of Peterborough, in the Province of Ontario.

The Board is constituted of six directors, holding office for one year.

The directors and chief executive officers of the Corporation at the 31st December, 1913, were as follows, together with their respective terms of office:

Hon. Geo. A. Cox, President, Toronto;   24th January, 1913; 23rd January, 1914.
W. G. Morrow, Vice-President, Peterborough;   "   "
Richard Hall, Vice-President, Peterborough;   "   "
E. W. Cox, Director, Toronto;
D. W. Dumble, Director, Peterborough;
H. C. Cox, Director, Toronto;
W. G. Morrow, Managing Director, Peterborough;
H. W. Morphet, Secretary, Peterborough.

A. Permanent capital stock: Total amount authorized, $2,000,000; total amount subscribed, $1,000,000, as more particularly set out in Schedule A hereto.

SCHEDULE A.

Class 2.—Fixed and permanent capital stock created by virtue of Joint Stock Companies' Acts or by Private Acts.

Last call made, date 31st May, 1902; rate per cent., 40 per cent; gross amount, $400,000. Amount paid thereon, $400,000.

Description.	No. of shares.	Par value of shares.	Total amount held.	Total amount paid thereon.	Total remaining unpaid thereon.
		$	$	$	$
2. Fully called	10,000	100	1,000,000	1,000,000	....

LIST OF SHAREHOLDERS AS AT 31st DECEMBER, 1913.

(Not printed.)

BALANCE SHEET AS AT 31st DECEMBER, 1913.

Dr. Capital and Liabilities.

Capital Liabilities to Stockholders or Shareholders.

A.—Permanent Capital Stock or Shares.

1. (a) Ordinary joint stock capital fully called; total called, $1,000,000; total paid thereon $1,000,000 00		
4. (d) Divindends declared in respect of (1), but not yet paid..	25,000 00	
6. (f) Reserve fund in respect of (1)	850,000 00	
7. (g) Contingent fund in respect of (1)	60,334 55	
		$1,935,334 55

·Liabilities to the Public.

27. Deposits: Right reserved to require 30 days' notice of withdrawal	$445,320 59	
28. Interest on deposits, due or accrued or capitalized	3,865 79	
29. Debentures issued in Canada	408,290 00	
30. Interest due and accrued on (29)	7,358 17	
31. Debentures issued elsewhere than in Canada	1,073,858 81	
32. Interest accrued on (31)	6,278 28	
40. Other liabilities to the public, viz.:		
41. (a) Sundry accounts due by Company	3,949 77	
		1,948,921 41
Total liabilities		$3,884,255 96

Cr. Assets.

I.—Assets of which the Corporation is the Beneficial Owner.

A.—Immovable Property Owned Beneficially by Corporation.

5. (b) Freehold land (including buildings) other than foregoing.	$559,861 82	
6. (c) Leasehold land (including buildings) other than foregoing	40,000 00	
		$599,861 82

B.—Debts secured by Mortgages of Land.

9. (a) Debts (other than item 10) secured by mortgages of land	$370,419 77	
11. (c) Interest due and accrued on item (9)	10,179 15	
		380,598 92

C.—Debts not above enumerated for which the Corporation holds securities as follows:

22. (j) Debts secured by stocks and bonds.................$2,752,335 28		
26. (n) Interest due or accrued on item (22) and not included therein	44,982 50	
		2,797,317 78

D.—Unsecured Debts.

27. (a) Sundry accounts due to Company		4,449 23

BALANCE SHEET.—Continued.

E.—Cash.

31. (*a*) On hand	$2,429 36	
32. (*b*) In banks	99,598 85	
		$102,028 21
Total assets		$3,884,255 96

CASH ACCOUNT.

Receipts for the year ending December, 1913.

	(Col. 1.)	(Total Col. 4.)
I.—Received by the Corporation for its Own Use.		
A.—Balances from 31st December, 1912.		
1. (*b*) Cash (not already shown under (1)):		
2.　　　　(i) On hand	....	$2,487 65
3.　　　　(ii) In bank	....	55,059 39
C.—Receipts on account of Investments, Loans or Debts.		
(*a*) On mortgages of realty:		
10.　　　　(i) Principal	$115,430 03	
11.　　　　(ii) Interest	12,560 03	
		127,990 06
(*b*) Stocks and bonds owned by Company:		
12.　　　　(i) Principal	$627,650 07	
13.　　　　(ii) Interest or dividends together with profits on stocks and bonds	155,483 13	
		783,133 20
D.—Receipts from Real Estate Owned Beneficially by Corporation.		
16. (*a*) Sales (not included in any of the foregoing items)	$397,872 72	
17. (*b*) Rents, together with profit from sales of property	90,597 24	
		488,469 96
F.—Borrowed Money.		
26. (*b*) Borrowed by taking deposits	....	656,480 79
27. (*c*) Borrowed on debentures	....	198,955 10
G.—Receipts from other sources, viz.:		
30. (*a*) Sundry accounts due to Company	....	6,702 49
Total		$2,319,278 64

CASH ACCOUNT.

Expenditure for the year ending 31st December, 1913.

I.—Expended on Corporation Account.

A.—Sums Loaned or Invested on Capital Account.

CASH ACCOUNT.—Continued.

Expenditure for the year ending 31st December, 1913.

	Col. 1.)	(Total, Col. 4.)
1. (a) Loaned on mortgages of realty	....	$387,137 00
(b) Loaned on or invested in other securities, viz.:		
2. (ii) Stocks, bonds and debentures	....	497,765 19
6. (c) Real estate purchased	....	392,810 27

B.—Expended on Stock Account.

8. Dividends paid on permanent stock	....	100,000 00

C.—Borrowed Money (other than foregoing) or interest thereon paid.

19. (b) Deposits: Principal, $620,287.94; interest, $15,154.50.	....	635,442 44
20. (c) Debentures issued in Canada: Principal, $70,892.00; interest, $17,068.84	....	87,960 84
21. (d) Debentures issued elsewhere: Principal, $18,250.00; interest, $43,728.03	....	61,978 03

D.—Management Expenses other than foregoing.

25. (a) Salaries, wages and fees	$26,662 15	
26. (b) Commission and brokerage	6,050 53	
28. (d) Stationery, postage, printing and advertising.......	781 31	
29. (e) Law costs	497 94	
30. (f) Fuel, rent, taxes (other than 7 and 32) and rates....	1,910 01	
32. (h) Registration fees	200 00	
		36,101 94

E.—Other Expenditures, viz.:

34. (a) Repairs and improvements to property owned......	$5,072 21	
35. (b) Taxes on property owned	5,379 34	
36. (c) Insurance on property owned	3,523 20	
(d) Ground rent on leasehold property	1,500 00	
(e) Sundry accounts due by Company................	2,579 97	
		18,054 72

F.—Balance.

37. (a) Cash on hand and in banks	....	102,028 21
Total		$2,319,278 64

MISCELLANEOUS STATEMENT FOR THE YEAR ENDING 31ST DECEMBER, 1913.

1. Amount of debentures maturing in 1914: Issued in Canada, $80,565.00; Issued elsewhere, £39,896.
2. Amount of other existing obligations which will mature in 1914: Exclusive of deposits, none.
3. Amount of securities held by the Corporation which will mature and become payable to the Corporation in 1914: None, except $2,752,335 28 of cashable stocks and bonds.
4. Average rate of interest per annum paid by the Corporation during 1913: On deposits, 3½%; on debentures, 4.23%; on debenture stock, none.
5. Average rate of interest per annum received by the Corporation during 1913: (a) On mortgages of realty; (b) on other securities:
   (i) Owned beneficially by the Corporation: (a) 5.90%; (b) fluctuates.
   (ii) Not owned beneficially: (a) nil; (b) nil.

6. Of the mortgages owned beneficially by the Corporation, $370,419.72 is on realty situate in Ontario, and nil is on realty situate elsewhere.

7. Of the mortgages not owned beneficially by the Corporation, nil is on realty situate in Ontario, and nil is on realty situate elsewhere.

8. Loans written off or transferred to real estate account during 1913, viz.:
   (i) Funds or securities owned beneficially, nil.
   (ii) Not so owned, nil.

9. Number and aggregate amount of mortgages upon which compulsory proceedings have been taken by the Corporation in 1913, viz.:
   (i) Owned beneficially, No., nil; amount, nil.
   (ii) Not so owned, No., nil; amount, nil.

10. Aggregate market value of land mortgaged to the Corporation:
    (i) Mortgages owned beneficially, $438,300.00.
    (ii) Not so owned, nil.

11. How often are the securities held by the Corporation valued? All within one year.

12. (a) Specify the officers of the Corporation who are under bond and for what sum respectively. Manager $5,000; Secretary, $3,000; Accountant, $2,000; Cashier, $5,000.

    (b) Are the said bonds executed by private sureties or by Guarantee Companies? Guarantee Company.

13. Date when the accounts of the Corporation were last audited? To 31st December, 1913.

14. Names and addresses of the auditors respectively for 1913, and for 1914 (if appointed):
    For 1913: James A. Hall and F. J. A. Hall.
    For 1914: James A. Hall and F. J. A. Hall.

15. What were the dividend days of the Corporation in 1913, and what rate or rates of dividend were paid on those days respectively? First days of January, April, July and October, 2½% each (10% for the year).

16. What is the date appointed for the Annual Meeting? 23rd January, 1914. Date of last Annual Meeting? 24th January, 1913.

17. Special General Meetings held in 1913. Dates: None.

THE CANADIAN NORTHERN PRAIRIE LANDS COMPANY, LIMITED.

Head Office, Toronto, Ontario.

Incorporated by Letters Patent of Ontario, issued under The Ontario Companies Act and bearing date 30th May, 1905.

The Company was, by Supplementary Letters Patent, issued under The Loan Corporations Act, bearing date 2nd March, 1909, given the additional powers of a Loaning Land Company, except the power of taking deposits, and was on the 27th May, 1910, granted registry on the Loaning Land Company Register.

ANNUAL STATEMENT

Of the condition and affairs of the Canadian Northern Prairie Lands Company, Limited, at 31st December, 1913, and for the year ending on that day made to the Registrar of Loan Corporations for the Province of Ontario, pursuant to the laws of the said Province.

The head office of the Corporation is at No. 11 Toronto Street, in the City of Toronto, in the Province of Ontario.

The Board is constituted of seven directors, holding office for one year, or until their successors are appointed.

The directors and chief executive officers of the Corporation at 31st December, 1913, were as follows, together with their respective terms of office:

Hugh Sutherland, President, Winnipeg, Man.; April 10th, 1913; April 14th, 19··
D. B. Hanna, Vice-President, Toronto, Ont.;   "   "
Col. A. D. Davidson, Director, Toronto, Ont.;   "   "
A. J. Mitchell, Director, Toronto, Ont.;
Lewis Lukes, Director, Toronto, Ont.;
Norman Scott Russell, Director, London, England;   "
T. Blundell Brown, Director, London, England;   "
L. W. Mitchell, Secretary, Toronto, Ont.

A.—Permanent capital stock: Total amount authorized, $5,000,000; total amount subscribed, $1,500,000, as more particularly set out in Schedule A hereto.

SCHEDULE A.

Class 2.—Fixed and permanent capital stock created by virtue of Joint Stock Companies' Acts or Private Acts.

Description.	No. of shares.	Par value.	Total amount held.	Total amount paid thereon.	Total remaining unpaid on calls.
		$	$	$	
Fully called	300,000	5	1,500,000	1,500,000	fully paid.

LIST OF SHAREHOLDERS AS AT 31st DECEMBER, 1913.

(Not printed.)

BALANCE SHEET AS AT 31st DECEMBER, 1913.

Dr.   Capital and Liabilities.

Capital (Liabilities to Stockholders or Shareholders).

A.—Permanent Capital Stock or Shares.

1. (a) Ordinary joint stock capital fully called; total called, $1,500,000; total paid thereon	$1,500,000 00
5. (e) Unappropriated profits in respect of (1)	422,345 09
6. (f) Reserve fund in respect of (1)	1,500,000 00

Liabilities to the Public.

40. Other liabilities to the public, viz.:	
42. (b) Commissions due and deferred	52,823 91
43. (c) Sundry accounts	1,493 06
Total liabilities	$3,476,662 06

Cr.   Assets.

I.—Assets of which the Corporation is the Beneficial Owner.

A.—Immovable Property Owned Beneficially by Corporation.

5. (b) Freehold land (including buildings) other than foregoing—land account	$200,998 05

B.—Debts secured by Mortgages of Land, etc.

9. (a) Debts (other than item 10) secured by mortgages of land	441,209 12
10. (b) Debts secured, land sales, contracts	639,394 21
(bb) Debts secured by land held by the Company as mortgagee in possession, or secured by land for the rents and profits of which the Company is accountable	234,151 57
11. (c) Interest due or accrued on items 9 and 10, and not included therein	105,241 22

C.—Debts not above enumerated, for which the Corporation holds security, as follows:

22. (j) Debts secured by stocks, bonds, etc.—Call loans	1,180,712 68
23. (k) Debts secured by stocks and bonds, etc.	251,068 00
24. (l) Debts secured by municipal securities	12,016 11
25. (m) Debts secured by mortgage securities	26,773 91

E.—Cash.

32. (b) In banks	42,044 46
Accrued interest, bank balances	26 24

F.—Assets not hereinbefore mentioned.

37. (a) Bonds and debentures	310,941 46
38. (b) Accrued interest on 37 (a)	21,101 01
39. (c) Tax certificates	10,984 02
Total assets	$3,476,662 06

CASH ACCOUNT.

Receipts for the year ending 31st December, 1913.

I.—Received by the Corporation for its Own Use.

Balances from 31st December, 1912.

	(Total, Col. 4.)
(b) **Cash** (not already shown under (1)):	
3. (ii) In banks	$64,064 94

C.—Receipts on account of Investments, Loans or Debts.

(a) On mortgages of realty:	
10. (i) Principal	203,426 76
11. (ii) Interest	53,246 95
(b) On other securities:	
12. (i) Principal	} 186,539 55
13. (ii) Interest or dividends	}
(c) Unsecured debts:	
14. (i) Principal	} 2,368 62
15. (ii) Interest	}

E.—Miscellaneous.

G.—Receipts from Other Sources.

30. (a) **Miscellaneous**	197 08
Total	$509,843 90

CASH ACCOUNT.

Expenditure for the year ending 31st December, 1913.

I.—Expended on Corporation Account.

A.—Sums Loaned or Invested on Capital Account.

	(Total, Col. 4.)
1. (a) Loaned on mortgages of realty	$58,062 85
(b) Loaned or invested in other securities:	
2. (i) Call loans	227,835 75
3. (ii) Mortgage securities	24,000 00
4. (iii) Tax certificates	10,984 02
5. (iv) Municipal securities	12,000 00

B.—Expended on Stock Account.

8. Dividend paid on permanent stock	116,464 80

D.—Management Expenses.

30. (f) Salaries, wages, commission, taxes, office expense, etc............	4,239 37

E.—Other Expenditures.

34. (a) Re land sales commissions, expenses, refunds and miscellaneous	14,162 65

F.—Balance.

37. (b) Cash in banks	42,044 46
Total	$509,843 90

MISCELLANEOUS STATEMENT FOR THE YEAR ENDING 31ST DECEMBER, 1913.

1. Amount of debentures maturing in 1914: Issued in Canada, nil; Issued elsewhere, nil.
2. Amount of other existing obligations which will mature in 1914: Nil.
3. Amount of securities held by the Corporation which will mature and become payable to the Corporation in 1914: $170,843.49 approximately .
4. Average rate of interest per annum paid by the Corporation during 1913: On deposits, nil; on debentures, nil; on debenture stock, nil.
5. Average rate of interest per annum received by the Corporation during 1913: (a) On mortgages of realty; (b) on other securities:
   (i) Owned beneficially by the Corporation: (a) 6½%; (b) 6%.
   (ii) Not owned beneficially; (a) nil; (b) nil.
6. Of the mortgages owned beneficially by the Corporation, $2,500.00 is on realty situate in Ontario, and $438,709.12 is on realty situate elsewhere.
7. Of the mortgages not owned beneficially by the Corporation, nil is on realty situate in Ontario, and nil is on realty situate elsewhere.
8. Loans written off or transferred to real estate account during 1913, viz.:
   (i) Funds or securities owned beneficially, nil.
   (ii) Not so owned, nil.
9. Number and aggregate amount of mortgages upon which compulsory proceedings have been taken by the Corporation in 1913, viz.:
   (i) Owned beneficially, nil; amount, nil.
   (ii) Not so owned, nil; amount, nil.
10. Aggregate market value of land mortgaged to the Corporation:
    (i) Mortgages owned beneficially—
    (ii) Not so owned: None.
11. How often are the securities held by the Corporation valued? Running valuation.
12. (a) Specify the officers of the Corporation who are under bond, and for what sum respectively. Davidson & McRae, Sales Agents, $10,000.00.
    (b) Are the said bonds executed by private sureties or by Guarantee Companies? Guarantee Company.
13. Date when the accounts of the Corporation were last audited? December 31st, 1913.
14. Names and addresses of the auditors respectively for 1913 and for 1914 (if appointed):
    For 1913: T. J. Macabe and H. G. Foreman.
    For 1914:
15. What were the dividend days of the Corporation in 1913, and what rate or rates of dividend were paid on those days respectively? April 1st and October 1st, 12% per annum.
16. What is the date appointed for the Annual Meeting? Fourth Wednesday in January. Date of last Annual Meeting? April 10th, 1913.
17. Special General Meetings held in 1913. Dates: Nil.

THE SCOTTISH ONTARIO AND MANITOBA LAND COMPANY (LIMITED).

Head Office, Glasgow, Scotland.

CONSTATING INSTRUMENTS.

Certificate of Incorporation (15th Dec., 1879), issued by Registrar of Joint Stock Companies for Scotland, under the Companies Act, 1862, 1867 and 1877.

Memorandum of Association and Articles of Association (both of the 12th Dec., 1870) under the above Acts and amendment to 73rd Article made 24th April, 1882.

For the lending and borrowing powers see the Memorandum of Association and the Articles of Association, and the (Imp.) Companies' Act 1862 to 1893; also for transactions in Ontario, see the Loan and Trust Corporations Act, 2 Geo. V., c. 34.

ANNUAL STATEMENT

Of the condition and affairs of the Scottish Ontario and Manitoba Land Company (Limited), of Glasgow, Scotland, at the 31st December, 1913, and for the year ending on that day, made to the Registrar of Loan Corporations for the Province of Ontario, pursuant to the laws of the said Province.

The head office of the Company is at No. 205 St. Vincent Street, in the City of Glasgow, Scotland.

The chief agency for Ontario is situate at No. 156 Yonge Street, in the City of Toronto, in the Province of Ontario.

The Chief Agents and Attorneys for Ontario are Thomas Langton, Herbert Macdonald Mowat, and Roderick James Maclennan (or any one of them), and their address is 156 Yonge Street, Toronto, in the Province of Ontario.

The Board is constituted of six directors, holding office for the term of three years.

The directors and chief executive officers of the Corporation at the 31st December, 1913, were as follows, together with their respective terms of office:

Robert Anderson, Chairman, Glasgow;	13 April, 1911; April, 1914.
Geo. D. Sterling, C.A., Director & Interim Chairman, Glasgow;	11 April, 1912; April, 1915.
*David Sturrock, Director, Glasgow;	13 April, 1913; April, 1916.
R. W. Henry, Director, Glasgow;	14 April, 1913; April, 1916.
George W. Currie, C.A., Director, Edinburgh;	11 April, 1912; April, 1915.
Frederick P. Milligan, Director, Edinburgh;	11 April, 1912; April, 1914.
James Muirhead, Secretary, Glasgow, Scotland.	

A.—Permanent capital stock: Total amount authorized, $730,000.00; total amount subscribed, $547,500, as more particularly set out in Schedule A hereto.

SCHEDULE A.

Class 2.—Fixed and permanent Capital Stock created by virtue of Joint Stock Companies' Acts or Private Acts.

Last call made:—Date, 30th June, 1913; rate per cent., 66⅔ on 12,500 shares; gross amount, $121,666.67; amount paid thereon, $121,666.67.

Description.	No. of shares.	Par value of shares.	Total amount held.	Total amount paid thereon.	Total remaining unpaid on calls.
		$ c.	$ c.	$ c.	$
66⅔ per cent. called stock............	37,500	14.60	547,500 00	365,000 00	....

LIST OF SHAREHOLDERS AS AT 31st DECEMBER, 1913.
(Not printed.)

*Deceased.

BALANCE SHEET AS AT 31st DECEMBER, 1913.

Dr.   Capital and Liabilities.

Capital (Liabilities to Stockholders or Shareholders).

A.—Permanent Capital Stock or Shares.

2. (b) Ordinary joint stock capital, 66⅔ per cent. called; total called, $365,000; total paid thereon........	$365,000 00	
4. (d) Dividends declared in respect of (2), but not yet paid	431 92	
5. (e) Unappropriated profits in respect of (2)............	220,854 91	
6 (f) Reserve fund in respect of (2).....................	39,408 62	$625,695 45

Liabilities to the Public.

31. Debentures issued elsewhere than in Canada............	$419,263 33	
32. Interest due and accrued on (31)......................	2,393 61	
40. Other liabilities to the public, viz.:		
42. (a) Suspense account for unadjusted balance on joint account	11,557 46	
43. (b) Sundry debts	7,822 61	441,037 01

Total liabilities		$1,066,732 46

Cr.   Assets.

I.—Assets of which the Corporation is the Beneficial Owner.

A.—Immovable Property Owned Beneficially by Corporation.

1. (a) Office premises, situate as follows:		
2. (1) At Main Street, Winnipeg, held in freehold..	20,000 00	
5. (b) Freehold land (including buildings) other than foregoing	140,231 35	$160,231 £

B.—Debts secured by Mortgages of Land.

9. (a) Debts secured by mortgages of land...............	$861,103 35	
11. (c) Interest due or accrued on item (9) and not included therein	19,719 53	880,822 88

D.—Unsecured Debts.

27. (a) Sundry small debts		1,340 95

E.—Cash.

31. (a) On hand	$42 30	
32. (b) In banks	24,294 98	24,337 28

Total assets		$1,066,732 46

17 L.O.

CASH ACCOUNT.

Receipts for the year ending 31st December, 1913.

I.—Received by the Corporation for its Own Use.

A.—Balances from 31st December, 1912.

		(Col. 1.)	(Col. 3.)	(Total, Col. 4.)
	(b) Cash (not already shown under (1)):—			
2.	(i) On hand			$29 54
3.	(ii) In bank			21,726 22

B.—Sums Received Wholly or Partly on Capital Stock.

		(Col. 1.)	(Col. 3.)	(Total, Col. 4.)
4.	(a) Calls on joint stock permanent capital		$14,603 22	

C.—Receipts on account of Investments, Loans or Debts.

		(Col. 1.)	(Col. 3.)	(Total, Col. 4.)
	(a) On mortgages of realty:—			
10.	(i) Principal		95,432 34	
11.	(ii) Interest	$59,092 32		
	(b) On other securities:			
13.	(ii) Interest or dividends, bank interest	804 77		

D.—Receipts from Real Estate Owned Beneficially by Corporation.

		(Col. 1.)	(Col. 3.)	(Total, Col. 4.)
16.	(a) Sales	....	4,285 98	
17.	(b) Rents	271 35		

F.—Borrowed Money.

		(Col. 1.)	(Col. 3.)	(Total, Col. 4.)
25.	(a) Bank or other advances, discounts or overdrafts, temporary loans	....	39,234 12	
27.	(c) Borrowed on debentures	....	58,643 33	

G.—Receipts from other sources, viz.:

		(Col. 1.)	(Col. 3.)	(Total, Col. 4.)
30.	(a) Transfer fees	33 95		
	(b) Contributions from other companies for office expenses	998 83		
	(c) Refund of taxes	68 90		
	(d) On account of property held jointly with third parties	....	1,286 51	
	(e) Exchange	72 59		
	Totals	$61,342 71	$213,485 50	$21,755 76
				61,342 71
				213,485 50
				$296,583 97

CASH ACCOUNT.

Expenditure for the year ending 31st December, 1913.

I.—Expended on Corporation Account.

A.—Sums Loaned or Invested on Capital Account.

		(Col. 1.)	(Col. 3.)	(Total, Col. 4.)
1.	(a) Loaned on mortgages of realty		$141,581 20	
6.	(c) Real estate purchased		15,765 16	

CASH ACCOUNT.—Continued.

'Expenditure for the year ending 31st December, 1913.

	(Col. 1.)	(Col. 3.)	(Total, Col. 4.)
B.—Expended on Stock Account.			
8. Dividends paid on permanent stock........	$30,194 19		
C.—Borrowed Money (other than foregoing), or Interest thereon paid, viz.:			
18. (a) Bank account (Principal and interest): Temporary advances	756 13	38,466 56	
21. (d) Debentures issued elsewhere: Interest	14,966 23		
Principal	....	1,946 66	
D.—Management Expenses (other than foregoing).			
25. (a) Salaries, wages and fees	9,458 65		
26. (b) Commission or brokerage	913 14		
28. (d) Stationery, postage, printing and advertising	332 21		
29. (e) Law costs	251 67		
30. (f) Fuel, rent, taxes (other than in 7 and 32) and rates	11,340 64		
31. (g) Travelling expenses	263 45		
33. (i) Other management expenditure	659 10		
E.—Other Expenditures, viz.:			
35. (b) Payments to third parties of share of price of properties sold.............	....	5,351 70	
F.—Balance.			
37. (a) Cash on hand and in banks............	....	....	24,337 28
	$69,135 41	$203,111 28	
			69,135 41
			203,111 28
Total			$296,583 97

MISCELLANEOUS STATEMENT FOR THE YEAR ENDING 31ST DECEMBER, 1913.

---

1. Amount of Debentures maturing in 1914: Issued in Canada, none; Issued elsewhere, none.
2. Amount of other existing obligations which will mature in 1914: None, except small current accounts.
3. Amount of other securities held by the Corporation which will mature and become payable to the Corporation in 1914, $172,221.
4. Average rate of interest per annum paid by the Corporation during 1913: On deposits, none; on debentures, 4¼%; on debenture stock, none.
5. Average rate of interest per annum received by the Corporation during 1913:
   (a) On mortgages of realty; (b) On other securities.
   (i) Owned beneficially by the Corporation (a) 7½%; (b) none.
   (ii) Not owned beneficially: (a) None; (b) none.

6. Of the mortgages owned beneficially by the Corporation, $42,915.97 is on realty situate in Ontario, and $818,187.38 is on realty situate elsewhere.

7. Of the mortgages not owned beneficially by the Corporation, none is on realty situate in Ontario, and none is on realty situate elsewhere.

8. Loans written off or transferred to real estate account during 1913, viz.:
   (i) Funds or securities owned beneficially, $7,896.80.
   (ii) Not so owned, none.

9. Number and aggregate amount of mortgages upon which compulsory proceedings have been taken by the Corporation in 1913, viz.:
   (i) Owned beneficially: Number, none; Amount, none.
   (ii). Not so owned: Number, none; Amount, none.

10. Aggregate market value of land mortgaged to the Corporation:
   (i) Mortgages owned beneficially, $1,922,206.
   (ii) Not so owned, none.

11. How often are securities held by the Corporation valued? At regular intervals.

12. (a) Specify the officers of the Corporation who are under bond, and for what sum respectively: Alexander Bain, Manager in Manitoba; William Bain, Assistant Manager in Manitoba; H. J. Skynner, Agent, Brandon—General Policy, £5,000.

   (b) Are the said bonds executed by private sureties or by Guarantee Companies? Guarantee Company.

13. Date when the accounts of the Corporation were last audited? March, 1913.

14. Names and addresses of the auditors respectively. for 1913 and for 1914 (if appointed):
   For 1913: Moores, Carson & Watson, C.A., Glasgow.
   For 1914: Same.

15. What were the dividend days of the Corporation in 1913, and what rate or rates of dividend were paid on those days respectively? 11th April, 1913, 10%; 30th June, 1913, 50% bonus.

16. What is the date appointed for the Annual Meeting? In March or April. Date of last Annual Meeting? 10th April, 1913.

17. Special General Meetings held in 1913: Dates, none.

IV. TRUST COMPANIES.

DETAILED REPORTS OF THE SEVERAL COMPANIES.

THE BRANTFORD TRUST COMPANY, LIMITED.

CONSTATING INSTRUMENTS.

The Brantford Trust Company was incorporated by Letters Patent of Ontario, bearing date 16th December, 1907. See The Loan and Trust Corporations Act, 2 Geo. V., c. 34.

ANNUAL STATEMENT

Of the condition and affairs of The Brantford Trust Company, Limited, of Brantford, Ont., at the 31st December, 1913, and for the year ending on that day, made to the Registrar of Loan Corporations for the Province of Ontario, pursuant to the laws of the said Province.

The head office of the Corporation is at No. 38 and 40 Market Street, in the City of Brantford, in the Province of Ontario.

The Board is constituted of six directors, holding office for the term of one year.

The directors and chief executive officers of the Corporation at 31st December, 1913, were as follows, together with their respective terms of office:

Christopher Cook, President, Brantford;   February, 1913; February, 1914.
Charles B. Heyd, Vice-President, Brantford;   "   "
John Mann, Director, Brantford;   "   "
A. J. Wilkes, K.C., Director, Brantford;
A. K. Bunnell, C.A., Director, Brantford;
Franklin Grobb, Director, Brantford;
W. G. Helliker, Manager, Secretary, Brantford.

A.—Permanent capital stock: Total amount authorized, $300,000; total amount subscribed, $300,000, as more particularly set out in Schedule A hereto.

SCHEDULE A.

Class 2.—Fixed and Permanent Capital Stock created by virtue of Joint Stock Companies Acts or Private Acts.

Description.	No. of shares.	Par value.	Total amount held.	Total amount paid thereon.	Total remaining unpaid on calls.
1. Fully called..........	3,000	$ 100	$ 300,000	- $ 300,000	....

LIST OF SHAREHOLDERS AS AT 31st DECEMBER, 1913.

(Not printed.)

BALANCE SHEET AS AT 31st DECEMBER, 1913.

Dr.   Capital and Liabilities.

Capital (Liabilities to Stockholders or Shareholders).

A.—Permanent Capital Stock or Shares.

1. (a) Ordinary joint stock capital fully called; total called, $300,000; total paid thereon $300,000 00

BALANCE SHEET.—Continued.

4. (d) Dividends declared in respect of (1), but not yet paid $7,500 00
5. (e) Unappropriated profits in respect of (1) 11,710 33
                                                                              $319,210 33

Total actual liabilities 319,210 33

II.—Contingent Liabilities.

49. Money for which the Corporation is contingently liable:
50. (a) Principal guaranteed 20,886 50
51. (b) Interest guaranteed 260 00
56. (e) Other contingent liabilities, value of trusts and
estates under administration 191,644 27

Total contingent liabilities 212,790 77

Gross total liabilities, actual and contingent.............. $532,001 10

Cr.   Assets.

I.—Assets of which the Corporation is the Beneficial Owner.

B.—Debts secured by Mortgages of Land.

9. (a) Debts (other than item 10) secured by mortgages of
land $280,893 88
11. (c) Interest due and accrued on item (9), not included
therein 4,904 40
                                                                              $285,798 28

C.—Debts not above enumerated, for which the Corporation holds security,
as follows:

14. (b) Debts secured by municipal bonds or debentures................   21,486 83

E.—Cash.

32. (b) In bank 11,925 22

Total assets owned beneficially by Corporation........... $319,210 33

II.—Assets not owned beneficially by Corporation, but for which the Corporation is Accountable.

A.—As Guarantor.

(a) Mortgage securities:
43.   (i) Principal $14,660 00
44.   (ii) Interest due and accrued 453 58

(b) Other securities:
(i) Cash in Standard Bank, Brantford 6,032 92

B.—As Trustee, Representative, Guardian or Agent (without guarantee).

52. (d) Value of trusts and estates under administration... $191,644 27
Total of assets II. 212,790 77

Gross total of assets I. and II. $532,001 10

CASH ACCOUNT.

Receipts for the year ending 31st December, 1913.

I.—Received by the Corporation for its Own Use.

A.—Balance from 31st December, 1912.

(b) Cash (not already shown under (1)):

3.	(ii) In bank	$8,500 32

C.—Receipts on account of Investments, Loans or Debts.

(a) On mortgages of realty:

10.	(i) Principal	52,876 89
11.	(ii) Interest	18,287 08

(b) On other securities:

12.	(i) Principal	842 58
13.	(ii) Interest or dividends	499 47

E.—Miscellaneous.

18. (a)	Commission, brokerage (or remuneration as corporate agent, trustee, etc.)	542 86
	Total	$81,548 70

II.—Received as Corporate Trustee, Representative, Guardian or Agent in Trust.

A.—Balance from 31st December, 1912.

(b) Cash:

(ii) In bank	$7,491 34

B.—Receipts on account of Investments, etc.

34. (a) Mortgages: Principal, $8,967.77; interest, $1,273.16	10,240 93

D.—Receipts from other sources.

39. (a) From guaranteed investments	3,185 48
40. (b) Interest, extra from banks, etc.	55 07
41. (c) On account of trusts and estates	13,139 75
Total	$39,062 57

CASH ACCOUNT.

Expenditure for the year ending 31st December, 1913.

I.—Expended on Corporation Account.

A.—Sums Loaned or Invested on Capital Account.

	(Col. 1.)	(Total, Col. 4.)
1. (a) Loaned on mortgages of realty	$39,423 16	
2. (b) Loaned on or invested in other securities, viz.:		
(i) Municipal debentures	13.578 (ℓ	

CASH ACCOUNT.—Continued.

Expenditure for the year ending 31st December, 1913.

B.—Expended on Stock Account.

8. Dividend paid on permanent stock	$15,000 00	15,000 00

D.—Management Expenses.

25. (a) Salaries and auditors' fees	700 00
26. (b) Commission or brokerage on loans	293 87
28. (d) Stationery, postage, printing and advertising	125 45
29. (e) Law costs, solicitor's costs	8 00
32. (h) Registration and Government fees	460 00
33. (i) Guarantee company	35 00

F.—Balance.

37. (a) Cash in bank	11,925 22
Total	$81,548 70

II.—Expended on Trust or Agency Account.

A.—Loaned on Invested on Capital Account.

42. (a) Loaned on mortgages of realty		$7,524 42
(b) Loaned or invested on or in other securities:		
44. (ii) Principal	$735 48	
45. (iii) Paid on guaranteed investments: Interest..	832 92	1,568 40

B.—Other Expenditures.

50. (a) Remuneration paid Brantford Trust Company, Limited, as agent, executor, etc.	542 36
51. (b) Commission on loans	76 75
53. (d) Cash invested for estates and paid out for various purposes.....	16,617 89

C.—Balances.

Cash in banks and loan company	12,732 75
Total	$39,062 57

MISCELLANEOUS STATEMENT FOR THE YEAR ENDING 31ST DECEMBER, 1913.

1. Amount of Debentures maturing in 1914: Issued in Canada, none; Issued elsewhere, none.
2. Amount of other existing obligations which will mature in 1914, none.
3. Amount of securities held by the Corporation which will mature and become payable to the Corporation in 1914, $34,375.00.
4. Average rate of interest per annum paid by the Corporation during 1913: On deposits, none; on debentures, none; on debenture stock, none.
5. Average rate of interest per annum received by the Corporation during 1913:
   (a) On mortgages of realty; (b) On other securities.
   (i) Owned beneficially by the orporation: (a) 6.19%; (b) 7.05%.
   (ii) Not owned beneficially: (a) 6.33%; (b) None.

6. Of the mortgages owned beneficially by the Corporation, $280,893.88 is on realty situate in Ontario, and none is on realty situate elsewhere.

7. Of the mortgages not owned beneficially by the Corporation, $14,660.00 is on realty situate in Ontario, and none is on realty situate elsewhere.

8. Loans written off or transferred to real estate account during 1913, viz.:
   (i) Funds or securities owned beneficially, none.
   (ii) Not so owned, none.

9. Number and aggregate amount of mortgages upon which compulsory proceedings have been taken by the Corporation in 1913, viz.:
   . (i) Owned beneficially: Number, none; Amount, none.
   (ii) Not so owned: Number, none; Amount, none.

10. Aggregate market value of land mortgaged to the Corporation: (i) Mortgages owned beneficially, $712,396.00; (ii) Not so owned, $32,620.00.

11. How often are the securities held by the Corporation valued? Yearly.

12. (a) Specify the officers of the Corporation who are under bond and for what sum respectively: Manager, $5,000.00; Accountant, $2,500.00; Teller, $2,500.00.
   (b) Are the said bonds executed by private sureties or by Guarantee Companies? Guarantee Companies.

13. Date when the accounts of the Corporation were last audited? 31st December, 1912, to 31st December, 1913.

14. Names and addresses of the auditors respectively for 1913 and for 1914 (if appointed):
   For 1913: F. W. Frank and C. J. Parker, Brantford.
   For 1914: F. W. Frank and C. J. Parker, Brantford.

15. What were the dividend days of the Corporation in 1913 and what rate or rates of dividend were paid on those days respectively: January 2nd, 1913, 2½%; July 2nd, 1913, 2½%.

16. What is the date appointed for the Annual Meeting? 2nd Wednesday in February. Date of last Annual Meeting? February 11th, 1914.

17. Special General Meetings held in 1913: Dates, none.

THE UNION TRUST COMPANY, LIMITED.

Incorporated by Letters Patent of Ontario, dated 7th August, 1901. The Letters Patent authorized the Company to acquire and take over the assets, business and goodwill of the Provincial Trust Company of Ontario, Limited.

The Authorized Capital Stock of the Union Trust Company was at first $2,000,000 (F. p. 106); then, by Supplementary Letters Patent of 27th December, 1905, was increased to $2,500,000 (F. p. 205); finally, by Supplementary Letters Patent of 25th November, 1908, was decreased to $1,000,000 (F. p. 393).

ANNUAL STATEMENT

Of the condition and affairs of the Union Trust Company, Limited, of Toronto, as at 31st December, 1913, and for the year ending on that day, made to the Registrar of Loan Corporations for the Province of Ontario, pursuant to the laws of the said Province.

The head office of the Corporation is at No. 176 Bay Street, in the City of Toronto and Province of Ontario.

The Board is constituted of fifteen directors holding office for one year.

The directors and chief executive officers at 31st December, 1913, were as follows, together with their respective terms of office:

Charles Magee, Chairman of the Board, Ottawa, Ont.; February, 1913; February, 1914
H. H. Beck, President, Toronto, Ont.;   "   "
Hon. E. G. Stevenson, 1st Vice-Pres., Toronto, Ont.;   "   "
E. E. A. DuVernet, K.C., 2nd Vice-Pres., Toronto, Ont.;   "
Samuel Barker, M.P., Director, Hamilton, Ont.;
T. Willes Chitty, Director, London, England;
Henry F. Gooderham, Director, Toronto, Ont.;
Right Hon. Lord Hindlip, Director, Worcester, Eng.;   "
Chas. H. Hoare, Director, London, Eng.;
S. F. Lazier, K.C., Director, Hamilton, Ont.;
George S. May, Director, Ottawa, Ont.;
J. H. McConnell, M.D., Director, Toronto, Ont.;
Hon. Sir George W. Ross, Director, Toronto, Ont.;   "
H. S. Strathy, Director, Toronto, Ont.;
J. M. McWhinney, Director and General Manager,
          Toronto, Ont.;

A.—Permanent capital stock: Total amount authorized, $1,000,000; total amount subscribed, $1,000,000, as more particularly set out in Schedule A hereto.

SCHEDULE A.

Class 2.—Fixed and permanent capital stock created by virtue of Joint Stock Companies' Acts or Private Acts.

Description.	No. of shares.	Par value of shares.	Total amount held.	Total amount paid thereon.	Total remaining unpaid on calls.
		$	$	$	$
1. Fully called..	10,000	100	1,000,000	1,000,000	....

LIST OF SHAREHOLDERS AS AT 31st DECEMBER, 1913.

(Not printed.)

BALANCE SHEET AS AT 31st DECEMBER, 1913.

Dr.   Capital and Liabilities.

Capital (Liabilities to Stockholders or Shareholders).

A.—Permanent Capital Stock or Shares.

1. (a) Ordinary joint stock capital, fully called: Total called, $1,000,000; total paid thereon	$1,000,000 00
4. (d) Dividends declared in respect of (1), but not yet paid..........	25,000 00
5. (e) Unappropriated profits in respect of (1)	39,736 78
6. (f) Reserve fund in respect of (1)...............................	950,000 00

Liabilities to the Public.

41. Other liabilities to the public, viz.:	
42. (a) Interest accrued, but not yet payable, on guaranteed investments	8,010 35
43. (b) Sundries	19,706 44
Total actual liabilities	$2,042,453 57

II. Contingent Liabilities.

48. Money for which the Corporation is contingently liable:		
50. (a) Principal guaranteed		7,001,691 93
52. (c) Trust funds invested, but not guaranteed:		
53. (i) Principal	529,855 55	
54. (ii) Interest	4,160 32	
55. (d) Trust funds uninvested, bearing interest, and not guaranteed ... .\....	58,803 25	
56. (e) Other contingent liabilities	4,723,095 07	
		5,315,914 19
Total contingent liabilities		$12,317,606 12
Gross total liabilities, actual and contingent		$14,360,059 69

Cr.   Assets.

I.—Assets of which the Corporation is the Beneficial Owner.

A.—Immovable Property Owned Beneficially by Corporation.

5. (b) Freehold land, including buildings other than foregoing..........		$619,491 11

B.—Debts secured by Mortgages of Land.

9. (a) Debts (other than item 10) secured by mortgages of land	$695,908 51	
10. (b) Debts secured by mortgaged land held for sale......	8,615 33	
11. (c) Interest due or accrued on items 9, 10 and 43 (1) and not included therein	143,747 70	
		848,271 54

C.—Debts not above enumerated, for which the Corporation holds security, as follows:

22. (j) Debts secured by stocks and bonds	$181,804 18	
26. (n) Interest due and accrued on item 22, and not included therein	34,683 55	
		216,487 73

BALANCE SHEET.—Continued.

E.—Cash.

31. (a) On hand	$41,623 55	
32. (b) In banks	17,466 81	
		$59,095 36

F.—Assets not hereinbefore mentioned.

37. (a) Bonds, stocks and debentures	$168,019 17	
38. (b) Interest on bonds, stocks and debentures (due and accrued)	70,226 57	
		238,245 74
39. (c) Sundry assets		60,862 09
Total assets owned beneficially by Corporation		$2,042,453 57

II.—Assets Not Owned Beneficially by Corporation, but for which the Corporation is Accountable.

A.—As Guarantors.

(a) Mortgage securities:		
43. (i) Principal	$3,297,759 72	
(b) Other securities:		
45. (i) Principal	3,482,493 11	
Cash on hand and in bank	221,439 10	
		$7,001,691 93

B.—As Trustee, Representative, Guardian or Agent (without guarantee).

(a) Mortgage securities:		
47. (i) Principal	514,667 55	
48. (ii) Interest due	4,160 32	
(b) On other securities:		
49. (i) Principal	15,188 00	
52. (d) Uninvested trust funds	58,803 25	
Inventoried value of unrealized original assets of trusts, estates, etc.	4,723,095 07	
		5,315,914 19
Total of assets II.		$12,317,606 12
Gross total assets I. and II.		$14,360,059 69

CASH ACCOUNT.

Receipts for the year ending 31st December, 1913.

I.—Received by the Corporation for Its Own Use.

A.—Balances from 31st December, 1912.

		(Col. 1.)	(Col. 3.)	(Total, Col. 4.)
2.	(i) On hand	....	$22,293 56	
3.	(ii) In bank	....	42,436 27	

CASH ACCOUNT.—Continued.

Receipts for the year ending 31st December, 1913.

		(Col. 1.)	(Col. 3.)	(Total, Col. 4.)
C.—Receipts on Account of Investments, Loans or Debts.				
	(a) On mortgages of realty:			
10.	(i) Principal	. . . .	$121,063 22	
11.	(ii) Interest	$307,852 64		
	(b) On other securities:			
12.	(i) Principal	. . . .	26,606 48	
13.	(ii) Interest or dividends	158,564 45		
D.—Receipts from Real Estate Owned Beneficially by Corporation.				
17.	*(b)* Rents	14,303 24		
E.—Miscellaneous.				
18.	*(a)* Commission, brokerage (or remuneration as Corporate Agent, Trustee, etc.)	139,287 26		
19.	*(b)* Premiums or bonus on loans	3,458 33		
G.—Receipts from Other Sources.				
30.	*(a)* Insurance department	. . . .	25,355 33	
	(b) Sundry suspense items	. . . .	17,953 84	
	(c) Safe deposit department	3,364 50		
	(d) Bank interest	3,355 03		
	Totals	$630,185 45	$255,763 70	$885,954 15

II.—Received as Corporate Trustee, Representative, Guardian or Agent in Trust.

A.—Balance from 31st December, 1912.

	(b) Cash:		
32.	(i) On hand	$50,287 16	
33.	(ii) In bank	292,974 68	

B.—Received on account of Investments, Loans or Debts.

34.	*(a)* On mortgages: Principal, $487,216.22; interest, $44,920.63	532,136 85	
35.	*(b)* On other securities: Principal	500,794 76	

C.—Receipts from Real Estate.

38.	*(b)* Rents	47,708 12	

D.—Receipts from Other Sources, viz.:

39.	*(a)* On guaranteed investment account	6,831,596 62	
40.	*(b)* As executor, trustee, agent, etc.	312,325 20	
	Totals		$8,567,823 39

I.—Expended on Corporation Account.

A.—Sums Loaned or Invested on Capital Account.

CASH ACCOUNT.—Continued.

Expenditure for the year ending 31st December, 1913.

	(Col. 1.)	(Col. 3.)	(Total, Col. 4.)
1. (a) Loaned on mortgages of realty.........	....	$108,750 12	
(b) Loaned or invested in other securities:			
2. (i) Stocks, bonds and debentures...	....	6,341 16	
6. (c) Real estate purchased	....	140,605 05	
7. (d) Incumbrances on realty paid off........	$2,537 46		
(e) Insurance or taxes advanced on property mortgaged to the Corporation......	....	14,316 53	

B.—Expended on Stock Account.

8. Dividends paid on permanent stock	100,000 00		

C.—Borrowed Money (other than foregoing) or interest thereon paid, viz.:

24. (g) Guarantees paid (interest)	277,952 04		

D.—Management Expenses (other than foregoing).

25. (a) Salaries, wages and fees	81,498 54		
26. (b) Commission or brokerage	2,546 18		
28. (d) Stationery, postage, printing and advertising	25,822 80		
29. (e) Law costs	182 00		
30. (f) Fuel, rent and taxes (other than in 7 and 32) and rates	15,131 39		
31. (g) Travelling expenses	6,955 47		
32. (h) Registration fees	310 00		
33. (i) Other management expenditure	11,609 56		

E.—Other Expenditure, viz.:

34. (a) Insurance Department	....	27,553 18	
35. (b) Interest on bank (overdraft)	4,247 31		

F.—Balance.

37. (a) Cash on hand and in banks.. $59,095 36			
Totals $59,095 36	$528,792 75	$298,066 04	$885,954 15

II.—Expended on Trust or Agency Account.

A.—Loaned or Invested on Capital Account.

42. (a) Loaned on mortgages of realty	$482,701 52
(b) Loaned and invested on or in other securities:	
43. (1) Stocks, bonds and debentures	665,853 66

B.—Other Expenditures.

51. (b) Insurance re mortgages	1,323 95
53. (d) On Guaranteed Investment Account	6,686,971 15
(e) As executor; trustee, agent, etc.	450,730 76

C.—Balance.

54. (a) Cash on hand and in banks	280,242 35
Total	$8,567,823 39

1. Amount of Debentures maturing in 1914: Company does not issue debentures.
2. Amount of other existing obligations which will mature, in 1914, $84,200.05.
3. Amount of securities held by the Corporation which will mature and become payable to the Corporation in 1914, $1,261,950.92.
4. Average rate of interest per annum paid by the Corporation during 1913: On trust accounts, 4%; on debentures, none; on debenture stock, none.
5. Average rate of interest per annum received by the Corporation during 1913:
   (a) On mortgages of realty; (b) On other securities.
   (i) Owned beneficially by the Corporation: (a) 6.16%; (b) 5.18%.
   (ii) Not owned beneficially: (a) 7½%; (b) 5.62%.
6. Of the mortgages owned beneficially by the Corporation, $304,265.98 is on realty situate in Ontario, and $535,390.23 is on realty situate elsewhere.
7. Of the mortgages not owned beneficially by the Corporation, $1,443,337.38 is on realty situate in Ontario, and $2,369.089.89 is on realty situate elsewhere.
8. Loans written off or transferred to real estate account during 1913, viz.:
   (i) Funds or securities owned beneficially, none.
   (ii) Not so owned, $1,955.00.
9. Number and aggregate amount of mortgages upon which compulsory proceedings have been taken by the Corporation in 1913, viz.:
   (i) Owned beneficially: Number, none; Amount, none.
   (ii) Not so owned: Number, 5; Amount, $13,800.00.
10. Aggregate market value of land mortgaged to the Corporation:
    (i) Mortgages owned beneficially, $1,787,810.90.
    (ii) Not so owned, $11,077.412.00.
11. How often are the securities held by the Corporation valued? Annually.
12. (a) Specify the officers of the Corporation who are under bond and for what sum respectively: Thirty-six, $132,000.00.
    (b) Are the said bonds executed by private sureties or by Guarantee Companies? Guarantee Companies.
13. Date when the accounts of the Corporation were last audited? December 31st, 1913.
14. Names and addresses of the auditors respectively for 1913 and for 1914 (if appointed):
    For 1913: A. C. Neff, F.C.A., and C. R. Cumberland.
    For 1914: A. C. Neff, F.C.A., and C. R. Cumberland.
15. What were the dividend days of the Corporation in 1913, and what rate or rates of dividend were paid on those days respectively? April 1st, July 1st, October 1st, balance of 1913; dividend payable January 2nd, 1914. Dividend at rate of 10% per annum.
16. What is the date appointed for the Annual Meeting? February 5th, 1914. Date of last Annual Meeting? February 6th, 1913.
17. Special General Meetings held in 1913: Dates, none held.

THE CANADA TRUST COMPANY.

Incorporated on the 23rd July, 1894, by special Act of the Dominion of Canada, 57.8 Vict. (1894) Chap. 115, under the name of The General Trusts Corporation of Canada.

By a subsequent special Act, 62.3 Vict., Chap. 111 (D.) passed on the 11th August, 1899, the corporate name was changed to The Canada Trust Company, and certain other amendments were made in the incorporating Act.

The powers of the Company are defined by sections 3 of the incorporating Act, which powers are (section 4) to be deemed subject to the laws of the Province.

ANNUAL STATEMENT

Of the condition and affairs of The Canada Trust Company, of London, Ontario, at the 31st December, 1913, and for the year ending on that day, made to the Registrar of Loan Corporations for the Province of Ontario, pursuant to the laws of the said Province.

The head office of the Corporation is at No. 442 Richmond Street, in the City of London, in the Province of Ontario.

The Board is constituted of seventeen directors holding office for one year.

The directors and chief executive officers of the Corporation at the 31st December, 1913, were as follows, together with their respective terms of office.

Thomas G. Meredith, K.C., Pres., London, Ont.;   February, 1913; February, 1914.
Dr. F. R. Eccles, Vice-Pres., London, Ont.;   "   "
Frank E. Leonard, Director, London, Ont.;
H. S. Blackburn, Director, London, Ont.;
H. E. Gates, Director, London, Ont.;
J. B. McKillop, Director, London, Ont.;
John Cowan, K.C., Director, Sarnia, Ont.;
Philip Pocock, Director, London, Ont.;
W. J. Christie, Director, Winnipeg, Man.;
Robert Fox, Director, London, Ont.;
George T. Brown, Director, London, Ont.;   "
George A. Sommerville, Director, Toronto, Ont.;   "
Prof. Wm. Saunders, C.M.G., Director, London, Ont.;   "
E. P. Clement, K.C., Director, Berlin, Ont.;   "
R. O. McCulloch, Director, Galt, Ont.;   "
Verschoyle Cronyn, K.C., Director, London, Ont.;   "
Hume Cronyn, Managing Director, London, Ont.;

A.—Permanent capital stock: Total amount authorized, $5,000,000; total amount subscribed, $1,000,000, as more particularly set out in Schedule A hereto.

SCHEDULE A.

Class 2.—Fixed and permanent Capital Stock created by virtue of Joint Stock Companies' Acts or Private Acts.

Description.	No. of shares.	Par value of shares.	Total amount held.	Total amount paid thereon.	Total amount unpaid and constituting an asset of the corporation.
		$	$	$	$
1. Fully called..........	6,947	100	694,700	694,700	....
2. Partly called	551	100	55,100	13,775	....
4. Calls due 2nd January, 1914.................	2,502	100	250,200	....	250,200*
Totals	10,000	....	1,000,000	708,475	250,200

*Paid January 2nd, 1914.

LIST OF SHAREHOLDERS AS AT 31st DECEMBER, 1913.

(Not printed.)

18 L.C.

BALANCE SHEET AS AT 31st DECEMBER, 1913.

Dr. Capital and Liabilities.

Capital (Liabilities to Stockholders or Shareholders).

A.—Permanent Capital Stock or Shares.

1. (a) Ordinary joint stock capital fully called; total called, $694.700, total paid thereon	$694,700 00	
2. (b) Ordinary joint stock capital, 25 per cent. called: Total called, $13.775, total paid thereon	13,775 00	
3. (c) Ordinary joint stock capital, subscribed but not called	41,325 00	
(cc) Joint stock capital, calls on 2,502 fully paid, due 2 January, 1914, paid on that date	250,200 00	
4. (d) Dividends declared in respect of (1) and (2) but not yet paid	17,511 87	
5. (e) Unappropriated profits in respect of (1) and (2) ..	8,684 76	
6. (f) Reserve fund in respect of (1) and (2) or (3), including $62,550. premium on calls due, January 14th, paid January 2nd, 1914	325,000 00	

Total actual liabilities $1,351,196 63

Liabilities to the Public. None.

Contingent Liabilities.

49. Money for which the Corporation is contingently liable, viz.:		
50. (a) Principal guaranteed	$1,886,946 75	
51. (b) Interest guaranteed	25,672 49	
52. (c) Trust funds invested but not guaranteed:		
53. (i) Principal	1,043,749 40	
54. (ii) Interest	43,170 60	
56. (e) Unrealized assets of estates, estimated	479,427 00	

Total contingent liabilities $3,478,966 24

Gross total liabilities, actual and contingent $4,830,162 87

Cr. Assets.

I.—Assets of which the Corporation is the Beneficial Owner:

B.—Debts secured by Mortgages of Land.

9. (a) Debts (other than item 10) secured by mortgages of land	$815,181 29	
Less retained to pay prior mortgages	39,797 62	
		$775,383 67

C.—Debts not above enumerated for which the Corporation holds securities as follows:

14. (b) Municipal bonds or debentures owned by company .	$47,194 00	
15. (c) Public school debentures owned by company	32,820 00	
16. (d) Debts secured by loan corporation debentures	26,362 00	
22. (j) Debts secured by loan corporations' permanent stock	11,923 00	
23. (k) Debts secured by stock of other corporations	32,601 00	
		150,900 00

BALANCE SHEET.—Continued.

E.—Cash.

32. (b) In banks in Canada $70,837 96

F.—Assets not Hereinbefore Mentioned.

37. (a) Calls on stock due January 2nd, 1914, with premium thereon, paid January 2nd, 1914 .... $312,750 00
38. (b) Uncalled subscribed stock 41,325 00

                                                                354,075 00

          Total assets owned beneficially by Corporation $1,351,196 63

II.—Assets not owned Beneficially by Corporation, but for
which the Corporation is Accountable.

A.—As Guarantor.

(a) Mortgage securities:

43.   (i) Principal $1,422,504 00

44.   (ii) Interest 41,977 72

(b) Other securities:

45.   (i) Principal 380,441 20
46.   (ii) Interest due and accrued 4,749 80
             (iii) Cash in bank 62,946 52

                                                                $1,912,619 24

B.—As Trustee, Representative, Guardian or Agent
(without guarantee).

(a) Mortgage securities:

47.   (i) Principal $598,977 67
48.   (ii) Interest due and accrued 19,992 33

(b) Other securities:

49.   (i) Principal 374,943 10
50   (ii) Interest due and accrued 6,162 90
51. (c) Unrealized assets of estates, estimated 479,427 00
52. (d) Trust funds deposited in banks bearing interest, but
not guaranteed 86,844 00

          Total assets II. $1,566,347 00

          Grand total of assets I. and II. $4,830,162 87

CASH ACCOUNT.

Receipts for the year ending 31st December, 1913.

I.—Received by the Corporation for its Own Use.

A.—Balance from 31st December, 1912.

Cash (not already shown under (1)):

3.   (ii) In bank $40,097 58

CASH ACCOUNT.—Continued.

Receipts for the year ending 31st December, 1913.

B.—Sums received wholly or partly on Capital Stock.

4. (a) Calls on joint stock, permanent capital	$231,550 00		
5. (b) Premiums on (4)	57,887 50		$289,437 50

C.—Receipts on account of Investments, Loans or Debts.

(a) On mortgages of realty:

10.	(i) Principal	$207,615 10	
11.	(ii) Interest	44,135 88	

(b) On other securities:

12.	(i) Principal	$65,864 13	
13.	(ii) Interest or dividends	7,410 09	325,025 20

E.—Miscellaneous.

18. (a) Commission, brokerage (or remuneration as corporate agent, trustee, etc.)		21,197 10

G.—Receipts from other sources.

30. (a) Safety deposit box rentals	$143 25	
(b) Bank interest	2,333 71	2,376 96
Total		$678,134 34

II.—Received as Corporate Trustee, Representative, Guardian or Agent in Trust

A.—Balance from 31st December, 1912.

33.	(ii) In bank	$115,986 00

B.—Receipts on Account of Investments, etc.

34. (a) Mortgages: Principal, $711,996.87; interest, $130,890.49	$842,887 36	
35. (b) On other securities: Principal, $43,699.36; Interest, $29,596.50	73,295 86	916,183 22

C.—Receipts from Real Estate.

38. (b) Rents		27,529 72

D.—Receipts from other Sources, viz.:

39. Estates moneys received for investments, etc.		1,104,927 89
		$2,164,626 83

CASH ACCOUNT.

Expenditure for the year ending 31st December, 1913.

I.—Expended on Corporation Account.

A.—Sums Loaned or Invested on Capital Account.

1. (a) Loaned on mortgages of realty $412,383 61			
Assumed mortgages 38,488 57	$450,872 18		
(b) Loaned on or invested in other securities, viz.:			
2. (i) Bonds and debentures	109,513 15		
			$560,385 33

B.—Expended on Stock Account.

3., Dividends on permanent stock .... $28,047 88   ......   28,047 88

D.—Management Expenses.

25. (a) Salaries, wages and fees	7,815 57
26. (b) Commission or brokerage	2,428 31
28. (d) Stationery, postage, printing and advertising	4,365 60
29. (e) Law costs	835, 81
32. (h) Registration fees	1,083 88
	16,529 17

E.—Other Expenditures, viz.:

34. (a) Safety deposit boxes 2,334 00

F.—Balances.

37. (a) Cash in banks in Canada 70,837 96

Totals $678,134 34

II.—Expended on Trust or Agency Account.

Loaned or invested on Capital Account.

42. (a) Loaned on mortgages of realty $1,349,316 90

(b) Loaned or invested on or in other securities:		
43. (i) Stocks of other corporations and bonds	102,580 90	
		$1,451,897 80

B.—Other Expenditures.

53. (d) Sundry returns, payments and disbursements 562,938 51

C.—Balance.

54. (b) (i) Cash in bank, London, England	$57,110 40	
(ii) Cash in banks in Canada	92,680 12	
		149,790 52

Total $2,164,626 83

1. Amount of debentures maturing in 1914: Issued in Canada, none; Issued elsewhere, none.
2. Amount of other existing obligations which will mature in 1914: $191,418.46.
3. Amount of securities held by the Corporation which will mature and become payable to the Corporation in 1914: $47,589.72.
4. Average rate of interest per annum paid by the Corporation during 1913: on deposits, none; on debentures, none; on debenture stock, none.
5. Average rate of interest per annum received by the Corporation during 1913:
    (a) On mortgages of realty; (b) On other securities.
    (i) Owned beneficially by the Corporation; (a) 7.014%; (b) 6.323%.
    (ii) Not owned beneficially; (a) 6.808%; (b) 8.44%.
6. Of the mortgages owned beneficially by the Corporation, $619,581.29 is on realty situate in Ontario, and $437,399.00 is on realty situate elsewhere.
7. Of the mortgages not owned beneficially by the Corporation, $1,335,255.72 is on realty situate in Ontario, and $748,196.00 is on realty situate elsewhere.
8. Loans written off or transferred to real estate account during 1913, viz.:
    (i) Funds or securities owned beneficially, none;
    (ii) Not so owned, none.
9. Number and aggregate amount of mortgages upon which compulsory proceedings have been taken by the Corporation in 1913, viz.:
    (i) Owned beneficially: No., three; amount, $9,501.28.
    (ii) Not so owned: No., five; amount, $5,770.00.
10. Aggregate market value of land mortgaged to the Corporation:
    (i) Mortgages owned beneficially, $1,915,342.00.
    (ii) Not so owned, $5,111,443.00.
11. How often are the securities held by the Corporation valued, Annually.
12. (a) Specify the officers of the Corporation who are under bond and for what sum respectively: Managing Director, $10,000.00; and other officers $40,000.00; $50,000.00 in all.
    (b) Are the said bonds executed by private sureties or by Guarantee Companies? Guarantee Companies.
13. Date when the accounts of the Corporation were last audited: As at 31st December, 1913.
14. Names and addresses of the auditors respectively for 1913 and for 1914 (if appointed):
    For 1913: M. H. Rowland and J. F. Kern.
    For 1914: M. H. Rowland and J. F. Kern.
15. What were the dividend days of the Corporation in 1913 and what rate or rates of dividend were paid on those days respectively: 2nd January, 1913, 2½%, and 2nd July, 1913, 2½%.
16. What is the date appointed for the Annual Meeting, February 10th, 1914. Date of last Annual Meeting? February 4th, 1913.
17. Special General Meetings held in 1913: Dates, February 4th, 1913.

THE NATIONAL TRUST COMPANY, LIMITED.
Head Office, Toronto.

Incorporated on the 12th day of August, 1898, by Letters Patent issued under the Ontario Companies Act (R.S.O. 1887, c. 191), subject to the provisions of the Ontario Trust Companies' Act (R.S.O. 1897, c. 206). See the Loan and Trust Corporations Act (2 Geo. V., c. 34).

ANNUAL STATEMENT

Of the condition and affairs of the National Trust Company, Limited, at the 31st December, 1913, and for the year ending on that day, made to the Registrar of Loan Corporations for the Province of Ontario, pursuant to the laws of the said Province.

The head office of the Corporation is at Nos. 18-22 King Street East, in the City of Toronto, in the Province of Ontario.

The Board is constituted of twenty-four directors, holding office for one year.

*The directors and chief executive officers of the Corporation at 31st December, 1913, were as follows, together with their respective terms of office:

J. W. Flavelle, President, Toronto, Ont.;
Z. A. Lash, K.C., Vice-President, Toronto, Ont.;
E. R. Wood, Vice-President, Toronto, Ont.;
Hon. Geo. A. Cox, Director, Toronto, Ont.;
Hon. Mr. Justice Britton, Director, Toronto, Ont.;
E. W. Cox, Director, Toronto, Ont.;
Elias Rogers, Director, Toronto, Ont.;
Robert Kilgour, Director, Toronto, Ont.;
H. H. Fudger, Director, Toronto, Ont.;
A. E. Kemp, Director, Toronto, Ont.;
Sir Wm. MacKenzie, Director, Toronto, Ont.;
H. B. Walker, Director, Montreal, Que.;
Chester D. Massey, Director, Toronto, Ont.;   } Elected at Annual Meeting,
G. H. Watson, K.C., Director, Toronto, Ont.;
J. H. Plummer, Director, Toronto, Ont.;
Wm. McMaster, Director, Montreal, Que.;
F. H. Phippen, K.C., Director, Toronto, Ont.;
Alexander Laird, Director, Toronto, Ont.;
Alex. Bruce, K.C., Director, Toronto, Ont.;
H. J. Fuller, Director, New York. N.Y.;
F. W. Molson, Director, Montreal, Que.;
T. B. Macauley, Director, Montreal, Que.;
W. M. Birks, Director, Montreal, Que.;
W. E. Rundle, General Manager, Toronto, Ont.;
J. C. Breckenridge, Assistant Manager, Toronto, Ont.;
E. Cassidy, Secretary, Toronto;

A.—Permanent capital stock: Total amount authorized, $2,000,000; total amount subscribed, $1,500,000, as more particularly set out in Schedule A hereto.

SCHEDULE A.

Class 2.—Fixed and Permanent Capital Stock created by virtue of Joint Stock Companies Acts or Private Acts.

Description	No. of shares	Par value of shares	Total amount held	Total amount paid thereon
		$	$	$
1. Fully called....	15,000	100	1,500,000	1,500,000

LIST OF SHAREHOLDERS AS AT 31st DECEMBER, 1913.
(Not printed.)

*At annual meeting succeeding appointment. No permanent date fixed for annual

BALANCE SHEET AS AT 31st DECEMBER, 1913.

Dr.   Capital and Liabilities.

Capital (Liabilities to Stockholders or Shareholders).

A.—Permanent Capital Stock or Shares.

1. (a) Ordinary joint stock capital, fully called; total
          called, $1,500,000; total paid thereon $1,500,000 00
4. (d) Dividends declared in respect of (1), but not yet
          paid 37,500 00
5. (e) Unappropriated profits on (1) 16,788 41
6. (f) Reserve fund in respect of (1) 1,500,000 00
                                                                              $3,054,288 41

Liabilities to the Public.

39. Due on loans in process of completion or to pay assumed mortgages.   59,213 47

          Total actual liabilities $3,113,501 88

II.—Contingent Liabilities.

49. Money for which the Corporation is contingently liable,
          viz.:
50. (a) Principal, guaranteed, together with trust deposits ⎰ $6,527,244 14
51. (b) Interest guaranteed .... ⎱
52. (c) Trust funds invested but not guaranteed:
53.   (1) Principal . . .. ⎱ 31,094,121 66
54.   (2) Interest . . . . ⎰
55. (d) Trust fund uninvested not bearing interest and
          not guaranteed 3,780,634 49

          Total contingent liabilities 41,402,000 29

          Gross total liabilities, actual and contingent............... $44,515,502 17

Cr.   Assets.

I.—Assets of which the Corporation is the Beneficial Owner.

A.—Immovable Property Owned Beneficially by Corporation.

1. (a) Office premises situate in Toronto, held in freehold... $145,618 80
        (ii) Office premises situate at Winnipeg, Edmonton
              and Saskatoon, held in freehold 171,791 87
        (iii) Office premises situate at Montreal, held in
              freehold 103,162 29
5. (b) Freehold land (including buildings) other than fore-
          going 57,012 00
7. (d) Safe deposit vaults 51,290 00
8. (e) Rents due and accrued re vaults 874 98
                                                                              $529,749 94

B.—Debts secured by Mortgages of Land.

9. (a) Debts (other than item 10) secured by mortgages of
          land $1,209,458 38
11. (c) Interest due or accrued on item (9), and not in-
          cluded therein, including accrued interest on
          certain mortgages held for guaranteed trust
          account 306,897 25
                                                                              1,516,355 63

BALANCE SHEET.—Continued.

C.—Debts not above enumerated, for which the Corporation holds securities as follows:

22. (j) Debts secured by call loans on stocks and bonds, etc............		$582,841 83

E.—Cash.

31. (a) On hand	$1,569 04	
32. (b) In sundry banks	137,645 76	139,214 80

F.—Assets not hereinbefore mentioned.

37. (a) Stocks of other corporations	$98,592 36	
38. (b) Railway and other bonds	246,747 32	345,339 68

Total assets owned beneficially by the Corporation.......... $3,113,501 88

II.—Assets not owned Beneficially by Corporation, but for which the Corporation is Accountable.

A.—As Guarantors.

(a) Mortgage securities:

43.	(i) Principal	$5,785,583 08
44.	(ii) Interest due and accrued	16,844 76

(b) On other securities:

45.	(i) Principal	$536,575 15
46.	(ii) Interest due and accrued	1,928 90
	(iii) Cash on hand and in banks...............	186,312 25
		6,527,244 14

B.—As Trustee, Representative, Guardian or Agent (without Guarantee).

(a) Mortgage securities:

47.	(i) Principal	$12,732,779 61
48.	(ii) Interest due	35,494 98

(b) On other securities:

49.	(i) Principal	18,319,130 27
50.	(ii) Interest due, rents, etc.	6,716 80
52. (d) Uninvested trust funds		3,780,634 49
		34,874,756 15

Total assets of II. 41,402,000 29
Gross total assets I. and II. $44,515,502 17

CASH ACCOUNT.

Receipts for the year ending 31st December, 1913.

I.—Received by the Corporation for Its Own Use.

A.—Balance from 31st December, 1912.

	(Col. 1.)	Total (Col. 4.)
3. { (i) On hand .... { (ii) In bank		} $193,726 90

C.—Receipts on account of Investments, Loans or Debts.

(a) On mortgages of realty:

CASH ACCOUNT.—Continued.

Receipts for the year ending 31st December, 1913.

		(Col. 1.)	(Total, Col. 4.)
10.	(i) Principal		$2,119,303 95
11.	(ii) Interest	$90,811 19	

(b) On other securities:

12.	(i) Principal	....	965,544 90
13.	(ii) Interest or dividends	67,109 86	

D.—Receipts from Real Estate Owned Beneficially by Corporation.

16. (a)	Sales	....	4,574 45
17. (b)	Rent	64,697 36	

E.—Miscellaneous.

18. (a)	Commission, brokerage (or remuneration as corporate agent, trustee, etc.)	377,109 09	
19. (b)	Premiums or bonus on loans	3,273 50	
			603,001 00
	Total		$3,886,151 20

II.—Received as Corporate Trustee, Representative, Guardian or Agent in Trust.

A.—Balance from 31st December, 1912.

(b) Cash:

32.	(i) On hand	}	$4,717,235 01
33.	(ii) In bank		

B.—Received on account of Investments, Loans or Debts.

34. (a)	On mortgages: Principal, $4,595,705.13; interest, $627,058.24	5,222,763 37
35. (b)	On other securities: Principal, $7,674,379.09; interest, $617,512.89.	8,291,891 98

C.—Receipts from Real Estate.

37. (a)	Sales (not included in foregoing items)	732,824 42
38. (b)	Rents	135,241 45

D.—Received from other sources.

39. (a)	Estates, capital and revenue (including guaranteed funds)	12,855,213 33
	Total	$31,955,169 56·

CASH ACCOUNT.

Expenditure for the year ending 31st December, 1913.

I.—Expended on Corporation Account.

A.—Sums Loaned or Invested on Capital Account.

	(Col. 1.)	(Total, Col. 4.)
1. (a) Loaned on mortgages of realty		$1,979,204 80

CASH ACCOUNT.—Continued.

Expenditure for the year ending 31st December, 1913.

	(Col. 1.)	(Total, Col. 4.)
(b) Loaned or invested in other securities:		
2. (i) Call loans, stocks, bonds, etc.		$1,182,723 69
6. (c) Real estate purchased		9,550 32
(e) Insurance or taxes advanced on property mortgaged to the Corporation		52,691 12

B.—Expended on Stock Account.

8. Dividend paid on permanent stock $150,000 00

D.—Management Expenses.

25. (a) Salaries, wages and fees	211,011 21
26. (b) Commission or brokerage	6,733 78
28. (d) Stationery, postage, printing, etc.	29,514 37
29. (e) Law costs	4,080 91
30. (f) Fuel, rent, taxes (other than 7 and 32) and rates...	33,832 52
31. (g) Travelling expenses and inspection expenses	26,540 55
32. (h) Registration fees	680 00
33. (i) Other management expenditure	19,276 21

E.—Other Expenditure.

34. Real estate charges	41,146 42	
		522,765 97

F.—Balance.

37. (a) Cash on hand and in banks	139,214 30
Total	$3,886,151 20

II.—Expended on Trust or Agency Account.

A.—Loaned or Invested on Capital Account.

42. (a) Loaned on mortgages of realty $3,775,073 46

Loaned or invested on or in other securities:

43. (i) Call loans, bonds, etc.	5,570,063 13
47. (a) Real estate purchased	20,000 00

B.—Other Expenditure.

53. (d) Estates, capital and revenue, including guaranteed funds........ 18,623,086 23

C.—Balance.

54. (a) On hand and in banks	3,966,946 74
Total	$31,955,169 56

1. Amount of Debentures maturing in 1914: Issued in Canada, none; Issued elsewhere, none.
2. Amount of other existing obligations which will mature in 1914: Assumed mortgages and loans in process of completion, $19,502.30; guaranteed funds, etc., $474,560.22.
3. Amount of securities held by the Corporation which will mature and become payable to the Corporation in 1914: Company funds, $141,758.30.
4. Average rate of interest per annum paid by the Corporation during 1913: On trusts deposits, 3¾%; On debentures, none; On debenture stock, none.
5. Average rate of interest per annum received by the Corporation during 1913:
   (a) On mortgages of realty; (b) On other securities.
   (i) Owned beneficially by the Corporation: (a) 7%; (b) 5½%.
   (ii) Not owned beneficially: (a) 7%; (b) 5½%.
6. Of the mortgages owned beneficially by the Corporation, $215,598.40 is on realty situate in Ontario, and $1,300,757.23 is on realty situate elsewhere.
7. Of the mortgages not owned beneficially by the Corporation, $5,085,528.66 is on realty situate in Ontario, and $13,485,173.77 is on realty situate elsewhere.
8. Loans written off or transferred to real estate account during 1913, viz.:
   (i) Funds or securities owned beneficially, $2,650.00.
   (ii) Not so owned, $800.00.
9. Number and aggregate amount of mortgages upon which compulsory proceedings have been taken by the Corporation in 1913, viz.:
   (i) Owned beneficially: Number, 14; Amount, $35,799.09.
   (ii) Not so owned; Number, 142; Amount, $214,572.73.
10. Estimated aggregate market value of land mortgaged to the Corporation:
    (i) Mortgages owned beneficially, $3,050,000.00.
    (ii) Not so owned, $37,000,000.00.
11. How often are the securities held by the Corporation valued? Yearly.
12. (a) Specify the officers of the Corporation who are under bond and for what sum respectively: All officers for a total of $298,500.00.
    (b) Are the said bonds executed by private sureties or by Guarantee Companies? Guarantee Company.
13. Date when the accounts of the Corporation were last audited? To 31st December, 1913.
14. Names and addresses of the auditors respectively for 1913 and for 1914 (if appointed):
    For 1913: John MacKay, Geo. Edwards, G. Dunford, C.A.; Webb, Read, Hegan, Callingham & Co.
    For 1914: The same.
15. What were the dividend days of the Corporation in 1913, and what rate or rates of dividend were paid on those days respectively? January 2nd, April 1st, July 2nd, October 1st; 2½% on each.
16. What is the date appointed for the Annual Meeting? None. Date of last Annual Meeting, January 29th, 1913.
17. Special General Meetings held in 1913: Dates, none.

THE LONDON AND WESTERN TRUSTS COMPANY, LIMITED.

Head Office, London, Ontario.

Incorporated on the 17th September, 1896, by Letters Patent of Ontario, issued under the Ontario Joint Stock Companies' Letters Patent Act, R.S.O., 1887, chapter 157. See also Loan and Trust Corporations Act, 2 Geo. V., c. 34.

ANNUAL STATEMENT

Of the condition and affairs of the London and Western Trusts Company, Limited, of London, Ontario, at the 31st December, 1913, and for the year ending on that day made to the Registrar of Loan Corporations for the Province of Ontario, pursuant to the laws of the said Province.

The head office of the Corporation is at No. 382 Richmond Street, in the City of London, in the Province of Ontario.

The Board is constituted of twenty-five directors, holding office for one year.

The directors and chief executive officers of the Corporation at the 31st December, 1913, were as follows, together with their respective terms of office:

Sir George C. Gibbons, Pres., London, Ont.;　　February 20, 1913; February 19, 1914.
John Labatt, Vice-President, London, Ont.;　　　　"　　　　　　"
J. L. Englehart, Vice-Pres., Petrolea, Ont.;　　　 "　　　　　　"
John McClary, Director, London, Ont.;
George Robinson, Director, London;　　　　　　　 "
T. H. Smallman, Director, London;　　　　　　　　"
E. Meredith, K.C., Director, London:　　　　　　　"
G. B. Harris, Director, London;　　　　　　　　　"
Geo. Mair, Director, Windsor;
Major Thos. Beattie, M.P., Director, London;　　 "
J. C. Duffield, Director, London;
D. Milne, Director, Sarnia;
M. Masuret, Director, London;
M. D. Fraser, K.C., Director, London;
R. W. Puddicombe, Director, London;
Col. T. R. Atkinson, Director, Simcoe;
W. J. Reid, Director, London;
Hon. C. S. Hyman, Director, London;
A. M. Smart, Director, London;
John S. Moore, Manager, London, Ont.

A.—Permanent capital stock: Total amount authorized, $500,000; total amount subscribed, $500,000, as more particularly set out in Schedule A hereto.

SCHEDULE A.

Class 2.—Fixed and Permanent capital stock created by virtue of Joint Stock Companies Acts or Private Acts.

Last call made:—Date, 1913; rate, 10 per cent.; gross amount, $50,000; amount paid thereon, $50,000.

Description.	No. of shares.	Par value of shares.	Total amount held.	Total amount paid thereon.	Total remaining unpaid.
		$	$	$	$
2. 80 per cent. called	5,000	100	500,000	400,000	100,000 00

LIST OF SHAREHOLDERS AS AT 31st DECEMBER, 1913.

(Not printed.)

BALANCE SHEET AS AT 31st DECEMBER, 1913.

Dr.   Capital and Liabilities.

Capital (Liabilities to Stockholders or Shareholders),

A.—Permanent Capital Stock or Shares.

2. (*b*) Ordinary joint stock capital, 80 per cent. called, $400,000; total paid thereon	$400,000 00	
4. (*d*) Dividends declared in respect of (2), but not yet paid	11,891 01	
5. (*e*) Unappropriated profits in respect of (2)	3,702 53	
6. (*f*) Reserve fund in respect of (2)	90,000 00	
Total actual liabilities		$505,593 54

II.—Contingent Liabilities.

48. Money for which the Corporation is contingently liable, viz.:		
49. (*a*) Principal guaranteed	$220,981 17	
50. (*b*) Interest guaranteed	2,554 00	
51. (*c*) Trust funds invested, but not guaranteed:		
52. (i) Principal	2,176,010 45	
53. (ii) Interest	65,412 22	
54. (*d*) Trust funds uninvested, bearing interest and not guaranteed	15,496 49	
Total contingent liabilities		$2,480,454 33
Gross total liabilities, actual and contingent...............		2,986,047 87
Unrealized original assets of estates (estimated value)......		2,980,100 38
Grand total		$5,966,148 25

Cr.   Assets.

1.—Assets of which the Corporation is the Beneficial Owner.

1. (*a*) Office premises situate as follows:		
(i) At London, held in freehold	$20,000 00	
7. (*d*) Office fittings	5,000 00	
		$25,000 00

B.—Debts secured by Mortgages of Land.

9. (*a*) Debts secured by mortgages of land	$395,083 09	
11. (*c*) Interest due or accrued on item (9) and not included therein	7,827 42	
		402,910 51

C.—Debts not above enumerated for which the Corporation holds securities as follows:

14. (*b*) Debts secured by municipal bonds or debentures....	$730 03	
22. (*j*) Debts secured by Loan Corporations' stocks........	48,461 80	
23. (*k*) Debts secured by legacies and life insurance policies	6,276 83	
26. (*n*) Interest due or accrued on items (14), (16), (22), (23), and not included therein	1,351 69	
		56,820 35

BALANCE SHEET.—Continued.

E.—Cash.

32. (b) In bank	$20,862 68
Total assets owned beneficially by Corporation.............	$505,593 54

II.—Assets not owned Beneficially by Corporation, but for which the Corporation is Accountable.

A.—As Guarantor.

(a) Mortgage securities:

43.	(i) Principal	$220,906 49
44.	(ii) Interest due and accrued	6,872 94

B.—As Trustee, Representative, Guardian or Agent (without guarantee).

(a) Mortgage securities:

47.	(i) Principal , ...	2,027,499 34
48.	(ii) Interest due or accrued	57,267 31

(b) Other securities:

49.	(i) Principal	148,585 79
50.	(ii) Interest due and accrued	3,825 97
52. (d) Uninvested trust funds		15,496 49

Total assets of II. ....:...........................	2,480,454 33
Gross total assets I. and II.	2,986,047 87
Unrealized original assets of estates (estimated value) ...	2,980 100 38
Grand total	$5,966,148 25

CASH ACCOUNT.

Receipts for the year ending 31st December, 1913.

I.—Received by the Corporation for its Own Use.

A.—Balance from 31st December, 1912.

	(Col. 1.)	(Total, Col. 4.)
3. (ii) Cash in bank	....	$4,180 42

B.—Sums Received Wholly or Partly on Capital Stock.

4. (a) Calls on joint stock capital	....	50,000 00

C.—Receipts on account of Investments, Loans or Debts.

(a) On mortgages of realty:

10.	(i) Principal	....	106,658 13
11.	(ii) Interest	22,634 13	22,634 13

(b) On other securities:

12.	(i) Principal		36,067 18
13.	(ii) Interest	$7,116 58	7,116 58

CASH ACCOUNT.—Continued.

Receipts for the year ending 31st December, 1913.

D.—Receipts from Real Estate Owned Beneficially by Corporation.

		(Col. 1.)	(Total, Col. 4.)
17. (b) Rents, office building		$648 88	$648 88

E.—Miscellaneous.

18. (a) Commission, brokerage (or remuneration as corporate agent, trustee, etc.)	24,998 39	24,998 39

G.—Receipts from other sources.

30. (a) Safe deposit rentals	505 50	505 50
Total		$252,809 21

II.—Received as Corporate Trustee, Representative, Guardian or Agent in Trust.

A.—Balances from 31st December, 1912.

33. (ii) In bank	$37,848 17

B.—Received on account of Investments, Loans or Debts.

34. (a) On mortgages: Principal, $337,407.25; interest, $109,910.57..	447,317 82
35. (b) On other securities: Principal, $36,067.18; interest, $7,116.58....	43,183 76
36. (c) On unsecured debts: Principal, $216,328.43; interest, $156,319.68.	372,648 11

C.—Receipts from Real Estate.

37. (a) Sales (not included in foregoing items)........................	42,431 63
38. (b) Rents , ...	13,524 00

D.—Receipts from other sources, viz.:

*39. (a) Cash in banks, fire and life insurance collected	720,400 01
40. (b) Sundry other receipts	321,083 23
Total	$1,998,436 73

CASH ACCOUNT.

Expenditure for the year ending 31st December, 1913.

I.—Expended on Corporation Account.

A.—Loaned or Invested on Capital Account.

1. (a) Loaned on mortgages of realty	$120,912 74
(b) Loaned on other securities:	
2. (i) Legacies and life insurance policies	546 91
3. (ii) Loan Company stocks	65,627 80
4. (iii) Loan Company debentures	3,615 00

---

* Including fire insurance collected re Point Edward Elevator Co., $102,998.67.

CASH ACCOUNT.—Continued.

Expenditure for the year ending 31st December, 1913.

B.—Expended on Stock Account.

8. Dividends paid on permanent stock	$21,983 70	$21,983 70

D.—Management Expenses.

25. (a) Salary, wages and fees	$13,167 26
26. (b) Commission or brokerage	954 71
28. (d) Stationery, postage, printing and advertising	1,303 86
29. (e) Law costs	19 40
30. (f) Fuel, rent and rates	195 05
31. (g) Travelling expenses	27 55
32. (h) Registration fees	250 00
33. (i) Other management expenditure	371 06

E.—Other Expenditure, viz.:

34. (a) Government and municipal tax	971 49	17,260 38

F.—Balance.

38. (i) Cash in bank, London, Ont.	20,862 68
Total	$252,809 21

II.—Expended on Trust or Agency Account.

A—Sums Loaned or Invested on Capital Account.

42. (a) Loaned on mortgages of realty	$460,899 89

Loaned on other securities:

43. (i) Life insurance policies and Loan Company stock........	78,789 71
(b) Incumbrances on realty paid off, viz.:	
48. (i) Principal (including payments on assumed mortgage, $19,989.84)	39,721 04
49. (ii) Interest	1,495 88

B.—Other Expenditures.

50. (a) Commission or remuneration paid for management of estate, trust or agency	19,384 52
51. (b) Rents, taxes and rates	8,649 59
*52. (c) Debts or obligations wholly or partly paid: Principal, $213,116.07; interest, $4,107.09	217,223 16
53. (d) Allowances and disbursements of estates, etc.	1,156,776 45

C.—Balance.

54. (b) Cash in banks	15,496 49
Total	$1,998,436 73

* Including Point Edward Elevator bonds retired, $99,800.69.

19 L.C.

1. Amount of debentures maturing in 1914: Issued in Canada, none; issued elsewhere, none.
2. Amount of other existing obligations which will mature in 1914: Guaranteed Trust receipts, $17,777.07.
3. Amount of securities held by the Corporation which will mature and become payable to the Corporation in 1914: $104,776.14.
4. Average rate of interest per annum paid by the Corporation during 1913: On deposits, none; on debentures, none; on debenture stock, none.
5. Average rate of interest per annum received by the Corporation during 1913: (a) On mortgages of realty; (b) on other securities:
   (i) Owned beneficially by the Corporation: (a) 6.437; (b) 6.455.
   (ii) Not owned beneficially: (a) 5.650; (b) 5.553.
6. Of the mortgages owned beneficially by the Corporation, all is on realty situate in Ontario, and none is on realty situate elsewhere.
7. Of the mortgages not owned beneficially by the Corporation, all is on realty situate in Ontario, and none is on realty situate elsewhere.
8. Loans written off or transferred to real estate account during 1913, viz.:
   (i) Funds or securities owned beneficially, none.
   (ii) Not so owned, none.
9. Number and aggregate amount of mortgages upon which compulsory proceedings have been taken by the Corporation in 1913, viz.:
   (i) Owned beneficially, No., one. Amount, $2,278.00.
   (ii) Not so owned, No., none. Amount, none.
10. Aggregate market value of land mortgaged to the Corporation:
    (i) Mortgages owned beneficially, $1,240,995.
    (ii) Not so owned, $5,498,100.
11. How often are the securities held by the Corporation valued? Annually.
12. (a) Specify who the officers of the Corporation who are under bond and for what sum respectively. Manager, $10,000; other officers, $5,000.
    (b) Are the said bonds executed by private sureties or by Guarantee Companies? Both.
13. Date when the accounts of the Corporation were last audited? December 31st, 1913.
14. Names and addresses of the auditors respectively for 1913 and for 1914 (if appointed):
    For 1913: Alfred A. Booker, C.A., F. G. Jewell, C.A.
    For 1914: Same.
15. What were the dividend days of the Corporation in 1913, and what rate or rates of dividend were paid on those days respectively: January 2nd, July 2nd; 6% per annum each.
16. What is the date appointed for the Annual Meeting? February 19th, 1914; third Thursday in February. Date of last Annual Meeting? February 20th, 1913.
17. Special General Meetings held in 1913. Dates: None.

THE TORONTO GENERAL TRUSTS CORPORATION.

Head Office, Toronto, Ontario.

———

The Toronto General Trusts Corporation was constituted on the 1st April, 1899, by special Act of Ontario, 62 Vict. (2), chap. 109, amalgamating into one Company under the above name:

(1) The Toronto General Trusts Company, and (2) The Trusts Corporation of Ontario.

By an agreement made under The Loan Corporations Act in two indentures dated respectively 13th and 30th July, 1903, approved by Order-in-Council (Ontario), 11th September, 1903, the Toronto General Trusts Corporation acquired the assets and assumed the liabilities and duties of the Ottawa Trusts and Deposit Company. See also special Act of the Province of Quebec (2nd June, 1904), 4 Edw. VII., chapter 93.

———

ANNUAL STATEMENT

Of the condition and affairs of the Toronto General Trusts Corporation, of Toronto, Ontario, at the 31st December, 1913, and for the year ending on that day, made to the Registrar of Loan Corporations for the Province of Ontario, pursuant to the laws of the said Province.

The head office of the Corporation is at No. 83 Bay Street, in the City of Toronto, in the Province of Ontario.

The Board is constituted of twenty-one directors, holding office for one year.

The directors and chief executive officers of the Corporation at the 31st December, 1913, were as follows:

Hon. Featherston Osler, K.C., President, Toronto;
J. W. Langmuir, Vice-President and Managing Director, Toronto;
Hon. J. J. Foy, K.C., M.P.P., Vice-President, Toronto;
W. R. Brock, Director, Toronto;
Hamilton Cassels, K.C., Director, Toronto;
Sir Wm. Mortimer Clark, K.C., Toronto;
Hon. W. C. Edwards, Director, Ottawa;
A. C. Hardy, Director, Brockville;
Hon. J. M. Gibson, K.C., Director, Toronto;
John Hoskin, K.C., LL.D., Director, Tunbridge Wells, Eng.;
Hon. Robert Jaffray, Director, Toronto;
Thomas Long, Director, Toronto;
W. D. Matthews, Director, Toronto;
Hon. Peter Maclaren, Director, Perth, Ont.;
J. Bruce Macdonald, Director, Toronto;
Hon. Sir Daniel H. McMillan, K.C.M.G., Director, Winnipeg, Man.;
Sir Edmund Osler, M.P., Director, Toronto;
J. G. Scott, K.C., Director, Toronto;
Sir Edmund Walker, Director, Toronto;
D. R. Wilkie, Director, Toronto;
Major R. W. Leonard, Director, St. Catharines, Ont.;
William G. Watson, Secretary, Toronto.

A.—Permanent capital stock: Total amount authorized, $2,000,000; total amount subscribed, $1,500,000 as more particularly set forth in Schedule A hereto.

Class 2.—Fixed and Permanent Capital Stock created by virtue of Joint Stock Companies Acts or Private Acts.

Description.	No. of shares.	Par value of shares.	Total amount held.	Total amount paid thereon.	Total remaining unpaid on calls.
		$	$	$	$
1. Fully called	15,000	100	1,500,000	1,500,000	None

LIST OF SHAREHOLDERS AS AT 31st DECEMBER, 1913.

(Not printed.)

BALANCE SHEET AS AT 31st DECEMBER, 1913.

Dr.   Capital and Liabilities.

Capital (Liabilities to Stockholders or Shareholders).

A.—Permanent Capital Stock or Shares.

1. (a) Ordinary joint stock capital fully called: Total
   called, $1,500,000; total paid thereon.........$1,500,000 00
4. (d) Dividends declared in respect of (1), but not yet paid   36,220 20
5. (e) Unappropriated profits in respect of (1) 42,232 75
6. (f) Reserve fund in respect of (1) 1,500,000 00

C.—Liabilities to Stockholders, other than already shown under A or B.

26. Profits on municipal debentures held in suspense 12,813 39
26½ Reserve re office furniture 2,000 00
                                                                           _____
                                                                           $3,093,266 34

        Total actual liabilities $3,093,266 34

Contingent Liabilities.

48. Money for which the Corporation is contingently liable:
49. (a) Principal guaranteed $8,785,687 87

51. (c) Trust funds invested, but not guaranteed:
52.   (i) Principal 19,792,629 45
53.   (ii) Interest 48,829 33
54. (d) Trust and agency funds uninvested bearing bank
            interest and not guaranteed 471,205 17
56. (e) Other contingent liabilities 64,817 81
                                                                           _____
                                                                           29,163,169 63
     Inventory value of unrealized original assets of estates
        and agencies under administration by the Cor-
        poration 30,799,448 00

        Gross total liabilities, actual and contingent $63,055,883 97

BALANCE SHEET.—Continued.

Cr. Assets.

I.—Assets of which the Corporation is the Beneficial Owner.

A.—Immovable Property Owned Beneficially by Corporation.

1. (a) Office premises situate as follows:
2.   (i) At Toronto, held in freehold $650,000 00
3.   (ii) At Ottawa, held in freehold 175,000 00 $825,000 00

    B.—Debts secured by Mortgages of Land.

9. (a) Debts (other than item 10) secured by mortgages of land $1,660,716 79
11. (c) Interest due or accrued on item 9 and not included therein 48,971 39   1,709,688 18

C.—Debts not above enumerated for which the Corporation holds securities as follows:

22. (j) Debts secured by Joint Stock Company bonds and debentures $81,600 00
23. (k) Debts secured by call loans on stock and bonds .. 133,570 00
26. (n) Interest due and accrued on items 22 and 23 and not included therein 1,141 37   216,311 37

    E.—Cash.

32. (b) On hand and in banks 133,977 35

    F.—Assets not hereinbefore mentioned.

37. (a) Accrued rent, office building and vaults $5,464 96
38. (b) Commission accrued 359 44
39. (c) Loans on corporations guarantee of mortgage account 200,000 00
40. (d) Sundry assets 2,465 04   203,289 44

    Total of assets owned beneficially by Corporation........... $3,093,266 34

II.—Assets not owned beneficially by the Corporation, but for which the Corporation is Accountable.

    A.—As Guarantor.

(a) Mortgage securities:
43.   (i) Principal $7,202,225 82
44.   (ii) Interest due and accrued 206,690 96

(b) Other securities:
45.   (i) Principal 1,189,086 82
46.   (ii) Interest due and accrued 1,747 26
     Cash in bank 185,937 01 $8,785,687 87

    B.—As Trustee, Representative, Guardian or Agent (without guarantee).

(a) Mortgage securities:
47.   (i) Principal 14,114,608 53
48.   (ii) Interest due and accrued 48,829 33

BALANCE SHEET.—Continued.

(b) Other securities:
49.   (1) Principal $5,705,081 61
51. (c) Unsecured debts, sundries 3,013 70
52. (d) Uninvested trust funds 505,948 59
                                                                                ——————————
                                                                                $20,377,481 76

       Total of assets II. $29,163,169 63

Unrealized original assets, including · real estate, mortgages,
       debentures, stock and bonds, etc., at inventory
       value 30,799,448 00

       Gross total of assets I. and II. $63,055,883 97

· CASH ACCOUNT.

Receipts for the year ending 31st December, 1913.

I.—Received by the Corporation for its Own Use.

A.—Balance from 31st December, 1912.

(b) Cash not already shown under (1):

		(Col. 1.)	(Total Col. 4.)
2.	(i) On hand	$150 00	
3.	(ii) In bank	50,523 74	
			$50,673 74

B.—Sums Received Wholly or Partly on Capital Stock.

4. (a) Calls on joint stock permanent capital $250,581 25
5. (b) Premiums on (4) 212,979 61
                                                                               ——————————
                                                                               463,560 86

C.—Receipts on account of Investments, Loans or Debts.

(a) On mortgages of realty:
10.   (i) Principal 405,686 62
11.   (ii) Interest, including profits on guaranteed funds   238,646 46

(b) On other securities:
12.   (i) Principal 474,224 83
13.   (ii) Interest or dividends 10,849 71

(c) Unsecured debts:
15.   (ii) Interest received from bank 2,214 00

D.—Receipts from Real Estate Owned Beneficially by
                Corporation

17. (b) Rents 87,228 18

E.—Miscellaneous.

18. (a) Commission, brokerage (or remuneration as corpor-
       ate agent, trustee, etc.) 223,135 10
                                                                               ——————————
                                                                               562,073 45

CASH ACCOUNT.—Continued.

Receipts for the year ending 31st December, 1913.

G.—Receipts from Other Sources.

30. (a) Returns from borrowers .....:.....................	......	$62,587 10
(b) Sundry items in suspense	......	3,010 47
Total		$2,021,817 07

II.—Received as Corporate Trustee, Representative, Guardian or Agent in Trust.

A.—Balance from 31st December, 1912.

(b) Cash (not included in 31):

32. (i) On hand	$55 37	
33. (ii) In bank ....·....:	943,834 04	$943,889 41

B.—Received on account of Investments, Loans or Debts.

34. (a) On mortgages: Principal, $3,612,960.91; Interest, $1,466,447.84 ..	5,079,408 75
35. (b) On other securities: Principal,$1,791,340.90; interest, $1,504,426.52	3,295,767 42

C.—Receipts from Real Estate.

37. (a) Sales (not included in foregoing items)	336,589 08
38. (b) Rents	467,867 47

D.—Receipts from other sources, viz.:

39. (a) For investments	2,617,810 84
40. (b) Sundry realizations	1,969,558 71
Total	$14,710,891 68

CASH ACCOUNT.

Expenditure for the year ending 31st December, 1913.

I.—Expended on Corporation Account.

A.—Sums Loaned or Invested on Capital Account.

	(Col. 1.)	(Total Col. 4.)
1. (a) Loaned on mortgages of realty	......	$868,854 40
(b) Loaned or invested in other securities, viz.:		
2. (i) Call loans on stocks and bonds	......	313,888 89
(ii) Loaned on Corporation guaranteed mortgage account	......	200,000 00
6. (c) Real estate purchased (new head office construction)	......	21,112 55
(e) Insurance or taxes advanced on property mortgaged to the Corporation	......	71,875 32

B.—Expended on Stock Account.

8. Dividends paid on permanent stock	$129,535 71	129,535 71

CASH ACCOUNT.—Continued.

Expenditure for the year ending 31st December, 1913.

D.—Management Expenses (other than foregoing).

25.	(a)	Salaries, wages and fees	$159,694 61
26.	(b)	Commission or brokerage	17,302 60
28.	(d)	Stationery, postage, printing and advertising	23,352 07
29.	(e)	Law costs	59 00
30.	(f)	Rent, taxes (other than in 7 and 32) and rates	31,728 15
31.	(g)	Travelling expenses	6,840 67
32.	(h)	Registration fees	1,389 35
33.	(i)	Other management expenditure	8,664 91

$249,031 36

(j) Wages, fuel, taxes, repairs, etc., to Corporation's premises at Toronto and Ottawa 31,168 22

E.—Other Expenditures, viz.:

34. (a) Office and vault furniture and fixtures purchased $2,373 27

F.—Balance.

37. (a) Cash on hand and in bank 133,977 35

Total . . . .:.. $2,021,817 07

II.—Expended on Trust or Agency Account.

A.—Loaned or Invested on Capital Account.

42.	(a)	Loaned on mortgages of realty	$4,881,356 97
	(b)	Loaned or invested on or in other securities	2,709,839 77
47.	(a)	Real estate purchased	99,747 52
	(b)	Incumbrances of realty paid off:	
48.		(i) Principal $165,301 92	
49.		(ii) Interest 144,530 29	

309,832 21

B.—Other Expenditures.

50.	(a)	Commission or remuneration paid for management of estate, trust or agency (including item 26)	261,104 21
51.	(b)	Rents, taxes and rates	133,763 16
53.	(d)	Sundry distributions to beneficiaries, etc.	5,623,362 24

C.—Balance.

54. (a) Cash on hand and in various banks 691,885 60

Total $14,710,891 68

MISCELLANEOUS STATEMENT FOR THE YEAR ENDING 31ST DECEMBER, 1913.

1. Amount of debentures maturing in 1914, issued in Canada. This Corporation does not issue debentures.
2. Amount of other existing obligations which will mature in 1914. Guaranteed funds, $776,804.60.
3. Amount of securities held by the Corporation which will mature and become payable to the Corporation in 1914. Beneficially owned, $140,336.35.
4. Average rate of interest per annum paid by the Corporation during 1913, on deposits, none; on debentures, none; on debenture stock, Corporation does not take deposits and does not issue debentures or debenture stock.
5. Average rate of interest per annum received by the Corporation during 1913:
    (a) On mortgages of realty; (b) On other securities.
    (i) Owned beneficially by the Corporation: (a) 7.26%; (b) 5.37%.
    (ii) Not owned beneficially: (a) 6.33%; (b) 4.79%.
6. Of the mortgages owned beneficially by the Corporation, $479,182.98 is on realty situate in Ontario, and $1,172,695.26 is on realty situate elsewhere.
7. Of the mortgages not owned beneficially by the Corporation, $14,722,651.22 is on realty situate in Ontario, and $6,572,197.79 is on realty situate elsewhere.
8. Loans written off or transferred to real estate account during 1913, viz.:
    (i) Funds or securities owned beneficially, none.
    (ii) Not so owned, none.
9. Number and aggregate amount of mortgages upon which compulsory proceedings have been taken by the Corporation in 1913, viz.:
    (i) Owned beneficially: No., none. Amount, none.
    (ii) Not so owned: No., none. Amount, none.
10. Aggregate market value of land mortgaged to the Corporation:
    (i) Mortgages owned beneficially, $3,400,000.00.
    (ii) Not so owned, $43,000,000.00.
11. How often are the securities held by the Corporation valued? On renewal or transfer of mortgages.
12. (a) Specify the officers of the Corporation who are under bond and for what sum respectively: All officers and members of the staff are under bond aggregating $191,500.
    (b) Are the said bonds executed by private sureties or by Guarantee Companies? By Guarantee Companies.
13. Date when the accounts of the Corporation were last audited? 31st December, 1913.
14. Names and addresses of the auditors respectively for 1913 and for 1914 (if appointed):
    For 1913: R. F. Spence and Geo. Macbeth.
    For 1914: R. F. Spence and Geo. Macbeth, Toronto.
15. What were the dividend days of the Corporation in 1913, and what rate or rates of dividend were paid on those days respectively: January 2nd, 2½%; April 1st 2½%; July 2nd, 2½%; October 1st, 2½%.
16. What is the date appointed for the Annual Meeting? 1st Wednesday in February. Date of last Annual Meeting? 5th February, 1913.
17. Special General Meetings held in 1913: Dates, none.

THE TITLE AND TRUST COMPANY.

Head Office, Toronto, Ont.

CONSTATING INSTRUMENTS.

The Title and Trust Company was incorporated in 1905, by Special Act of the Parliament of Canada, 4.5 Edward VII., Chapter 162 (Royal Assent 20th July, 1905). By Section 19 of this Act the Company was required to make an initial deposit with the Receiver-General of Canada to carry on the business of Title Insurance, the said deposit to be increased to $75,000 within two years from the date of the issue of such license, and to be further increased as the Treasury Board may from time to time require.

In 1907, by Special Act of the Province of Ontario, 7 Edward VII., Chapter 118, the Company was upon the conditions therein specified made admissible to registry under *The Loan Corporations Act;* and initial registry was granted on the 30th August, 1907.

ANNUAL STATEMENT

Of the condition and affairs of the Title and Trust Company at 31st December, 1913 and for the year ending on that day, made to the Registrar of Loan Corporations for the Province of Ontario, pursuant to the laws of the said Province.

The head office of the Corporation is at 61 Yonge Street, in the City of Toronto, in the Province of Ontario.

The Board is constituted of fourteen directors, holding office for the term of one year.

The directors and chief executive officers of the Corporation at 31st December, 1913, were as follows, together with their respective terms of office:

E. F. B. Johnston, K.C., Pres., Toronto, Ont.;   January, 24th, 1913; February, 6th, 1914.
Hon. W. A. Charlton, Vice-Pres., Toronto, Ont.;   "   "
Noel Marshall, Vice-President, Toronto, Ont.;   "   "
W. J. Gage, Vice-President, Toronto, Ont.;
Geo. H. Hees, Director, Toronto, Ont.;
W. K. George, Director, Toronto, Ont.;
W. R. Hobbs, Director, Toronto, Ont.;
R. Wade, Director, Orillia, Ont.;
J. B. Tudhope, Director, Orillia, Ont.;
Allan McPherson, Director, Longford Mills, Ont.;   "
Jacob Kohler, Director, Cayuga, Ont.;
J. A. Kammerer, Director, Toronto, Ont.;
D. B. Hanna, Director, Toronto, Ont.;
John J. Gibson, Managing Director, Toronto, Ont.;   "
J. M. Prentiss, Secretary, Toronto, Ont.

A.—Permanent capital stock: Total amount authorized, $1,000,000, total amount subscribed, $273,000.00, as more particularly set out in Schedule A hereto.

SCHEDULE A.

Class 2.—Fixed and permanent capital stock created by virtue of Joint Stock Companies' Acts or Private Acts.

Description.	No. of shares.	Par value.	Total amount held.	Total amount paid thereon.	Total remaining unpaid,
		$	$	$	$
2. 60 per cent. called	2,730	100	273,000	15,650	107,350
Totals.............	2,730	....	273,000	165,650	107,350

LIST OF SHAREHOLDERS AS AT 31st DECEMBER, 1913.
(Not printed.)

BALANCE SHEET AS AT 31st DECEMBER, 1913.

Dr.   Capital and Liabilities.

Capital (Liabilities to Stockholders or Shareholders).

A.—Permanent Capital Stock or Shares.

2. (b) Ordinary joint stock capital, 60 per cent. called, $163,800.00; total paid thereon	$159,850 00		
3. (c) Joint stock capital paid in advance of calls	5,800 00		
4. (d) Dividends declared in respect of (2), (3), but not yet paid	4,493 06		
5. (e) Unappropriated profits	1,474 93		
6. (f) Reserve fund	45,000 00	$216,617 99	

Total actual liabilities $216,617 99

Contingent Liabilities.

48. Money for which the Corporation is contingently liable, viz.:

52. (c) Trust funds invested, but not guaranteed, including profits in land contracts	$1,031,271 18	
55. (d) Trust funds uninvested not bearing interest and not guaranteed, in banks	5,363 46	

Total contingent liabilities 1,036,634 64

Gross total liabilities, actual and contingent $1,253,252 63

Assets.

I.—Assets of which the Corporation is the Beneficial Owner.

B.—Debts secured by Mortgages of Land.

9. (a) Debts secured by mortgages of land	$50,780 04
11. (c) Interest due and accrued on item 9	1,157 16

C.—Debts, not above enumerated for which the Corporation holds securities as follows:

14. (b) Debts secured by Municipal Bonds or Debentures	101,785 95
22. (f) Debts secured by Bank and other stocks for Call Loans	7,801 50
26. (n) Interest due and accrued on items (14), (22) and not included therein	1,476 32

D.—Unsecured Debts.

27. (a) Sundry accounts receivable	75 74

E.—Cash.

31. (a) On hand	1,534 18
32. (b) In banks	8,020 21

BALANCE SHEET.—Continued.

F.—Assets not Hereinbefore Mentioned.

37. (a) Stock in Provident Land Co.	$13,600 00	
38. (b) Equity in Real Estate	5,000 00	
39. (c) Office furniture	1,863 15	
40. (d) Automobile—depreciation written off	500 00	
41. (e) Stocks and accrued Dividends	23,023 74	
		$216,617 99

Total of assets owned beneficially by Corporation $216,617 99

II.—Assets not owned Beneficially by Corporation but for which the Corporation is Accountable.

B.—As Trustee, Representative, Guardian or Agent (without guarantee).

(a) Mortgage securities:		
47.　　　(i) Principal	$163,054 46	
(b) Other securities:		
49.　　　(i) Real Estate and accounts receivable	868,216 72	
52. (d) Uninvested Trust Fund—cash in banks	5,363 46	
Total of assets II.		$1,036,634 64

Gross total of assets I. and II. $1,253,252 63

CASH ACCOUNT.

Receipts for the year ending 31st December, 1913.

I.—Received by the Corporation for Its Own Use.

A.—Balances from 31st December, 1912.

	(Col. 1.)	(Col. 3.)	(Total Col. 4.)
(a) Cash not already shown under (1):			
2.　　　(i)　On hand	......	$274 97	$274 97
3.　　　(ii) In bank	......	7,599 18	7,599 18
B.—Sums Received Wholly or Partly on Capital Stock.			
4. (a) Calls on joint stock permanent capital	......	53,100 00	53,100 00
C.—Receipts on Account of Investments, Loans or Debts.			
(a) On mortgages of realty:			
10.　　　(i) Principal	......	23,523 76	23,523 76
11.　　　(ii) Interest	$2,291 69	......	2,291 69
(b) On other securities:			
12.　　　(i) Principal	......	18,772 25	18,772 25
13.　　　(ii) Interest or dividend	16,057 82	......	16,057 82

CASH ACCOUNT.—Continued.

Receipts for the year ending 31st December, 1913.

		(Col. 1.)	(Col. 3.)	(Total Col. 4.)
	(c) Unsecured debts:			
14.	(i) Principal	......	$5,181 17	$5,181 17
15.	(ii) Interest . . . :	$2,256 68	......	2,256 68
	E.—Miscellaneous.			
18.	*(a)* Commission, brokerage (or remuneration as corporate agent, trustee etc.)	30,134 74	......	30,134 74
	G.—Receipts from other sources.			
30.	*(a)* Insurance, registration fees, valuation fees, transfer fees	414 65	......	414 65
	(b) Title insurance premiums	451 69	......	451 69
	Totals	$51,607 27	$108,451 33	$160,058 60

		(Col. 1.)	(Col. 3.)	(Total Col. 4.)
II.—Received as Corporate Trustee, Representative, Guardian or Agent in Trust.				
	A.—Balance from 31st December, 1912.			
	(b) Cash (not included in 31):			
33.	(ii) In banks	......	$22,361 67	$22,361 67
	B.—Receipts on account of investments, loans:			
34.	*(a)* On mortgages Principal, $100,382.55; Interest, $27,389.27	27,389 27	100,382 55	127,771 82
35.	*(b)* On other securities, principal	......	61,465 50	61,465 50
36.	*(c)* Unsecured debts, principal	......	23,245 83	23,245 83
	C.—Receipts from Real Estate.			
37.	*(a)* Sales	......	423,873 78	423,873 78
38.	*(b)* Rents	8,850 55	......	8,850 55
	D.—Receipts from Other Sources, viz.:			
39.	*(a)* From clients for investment	......	361,012 02	361,012 02
	Totals	$36,239 82	$992,341 35	$1,028,581 17

CASH ACCOUNT.

Expenditure for the year ending 31st December, 1913.

		(Col. 1.)	(Col. 3.)	(Total Col. 4.)
I.—Expended on Corporation Account.				
A.—Sums Loaned or Invested on Capital Account.				
1.	*(a)* Loaned on mortgage of realty	......	$57,559 40	$57,559 40
	(b) Loaned on, or invested in, other securities, viz.:			
2.	(i) Bank and other Stocks	......	32,158 29	32,158 29
3.	(ii) Invested in Provident Land Co., stocks	......	8,350 00	8,350 00
4.	(iii) Bonds and debentures	......	10,132 42	10,132 42

CASH ACCOUNT.—Continued.

Expenditure for the year ending 31st December, 1913.

B.—Expended on Stock Account.

8. Dividends paid on permanent stock .... $7,197 25 ...... $7,197 25

D.—Management Expenses.

25. (a) Salaries, wages and fees	15,722 12	......	15,722 12
26. (b) Commission or brokerage	1,913 43	......	1,913 43
28. (d) Stationery, postage printing, etc.	4,130 28	......	4,130 28
29. (e) Law costs....	198 93	......	198 93
30. (f) Fuel, rent, taxes (other than 7 and 32) and rates	3,200 04	......	3,200 04
31. (g) Travelling expenses	14 00	......	14 00
32. (h) Registration fees	18 55	......	18 55
33. (i) Other management expenditure, Directors' fees	1,220 00		1,220 00

E.—Other Expenditures, viz.:

34. (a) Sundry expenses, other than above....	7,624 17	......	7,624 17
35. (b) Statutory and license fees	1,065 33	......	1,065 33

F.—Balance.

37. (a) Cash on hand and in banks............ ...... $9,554 39 9,554 39

Totals $42,304 10 $117,754 50 $160,058 60

II.—Expended on Trust or Agency Account.

A.—Loaned or Invested on Capital Account.

42. (a) Loaned on mortgages of realty $221,430 29 $221,430 29

(b) Loaned or invested on or in other securities, viz.:

43. (1) Stocks and bonds	......	62,265 50	62,265 50
47. (a) Real estate purchased	......	52,635 90	52,635 90

(b) Incumbrances on Realty paid off, viz.:

48. (1) Principal		139,132 69	139,132 69
49. (ii) Interest	$24,111 47	......	24,111 47

B.—Other Expenditures.

50. (a) Commission or remuneration paid for management of estate, trust or agency (including item 26)	32,569 98	......	32,569 98
53. (d) Expenses in behalf of estates	39,471 40	......	39,471 40
Distributed to clients	......	451,600 48	451,600 48

C.—Balance.

54. (b) Cash on hand and in banks 5,363 46 5,363 46

Totals $96,152 85 $932,428 32 $1,028,581 17

MISCELLANEOUS STATEMENT FOR THE YEAR ENDING 31ST DECEMBER, 1913.

1. Amount of debentures maturing in 1914: Issued in Canada, none; issued elsewhere, none.
2. Amount of other existing obligations which will mature in 1914: none.
3. Amount of securities held by the Corporation which will mature and become payable to the Corporation in 1914: $23,331.46.
4. Average rate of interest per annum paid by the Corporation during 1913: On deposits, no deposits; on debentures, none; on debenture stock, none.
5. Average rate of interest per annum received by the Corporation during 1913:
   (a) On mortgages of realty; (b) On other securities.
   (i) Owned beneficially by the Corporation: (a) 6¼%; (b) 5.85%.
   (ii) Not owned beneficially: (a) 6½%; (b) nil.
6. Of the mortgages owned beneficially by the Corporation, $50,780.04 is on realty situate in Ontario, and none is on realty situate elsewhere.
7. Of the mortgages not owned beneficially by the Corporation, $163,054.46 is on realty situate in Ontario, and none is on realty situate elsewhere.
8. Loans written off or transferred to real estate account during 1913, viz:
   (i) Funds or securities owned beneficially, none.
   (ii) Not so owned, none.
9. Number and aggregate amount of mortgages upon which compulsory proceedings have been taken by the Corporation in 1913, viz.:
   (i) Owned beneficially, No., none; amount, nil.
   (ii) Not so owned, No., none; amount, nil.
10. Aggregate market value of land mortgaged to the Corporation:
    (i) Mortgages owned beneficially, $196,850.00.
    (ii) Not so owned, $430,552.00.
11. How often are the securities held by the Corporation valued? Annually.
12. (a) Specify the officers of the Corporation who are under bond and for what sum respectively: Manager, $4,000.00; Secretary, $2,000.00; Bookkeeper, $2,000.00; Cashier, $2,000.00.
    (b) Are the said bonds executed by private sureties or by Guarantee Companies? Guarantee Company.
13. Date when the accounts of the Corporation were last audited? January 16th, 1914.
14. Names and addresses of the auditors respectively for 1913 and for 1914, (if appointed):
    For 1913: Thomas Jenkins, James Hardy.
    For 1914: Thomas Jenkins, James Hardy.
15. What were the dividend days of the Corporation in 1913, and what rate or rates of dividend were paid on those days respectively: 3% 1st January, 1913; 3% 1st July, 1913.
16. What is the date appointed for the Annual Meeting? February 6th, 1914; Date of last Annual Meeting? January 24th, 1913.
17. Special General Meetings held in 1913: Dates February 21st, 1913.

THE ROYAL TRUST COMPANY.

Head Office, Montreal, Que.

CONSTATING INSTRUMENTS.

The Royal Trust Company was incorporated in 1892, by Special Act of the Province of Quebec, 55 56 Vict., chap. 79, which was amended by 55 56 Vict. (1892), chap. 80 (Q.), and by 59 Vict. (1895), chap. 67 (Q.), and by 63 Vict. (1900), chap. 76 (Q.).

Authorized by Special Act of the Legislature of Ontario, 2 Edw. VII., chap. 103, to transact business therein as specified in section 1 (55) of the said Act, which enacts as follows:

"(5) The Company shall be limited in respect to all business relating to property, rights or interests in the Province of Ontario, to the powers mentioned in the schedule to the Ontario Trusts Companies' Act, and shall be subject to the general provisions of the said Act and of the general public law of the said Province relating to trust companies and trusts."

The Company has a deposit in the Province of Ontario amounting to $200,000.

────

ANNUAL STATEMENT

Of the condition and affairs of the Royal Trust Company at the 31st December, 1913, and for the year ending on that day, made to the Registrar of Loan Corporations for the Province of Ontario, pursuant to the laws of the said Province.

The head office of the Corporation is at No. 107 St. James Street, in the City of Montreal, Quebec.

The chief agency for Ontario is situate at corner of Queen and Yonge Streets, in the City of Toronto, in the Province of Ontario.

The chief agent and attorney for Ontario is M. S. L. Richey, and his address is Royal Trust Company, Toronto, Ontario.

The Board is constituted of seventeen directors, holding office for one year.

The directors and chief executive officers of the Corporation at the 31st December, 1913, were as follows, together with their respective terms of office:

Rt. Hon. Lord Strathcona and Mount Royal, G.C.M.G.,
   President, Montreal;   11th Nov., 1913; 10th Nov., 1914.
H. V. Meredith, Vice-President, Montreal;   "   "
Sir H. Montague Allan, Director, Montreal;   "   "
R. B. Angus, Director, Montreal;   "
A. Baumgarten, Director, Montreal;
E. B. Greenshields, Director, Montreal;
C. R. Hosmer, Director, Montreal;
Sir W. C. Macdonald, Director, Montreal;
Hon. R. Mackay, Director, Montreal;
Sir Wm. C. Van Horne, K.C.M.G., Director, Montreal;   "
A. Macnider, Director, Montreal;
David Morrice, Director, Montreal;
Sir T. G. Shaughnessy, K.C.V.O., Director, Montreal;   "
A. D. Braithwaite, Director, Montreal;
C. B. Gordon, Director, Montreal;   "
Hon. Sir Lomer Gouin, K.C.M.G., Director, Montreal; 14th Jan., 1913;   "
H. R. Drummond, Director, Montreal;   9th Dec., 1913;   "
A. E. Holt, Manager, Montreal;   11th Nov., 1913;   "
G. K. Ross, Secretary;   "

A.—Permanent capital stock: Total amount authorized, $5,000,000; total amount subscribed, $1,000,000, as more particularly set out in Schedule A hereto.

SCHEDULE A.

Class 2.—Fixed and Permanent Capital Stock created by virtue of Joint Stock Companies Acts or Private Acts.

Last call made: Date 30th June, 1909; rate 30%; gross amount, $300,000; amount paid thereon, $300,000.

Description.	No. of shares.	Par value.	Total amount held.	Total amount paid thereon.	Total remaining unpaid on calls.
		$	$	$	$
1. Fully called	10,000	100	1,000,000	1,000,000	....

LIST OF SHAREHOLDERS AS AT 31st DECEMBER, 1913.

(Not printed.)

BALANCE SHEET AS AT 31st DECEMBER, 1913.

Dr.   Capital and Liabilities.

Capital (Liabilities to Stockholders or Shareholders).

A.—Permanent Capital Stock or Shares.

1. (a) Ordinary joint stock capital; fully called; total called, $1,000,000; total paid thereon..........$1,000,000 00		
4. (d) Dividends declared in respect of (1), but not yet paid	30,000 00	
5. (e) Unappropriated profits on (1)	440,315 48	
6. (f) Reserve fund in respect of (1)	1,000,000 00	$2,470,315 48

Liabilities to the Public.

37. Owing to banks (including interest due or accrued)................		1,938,431 96
40. Other liabilities to the public:		
41. (a) Charges accrued to date ....,...	$7,085 89	7,085 89

Total actual liabilities $4,415,833 33

II.—Contingent Liabilities.

49. Money for which the Corporation is contingently liable, viz.:		
51. (b) Interest guaranteed	$330,318 03	
52. (c) Trust funds invested, but not guaranteed:		
52. (i) Principal	66,921,138 07	
55. (d) Trust funds uninvested	2,772,690 94	
56. (e) Agency funds uninvested	9,065 47	
57. (f) Judicial surety, indemnity and other bonds.......	441,360 20	

Total contingent liabilities 70,474,572 71

Gross total liabilities, actual and contingent............... $74,890,406 04

20 L.C.

BALANCE SHEET.—Continued.

Cr.   Assets.

I.—Assets of which the Corporation is the Beneficial Owner.

A.—Immovable Property Owned Beneficially by Corporation.

B.—Debts secured by Mortgages of Land.

9. (a) Debts (other than item 10) secured by mortgages of land and buildings	$705,959 35	
11. (c) Interest due and accrued on item (9) and not included therein	10,437 81	
		$716,397 16

C.—Debts not above enumerated for which the Corporation holds securities, as follows:

14. (b) Municipal bonds and debentures	$5,583 95	
18. (f) Stocks or bonds of any of the Provinces of Canada.	25,000 00	
22. (j) Railway and other corporation securities	1,316,279 63	
23. (k) Deposits with Provincial Governments	270,000 00	
24. (l) Debts secured by bonds, stocks, etc.	1,931,681 69	
26. (n) Interest due or accrued on items 14 to 24 and not included therein	19,086 95	
		3,617,632 22

D.—Unsecured Debts.

27. (a) Balances on sundry accounts, including commissions, fees, etc., due	79,722 87

E.—Cash.

31. (a) On hand	370 00
37. Office furniture	1,711 08
Total assets owned beneficially by the Corporation.........	$4,415,833 33

NOTE.—Assets reported in 1912, but written off in 1913 (not extended), $14,431.49.

II.—Assets not owned beneficially by the Corporation but for which the Corporation is accountable.

A.—As Guarantors.

(a) Mortgage securities:

43.	(1) Principal	$268,818 03

(b) On other securities:

45.	(1) Principal	61,500 00
		$330,318 03

B.—As Trustee, Representative, Guardian or Agent (without guarantee).

(a) Mortgage securities:

47.	(1) Principal	$15,759,479 48

BALANCE SHEET.—Continued.

(b) On other securities:

49.	(i) Principal	$51,161,658 59
52. (d)	Uninvested trust funds	2,772,690 94
53. (e)	Uninvested agency funds	9,065 47
54. (f)	Securities held against judicial surety, indemnity, and other bonds	441,360 20
		$70,144,254 68

Total assets of II. $70,474,572 71

Gross total of assets I. and II. $74,890,406 04

CASH ACCOUNT.

Receipts for the year ending 31st December, 1913.

I.—Received by the Corporation for its Own Use.

A.—Balances from 31st December, 1912.

		(Col. 1.)	(Total, Col. 4.)
1. (b) Cash (not already shown under (i)):			
2.	(i) On hand	....	$370 00
3.	(ii) In bank	....	2,745 45

C.—Receipts on account of Investments, Loans or Debts.

(a) On mortgages of realty:

10.	(i) Principal	....	1,177,903 52
11.	(ii) Interest	$49,703 89	

(b) On other securities:

12.	(i) Principal	....	755,964 69
13.	(ii) Interest or dividends	51,037 03	

(c) Secured debts:

14.	(i) Principal	....	1,492,873 66
15.	(ii) Interest	29,076 47	

E.—Miscellaneous.

18. (a)	Commission, brokerage (or remuneration as Corporate Agent, etc.)	463,210 76	
			593,028 15

F.—Borrowed Money.

25. (a) Bank or other advances, discounts or overdrafts...............		1,938,431 96

Total $5,961,317 43

CASH ACCOUNT.—Continued.

Receipts for the year ending 31st December, 1913.

II.—Received as Corporate Trustee, Representative, Guardian or Agent in Trust.

A.—Balance from 31st December, 1912.

(b) Cash:

33.	(ii) In bank	$4,445,969 68

B.—Received on account of Investments, Loans or Debts.

34. (a)	On mortgages: Principal, $1,916,903.15; interest, $1,129,141.43	3,046,044 58
35. (b)	On other securities: Principal, $9,396,390.41; interest, $4,861,288.72	14,257,679 13

C.—Receipts from Real Estate.

37. (a)	Sales (not included in foregoing items)	504,565 32
38. (b)	Rents	181,867 79

D.—Receipts from Other Sources.

39. (a)	Estate and agencies (Capital and Revenue Account) realizations, receipts, etc.	33,285,100 64	
			$55,731,227 14
	Total		$61,682,544 57

CASH ACCOUNT.

Expenditure for the year ending 31st December, 1913.

I.—Expended on Corporation Account.

A.—Sums Loaned or Invested on Capital Account.

	(Col. 1.)	(Total, Col. 4.)
1. (a) Loaned on mortgages of realty	....	$981,197 82
(b) Loaned or invested in other securities	....	4,498,661 98

B.—Expended on Stock Account.

8. Dividend paid on permanent stock	$160,000 00	
		$160,000 00

D.—Management Expenses.

25. (a) Salaries, wages and fees	$197,520 12	
26. (b) Commission or brokerage	2,754 69	
28. (d) Stationery, postage, printing and advertising....	26,409 15	
29. (e) Law costs	2,731 25	
30. (f) Fuel, rent, taxes (other than 7 and 32) and rates.	49,766 33	
31. (g) Travelling expenses	10,322 41	
32. (h) Registration fees	615 00	
33. (i) Other management expenditure	23,079 10	
		313,198 05

CASH ACCOUNT.—Continued.

Expenditure for the year ending 31st December, 1913.

E.—Other Expenditures, viz.:

34. (a) Office furniture 7,889 58

F.—Balance.

37. (a) Cash on hand and in bank 370 00

Total $5,961,317 43

II.—Expended on Trust or Agency Account.

A.—Loaned or Invested on Capital Account.

42. (a) Loaned on mortgages of realty $4,344,648 30
    (b) Loaned or invested on or in other securities...... 15,265,229 95
47. (a) Real estate purchased 180,730 75

    (b) Incumbrances on realty paid off, viz.:

48.   (i) Principal 56,168 05
49.   (ii) Interest 8,435 61

B.—Other Expenditures.

53. (d) Estate and agencies, payments on account of
        capital and revenue 33,084,258 07

C.—Balances.

54. (b) Cash in bank 2,781,756 41
                                                         ───────────── $55,721,227 14

        Total $61,682,544 57

Miscellaneous Statement for the Year Ending 31st December, 1913.

1. Amount of Debentures maturing in 1914: No debentures issued.
2. Amount of other existing obligations which will mature in 1914, none.
3. Amount of securities held by the Corporation which will mature and become payable
   to the Corporation in 1914, $85,000.
4. Average rate of interest per annum paid by the Corporation during 1913: No
   deposits taken nor debentures issued.
5. Average rate of interest per annum received by the Corporation during 1913:
        (a) On mortgages of realty; (b) on other securities.
        (i) Owned beneficially by the Corporation: (a) About 6%; (b) about 5%.
        (ii) Not owned beneficially: (a) About 6%; (b) about 5%.
6. Of the mortgages owned beneficially by the Corporation, $17,528.35 is on realty
   situate in Ontario, and $688,431.00 is on realty situate elsewhere.
7. Of the mortgages not owned beneficially by the Corporation, $1,180,755.10 is on
   realty situate in Ontario, and $14,847,542.41 is on realty situate elsewhere.
8. Loans written off or transferred to real estate account during 1913, viz.:
        (i) Funds or securities owned beneficially, none.
        (ii) Not so owned, none.
9. Number and aggregate amount of mortgages upon which compulsory proceedings
   have been taken by the Corporation in 1913, viz.:
        (i) Owned beneficially: No., 6; amount, $5,306.70.
        (ii) Not so owned: No., 1; amount, $2,000.

10. Aggregate market value of land mortgaged to the Corporation:
    (i) Mortgages owned beneficially, $1,229,912.00.
    (ii) Not so owned, $38,507,387.16.
11. How often are the securities held by the Corporation valued? Quarterly.
12. (a) Specify the officers of the Corporation who are under bond and for what sum respectively: All the officers of the company, for total of $212,000.00.
    (b) Are the said bonds executed by private sureties or by Guarantee Companies? Guarantee Company.
13. Date when the accounts of the Corporation were last audited? 30th September, 1913.
14. Names and addresses of the auditors respectively for 1913, and for 1914 (if appointed):
    For 1913: James Hutchinson, C.A., Montreal.
    For 1914: James Hutchinson, C.A., Montreal.
15. What were the dividend days of the Corporation in 1913, and what rate or rates of dividend were paid on those days respectively? 31st March, 3%; 30th June, 3%; 30th September, 3% and bonus of 4%; 31st December, 3%.
16. What is the date appointed for the Annual Meeting? 2nd Tuesday in November. Date of last Annual Meeting? 11th November, 1913.
17. Special General Meetings held in 1913: Dates, none.

MERCANTILE TRUST COMPANY OF CANADA, LIMITED.

Head Office, Hamilton, Ont.

CONSTATING INSTRUMENTS.

The Mercantile Trust Company of Canada, Limited, was incorporated by Letters Patent of the Dominion of Canada, bearing date 12th November, 1906.

Authorized by special Act of the Legislature of Ontario, 7 Edw. VII., chap. 115, to transact business therein as specified in section 1 (3) of the said Act, which enacts as follows:

" (3) The Company shall be limited in respect of all business relating to property, rights or interests in the Province of Ontario, to the powers mentioned in the schedule to The Trust Companies Act, and shall be subject to the general provisions of the said Act, and of the general public law of the said Province relating to trust companies and trusts."

ANNUAL STATEMENT

Of the condition and affairs of the Mercantile Trust Company at 31st December, 1913, and for the year ending on that day, made to the Registrar of Loan Corporations for the Province of Ontario, pursuant to the laws of the said Province.

The head office of the Corporation is at Bank of Hamilton Building, in the City of Hamilton, in the Province of Ontario.

The Board is constituted of fifteen directors, holding office for one year.

The directors and chief executive officers of the Corporation at 31st December, 1913, were as follows, together with their respective terms of office:

Hon. William Gibson, Pres., Beamsville, Ont.;   February 3rd, 1913; February 2nd, 1914.
Cyrus A. Birge, Vice-President, Hamilton, Ont.;   "   "
Henry L. Roberts, Vice-President, Hamilton, Ont.;   "   "
George Rutherford, Vice-President, Hamilton, Ont.;   "
Hon. John S. Hendrie, Director, Hamilton, Ont.;   "
J. J. Green, Director, Hamilton, Ont.;
T. C. Haslett, K.C., Director, Hamilton;
A. E. Dyment, Director, Toronto, Ont.;   "
Stanley Mills, Director, Hamilton, Ont.;   "
W. H. Merritt, M.D., Director, St. Catharines, Ont.;   "
James Turnbull, Director, Hamilton, Ont.;   "
J. F. Kavanagh, Director, Hamilton, Ont.;
C. C. Dalton, Director, Toronto, Ont.;
W. A. Wood, Director, Hamilton;
John I. McLaren, Director, Hamilton;
S. C. Macdonald, Manager-Secretary, Hamilton, Ont.;   "   "

A. Permanent capital stock: Total amount authorized, $1,000,000; total amount subscribed, $462,200.

SCHEDULE A.

Class 2.—Fixed and Permanent Capital Stock created by virtue of Joint Stock Companies Acts or Private Acts.

Description.	No. of shares.	Par value.	Total amount held.	Total amount paid thereon.	Total remaining unpaid on calls.
2. Fully called	4,622	$ 100	$ 462,200	$ 452,100	$ 10,100

LIST OF SHAREHOLDERS AS AT 31st DECEMBER, 1913.

(Not printed.)

BALANCE SHEET AS AT 31st DECEMBER, 1913.

Dr.   Capital and Liabilities.

Capital (Liabilities to Stockholders or Shareholders).

A.—Permanent Capital Stock or Shares.

2. (b) Ordinary joint stock capital, fully called; total called, $462,200, total paid thereon	$452,100 00	
4. (d) Dividends declared in respect of (2), but not yet paid	12,712 98	
5. (e) Unappropriated profits in respect of (2)............	4,461 37	
6. (f) Reserve fund	70,000 00	
7. (g) Contingent fund	5,000 00	
		$544,274 35

Liabilities to the Public.

27. Deposits, special	$25,006 22	
39. Due on loans in process of compilation or to pay assumed mortgages	8,000 00	
		33,006 22
Total actual liabilities		$577,280 57

Contingent Liabilities.

49. Money for which the Corporation is contingently liable, viz.:		
50. (a) Principal guaranteed	$478,658 01	
51. (b) Interest guaranteed	4,454 73	
52. (c) Trust funds invested but not guaranteed:		
53. (i) Principal	249,160 53	
54. (ii) Interest	72 68	
55 (d) Trust funds uninvested bearing bank interest and not guaranteed	71,121 18	
56. (e) Other contingent liabilities	1,044,650 16	
Total contingent liabilities		1,848,117 29
Gross total liabilities, actual and contingent		$2,425,397 86

I.—Assets of which the Corporation is the Beneficial Owner.

A.—Immovable Property Owned Beneficially by Corporation.

5. (b) Freehold land (including buildings) other than foregoing	......	$42,450 00

B.—Debts secured by Mortgages of Land.

9. (a) Debts other than item (10) secured by mortgages of land	$312,418 99	
11. (c) Interest due and accrued on item (9)	20,451 83	
		$332,870 82

C.—Debts not above enumerated for which the Corporation holds securities as follows:

22. (j) Debts secured by bonds and debentures	$66,279 82	
23. (k) Debts secured by collateral security	31,613 82	
26. (n) Interest due or accrued on items 22 and 23 and not included therein	2,483 42	
		100,377 06

BALANCE SHEET.—Continued.

Cr.   **Assets.**

E.—Cash.

31. (a) On hand	$361 46	
32. (b) In bank	95,502 49	$95,863 95

F.—Assets not hereinbefore mentioned.

37. (a) Sundry assets	$3,230 17	
38. (b) Office furniture and safe deposit boxes	2,488 57	5,718 74

Total assets owned beneficially by Corporation $577,280 57

II.—Assets not owned beneficially by Corporation, but for which the Corporation is accountable.

A.—As Guarantors.

(a) Mortgage securities:

43.	(i) Principal	$434.493 95	
44.	(ii) Interest due or accrued	19,615 72	$454,109 67

B.—As Trustee, Representative, Guardian or Agent (without guarantee).

(a) Mortgage securities:

47.	(i) Principal $204,857 44

(b) On other securities:

49.	(i) Principal	44,303 09	
50.	(ii) Interest accrued	72 68	
52. (d) Uninvested Trust funds	100,124 25	
53. (e) Inventoried value of unrealized original assets of estates, trusts, etc.	1,044,650 16	1,394,007 62

Total of assets II. $1,848,117 29

Gross total Assets I. and II. 2,425,397 86

CASH ACCOUNT.

Receipts for the year ending 31st December, 1913.

I.—Received by the Corporation for its Own Use.

A.—Balance from 31st December, 1912.

		(Col. 1.)	(Col. 3.)	(Total Col. 4.)
1. Cash:				
3.	(ii) In bank		$493 16	
2.	(i) On hand		17,815 80	

CASH ACCOUNT.—Continued.

Receipts for the year ending 31st December, 1913.

B.—Sums received wholly or partly on Capital Stock.

4. (a) Calls on joint stock permanent capital	......	$116,000 00		
5. (b) Premiums on (4)	$640 00			

C.—Receipts on Account of Investments, Loans or Debts.

(a) On mortgages of realty:

10.	(i) Principal . . , ...	......	286,240 73
11.	(ii) Interest, including profits on guaranteed funds, etc.	48,087 44	

(b) On other securities:

12.	(i) Principal , ...	......	270,490 80
13.	(ii) Interest or dividends	5,697 09	

D.—Receipts from Real Estate Owned Beneficially by Corporation.

17. (b) Rents	2,295 00

E.—Miscellaneous.

18. (a) Commission, brokerage (or remuneration as Corporate Agent, etc.)	17,782 37
19. (b) Premiums or bonus on loans	898 25

F.—Borrowed Money.

26. (b) Borrowed by taking deposits	......	50,787 02

G.—Receipts from other sources

30. (a) Safe deposit vaults	1,333 15	
(b) Sundry assets	......	96 50
(c) Suspense	......	683 50
Totals	$76,733 30	$742,607 51	$819,340 81

II.—Received as Corporate Trustee, Representative, Guardian or Agent in Trust.

A.—Balance from 31st December, 1912.

(b) Cash (not included in 31):

33. (ii) In bank	$62,330 26

B.—Received on account of Investments, Loans or Debts.

34. (a) On mortgages: Principal , $132,398.16; interest, $38,214.14	170,612 30
35. (b) On other securities: Principal, $50,512.82. interest, $3,653.99	54,166 81

CASH ACCOUNT.—Continued.

Receipts for the year ending 31st December, 1913.

C.—Receipts from Real Estate.

38. (b) Rents		$28,157 66

D.—Receipts from other sources.

39. (a) On guaranteed investment account		208,148 85
40. (b) As executor, trustee, etc.		1,060,990 48
Total		$1,579,406 26

CASH ACCOUNT.

Expenditure for the year ending 31st December, 1913.

I.—Expended on Corporation Account.

	(Col. 1.)	(Col. 3.)	(Total Col. 4.)
A.—Sums Loaned or Invested on Capital Account			
1. (a) Loaned on mortgages of realty	......	$115,395 87	
(b) Loaned on or invested in other securities			
2. (i) Stocks, bonds and debentures .	......	262,932 99	
3. (ii) Collateral loans	......	20,136 01	
6. (c) Real estate purchased		1,200 00	
7. (d) Incumbrances on realty paid off	$400 00		
B.—Expended on Stock Account.			
8. Dividends paid on permanent stock	21,020 25		
C.—Borrowed Money (other than foregoing) or interest thereon paid, viz.:			
18. (a) Bank account (principal and interest)..	4,877 46		
19. (b) Deposits: principal, $267,601.55; interest $1,634.24	1,634 24	267,601 55	
D.—Management Expenses (other than foregoing).			
25. (a) Salaries, wages and fees	13,818 82		
26. (b) Commission or brokerage	1,244 68		
28. (d) Stationery, postage, printing and advertising	3,521 96		
29. (e) Law costs	196 08		
30. (f) Fuel, rent, taxes (other than in 7 and 32) and rates	4,763 41		
31. (g) Travelling expenses	167 55		
32. (h) Registration fees	109 00		
33. (i) Other management expenditure	722 36		
E.—Other Expenditure, viz.:			
34. (a) Office furniture and safe deposit boxes .	......	356 17	
35. (b) Sundry assets	......	2,694 96	
36. (c) Suspense	......	683 50	
F.—Balance.			
37. (a) Cash on hand and in bank	......	95,863 95	
Totals	$52,475 81	$766,865 00	$819,340 81

CASH ACCOUNT.—Continued.

Expenditure for the year ending 31st December, 1913.

II.—Expended on Trust or Agency Account.

Loaned or Invested on Capital Account.

42.	(a) Loaned on mortgages of realty	$304,040 64
	(b) Loaned or invested on or in other securities	40,551 84

B.—Other Expenditures.

53.	(d) On guaranteed investment account	111,005 43
	(e) As executor, trustee, etc.	1,023,684 20

C.—Balances.

54.	(b) In banks	100,124 25

Total **$1,579,406 36**

MISCELLANEOUS STATEMENT FOR THE YEAR ENDING 31ST DECEMBER, 1913.

1. Amount of debentures maturing in 1914: Issued in Canada, None; issued elsewhere, none.
2. Amount of other existing obligations which will mature in 1914: $184,100, Guaranteed Investments.
3. Amount of securities held by the Corporation which will mature and become payable to the Corporation in 1914: $80,999.30.
4. Average rate of interest per annum paid by the Corporation during 1913: On Guaranteed deposits, $4.,852%; on debentures, none; on debenture stock, none.
5. Average rate of interest per annum received by the Corporation during 1913:
     (a) On mortgages of realty; (b) on other securities:
       (i) Owned beneficially by the Corporation: (a) 7.843; (b) 6%.
       (ii) Not owned beneficially: (a) 7.193; (b) 6%.
6. Of the mortgages owned beneficially by the Corporation, $33,477.27 is on realty situate in Ontario, and $278,302.12 is on realty situate elsewhere.
7. Of the mortgages not owned beneficially by the Corporation, $296,447.59 is on realty situate in Ontario, and $342,859.60 is on realty situate elsewhere.
8. Loans written off or transferred to real estate account during 1913, viz.:
       (i) Funds or securities owned beneficially: none.
       (ii) Not so owned: none.
9. Number and aggregate amount of mortgages upon which compulsory proceedings have been taken by the Corporation in 1913, viz.:
       (i) Owned beneficially, No. 5; amount $4,838.16.
       (ii) Not so owned: No., none; amount, none.
10. Aggregate market value of land mortgaged to the Corporation:
       (i) Mortgages owned beneficially: $1,267.650.
       (ii) Not so owned: $2,268.269.
11. How often are the securities held by the Corporation valued? Annually.
12. (a) Specify the officers of the Corporation who are under bond and for what sum respectively? Seven members of the staff aggregating $17,500.
     (b) Are the said bonds executed by private sureties or by Guarantee Companies? Employers' Liability Co.
13. Date when the accounts of the Corporation were last audited? January 28th, 1914.
14. Names and addresses of the auditors respectively for 1913 and for 1914 (if apointed):
       For 1913: C. S. Scott, F.C.A., G. E. F. Smith, C.A., Hamilton.
       For 1914: C. S. Scott, F.C.A., G. E. F. Smith, C.A., Hamilton.
15. What were the dividend days of the Corporation in 1913, and what rate or rates of dividend were paid on those days respectively: 2nd January and 2nd July; 6% per annum.
16. What is the appointed date for the Annual Meeting? Not appointed; date of last Annual Meeting? February 3rd, 1913.
17. Special General Meetings held in 1913: Dates, none.

THE TRUSTS AND GUARANTEE COMPANY, LIMITED.

Head Office, Toronto, Ontario.

Incorporated on the 24th February, 1897, by Letters Patent of Ontario issued under R.S.O., 1897, c. 191. See Ontario Trust Company Act (R.S.O. 1897, c. 206) and the Loan and Trust Corporations Act (2 Geo. V., chap. 34).

ANNUAL STATEMENT

Of the condition and affairs of The Trusts and Guarantee Company, Limited, of Toronto, Ont., at the 31st December, 1913, and for the year ending on that day, made to the Registrar of Loan Corporations for the Province of Ontario, pursuant to the laws of the said Province.

The head office of the Corporation is at No. 45 King Street West, in the City of Toronto, in the Province of Ontario.

The Board is constituted of thirteen directors, holding office for one year.

The directors and chief executive officers of the Corporation at the 31st December, 1913, were as follows, together with their respective terms of office:

James J. Warren, President, Toronto;   January 31st, 1913; January 30th, 1914.
D. W. Karn, Vice-President, Woodstock;   "   "
C. E. Ritchie, Vice-President, Akron, Ohio;   "   "
Hon. Senator McMillan, Director, Alexandria;   "
A. F. MacLaren, Director, Stratford;
W. Thoburn, M.P., Director, Almonte;
J. H. Adams, Director, Toronto;
G. P. Scholfield, Director, Toronto, Ont.;
Matthew Wilson, K.C., Director, Chatham;   .   "
Lloyd Harris, Director, Brantford;   "
A. C. Flumerfelt, Director, Victoria, B.C.;   "
W. D. Bell, Director, Chesley;
Edward Bentley Stockdale, Manager, Toronto;   "

A.—Permanent capital stock: Total amount authorized, $2,000,000; total amount subscribed, $2,000,000; as more particularly set out in Schedule A hereto.

SCHEDULE A.

Class 2.—Fixed and permanent capital stock created by virtue of Joint Stock Companies' Acts or Private Acts.

Description.	No, of shares.	Par value of shares.	Total amount held.	Total amount paid thereon.	Total remaining unpaid on calls.
		$	$	$ c,	$.
Fully called............	1,129½	100	112,950	112,950 00	....
20 per cent. called	18,870½	100	1,887,050	376,060 00	: 1,350 00
Paid in advance of calls..	....	....	....	861,536 18	....
Totals..........	20,000	....	2,000,000	1,350,546 18	1,350 00

LIST OF SHAREHOLDERS AS AT 31st DECEMBER, 1913.

(Not printed.)

BALANCE SHEET AS AT 31st DECEMBER, 1913.

Dr.   Capital and Liabilities.

Capital (Liabilities to Stockholders or Shareholders).

A.—Permanent Capital Stock or Shares.

1. (a) Ordinary joint stock capital fully called: Total called, $112,950.00; total paid thereon	$112,950 00	
2. (b) Ordinary joint stock capital, 20 per cent. called; total, $1,887,050.00; total paid thereon	376,060 00	
3. (c) Joint stock capital paid in advance of calls	861,536 18	
4. (d) Dividends declared in respect of (1), (2) and (3), but not yet paid	40,514 96	
(e) Unappropriated profits in respect of (1), (2) and (3)	348,695 05	
		$1,739,756 19

Liabilities to the Public.

42. (a) Open accounts		2,587 53
Total actual liabilities		$1,742,343 72

II.—Contingent Liabilities.

48. Moneys for which the Corporation is contingently liable, viz.:

49. (a) Principal guaranteed together with trust deposits .	$3,811,314 66	
50. (b) Interest guaranteed	10,372 96	
51. (c) Trust funds invested but not guaranteed	6,047,319 96	
54. (d) Trust funds uninvested bearing interest and not guaranteed..................................	151,176 43	
Total contingent liabilities		10,020,184 01
Grand total liabilities, actual and contingent		$11,762,527 73

Cr.   Assets.

I.—Assets of which the Corporation is Beneficial Owner.

A.—Immovable Property Owned Beneficially by the Corporation.

1. (a) Office premises as follows:		
2. (i) At Toronto, Calgary and Brantford, held in freehold and leasehold, including Safe Deposit Vaults....	$356,857 16	
5. (b) Freehold land (including buildings) other than foregoing	82,668 97	
		$439,526 13

B.—Debts secured by Mortgages of Land.

9. (a) Debts (other than item 10) secured by mortgages of land with interest accrued	......	704,507 54

C.—Debts not above enumerated, for which the Corporation holds securities as follows:

22. (i) Debts secured by stocks, bonds and miscellaneous securities, with interest accrued	......	491,472 02

BALANCE SHEET.—Continued.

D.—Unsecured Debts.

27. (a) Open accounts $42,763 08

E.—Cash.

32. (b) In banks 64,074 95

      Total assets owned beneficially by Corporation $1,742,343 72

II.—Assets not Owned Beneficially by Corporation, but for
which the Corporation is Accountable.

A.—As Guarantor.

(a) Mortgage securities:

43.   (i) Principal $2,829,807 72
44.   Interest due and accrued 101,137 15

(b) On other securities:

45.   (i) Principal 788,412 50
46.   (ii) Interest due and accrued 9,230 85
       (iii) Cash on hand and in banks 93,099 40
                                                                       3,821,687 62

B.—As Trustee, Representative, Guardian or Agent (without
guarantee).

(a) Mortgage securities:

47.   (i) Principal $1,512,266 57

(b) Other securities:

49.   (i) Principal, including unrealized original assets 4,535,053 39
52. (d) Uninvested trust funds 151,176 43

      Total assets of II. 6,198,496 39

      Gross total of assets I. and II. $11,762,527 73

CASH ACCOUNT.

Receipts for the year ending 31st December, 1913.

I.—Received by the Corporation for its Own Use.

A.—Balance from 31st December, 1912.

(b) Cash (not already shown under (1):   (Col. 1.) (Col. 3.) (Total, Col. 4.)

3.   (ii) In bank $90,716 43

B.—Sums received wholly or partly on Capital
Stock.

4. (a) Calls on joint stock permanent capital
and joint stock capital received in
advance of calls 5,645 52

CASH ACCOUNT.—Continued.

Receipts for the year ending 31st December, 1913.

C.—Received on account of Investments,
Loans or Debts.

(a) On mortgages of realty:

		(Col. 1.)	(Col. 3.)	(Total, Col. 4.)
10.	(i) Principal	......	$72,812 76	
11.	(ii) Interest, including profit on guaranteed trust account	$73,484 47		

(b) On other securities:

12.	(i) Principal	......	53,092 33	
13.	(ii) Interest or dividends	62,043 69		

D.—Receipts from Real Estate Owned Beneficially by Corporation.

16. (a) Sales (not included in any of the foregoing items)	......	8,495 99	

E.—Miscellaneous.

18. (a) Commission, brokerage (or remuneration as Corporate agent, trustee, etc.)	96,800 70		

G.—Receipts from Other Sources.

30. (a) Open accounts	......	10,608 75	
Totals	$232,328 86	$241,371 78	$473,700 64

II.—Received as Corporate Trustee, Representative,
Guardian or Agent in Trust.

A.—Balances from 31st December, 1912.

33.	(ii) Cash in bank	$369,980 76

B.—Receipts on account of Investments, etc.

34. (a) Mortgages: Principal, interest	694,758 87
35. (b) On other securities: Principal, interest	790,806 31

D.—Received from other sources.

39. (e) Estates, trusts and agencies: Capital and revenue realization, receipts, etc. 19,311,312 67
Total $21,166,858 61

CASH ACCOUNT.

Expenditure for the year ending 31st December, 1913.

I.—Expended on Corporation Account.

A.—Sums Loaned or Invested on Capital Account.

	(Col. 1.)	(Col. 3.)	(Total, Col. 4,)
1. (a) Loaned on mortgages of realty	......	$101,197 71	
(b) Loaned or invested on other securities:			
2. (i) Debentures, stocks and other securities	......	7,832 93	

B.—Expended on Stock Account.

| 3. Dividends paid on permanent stock and interest paid on joint stock capital received in advance of calls ...... | $80,733 95 | | |

D.—Management Expenses.

25. (a) Salaries, wages and fees	75,372 28		
28. (d) Stationery, postage, printing and advertising	14,948 39		
29. (e) Law costs	551 45		
30. (f) Fuel, rent, taxes (other than in 7 and 32) and rates	8,179 41		
31. (g) Travelling expenses	1,095 35		
32. (h) Registration fees	2,035 00		
33. (i) Other management expenditure ..	5,064 54		

E.—Other Expenditure, viz.:

| 34. (a) Open accounts . . . . | ...... | 17,635 05 | |
| 35. (b) Office premises, etc. .... | ...... | 94,979 63 | |

F.—Balance.

| 37. (a) Cash on hand and in bank ..$64,074.95 | | | |
| Totals . . ..$64,074 95 | $187,980 37 | $221,645 32 | $473,700 64 |

II.—Expended on Trust or Agency Account.

A.—Loaned or Invested on Capital Account.

42. (a) Loaned on mortgages of realty	......$1,319,843 74		
(b) In other securities, viz:.			
44. (ii) Call loans, stocks, bonds and other securities	......	536,626 76	

B.—Other Expenditures.

| 53. (d) Estates, trusts and agencies; payments on account of capital, revenue, etc. | ......19,166,112 28 | | |

C.—Balance.

| 54. (b) Cash on hand and in banks .... | $244,275 83 | | |
| Totals . . .. | $244,275 83 | $20,922,582 78 | $21,166,858 61 |

21 L.C.

Miscellaneous Statement for the Year Ending 31st December, 1913.

1. Amount of debentures maturing in 1914: Issued in Canada, none; issued elsewhere, none.
2. Amount of other existing obligations which will mature in 1914:   Guaranteed Funds, $144,666.47.
3. Amount of securities held by the Corporation which will mature and become payable to the Corporation in 1914: none.
4. Average rate of interest per annum paid by the Corporation during 1913: On deposits (trusts), for short term, 4%; for long term, about 5%.
5. Average rate of interest per annum received by the Corporation during 1913:
   (a) On mortgages of realty; (b) on other securities:
   (i) Owned beneficially by the Corporation: (a) 6%; (b) 6%.
   (ii) Not owned beneficially: (a) 7.10%; (b) 5.80%.
6. Of the mortgages owned beneficially by the Corporation, $21,428.57 is on realty situate in Ontario, and $683,078.97 is on realty situate elsewhere.
7. Of the mortgages not owned beneficially by the Corporation, $1,854,279.78 is on realty situate in Ontario, and $2,487,794.51 is on realty situate elsewhere.
8. Loans written off or transferred to real estate account during 1913, viz.:
   (i) Funds or securities owned beneficially, none.
   (ii) Not so owned, $12,767.22 transferred to real estate.
9. Number and aggregate amount of mortgages upon which compulsory proceedings have been taken by the Corporation in 1913, viz.:
   (i) Owned beneficially, No., none; amount, none.
   (ii) Not so owned, No. 2,; amount, $3,600.00.
10. Aggregate market value of land mortgaged to the Corporation:
    (i) Mortgages owned beneficially, $1,350.000.
    (ii) Not so owned, $8,000.000.
11. How often are the securities held by the Corporation valued? Yearly.
12. (a) Specify the officers of the Corporation who are under bond and for what sum respectively: All the staff for $55,000.00.
    (b) Are the said bonds executed by private sureties or by Guarantee Companies? Guarantee Company.
13. Date when the accounts of the Corporation were last audited? December 31st, 1913.
14. Names and addresses of the auditors respectively for 1913 and for 1914 (if appointed):
    For 1913: Harry Vigeon, Bryan Pontifex.
    For 1914: Harry Vigeon, Bryan Pontifex.
15. What were the dividend days of the Corporation in 1913 and what rate or rates of dividend were paid on those days respectively: January 2nd, July 2nd, 1913.
16. What is the date appointed for the Annual Meeting? Last Friday in January. Date of last Annual Meeting? January 30th, 1914.
17. Special General Meetings held in 1913: Dates, none.

THE IMPERIAL TRUSTS COMPANY OF CANADA.

Head Office, Toronto, Ontario.

Incorporated on the 23rd day of June, 1887, by Special Act of the Dominion of Canada, 50.51 Vic. c. 115 (D.), which in 1890 was amended by 53 Vic. c. 101 (D.).

ANNUAL STATEMENT

Of the condition and affairs of the Imperial Trusts Company of Canada, at the 31st December, 1913, and for the year ending on that day, made to the Registrar of Loan Corporations for the Province of Ontario, pursuant to the laws of the said Province.

The head office of the Corporation is at No. 15 Richmond Street West, in the City of Toronto, in the Province of Ontario.

The board is constituted of seven directors holding office for one year.

The directors and chief executive officers of the Corporation at the 31st December, 1913, were as follows, together with their respective terms of office:

James H. Mitchell, President, Toronto;   18th February, 1913; 10th February, 1914
A. J. Jackson, Vice-President, Toronto;
J. W. Seymour Corley, K.C., Director, Toronto;   "   "
W. A. Mitchell, Director, Toronto;
A. C. McMaster, Director, Toronto;
W. H. Cross, Director, Toronto;
E. J. B. Duncan, Director, Toronto;   "
W. H. Jackson, Manager, Toronto;   1st January, 1913.

A.—Permanent capital stock: Total amount authorized, $500,000; total amount subscribed, $400,000, as more particularly set out in Schedule A hereto.

SCHEDULE A.

Class 2.—Fixed and Permanent Capital Stock created by virtue of Joint Stock Companies Acts or Private Acts.

Last call made: Date, 1st October, 1913. Rate per cent., 25 per cent.; gross amount, $100,000. Amount paid thereon, $100,000.

Description.	No. of shares.	Par value of shares.	Total amount held.	Total amount paid thereon.	Total remaining unpaid.
		$	$	$	$
2. 50 per cent. called	4,000	100	400,000	200,000	....

LIST OF SHAREHOLDERS AS AT 31st DECEMBER, 1913.

(Not printed.)

BALANCE SHEET AS AT 31st DECEMBER, 1913.

Dr.   Capital and Liabilities.

1.—Capital (Liabilities to Stockholders or Shareholders).

    A.—Permanent Capital Stock or Shares.

2. (b) Ordinary joint stock capital, 25 per cent called:		
Total called, $200,000; total paid thereon	$200,000 00	
4. (d) Dividends declared in respect of (2)	3,000 00	
5. (e) Unappropriated profits in respect of (2)	10,741 57	
6. (f) Reserve fund in respect of (2)	50,000 00	
		$263,741 57

Liabilities to the Public.

39. Due on loans in process of completion or to pay assumed		
mortgages	$2,184 62	
41. Other liabilities to the public, viz.:		
42. (a) Advances obtained in real estate, including interest		
to 31st December, 1913	54,268 77	
43. (c) Sundry accounts payable, including rents paid in		
advance....................................	1,372 90	
		57,826 29

    Total actual liabilities $321,567 86

    II.—Contingent Liabilities.

48. Money for which the Corporation is contingently liable:		
49. (a) Trust funds received for investment, including trust		
deposits and interest to 31st December, 1913 ..	$501,514 08	
56. (e) Advances obtained on stocks for Investment	100,000 00	
Unclaimed balances	795 49	
		602,309 57

    Total Contingent Liabilities:

Estimated value of estates, assets, mortgages and other securities held in trust, etc., in hands of Company, and not invested by Company	3,140,796 27
Gross total liabilities, actual and contingent	$4,064,673 70

Cr.   Assets.

I.—Assets of which the Corporation is the Beneficial Owner.

A.—Immovable Property Owned Beneficially by the Corporation.

1. (a) Office premises situate as follows:		
3. (ii) At Toronto, held in leasehold	$94,382 63	
5. (b) Freehold land (including buildings) other than fore-		
going	139,911 00	
		$234,293 63

    B.—Debts secured by Mortgages of Land.

9. (a) Deed with right of redemption	......	16,500 00

BALANCE SHEET.—Continued.

D.—Unsecured Debts.

27. (a) Sundry accounts receivable **$2,468 67**

E.—Cash.

31. (a) On hand $716 79
32. (b) In bank 4,432 43
                                                             _____
                                                             5,149 22

F.—Assets not hereinbefore mentioned.

37. (a) office furniture $2,000 00
38. (b) Revenue stamps 14 34
39. (c) Port Hood Coal Company bonds 1 00
40. (d) Port Hood Coal Company stock 1 00
41. (e) Shares permanent preference stock of the Colonial
        Investment and Loan Co. 59,400 00
        Accrued dividend thereon 1,740 00
                                                             _____
                                                             63,156 34

    .   Total assets owned beneficially by Corporation **$321,567 86**

II.—Assets not owned beneficially by the Corporation but
      for which the Corporation is accountable.

A.—As Guarantor.

(a) Mortgage securities:
43.   (i) Principal $12,476 88
            (ii) Interest 121 05

(b) Other securities:
45. Call   and   time   loans: Principal, $36,901.27;   interest,
            accrued, $1,112.91 ....   38,014 18
            (i) Principal bonds and stocks of other Corpora-
            tions 492,434 69
46.   (ii) Interest accrued 12,386 16

B.—As Trustee, Representative. Guardian or Agent (without
            guarantee).

51. (c) Unsecured debts, accounts receivable 113 96
52. (d) Uninvested trust funds: Cash in hand and in banks.   46,762 65
                                                             _____
                                                             602,309 57

    Estimated value of mortgages and other securities held in trust, etc.,
        in hands of the Company as executors, agents, trustees, etc.,
        not invested by Company 3,140,796 27

        Gross total assets I. and II. **$4,064,673 70**

CASH ACCOUNT.

Receipts for the year ending 31st December, 1913.

I.—Received by the Corporation for its Own Use.

A.—Balances from 31st December, 1912.

	(Col. 1.)	(Col. 3.)	(Total Col. 4.)
(i) On hand	$7 19		
(ii) In bank	34,482 96	......	$34,490 15

CASH ACCOUNT.—Continued.

Receipts for the year ending 31st December, 1913.

C.—Receipts on account of Investments, Loans, or Debts.

	(Col. 1.)	(Col. 3.)	(Total Col. 4.)
(a) On mortgages of realty:			
11. (ii) Interest	. . . . . .	. . . . . .	$1,522 60
(b) On other securities:			
12. (i) Principal	. . . . . .	. . . . . .	58,830 00
D.—Receipts of Real Estate Owned Beneficially by Corporation.			
17. (b) Rents	. . . . . .	. . . . . .	10,629 92
E.—Miscellaneous.			
18. Commission, brokerage (or Remuneration as Corporation Agent, Trustee, etc.), including surplus interest and dividends on investments of trust funds	. . . . . .	. . . . . .	28,502 77
G.—Receipts from other sources.			
30. (a) Deposit on sales of real estate by Company as agent	$1,210 00		
(b) Rents for Safety Deposit Boxes	64 00		
(c) Refund amount overdrawn for salaries	74 00		
Stationery	91 79		
Law costs	142 62		1,582 41
Totals	. . . . . .		**$135,557 85**

II.—Received as Corporate Trustee, Representative, Guardian or Agent in Trust.

A.—Balance from 31st December, 1912.

31. (b) Cash:			
(i) On hand	. . . . . .	. . . . . .	$4,202 49
33. (ii) In bank	. . . . . .	. . . . . .	$1,691 18
B.—Received on Account of Investments, Loans or Debts.			
34. (a) On mortgages: Principal, $22,646.11; interest, $1,827.16	. . . . . .	. . . . . .	24,473 27
35. (b) On other securities: Principal, $198,373 35, interest, $103,072.27	. . . . . .	. . . . . .	301,445 62
D.—Receipts from other sources, viz.:			
39. (a) Trust deposits	. . . . . .	. . . . . .	2,053,382 09
40. (b) Funds borrowed for investment purposes	. . . . . .	. . . . . .	100,000 00
Sundry receipts, realizations, including guaranteed funds not otherwise itemized	. . . . . .	. . . . . .	45,457 89
Total			**$2,620,652 54**

CASH ACCOUNT.—Continued.

Expenditure for the year ending 31st December, 1913.

I.—Expended on Corporation Account.

A.—Sums Loaned or Invested on Capital Account.

		(Col. 1.)	(Col. 4.)
Loaned or invested on other securities, viz.:			
2.	(i) Stock of other corporations	......	$80,150 00
7. (d)	Incumbrances on realty paid off	......	4,117 38
(e)	Insurance and charges, or taxes advanced on property mortgaged to the Corporation	......	822 47

B.—Expended on Stock Account.

8. Dividends paid on permanent stock	......	6,003 00

D.—Management Expenses (other than foregoing).

25. (a) Salaries, wages and fees	$14,812 64	
26. (b) Commission or brokerage	2,936 34	
28. (d) Stationery, postage, printing and advertising	2,905 68	
29. (e) Law costs ...	296 90	
30. (f) Fuel, rent, taxes (other than 7 and 32), and rates ..	5,558 42	
32. (h) Registration fees and Government tax	1,260 00	
33. (i) Other management expenditure, insurance, etc.	1,610 08	29,379 96

E.—Other Expenditures, viz.:—

34. (a) Sundry repairs and improvements to real estate ..	$4,667 52	
35. (b) Office furniture	232 98	
36. (c) Interest on advances secured on real estate, etc. ...	2,566 72	
Ground rent office premises	2,088 60	
Deposits received on sales of real estate returned ..	380 00	9,935 82

F.—Balances.

37. (a) Cash on hand and in bank	5,149 22
Totals	$135,557 85

II.—Expended on Trust Agency Account.

A.—Sums Loaned or Invested on Capital Account.

42. (a) Loaned on mortgages of realty	$21,738 98
(b) Loaned or invested on or in other securities, viz.:	
43. (ii) Municipal Debentures	15,812 04
(iii) Stock and bonds of other corporations	309,783 31

B.—Other Expenditures.

52. (c) Debts or obligations wholly or partly paid: Principal, interest, $4,719.52	4,719 52
53. (d) Trust deposits repaid	2,188,920 36
50. (a) Sundry payments and disbursements, including guaranteed funds not otherwise itemized	32,915 68

C.—Balances.

54. (b) Cash on hand and in banks	46,762 65
Total	$2,620,652 54

MISCELLANEOUS STATEMENT FOR THE YEAR ENDING 31ST DECEMBER, 1913.

1. Amount of debentures maturing in 1914: Issued in Canada, none; issued elsewhere, none.
2. Amount of other existing obligations which will mature in 1914: Not including deposits, $6,947.42.
3. Amount of securities held by the Corporation which will mature and become payable to the Corporation in 1914: $43,362.77.
4. Average rate of interest per annum paid by the Corporation during 1913: On deposits, 4 1-8%; on debentures, none; on debenture stock, none.
5. Average rate of interest per annum received by the Corporation during 1913:
    (a) On mortgages of realty: (b) on other securities.
    (i) Owned beneficially by the Corporation: (a) Including deed with right of redemption, 9%; (b) 6 1-16%.
    (ii) Not owned beneficially: (a) 7½%; (b) 7%.
6. Of the mortgages owned beneficially by the Corporation, $16,500.00 is on realty situate in Ontario, and none is on realty situate elsewhere.
7. Of the mortgages not owned beneficially by the Corporation, none is on realty situate in Ontario, and none is on realty situate elsewhere.
8. Loans written off or transferred to real estate account during 1913, viz.:
    (i) Funds or securities owned beneficially, none.
    (ii) Not so owned, none.
9. Number and aggregate amount of mortgages upon which compulsory proceedings have been taken by the Corporation in 1913, viz.:
    (i) Owned beneficially: No., none; Amount, none.
    (ii) Not so owned: No., none; Amount, none.
10. Aggregate market value of land mortgaged to the Corporation:
    (i) Mortgages owned beneficially, $30,000 00.
    (ii) Not so owned, $44,500.00.
11. How often are the securities held by the Corporation valued? Yearly.
12. (a) Specify the officers of the Corporation who are under bond and for what sum respectively: Manager, $15.000; Accountant, $10.000; 5 Clerks, $5.000 each; two at $2.000 each and one at $1.000.
    (b) Are the said bonds executed by private sureties or by Guarantee Companies? Guarantee Companies.
13. Date when the accounts of the Corporation were last audited? 31st December, 1913.
14. Names and addresses of the auditors respectively for 1913 and for 1914 (if appointed):
    For 1913: Stiff Bros. and Sime & Riddell, Stead, Graham & Hutchinson.
    For 1914: Stiff Bros. and Sime & Riddell, Stead, Graham & Hutchinson.
15. What were the dividend days of the Corporation in 1913 and what rate or rates of dividend were paid on those days respectively? 1st January, 1913, 3%; 1st July, 1913, 3% and 1st October, special interim dividend of 25% upon the amount of subscribed capital stock.
16. What is the date appointed for the Annual Meeting? 10th February, 1914. Date of last Annual Meeting? 18th February, 1913.
17. Special General Meetings held in 1913: Dates, none.

THE GUARDIAN TRUST COMPANY, LIMITED.

Head Office, Toronto, Ontario.

Incorporated by Letters Patent of Ontario, dated the 8th day of April, 1910, issued under The Ontario Companies Act. Registered on the Trusts Company Register, 6th May, 1910.

ANNUAL STATEMENT

Of the condition and affairs of The Guardian Trust Company, Limited, of Toronto, as at 31st December, 1913, and for the year ending on that day, made to the Registrar of Loan Corporations for the Province of Ontario, pursuant to the laws of the said Province.

The head office of the Corporation is at No. 12 King Street East, in the City of Toronto, and Province of Ontario.

The Board is constituted of ten directors holding office for one year or until their successors are appointed.

The directors and chief executive officers of the Corporation at 31st December, 1913, were as follows, together with their respective terms of office:

Cawthra Mulock, President, Toronto,   March 1st, 1912.
E. H. Laschinger, Vice-President, Toronto,   "
A. M. Stewart, Director, Toronto,   "
Thomas Ahearn, Director, Ottawa,
Hon. J. A. Lougheed, Director, Calgary,
Chas. M. MacLean, Director, Brockville,
S. J. Moore, Director, Toronto,
W. D. Ross, Director, Toronto,
Geo. P. Scholfield, Director, Toronto,   "
W. S. Morden, General Manager, Toronto, 1st December, 1911.
E. W. McNeill, Secretary, Toronto, 1st May, 1910.

A.—Permanent capital stock: Total amount authorised, $2,000,000; total amount subscribed, $849,100.00, as more particularly set out in Schedule A hereto.

SCHEDULE A.

Class 2.—Fixed and permanent capital stock created by virtue of Joint Stock Companies' Act or Private Acts.

Last call made: Date, 1st March, 1912; rate per cent., 20%; gross amount, $169,-820.00; amount paid thereon, $169,420.00.

Description.	No. of shares.	Par value.	Total amount held.	Total amount paid thereon.	Total remaining unpaid calls.
		$	$	$	$
2. 20 per cent. called....	8,491	100	849,100	169,420	400
Paid in advance of calls.	....	....	....	75,120	....
Totals	8,491	....	849,100	244,540	400

LIST OF SHAREHOLDERS AS AT 31st DECEMBER, 1913.

(Not printed.)

BALANCE SHEET AS AT 31st DECEMBER, 1913.

Dr.   Capital and Liabilities.

Capital (Liabilities to Stockholders or Shareholders).

A.—Permanent Capital Stock or shares.

2. (b) Ordinary joint stock capital, 20 per cent. called; total called, $169,820; total paid theron	$169,420 00	
3. (cc) Joint stock capital paid in advance of calls	75,120 00	
5. (e) Unappropriated profits in respect of (2)	34,838 27	
		$279,378 27

Liabilities to the Public.

41. Other liabilities, to public, viz.:		
42. (a) Accounts payable, and suspense items		438 20
Total actual liabilities		$279,816 47

II.—Contingent Liabilities.

49. Money for which the Corporation is contingently liable, viz.:		
50. (a) Principal guaranteed ....}	$13,750 00	
51. (b) Interest guaranteed ....}		
52. (c) Trust funds invested, but not guaranteed:		
53. (i) Principal	1,188,472 35	
54. (ii) Interest	1,913 23	
55. (d) Trust funds uninvested bearing bank interest and not guaranteed	48,308 06	
Total contingent liabilities		1,252,443 64
Gross total liabilities, actual and contingent		$1,532,260 11

Cr.   Assets.

I.—Assets of which the Corporation is the Beneficial Owner.

B.—Debts Secured by Mortgages of Land.

9. (a) Debts (other than item 10) secured by mortgages of land	$44,288 57	
11. (c) Interest due and accrued on item 9 and not included thereon	1,996 98	
		$46,285 55

C.—Debts not above enumerated for which the Corporation holds Securities as follows:

23. (f) Debts secured by call loans on stocks and bonds ..	$177,205 00	
26. (n) Interest due or accrued (22)	547 48	
		177,752 48

D.—Unsecured Debts.

27. (a) Balance on sundry accounts, including commission, fees, etc., due		17,806 90

E.—Cash.

32. (b) On hand and in banks		9,648 09

BALANCE SHEET.—Continued.

F.—Assets not hereinbefore mentioned.

37. (a) Stocks and bonds	$26,298 00		
38. (b) Dividends and interest accrued on 37a	925 45		
39. (c) Office furniture and vault fixtures	1,100 00		
			$28,323 45
Total assets owned beneficially			$279,816 47

II.—Assets not owned beneficially by the Corporation, but for which the Corporation is accountable.

A.—As Guarantor.

(a) Mortgage securities:

43.	(1) Principal	......	$18,750 00

B.—As Trustee, Representative, Guardian or Agent (without guarantee).

(a) Mortgage securities:

47.	(1) Principal	$732,505 81	
48.	(ii) Interest due and accrued	1,426 94	
			733,932 75

(b) Other securities:

49.	(i) Principal	$454,178 28	
50.	(ii) Interest due and accrued	77 62	
51. (c) Unsecured debts	2,196 93	
52. (d) Uninvested trust funds	48,308 06	
			504,760 89
Gross total assets I. and II.			$1,532,260 11

CASH ACCOUNT.

Receipts for the year ending 31st December, 1913.

I.—Received by the Corporation for its Own Use.

A.—Balances from 31st December, 1912.

	(Col. 1.)	(Col. 3.)	(Col. 4.)
1. Cash:			
3. (ii) In bank	......	......	$6,540 86
B.—Sums received wholly or partly on Capital Stock.			
4. (aa) Joint stock capital received in advance of calls	......	.....	800 00

CASH ACCOUNT.—Continued.

Receipts for the year ending 31st December, 1913.

C.—Receipts on Account of Investments, Loans
            or Debts.

(a) On mortgage of realty:

10.	(i) Principal	. . . . . .	$35,011 30	
11.	(ii) Interest	$3,098 72	. . . . . .	$38,110 02

(b) On other securities:

12.	(i) Principal	. . . . . .	116,516 07	
13.	(ii) Interest or dividends	7,975 10	. . . . . .	124,491 17

(c) Unsecured debts:

14.	(i) Principal	. . . . . .	7,526 84	
15.	(ii) Interest	40 45	. . . . . .	7,567 29

E.—Miscellaneous.

18. (a)	Commission, brokerage (or remuneration as corporate agent, trustee, etc.)	7,508 90		
19. (b)	Premiums or bonus on loans	414 32	. . . . . .	7,923 22

G.—Receipts from other sources.

20. (a)	Bank interest	. . . . . .	. . . . . .	171 59
	Totals			$185,604 15

II.—Received as Corporate Trustee, Representative, Guardian or Agent in Trust.

A.—Balances from 31st December, 1912.

31. (a)	Capital account	. . . . . .	. . . . . .	$148,592 47

B.—Receipts on account of Investments, etc.

34. (a)	Mortgages: Principal, $50,751.20; interest, $29,079.92	79,831 12
35. (b)	On other securities: Principal, $90,532.90; interest, $5,741.51	96,274 41

C.—Receipts from Real Estate.

37. (a)	Sales (not included in foregoing items)	9,953 67
38. (b)	Rents and interest on agreements	1,334 17

D.—Received from Other Sources.

39. (e)	Estates, guaranteed investments	166,348 76
	Total	$502,334 60

CASH ACCOUNT.

Expenditure for the year ending 31st December 1913.

I.—Expended on Corporation Account.

A.—Sums Loaned or Invested on Capital Account.

	(Col. 1.)	(Col. 3.)	(Col. 4.)
1. (a) Loaned on mortgage of realty (including item 7 (e) if no separate account therefor)	......	$42,247 80	
(b) Loaned on or invested in other securities, viz.:—			
2. (i) Stocks and bonds	......	36,440 00	
3. (ii) Call loans	......	76,941 53	$155,629 33
C.—Borrowed Money (other than foregoing) or interest thereon paid, viz.:—			
18. (a) Bank account interest	29 85		
24. (g) Guarantees paid: Principal, interest, $659.44	659 44	......	689 29
D.—Management Expenses (other than foregoing):			
25. (a) Salaries, wages and fees	9,909 80		
26. (b) Commission or brokerage	1,038 22		
28. (d) Stationery, postage, printing, and advertising	537 91		
29. (e) Law costs	235 00		
30. (f) Fuel, rent, taxes (other than in 7 and 32) and rates	3,075 70		
31. (g) Travelling expenses	179 88		
32. (h) Registration fees	105 00		
33. (i) Other management expenditure	526 09		15,607 60
E.—Other Expenditure, viz.:			
34. (a) Advances to trusts and sundry accounts	......	$3,925 84	
35. (b) Office furniture	$104 00		4,029 84
F.—Balance.			
37. (a) Cash on hand and in banks			9,648 09
Totals			$185,604 13

· II.—Expended on Trust or Agency Account.

A.—Loaned or Invested on Capital Account .

42. (a) Loaned on mortgages of realty	$78,169 25
(b) Loaned or invested on or in other securities, viz.:	
43. (i) Bonds and debentures	$17,936 15
47. (a) Real estate purchased and improvements	135,226 77

CASH ACCOUNT.—Continued.

Expenditure for the year ending 31st December, 1913.

B.—Other Expenditures.

50.	(a) Commission or remuneration paid for management of estate, trust or agency (including item 26)	$3,914 55
51.	(b) Rents, taxes and rates	1,408 93
53.	(d) Estates, trust and agencies, payments on account, revenue, etc.	163,493 70

C.—Balance.

54.	(a) Cash on hand and in various banks	102,185 25
	Total	$502,334 60

MISCELLANEOUS STATEMENT FOR THE YEAR ENDING 31ST DECEMBER, 1913.

1. Amount of debentures maturing in 1914: Issued in Canada, none; issued elsewhere, none.
2. Amount of other existing obligations which will mature in 1914, none.
3. Amount of securities held by the Corporation which will mature and become payable to the Corporation in 1914, none.
4. Average rate of interest per annum paid by the Corporation during 1913: On deposits, none; on debentures, none; on debenture stock, none.
5. Average rate of interest per annum received by the Corporation during 1913:
   (a) On mortgages of realty; (b) on other securities.
   (i) Owned beneficially by the Corporation: (a) 6%;. (b) 5.85%.
   (ii) Not owned beneficially: (a) 5.84%; (b) 5%.
6. Of the mortgages owned beneficially by the Corporation, $44,288.57 is on realty situate in Ontario, and none is on realty situate elsewhere.
7. Of the mortgages not owned beneficially by the Corporation, $746,255.81 is on realty situate in Ontario, and none is on realty situate elsewhere.
8. Loans written off or transferred to real estate account during 1913, viz.:
   (i) Funds or securities owned beneficially, none.
   (ii) Not so owned, none.
9. Number and aggregate amount of mortgages upon which compulsory proceedings have been taken by the Corporation in 1913, viz.:
   (i) Owned beneficially, No., none; amount, none.
   (ii) Not so owned, No., none; amount, none.
10. Aggregate market value of land mortgaged to the Corporation:
    (i) Mortgages owned beneficially, $96,300.00.
    (ii) Not so owned, $1,858,737.50.
11. How often are the securities held by the Corporation valued? Yearly.
12. (a) Specify the officers of the Corporation who are under bond and for what sum respectively: All officers for a total of $10,000.00.
    (b) Are the said bonds executed by private sureties or by Guarantee Companies? Guarantee Company.
13. Date when the accounts of the Corporation were last audited? February 14th, 1913.
14. Names and addresses of the auditors respectively for 1913 and for 1914 (if appointed):
    For 1913: Edwards Morgan & Co., and O. Hudson Co.
    For 1914:
15. What were the dividend days of the Corporation in 1913 and what rate or rates of dividend were paid on those days respectively?
16. What is the date appointed for the Annual Meeting? Not fixed. Date of last Annual Meeting? March 1st, 1912.
17. Special General Meetings held in 1913: Dates, none.

THE FIDELITY TRUSTS COMPANY OF ONTARIO.

Head Office, London, Ontario.

Incorporated on the twenty-third of March, 1910, by Letters Patent of Ontario, issued under The Loan Corporations' Act, R.S.O. 1897, Chapter 205.

ANNUAL STATEMENT

Of the condition and affairs of the Fidelity Trusts Company of Ontario, London, Ontario, at the 31st December, 1913, and for the year ending on that day, made to the Registrar of Loan Corporations for the Province of Ontario, pursuant to the laws of the said Province.

The head office of the Corporation is at No. 371 Richmond Street, in the City of London, in the Province of Ontario.

The Board is constituted of eight directors, holding office for one year.

The directors and chief executive officers of the Corporation at the 31st December, 1913, were as follows, together with their respective terms of office:

T. H. Purdom, President, London, Ont.;   February 27th, 1914; February, 1915.
John Ferguson, Vice-President, London, Ont.;   "   "
W. J. McMurtry, Director, Toronto, Ont.;   "   "
John Purdom, Director, London, Ont.;
Samuel Wright, Director, London, Ont.;
John Milne, Director, London, Ont.;
Alex. Purdom, Director, London, Ont.;
Nathaniel Mills, Managing-Director, London, Ont.;   "
Wm. J. Harvey, Manager.

A.—Permanent capital stock: Total amount authorized, $500,000; total amount subscribed, $300,000, as more particularly set out in Schedule A hereto.

SCHEDULE A.

*Class 2.—Fixed and permanent capital stock created by virtue of Loan Corporations Act.

Last call made: Date, 1st December, 1913; rate per cent., 10%; gross amount, $8,500; amount paid thereon, $8,500.00.

Description.	Total amount issued and subsisting at 31st December, 1913.			Total amount of actual payments thereon.	Total amount unpaid and constituting an asset of the Corporation.
	No. of shares.	Par value of shares.			
		$	$	$	$
1. Fully called	1,050	100	105,000	105,000	....
2. 10% called	1,950	100	195,000	19,500	....
Totals	3,000	....	300,000	124,500	....

LIST OF SHAREHOLDERS AS AT 31st DECEMBER, 1913.

(Not printed.)

---

*See note, p. 336 *infra.*

BALANCE SHEET AS AT 31st DECEMBER, 1913.

Dr.   Capital and Liabilities.

Capital (Liabilities to Stockholders or Shareholders).

*A.—Permanent Capital Stock or Shares.

1. (a) Ordinary joint stock capital, fully called; total called, \$105,000; total paid thereon.............	\$105,000 00	
2. (b) Ordinary joint stock capital, 10 per cent. called; total called, \$19,500; total paid thereon........	19,500 00	
4. (d) Dividends declared in respect of (1) and (2) but not yet paid	2,875 00	
5. (e) Unappropriated profits in respect of (1) and (2)....	3,095 41	
Total actual liabilities		\$130,470 41

Contingent Liabilities.

43. Money for which the Corporation is contingently liable, viz.:

49. (a) Principal guaranteed	\$69,329 00	
51. (c) Trust funds invested but not guaranteed:		
52. (1) Principal	133,911 38	
56. (e) Other contingent liabilities, unrealized assets of estates and agencies under administration	411,600 00	
Total contingent liabilities		614,840 38
Gross total liabilities, actual and contingent		\$745,310 79

Cr.   Assets.

I.—Assets of which the Corporation is the Beneficial Owner .

C.—Debts not above enumerated, for which the Corporation holds securities as follows:

22. (j) Debts secured by stocks and bonds	\$112,950 40	
26. (n) Interest due and accrued on item 22 and not included therein	3,206 00	

E.—Cash.

32. (b) In bank and loan company	14,314 01	
Total assets owned beneficially by Corporation..............		\$130,470 41

II.—Assets not owned Beneficially by Corporation, but for which the Corporation is Accountable.

---

*10% paid up by certain stockholders, certain other stockholders were allowed to pay in full without a call having been made.

BALANCE SHEET.—Continued.

A.—As Guarantor.

(a) Mortgage securities:

43.   (1) Principal $59,761 70

(b) Other securities:

45.   (1) Uninvested trust funds 9,567 30

B.—As Trustee, Representative, Guardian or Agent (without guarantee).

(b) Other securities:

49.   (1) Principal 117,632 16
51. (c) Unsecured debts, unrealized assets of estates 411,600 00
52. (d) Uninvested trust funds, cash on hand 16,279 22

        Total of assets II. $614,840 38

        Gross total assets of I. and II. $745,310 79

CASH ACCOUNT.

Receipts for the year ending 31st December, 1913.

I.—Received by the Corporation for its Own Use.

A.—Balances from 31st December, 1912.

1. Cash:
3.   (ii) In bank $3,682 35

    B.—Sums Received Wholly or Partly on Capital Stock.

4. (a) Calls on joint stock permanent capital 9,500 00

C.—Receipts on account of Investments, Loans or Debts.

    (b) On other securities:

13.   (ii) Interest or dividends 6,958 90

E.—Miscellaneous.

18. (a) Commission, brokerage (or remuneration as corporate agents, etc.) 1,882 87

        Totals $22,024 12

II.—Received as Corporate Trustee, Representative, Guardian or Agent in Trust.

A.—Balances from 31st December, 1912.

' 33.   (ii) In bank $14,931 71

22 L.C.

CASH ACCOUNT.—Continued.

Receipts for the year ending 31st December, 1913.

B.—Received on account of Investments, Loans or Debts.

34. (a) On mortgages: Principal, $4,492.02; interest, $944.54.	$5,436	56
35. (b) On other securities: Principal, $8,000.00; interest, $115.61	8,115	61

C.—Receipts from Real Estate.

38. (b) Rents	3,508	99

D.—Receipts from other sources.

39. (a) Estates and agencies, capital and revenue monies received for investment	$89,858	63
40. (b) Guaranteed investment account	58,200	00
Totals . . . .,.........................	$380,051	50

CASH ACCOUNT.

Expenditure for the year ending 31st December, 1913.

I.—Expended on Corporation Account.

A.—Sums Loaned or Invested on Capital Account.

(Total, Col. 4.)

(b) Loaned or invested in other securities, viz.:

2. (i) Special deposit Dominion Savings and Investment Society	$9,500	00

B.—Expended on Stock Account.

8. Dividends paid on permanent stock	5,750	00

D.—Management Expenses.

25. (a) Salaries, wages and fees	1,250	00
28. (d) Stationery, postage, printing and advertising	262	21
31. (g) Travelling expenses	15	90
32. (h) Registration fee and Government taxes	367	00

E.—Other Expenditure, viz.:

34. (a) Guarantee insurance premiums	60	00
35. (b) Filing annual statement	5	00

F.—Balance.

37. (b) Cash in bank and loan company	4,814	01
Total	$22,024	12

II.—Expended on Trust or Agency Account.

A.—Loaned or Invested on Capital Account.

42. (a) Loaned on mortgages of realty	$50,088	72
(b) Loaned or invested on or in other securities:		
43. (i) Stocks	17,042	50

B.—Other Expenditures.

50. (a) Commission or remuneration paid for management
of estate, trust or agency (including item 26) .. $762 80
52. (c) Debts or obligations wholly or partly paid.......... 35,264 06
53. (d) On guaranteed investment account 3,698 90
Estates and agencies, payments on account capital and
revenue 247,348 00

C.—Balance.

54. (a) Cash in loan company 25,846 52

Totals $380,051 50

MISCELLANEOUS STATEMENT FOR THE YEAR ENDING 31ST DECEMBER, 1913.

1. Amount of Debentures maturing in 1914: Issued in Canada, none; Issued elsewhere,
none.
2. Amount of other existing obligations which will mature in 1914: Guaranteed investment receipts, $2,200.
3. Amount of securities held by the Corporation which will mature and become payable to the Corporation in 1914, $20,593.48.
4. Average rate of interest per annum paid by the Corporation during 1913: On
deposits, none; on debentures, none; on debenture stock, none.
5. Average rate of interest per annum received by the Corporation during 1913:
(a) On mortgages of realty; (b) On other securities.
(i) Owned beneficially by the Corporation: (a) None; (b) 5.68%.
(ii) Not owned beneficially: (a) 6%; (b) 5.83%.
6. Of the mortgages owned beneficially by the Corporation, none is on realty situate
in Ontario, and none is on realty situate elsewhere.
7. Of the mortgages not owned beneficially by the Corporation, $59,761.70 is on realty
situate in Ontario, and none is on realty situate elsewhere.
8. Loans written off or transferred to real estate account during 1913, viz.:
(i) Funds or securities owned beneficially, none.
(ii) Not so owned, none.
9. Number and aggregate amount of mortgages upon which compulsory proceedings
have been taken by the Corporation in 1913, viz.:
(i) Owned beneficially: No., none; Amount, none.
(ii) Not so owned: No., none; Amount, none.
10. Aggregate market value of land mortgaged to the Corporation:
(i) Mortgages owned beneficially, none.
(ii) Not so owned, $164,300.
11. How often are the securities held by the Corporation valued? Annually.
12. (a) Specify the officers of the Corporation who are under bond and for what sum
respectively: Manager, $10,000.00; Accountant, $5,000.00.
(b) Are the said bonds executed by private sureties or by Guarantee Companies?
Guarantee Company.
13. Date when the accounts of the Corporation were last audited? 31st December, 1913.
14. Names and addresses of the auditors respectively for 1913, and for 1914 (if
appointed):
For 1913: John Locheed, Francis B. Ware.
For 1914: John Locheed, Francis B. Ware.
15. What were the dividend days of the Corporation in 1913, and what rate or rates of
dividend were paid on those days respectively? January 1st, July 1st; at
rate of 5% per annum.
16. What is the date appointed for the Annual Meeting? February 27th, 1914. Date
of last Annual Meeting? February 25th, 1913.
17. Special General Meetings held in 1913: Dates, none.

THE PRUDENTIAL TRUST COMPANY, LIMITED.

Head Office, Montreal, Quebec.

CONSTATING INSTRUMENTS.

The Prudential Trust Company, Limited, was incorporated in 1909 by a special Act of the Parliament of the Dominion of Canada, 8.9 Edward VII., Chapter 124.

Authorised in 1911 by special Act of the Legislature, 1 Geo. V., Chapter 139, to transact business in the Province of Ontario as specified in Section 1 (5) of the said Act, which enacts as follows:

"(5) The Company shall be limited in respect of all business relating to property, rights or interests in the Province of Ontario, to the powers mentioned in this Act or granted from time to time to Trust Companies by any public Act or Order of the Lieutenant-Governor-in-Council of the said Province, and shall be subject to the general public law of the said Province relating to trust companies and trusts."

The Company has a deposit in the Province of Ontario amounting to $200,000.

ANNUAL STATEMENT

Of the condition and affairs of the Prudential Trust Company, Limited, at the 31st December, 1913, and for the year ending on that day, made to the Registrar of Loan Corporations for the Province of Ontario, pursuant to the laws of the said Province.

The head office of the Corporation is at No. 9 St. John Street, in the City of Montreal, Quebec.

The chief agency for Ontario is situate at No. 103 Bay Street, in the City of Toronto, in the province of Ontario.

The chief agent and attorney for Ontario is C. D. Henderson, and his address is No. 103 Bay Street, Toronto, Ontario.

The Board is constituted of twenty-three Directors, holding office for one year.

The directors and chief executive officers of the Corporation at the 31st December, 1913, were as follows, together with their respective terms of office:

Farquahar Robertson, Hon. President and Chairman, Montreal;	12th March, 1913; 25th March, 1914.
B. Hal. Brown, President, Montreal;	" "
W. G. Ross, Vice-President, Montreal;	" "
Edmund Bristol, K.C., M.P., Vice-Pres., Toronto;	
C. A. Barnard, K.C., Director, Montreal;	
R. C. Smith, K.C., Director, Montreal;	
Hon. J. M. Wilson. Director, Montreal;	
W. M. Doull, Director, Montreal;	
F. B. Pemberton, Director, Victoria;	
W. Grant Morden, Director, Montreal;	
C. J. Booth, Director, Ottawa;	
W. J. Morrice, Director, Montreal;	
Sir Geo Garneau, Director, Quebec;	
Robt. Bickerdike, Director, Montreal;	
Aemilius Jarvis, Director, Toronto;	
Lt.-Col. James Mason, Director, Toronto;	
W. J. Green, Director, Toronto;	
G. W. Ganong, Director, St. Stephen;	
W. Burton Stewart, Director, Montreal;	
C. F. Smith, Director, Montreal:	
W. T. Rodden, Director. Montreal;	
H. B. Ames, Director, Montreal;	
Paul Galibert. Director. Montreal;	
J. P. Steedman, Director, Hamilton;	
B. Hal. Brown, General Manager, Montreal;	

A. Permanent Capital Stock: Total amount authorized, $1,500,000. Total amount subscribed, $1,050,300, as more particularly set out in Schedule A hereto.

SCHEDULE A.

Class 2. Fixed and permanent Capital Stock created by virtue of Joint Stock Companies' Acts or private Acts.

Description.	No. of shares.	Par value.	Total amount held.	Total amount paid thereon.	Total remaining unpaid
			$	$	$
1. Fully called preferred stock.	876	100	37,600	37,600	....
2. 50 per cent. called.	9,193	100	919,300	459,650	459,650
3. 50 '' ''	751	100	75,100	13,010	62,090
4. Ordinary stock fully called	183	100	18,300	18,286	14
Totals	10,503	....	1,050,300	528,546	521,754

LIST OF SHAREHOLDERS AS AT 31st DECEMBER, 1913.

(Not printed.)

BALANCE SHEET AS AT 31st DECEMBER, 1913.

Dr. Capital and Liabilities.

Capital (Liabilities to Stockholders or Shareholders).

A.—Permanent Capital Stock or Shares.

1. (a) Ordinary joint stock capital, on which has been called, $18,300; total paid thereon $18,286 00
2. (b) Preferred joint stock, on which has been called $534,300; total paid thereon 510,260 00
   $528,546 00
4. (d) Dividends declared in respect of (1), (2) not yet paid....... 17,815 31

Liabilities to the Public.

40. Unclaimed dividends 291 44
41. Liabilities to the public, viz.:
42. (a) Loans payable $723,150 00
43. (b) Interest under Loans Payable accrued 4,543 88
44. (c) Accounts payable 14,223 88
    (d) Salaries, stationery and charges accrued to date ... 4,647 52
    (e) Contingent account 28,713 74
    (f) Mortgage on real estate 35,000 00
    810,278 97

Total actual liabilities $1,356,931 72

BALANCE SHEET.—Continued.

II.—Contingent Liabilities.

49. Money for which the Corporation is contingently liable, viz.:
51. (c) Trust funds invested but not guaranteed:
52.   (1) Principal $1,636,709 32
54. (d) Trust funds uninvested not bearing interest and
        not guaranteed 427,109 86
56. (e) Agency funds uninvested 2,953 50

        Total contingent liabilities $2,066,772 68

        Gross total liabilities, actual and contingent $3,423,704 40

Cr.   Assets.

I.—Assets of which the Corporation is the Beneficial Owner.

A.—Immovable Property Owned Beneficially by Corporation

2.   (1) At Montreal, held in freehold $71,054 75

B.—Debts secured by Mortgages of Land.

9. (a) Debts (other than item 10) secured by mortgages of
       land $233,504 26
11. (c) Interest due and accrued on item (9) and not in-
        cluded therein 6,084 96
                                                                                            ───────────
                                                                                            239,589 22

C.—Debts not above enumerated, for which the Corporation holds securities as follows:

14. (b) Debts secured by municipal bonds or debentures . . . $24,889 05
22. (j) Secured by other corporation securities 40,350 00
23. (k) Secured by deposit with Provincial Government 200,000 00
24. (l) Secured by loans on stocks, bonds, etc. 734,518 29
26. (n) Interest due or accrued on items 22 to 24 and not
        included therein 6,353 23
                                                                                            ───────────
                                                                                            1,006,110 57

D.—Unsecured Debts.

27. (a) Accounts receivable, including commissions, fees etc. $12,381 50
28. (b) Office furniture and fixtures (including vault and
        fittings 9,656 58
29. (c) Organization expenses 10,127 97

E.—Cash.

31. (a) On hand 150 00
32. (b) In banks 7,911 13
                                                                                            ───────────
                                                                                             40,177 18

        Total of assets owned beneficially by Corporation. $1,356,931 72

BALANCE SHEET.—Continued.

II.—Assets not owned beneficially by the Corporation, but for which the Corporation is Accountable.

B.—As Trustee, Representative, Guardian or Agent (without guarantee).

(a) Mortgage securities:
47.   (1) Principal $43,781 65

(b) On other securities:
49.   (1) Principal 1,592,977 67
52. (d) Uninvested trust funds 427,109 86
53. (e) Uninvested agency funds 2,953 50

Total of assets II. $2,066,772 68

Gross total assets I. and II. $3,423,704 40

CASH ACCOUNT.

Receipts for the year ending 31st December, 1913.

I.—Received by the Corporation for its Own Use.

A.—Balances from 31st December 1912.

		(Col. 1.)	(Col. 3.)	(Col. 4.)
1. Cash:				
2.	(i) On hand	......	......	$150 00
3.	(ii) In bank	......	......	26,254 47

B.—Sums received wholly or partly on Capital Stock.

4. (a) Calls on ordinary stock		......	$700 00	
(aa) Calls on preference stock		......	68,910 00	
				69,610 00
5. (b) Premiums on (4)		$2,800 00	......	

C.—Receipts on account of Investments, Loans, or Debts.

(a) On mortgages of realty:

10.	(1) Principal	......	......	38,521 75
11.	(ii) Interest	15,709 48		

(b) On other securities:

13.	(ii) Interest or dividends	1,182 90	

(c) Secured debts:

14.	(1) Principal	......	......	608,545 92
15.	(ii) Interest	125,164 26		

E.—Miscellaneous.

18. Commission, brokerage (or remuneration as corporation agent, trustee, etc.)—	18,404 05	......	163,260 69

CASH ACCOUNT.—Continued.

Receipts for the year ending 31st December, 1913.

	(Col. 1.)	(Col. 4.)
F.—Borrowed Money.		
25. (a) Loans payable		136,330 99
G.—Receipts from other sources.		
30. (a) Accounts payable		$5,869 39
Total		$1,048,543 21

II.—Received as Corporate Trustee, Representative, Guardian or Agent in Trust.

A.—Balances from 31st December, 1912.

		(Col. 4.)
31. (a) Capital account:		
33. (ii) In bank		.$386,286 64

B.—Received on account of Investments, Loans or Debts.

	(Col. 1.)	(Col. 4.)
34. (a) On mortgages: Principal, $4,700.00; interest, $2,315.39	$7,015 39	
35. (b) On other securities: Principal, $3,705,912.98; interest, $207,586.73	3,913,499 71	
		3,920,515 10

D.—Receipts from other sources, viz.:

		(Col. 4.)
39. (a) Estates, agencies (capital and revenue accounts, realizations, receipts, etc.)		6,913,572 11
Totals		$11,220,373 85

CASH ACCOUNT.

Expenditure for the year ending 31st December, 1913.

I.—Expended on Corporation Account.

A.—Sums Loaned or Invested on Capital Account.

	(Col. 1.)	(Col. 4.)
1. (a) Loaned on mortgages of realty	......	$65,519 21
(b) Loaned or invested in other securities	......	811,517 48
6. (c) Real estate purchased	......	7,612 75

B.—Expended on Stock Account.

	(Col. 1.)	(Col. 4.)
8. Dividends paid on permanent stock	21,690 32	

C.—Borrowed Money (other than foregoing) or interest thereon paid, viz.:

	(Col. 1.)	(Col. 4.)
18. (a) Repayment of loans	......	23,823 12
19. (b) Interest	33,973 12	

CASH ACCOUNT.—Continued.

Expenditure for the year ending 31st December, 1913.

	(Col. 1.)	(Col. 4.)
D.—Management Expenses (other than foregoing).		
25. (a) Salaries, wages and fees	42,587 85	
28. (d) Stationery, postage, printing and advertising	7,055 41	
29. (e) Law costs	1,711 82	
30. (f) Fuel, rent, taxes (other than in 7 and 32) and rates	11,622 46	
31. (g) Travelling expenses	2,269 71	
33. (i) Other management expenditure	1,076 72	
E.—Other Expenditure, viz.:		
34. (a) Office furniture and fixtures	......	1,872 11
35. (b) Commission paid on sale of stock	......	3,150 00
F.—Balance.		
37. (a) Cash on hand and in bank	......	8,061 13
		121,987 41
Total		$1,048,543 21

II.—Expended on Trust or Agency Account.

A.—Loaned or Invested on Capital Account.

42. (a) Loaned on mortgages of realty	$4,400 00
(b) Loaned and invested on or in other securities	1,903,650 77
B.—Other Expenditures.	
53. (d) Estates and agencies, payments on account of capital and revenue, etc.	8,882,259 72
C.—Balances.	
54. (b) Cash in banks	430,063 36
Total	$11,220,373 85

Miscellaneous Statement for the Year Ending 31st December, 1913.

1. Amount of debentures maturing in 1914: Issued in Canada, none; issued elsewhere, none.
2. Amount of other existing obligations which will mature in 1914: None.
3. Amount of securities held by the Corporation which will mature and become payable to the Corporation in 1914, none.
4. Average rate of interest per annum paid by the Corporation during 1913: On deposits, none; on debentures, none; on debenture stock, none.
5. Average rate of interest per annum received by the Corporation during 1913:
   (a) On mortgages of realty; (b) on other securities.
   (i) Owned beneficially by the Corporation: (a) 7½%; (b) 5%.
   (ii) Not owned beneficially: (a) 7%; (b) 5%.
6. Of the mortgages owned beneficially by the Corporation, none is on realty situate in Ontario, and $233,504.26 is on realty situate elsewhere.

7. Of the mortgages not owned beneficially by the Corporation, none is on realty situate in Ontario, and $43,731.65 is on realty situate elsewhere.

8. Loans written off or transferred to real estate account during 1913, viz.:

    (i) Funds or securities owned beneficially, none.

    (ii) Not so owned, none.

9. Number and aggregate amount of mortgages upon which compulsory proceedings have been taken by the Corporation in 1913, viz.:

    (i) Owned beneficially: No., none; amount, none.

    (ii) Not so owned: No., none; amount, none.

10. Aggregate market value of land mortgaged to the Corporation:

    (i) Mortgages owned beneficially, $467,000.00.

    (ii) Not so owned, $65,600.00.

11. How often are the securities held by the Corporation valued? Annually.

12. (a) Specify the officers of the Corporation who are under bond and for what sum respectively: All officers of the Company are under bond for sums not less than $2,000 each.

    (b) Are the said bonds executed by private sureties or by Guarantee Companies? Guarantee Company.

13. Date when the accounts of the Corporation were last audited? 13th February, 1914, for period ending 31st December, 1913.

14. Names and addresses of the auditors respectively for 1913 and for 1914 (if appointed):

    For 1913: Riddell, Stead, Graham & Hutchison.

    For 1914: Not appointed.

15. What were the dividend days of the Corporation in 1913 and what rate or rates of dividend were paid on those days respectively?

    (1) 27th March, 1913, for period 6 months ending 31st December, 1912, at 5%.

    (2) 15th July, 1913, for half year to 30th June, 1913, at 5%.

16. What is the date appointed for the Annual Meeting? 25th March, 1914. Date of last Annual Meeting? 12th March, 1913.

17. Special General Meetings held in 1913: Dates, none.

STANDARD TRUSTS COMPANY.

Head Office, Winnipeg, Man.

———

CONSTATING INSTRUMENTS.

The Standard Trusts Company was incorporated on the 1st day of March, 1902, by special Act of the Province of Manitoba (1.2 Edw. VII. Chap. 70).

Authorized to transact business in the Province of Ontario under the Loan and Trust Corporations Act (R.S.O. 1914, Chap. 184), by Order-in-Council passed the 14th day of January, 1914, subject to certain restrictions.

Registered on the Trust Companies Register, 1st July, 1913.

———

ANNUAL STATEMENT

Of the condition and affairs of the Standard Trusts Company of Winnipeg, Manitoba, at the 31st December, 1913, and for the year ending on that day, made to the Registrar of Loan Corporations for the Province of Ontario, pursuant to the laws of the said Province.

The Head Office of the Corporation is at No. 346 Main Street, in the City of Winnipeg, in the Province of Manitoba.

The Chief Agency for Ontario is situate at corner Wellington and Church Streets, in the City of Toronto, in the Province of Ontario.

The Chief Agent and Attorney for Ontario is Alex. Fasken, Esq., and his address is care Beatty, Blackstock & Co., Toronto, in the Province of Ontario.

The Board is constituted of fifteen Directors, holding office for the term of one year.

The directors and chief executive officers of the Corporation at the 31st December, 1913, were as follows:

J. T. Gordon, President, Winnipeg;   January 1st, 1913; December 31st, 1913.
Sir Wm. Whyte, Vice-President, Winnipeg;   "   "
M. Bull, Director, Winnipeg;
J. A. Girvin, Director, Winnipeg;
C. C. Castle, Director, Winnipeg;
John Persse, Director, Winnipeg;
P. C. McIntyre, Director, Winnipeg;
G. F. Stephens, Director, Winnipeg;
N. Bawlf, Director, Winnipeg;
K. Mackenzie, Director, Winnipeg;
E. S. Popham, Director, Winnipeg;
R. J. Blanchard, Director, Winnipeg;
Wm. Harvey, Managing Director and Vice-President, Winnipeg;
W. E. Lugsdin, Secretary-Treasurer, Winnipeg;   "
A. M. Fraser, Director, London, England;
Wm. Georgeson, Director, Calgary, Alberta;

A.—Permanent capital stock: Total amount authorized, $1,000,000; total amount subscribed, $750,000, as more particularly set out in Schedule A hereto.

Class 2.—Fixed and permanent capital stock created by virtue of Joint Stock Companies Acts or private Acts.

Description of Stock.	No. of shares.	Par value of shares	Total Amount held.	Total amount paid thereon.	Total remaining unpaid on calls.
			$	$	$
1. Fully called..........	15,000	50	750,000	750,000	None.

LIST OF SHAREHOLDERS AS AT 31st DECEMBER, 1913.

(Not printed.)

BALANCE SHEET AS AT 31st DECEMBER, 1913.

Dr.   Capital and Liabilities.

I.—Capital (Liabilities to Stockholders or Shareholders).

A.—Permanent Capital Stock or Shares.

1. (a) Ordinary joint stock capital fully called: total called, $750,000; total paid thereon	$750,000 00	
4. (d) Dividends declared in respect of (1) but not yet paid	33,019 75	
5. (e) Unappropriated profits in respect of (1)	3,027 13	
6. (f) Reserve fund in respect of (1)...................	400,000 00	

Liabilities to the Public.

37. Owing to banks (including interest due and accrued)....	55,785 14	
Total actual liabilities		$1,241,832 02

II.—Contingent Liabilities.

49. Money for which the Corporation is held contingently liable viz.:

50. (a) Principal guaranteed	$554,593 35	
52. (c) Trust funds invested but not guaranteed:		
53. (i) Principal	2,809,631 91	
54. (ii) Interest	88,045 64	
56. (e) Other contingent liabilities, gency accounts........	2,064,788 41	
Total contingent liabilities		$5,517,059 31
Gross total liabilities, actual and contingent................		$6,758,891 33

Cr.   Assets.

I.—Assets of which the Corporation is Beneficial Owner.

A.—Immovable Property Owned Beneficially by Corporation.

1. (a) Office premises situate as follows:		
2. (i) At Winnipeg, held in freehold	$99,625 00	
3. (ii) At Saskatoon, held in freehold	97,805 04	

BALANCE SHEET.—Continued.

B.—Debts secured by Mortgages of Land.

9. (a) Debts secured by mortgages of land................ 952,335 64

E.—Cash.

32. (b) In banks 92,066 34

Total of assets owned beneficially by Corporation.......... $1,241,832 02

II.—Assets not owned Beneficially by Corporation, but for which the Corporation is Accountable.

A.—As Guarantor.

(a) Mortgage securities:

43. (i) Principal 554,593 35

B.—As Trustee, Representative, Guardian, or Agent (without guarantee).

(a) Mortgage securities:

47. (i) Principal 3,135,852 56
48. (ii) Interest due and accrued 167,879 03

(b) Other securities:

49. (i) Principal 1,584,857 06
50. (ii) Interest due and accrued 50,615 49
52. (d) Uninvested trust funds 23,261 82

Total assets II. $5,517,059 31

Gross total of assets I. and II. $6,758,891 33

CASH ACCOUNT.

Receipts for the year ending 31st December, 1913.

Total Col. 4.

I.—Received by the Corporation for its Own Use.

A.—Balances from 31st December, 1912.

1. Cash:
2. (i) On hand and in bank $49,777 78

B.—Sums Received Wholly or Partly on Capital Stock.

4. (a) Calls on joint stock permanent capital, new issue... $250,000 00
5. (b) Premiums on (4) 62,500 00

312,500 00

C.—Receipts on account of Investments, Loans or Debts.

(a) On mortgages of realty:
10. (i) Principal 234,855 53
11. (ii) Interest . . . . $76,475 72 .... 76,475 72

CASH ACCOUNT.—Continued.

Receipts for the year ending 31st December, 1913.

D.—Receipts from Real Estate Owned Beneficially by Corporation.

17. (b) Rents $16,538 32	16,538 32

E.—Miscellaneous.

19. (b) Premiums or bonus on loans 151,311 04

G.—Receipts from Other Sources.

30. (a) Money received for investment on guaranteed basis.............	140,252 02
(b) Sundries	4,005 72
Total	**$985,716 13**

II.—Received as Corporate Trustee, Representative, Guardian or Agent in Trust.

B.—Received on Account of Investments, Loans or Debts. (Payments.)

34. (a) On mortgages: Principal, $605,441.00; interest, $256,944.05...... **$862,385 05**

D.—Receipts from Other Sources, viz.:

39. (a) Assets realized 199,004 59

40. (b) Sundry receipts, including money received from clients for investment 1,347,004 46

Total **$2,408,394 10**

CASH ACCOUNT.

Expenditures for the year ending 31st December, 1913.

I.—Expended on Corporation Account.

A.—Sums Loaned or Invested on Capital Account.

1. (a) Loaned on mortgages of realty	$574,280 78
7. (d) Incumbrances on realty paid off	57,626 38

B.—Expended on Stock Account.

8. Dividends paid on permanent stock 50,402 30

C.—Borrowed Money (other than foregoing) or Interest thereon paid, viz.:

18. (a) Bank account, interest on overdraft............................	6,389 40
24. (g) Guarantees paid: Principal, $88,868.21; interest, $35,319.60.......	124,187 81

CASH ACCOUNT.—Continued.

Expenditures for the year ending 31st December, 1913.

D.—Management Expenses (other than foregoing).

25. (a) Salaries, wages and fees	$76,921 30
26. (b) Commission or brokerage	4,386 68
28. (d) Stationery, postage, printing and advertising	22,264 61
30. (f) Fuel, rent, taxes and rates	13,499 01
31. (g) Travelling expenses	2,399 54
33. (i) Other management expenditure	217 10

E.—Other Expenditures, viz.:

34. (a) Inspectors	13,473 94
35. (b) Furniture	3,386 08

F.—Balance.

(b) Cash on hand and in banks	$92,066 34	
Less overdraft	55,785 14	36,281 20
Total		$985,716 13

II.—Expended on Trust or Agency Account.

A.—Loaned or Invested on Capital Account.

42. (a) Loaned on mortgages of realty	$598,366 27

B.—Other Expenditures.

50. (a) Commission or remuneration paid for management of estate, trust or agency	151,311 04
53. (d) Sundry payments, including payments of estates, liabilities and payments to clients	1,635,454 97

C.—Balance.

55. (1) Cash in bank	23,261 82
Total	$2,408,394 10

MISCELLANEOUS STATEMENT FOR THE YEAR ENDING 31ST DECEMBER, 1913.

1. Amount of Debentures maturing in 1914: Issued in Canada, none; Issued elsewhere, none.
2. Amount of other existing obligations which will mature in 1914, none.
3. Amount of securities held by the Corporation which will mature and become payable to the Corporation in 1914, none.
4. Average rate of interest per annum paid by the Corporation during 1913: On deposits, none; on debentures, none; on debenture stock, none.

5. Average rate of interest per annum received by the Corporation during 1913.
   (a) On mortgages of realty; (b) On other securities.
   (i) Owned beneficially by the Corporation: (a) 8½%; (b) None.
   (ii) Not owned beneficially: (a) 8%; (b) None.
6. Of the mortgages owned beneficially by the Corporation, none is on realty situate in Ontario, and $1,028,780.42 is on realty situate elsewhere.
7. Of the mortgages not owned beneficially by the Corporation, none is on realty situate in Ontario, and $2,809,631.91 is on realty situate elsewhere.
8. Loans written off or transferred to real estate account during 1913, viz.:
   (i) Funds or securities owned beneficially, none.
   (ii) Not so owned, none.
9. Number and aggregate amount of mortgages upon which compulsory proceedings have been taken by the Corporation in 1913, viz.:
   (i) Owned beneficially: No., 14; Amount, $27,900.00.
   (ii) Not so owned: No., 38; Amount, $43,074.84.
10. Aggregate market value of land mortgaged to the Corporation:
    (i) Mortgages owned beneficially, $2,500,000.
    (ii) Not so owned, $7,900,000.
11. How often are the securities held by the Corporation valued?
12. (a) Specify the officers of the Corporation who are under bond, and for what sum respectively:
    (b) Are the said bonds executed by private sureties or by Guarantee Companies?
13. Date when the accounts of the Corporation were last audited? 31st December, 1913.
14. Names and addresses of the auditors respectively for 1913 and for 1914 (if appointed):
    For 1913: John Scott & Company, C.A., Winnipeg.
    For 1914: John Scott & Company, C.A., Winnipeg.
15. What were the dividend days of the Corporation in 1913, and what rate or rates of dividend were paid on those days respectively? 2nd January, 2nd July; 9% per annum.
16. What is the date apointed for the Annual Meeting? Last Thursday in January each year. Date of last Annual Meeting? 29th January, 1914.
17. Special General Meetings held in 1913: Dates, none.

THE CANADA PERMANENT TRUST COMPANY.

Head office, Toronto, Ontario.

CONSTATING INSTRUMENTS.

The Canada Permanent Trust Company was incorporated in 1913 by a special Act of the Parliament of the Dominion of Canada.

Authorized by Order-in-Council (May 7th, 1913) to carry on business in the Province of Ontario as a Trust Company, pursuant to the provisions of The Loan and Trust Corporations Act, R.S.O., 1914, c. 184.

ANNUAL STATEMENT

Of the condition and affairs of the Canadian Permanent Trust Company, of Toronto, Ont., as at the 31st December, 1913, and for the year ending on that day, made to the Registrar of Loan Corporations for the Province of Ontario, pursuant to the laws of the said Province.

The head office of the Corporation is at No. 14-18 Toronto Street, in the City of Toronto, in the Province of Ontario.

The Board is constituted of nine Directors, holding office for the term of one year.

The directors and chief executive of the Corporation at the 31st December, 1913, were as follows, together with their respective terms of office:

W. G. Gooderham, President, Toronto;
W. D. Matthews, 1st Vice-President, Toronto;
George W. Monk, 2nd Vice-President, Toronto;
Lt.-Col. A. E. Gooderham, Director, Toronto;
R. S. Hudson, Director, Toronto;
F. Gordon Osler, Director, Toronto;
J. H. G. Hagerty, Director, Toronto;
John Massey, Director, Toronto;
John Campbell, Director, Edinburgh, Scotland;
John Massey and R. S. Hudson, Joint Managers, Toronto;
George H. Smith, Secretary-Treasurer, Toronto;

A permanent capital stock: Total amount authorized, $1,000,000.00. Total amount subscribed, $109,000,00, as more particularly set out in Schedule A hereto.

SCHEDULE A.

Class 2.—Fixed and permanent capital stock created by virtue of Joint Stock Companies' Acts or Private Acts.

Description.	No. of shares.	Par value of shares.	Total amount held.	Total amount paid thereon.	Total remaining unpaid.
		$	$	$	$
20 per cent. called.......	5,000	100	500,000	100,000	....
20 per cent. called.......	180	100	18,000	3,600	....
30 per cent. paid in advance of calls on 180 shares	....	....	....	5,400	....
Totals............	5,180	....	....	109,000	....

LIST OF SHAREHOLDERS AS AT 31st DECEMBER, 1913.

(Not printed.)

23 L.C.

BALANCE SHEET AS AT 31st DECEMBER, 1912.

Dr.   Capital and Liabilities.

I.—Capital (Liabilities to Stockholders or Shareholders).

A.—Permanent Capital Stock or Shares.

2. (b) Ordinary joint stock capital, 20% called: Total called, $103,600; total paid thereon, $103,600	$103,600 00		
(cc) Joint stock capital paid in advance of calls	5,400 00		
		$109,000 00	
5. (e) Unappropriated profits in respect of (2)		2,242 33	
Total actual liabilities		$111,242 33	

II.—Contingent Liabilities.

52. (c) Trust funds invested but not guaranteed:			
53. (i) Principal	$30,129 30		
54. (ii) Interest	166 43		
55. (d) Trust funds uninvested not bearing interest and not guaranteed	3,049 19		
Total contingent liabilities		33,344 92	
Gross total liabilities, actual and contingent		$144,587 25	

Cr.   Assets.

I.—Assets of which the Corporation is the Beneficial Owner.

B.—Debts secured by Mortgages of Land.

9. (a) Debts secured by mortgages of land	$102,692 45		
11. (c) Interest due and accrued on item 79) not included therein	371 84		
		$103,064 29	

E.—Cash.

22. (b) In banks and Loan Co.	……	8,178 04	
Total assets owned beneficially		$111,242 33	

II.—Assets not owned beneficially by Corporation, but for which the Corporation is Accountable.

B.—As Trustee, Representative, Guardian or Agent (without guarantee).

(a) Mortgage securities:			
47. (i) Principal	$21,355 30		
48. (ii) Interest due and accrued	76 43		
(b) Other securities:			
49. (i) Principal	8,774 00		
50. (ii) Interest due and accrued	90 00		
52. (d) Uninvested trust funds	3,049 19		
Total assets II.		$33,344 92	
Gross total assets, I and II		$144,587 25	

CASH ACCOUNT.

Receipts for the year ending 31st December, 1913.

I.—Received by the Corporation for Its Own Use.

B.—Sums received wholly or partly on Capital Stock.

4. (a) Calls on joint stock permanent capital .... ⎫
   (aa) Joint stock capital received in advance of calls .... ⎬ $109,000 00

C.—Receipts on account of Investments, Loans or Debts.

(a) On mortgages of realty:

10.	(i) Principal	581 30
11.	(ii) Interest	655 76

(b) On other securities:

13.	(ii) Bank interest	1,137 23

E.—Miscellaneous.

18. (a) Commission, brokerage (or remuneration as corporate agent, trustee, etc.) 20 00

G.—Receipts from Other Sources.

30. (a) Inspection 57 50

Totals 111,451 99

II.—Received as Corporate Trustee, Representative, Guardian or Agent in Trust.

B.—Received on Account of Investments, Loans or Debts.

34. (a) On mortgages: Principal.... $5,842 11 Interest.... $728 91		$8,204 77
35. (b) On other securities: Principal. 2,362 66 Interest.... 230 00		
	Bank interest.... 40 75	999 66

Totals $9,204 43

Expenditure for the year ending 31st December, 1913.

I.—Expended on Corporation Account.

A.—Sums Loaned or Invested on Capital Account.

1. (a) Loaned on mortgages of realty $103,273 95

F.—Balance.

37. (b) Cash in banks 8,178 04

Total $111,451 99

II.—Expended on Trust or Agency Account.

A.—Loaned or Invested on Capital Account.

42. (a) Loaned on mortgages of realty $4,086 75

24 L.C.

CASH ACCOUNT.—Continued.

Expenditure for the year ending 31st ·December, 1913.

B.—Other Expenditures.

50. (a) Commission or remuneration paid for management of estate, trust or agency, commission on loans		$10 00		
52. (c) Debts or obligations wholly or partly paid, viz.:				
Principal, $1,132.32; interest, $600.00	600 00	$1,132 32	610 00	1,132 32

C.—Balance.

55.	(i) Cash in Dominion Bank	$2,130 30	
57.	(ii) Cash in Canada Permanent ..	1,245 06	
			3,375 36
	Total		$9,204 43

MISCELLANEOUS STATEMENT FOR THE YEAR ENDING 31ST DECEMBER, 1913.

1. Amount of debentures maturing in 1914: Issued in Canada, none; issued elsewhere, none.
2. Amount of other existing obligations which will mature in 1914: None.
3. Amount of securities held by the Corporation which will mature and become payable to the Corporation in 1914, none.
4. Average rate of interest per annum paid by the Corporation during 1913: On deposits, none; on debentures, none; on debenture stock, none.
5. Average rate of interest per annum received by the Corporation during 1913:
   (a) On mortgages of realty; (b) on other securities.
   (i) Owned beneficially by the Corporation: (a) 8.09%; (b) none.
   (ii) Not owned beneficially; (a) 6.93%; (b) none.
6. Of the mortgages owned beneficially by the Corporation, $103,064.29 is on realty situate in Ontario, and none is on realty situate elsewhere.
7. Of the mortgages not owned beneficially by the Corporation, $21,431.73 is on realty situate in Ontario, and none is on realty situate elsewhere.
8. Loans written off or transferred to real estate account during 1913 ,viz.:
   (i) Funds or securities owned beneficially, none.
   (ii) Not so owned, none.
9. Number and aggregate amount of mortgages upon which compulsory proceedings have been taken by the Corporation in 1913, viz.:
   (i) Owned beneficially: No., none; amount, none.
   (ii) Not so owned: No., none; amount, none.
10. Aggregate market value of land mortgaged to the Corporation:
    (i) Mortgages owned beneficially, $280,760.00.
    (ii) Not so owned, $45,000.00.
11. How often are the securities held by the Corporation valued? ——
12. (a) Specify the officers of the Corporation(who are under bond and for what sum respectively: ——
    (b) Are the said bonds executed by private sureties or by Guarantee Companies?
13. Date when the accounts of the Corporation were last audited? 31st December, 1913.
14. Names and addresses of the auditors respectively for 1913 and for 1914 (if appointed):
    For 1913: A. E. Osler, A.C.A., Henry Barber, F.C.A.A., England, Toronto.
    For 1914: A. E. Osler, A.C.A., Henry Barber, F.C.A.A., England, Toronto.
15. What were the dividend days of the Corporation in 1913 and what rate or rates of dividend were paid on those days respectively? None
16. What is the date appointed for the Annual Meeting? Not appointed. Date of last Annual Meeting? February 11th, 1914.
17. Special General Meetings held in 1913: Dates, 9th April, 1913.

MONTREAL TRUST COMPANY.

Head Office, Montreal, Que.

CONSTATING INSTRUMENTS.

The Montreal Trust Company was incorporated on the 21st day of March, 1899, by special Act of the Province of Quebec, 52 Vic., c. 72 (Q) and subsequent special amending Act, under the name of the Montreal Safe Deposit Company.

By special Acts the name was changed in 1895 to the Montreal Trust and Deposit Company (59 Vic., c. 70 (Q)), and again in 1909 to the Montreal Trust Company (9 Edw. VII, c. 115 (Q)).

Authorized by Order-in-Council to carry on business in the Province of Ontario as from the 11th day of March, 1909, subject to certain conditions and limitations.

Registered on the Trust Companies Register, 21st January, 1913.

The Company has a deposit with the Province of Ontario, amounting to $200,000.00.

ANNUAL STATEMENT

Of the condition and affairs of the Montreal Trust Company of Montreal, Que., at the 31st December, 1913, and for the year ending on that day, made to the Registrar of Loan Corporations for the Province of Ontario, pursuant to the laws of the said Province.

The Corporation was incorporated under the laws of the Province of Quebec on the Twenty-first day of March, 1889.

The head office of the Corporation is at No. 142 Notre Dame Street West in the City of Montreal in the Province of Quebec.

The chief agency for Ontario is situate at No. 61 Yonge Street, in the City of Toronto, in the Province of Ontario.

The Chief Agent and Attorney for Ontario is John F. Hobkirk, and his address is 61 Yonge Street, Toronto, in the Province of Ontario.

The Board is constituted of twenty-one directors, holding office for the term of one year, there being one vacancy at 31st December, 1913.

The directors and chief executive officers of the Corporation at the 31st December, 1913, were as follows:—

H. S. Holt, President, Montreal, Que.;   14th January, 1913; 13th January, 1914
Robt. Archer, Vice-President, Montreal, Que.;   "   "
Sir W. M. Aitken, M.P., Director, London, Eng.;   "   "
J. E. Aldred, Director, New York, N.Y.;
V. J. Hughes, Director, Montreal, Que.;
A. J. Brown, Director, Montreal, Que.;
Fayette Brown, Director, Montreal, Que.;
Geo. Caverhill, Director, Montreal, Que.;
Hon. N. Curry, Director, Montreal, Que.;
Hon. A. Dandurand, Director, Montreal, Que.;
F. P. Jones, Director, Montreal, Que.;
Wm. Molson Macpherson, Director, Quebec, Que.;   "
C. E. Neill, Director, Montreal, Que.;
Hugh Payton, Director, Montreal, Que.;
E. L. Pease, Director, Montreal, Que.;
James Redmond, Director, Montreal, Que.;   "
F. W. Ross, Director, Quebec, Que.;
Hon. W. Ross, Director, Halifax, N.S.;   5th September, 1913;   "
A. Haig Sims, Director, Montreal, Que.;   14th January, 1913;   "
Jas. Reid Wilson, Director, Montreal, Que.;   ·   "
Vincent J. Hughes, Manager, Montreal;   at the will of the Directors
Ivan S. Ralston, Secretary, Montreal;   "   "

A.—Permanent capital stock: Total amount authorized, $1,000,000.00; total amount subscribed, $500,000; as more particularly set out in Schedule A hereto.

Class 2.—Fixed and permanent capital stock created by virtue of Joint Stock Companies' Acts or private Acts.

Last call made: Date, paid in full prior to 1900.

Description of Stock.	No. of shares.	Par value of shares.	Total amount held.	Total amount paid thereon.
1. Fully called	5,000	100	500,000	500,000

LIST OF SHAREHOLDERS AS AT 31st DECEMBER, 1913.

(Not printed.)

BALANCE SHEET AS AT 31st DECEMBER, 1913.

Dr.   Capital and Liabilities.

I.—Capital (Liabilities to Stockholders or Shareholders).

A.—Permanent Capital Stock or Shares.

1. (a) Ordinary joint stock capital, fully called; total called, $500,000; total paid thereon	$500,000 00	
5. (e) Unappropriated profits in respect of (1)	41,967 05	
6. (f) Reserve fund in respect of (1)	400,000 00	
		$941,967 05

Liabilities to the Public.

41. Other liabilities to the public, viz.:

42. (a) Guaranteed mortgage investment receipts	$30,416 63	
43. (b) Guaranteed funds withdrawable on notice not subject to cheque	1,479,674 79	
44. (c) Interest, etc., accrued to date	1,053 80	
		1,511,145 22

Total actual liabilities $2,453,112 27

II.—Contingent Liabilities.

49. Money for which the Corporation is contingently liable, viz.:

52. (c) Trust funds invested but not guaranteed (including securities actually held as trustee for bondholders)	$50,370,143 55	
55. (d) Trust funds uninvested	80,100 18	
56. (e) Other contingent liabilities, judicial surety indemnity and other bonds	471,250 00	

Total contingent liabilities $50,921,493 73

Gross total liabilities, actual and contingent............... $53,374,606 00

Cr. Assets.

I.—Assets of which the Corporation is the Beneficial Owner.

B.—Debts secured by Mortgages of Land.

9. (a) Debts secured by mortgages of land and buildings.. $121,130 89   **$121,130 89**

C.—Debts not above enumerated for which the Corporation holds securities as follows:—

·22. (j) Deposits with Provincial Governments............. $225,000 00
23. (k) Debts secured by railway and other corporation securities 1,948,127 03   **$2,173,127 03**

D.—Unsecured Debts.

27. (a) Office furniture $4,379 93
28. (b) Balances on sundry accounts, including commissions, fees, etc., due 38,845 11

E.—Cash.

31. (a) On hand $1,108 55
32. (b) In banks 114,520 76   **153,854 35**

Total of assets owned beneficially by Corporation............ **$2,453,112 27**

II.—Assets Not Owned Beneficially by the Corporation, but for which the Corporation is Accountable.

B.—As Trustee, Representative, Guardian or Agent (without guarantee).

   (a) Mortgage securities:

47.   (i) Principal $2,356,722 24

   (b) Other securities:

49.   (i) Principal (including securities actually held as trustees for bondholders) 48,013,421 31
51. (c) Security against judicial surety indemnity and other bonds 471,250 00
52. (d) Uninvested trust funds 80,100 18

Total assets II. **$50,921,493 73**

Gross total assets I. and II. **$53,374,606 00**

CASH ACCOUNT.

Receipts for the year ending 31st December, 1913.

	Col. 1.	Col. 4.
I.—Received by the Corporation for its Own Use.		
A.—Balances from 31st December, 1912.		
1. Cash		$1,055 00

CASH ACCOUNT.—Continued.

Receipts for the year ending 31st December, 1913.

		Col. 1.	Col. 4.
C.—Receipts on account of Investments, Loans or Debts.			
(a) On mortgages of realty:			
10.	(i) Principal		319,293 02
11.	(ii) Interest	$22,622 65	
(b) On other securities and demand loans:			
12.	(i) Principal		3,797,752 59
13.	(ii) Interest or dividends	65,494 51	
E.—Miscellaneous.			
18. (a) Commission, brokerage (or remuneration as corporate agent, trustee, etc.)		112,434 60	200,551 76
F.—Borrowed Money.			
26. (b) Borrowed by taking deposits			3,950,359 06
Total			$8,269,011 43

II.—Received as a Corporate Trustee, Representative, Guardian or Agent in Trust.

A.—Balances from 31st December, 1912.

31. (a) Capital Account:		
33.	(ii) In bank	$362,138 44
B.—Received on account of Investments, Loans or Debts.		
34. (a) On mortgages: Principal, $340,466.40; interest, $85,203.46		425,669 86
35. (b) On other securities: Principal, $10,114,985.28; interest, $229,643.39.		10,344,628 67
C.—Receipts from Real Estate.		
37. (a) Sales (not included in foregoing items)		189,017 74
38. (b) Rents		155,080 18
Total		$11,976,534 89

Expenditures for the year ending 31st December, 1913.

I.—Expended on Corporation Account.

A.—Sums Loaned or Invested on Capital Account.		
1. (a) Loaned on mortgages of realty		$88,681 75
(b) Loaned on or invested in other securities		3,873,303 36
B.—Expended on Stock Account.		
8. Dividends paid on permanent stock	$39,993 00	

CASH ACCOUNT.—Continued.

Expenditure for the year ending 31st December, 1913.

	(Col. 1.)	(Col. 2.)
C.—Borrowed Money (other than foregoing) or interest thereon paid, viz.:		
18. (a) Bank account		496,814 49
19. (b) Deposits: Principal, $3,582,223.10; interest, $21,591.71		3,603,814 81
D.—Management Expenses (other than foregoing):		
25. (a) Salaries, wages and fees	$36,663 76	
26. (b) Commission or brokerage	900 00	
28. (d) Stationery, postage, printing and advertising	7,115 23	
29. (e) Law costs	888 50	
30. (f) Fuel, rent, taxes and rates	6,322 34	
33. (i) Other management expenditure	5,705 29	97,588 12
F.—Balance.		
(b) Cash in various banks		108,808 90
Total		$8,269,011 43

II.—Expended on Trust or Agency Account.

A.—Loaned or Invested on Capital Account.

42. (a) Loaned on mortgages of realty	$280,707 78
(b) Loaned or invested on or in other securities	9,336,004 18
47. (a) Real estate purchased	150,645 27

B.—Other Expenditures.

50. (a) Commission or remuneration paid for management of estate, trust or agency	3,033 65
53. (d) Sundry distributions, etc.	2,122,869 93

C.—Balance.

(b) Cash in bank	83,274 08
Total	$11,976,534 89

MISCELLANEOUS STATEMENT FOR THE YEAR ENDING 31ST DECEMBER, 1913.

1. Amount of Debentures maturing in 1914: Issued in Canada, none; Issued elsewhere, none.
2. Amount of other existing obligations which will mature in 1914, none.
3. Amount of securities held by the Corporation which will mature and become payable to the Corporation in 1914, none.
4. Average rate of interest per annum paid by the Corporation during 1913: On guaranteed funds, about 3¼%; on debentures, none; on debenture stock, none.
5. Average rate of interest per annum received by the Corporation during 1913:
     (a) On mortgages of realty; (b) On other securities.
     (i) Owned beneficially by the Corporation: (a) 6.33%; (b) about 6%.
     (ii) Not owned beneficially: (a) 5.78%; (b) about 5¾%.
6. Of the mortgages owned beneficially by the Corporation, none is on realty situate in Ontario, and $121,130.89 is on realty situate elsewhere.

7. Of the mortgages not owned beneficially by the Corporation, none. is on realty situate in Ontario, and $2,356,722.24 is on realty situate elsewhere.

8. Loans written off or transferred to real estate account during 1913, viz.:
   (i) Funds or securities owned beneficially, none.
   (ii) Not so owned, none.

9. Number and aggregate amount of mortgages upon which compulsory proceedings have been taken by the Corporation in 1913, viz.:
   (i) Owned beneficially: No., none; amount, none.
   (ii) Not so owned: No., none; amount, none.

10. Aggregate market value of land mortgaged to the Corporation:
    (i) Mortgages owned beneficially, none.
    (ii) Not so owned, none.

11. How often are the securities held by the Corporation valued? Quarterly.

12. (a) Specify the officers of the Corporation who are under bond and for what sum respectively: All the officers of the company, for a total of $62,000.00.
    (b) Are the said bonds executed by private sureties or by Guarantee Companies? Guarantee Company.

13. Date when the accounts of the Corporation were last audited? 30th November, 1913.

14. Names and addresses of the auditors respectively for 1913, and for 1914 (if appointed):
    For 1913: George Dumford, C.A., Montreal; R. Carter, C.A., Halifax, N.S.; N. G. Hart, Royal Bank, Toronto.
    For 1914: R. Carter, C.A., Halifax, N.S.; N. G. Hart, Royal Bank, Toronto.

15. What were the dividend days of the Corporation in 1913, and what rate or rates of dividend were paid on those days respectively? 15th day of March, June, September and December, at 7% per annum on preferred stock and 8% per annum on common stock.

16. What is the date appointed for the Annual Meeting? 2nd Tuesday in January. Date of last Annual Meeting? 14th January, 1913.

17. Special General Meetings held in 1913: Dates, none held.

BRITISH EMPIRE TRUST COMPANY, LIMITED.

Head Office: London England.

CONSTATING INSTRUMENTS.

The British Empire Trust Company, Limited, was incorporated in London, on the 30th day of April, 1902 under the Companies Act, 1862 and 1890, England.

Authorized in 1913 by special Act of the Legislature of the Province of Ontario (3.4 Geo. V., C. 140) to transact business pursuant to Section 1 of the special Act. Registered on the Trust Companies Register, 18th August, 1913.

ANNUAL STATEMENT.

Of the condition and affairs of the British Empire Trust Company, Limited, at the 31st December, 1913, and for the year ending on that day, made to the Registrar of Loans Corporations for the Province of Ontario, pursuant to the laws of the said Province.

The head office of the Corporation is at No. 34 Nicholas Lane, in the City of London, England.

The chief agency for Ontario is situate at No. 9 Toronto Street, in the City of Toronto, in the Province of Ontario.

The chief agent and attorney for Ontario is Francis Charles Annesley, and his address is No. 1 Toronto Street, in the City of Toronto, Province of Ontario.

The board is constituted of eight directors, two of whom with the exception of the Managing Director retire in rotation every year.

The directors and chief executive officers of the Corporation at the 31st December, 1913, were as follows, together with their respective terms of office:

Robert Montgomery Horne-Payne, Chairman, Brentwood, England; 31st July, 1912; Annual Meeting, 1915.

John Davidson, Managing Director, Leigh-on-Sea; 9th July, 1912; no term fixed.

Tom Blundell Brown, Director, Brentwood, England; 25th July, 1911; Annual Meeting, 1915.

Dudley Northall Laurie, Director, London, England; 25th July, 1911; Annual Meeting, 1914.

Ernest Frederick Orby Gascoigne, Director, Ashtead, England; 25th July, 1911; Annual Meeting, 1914.

Sir William Mackenzie, Director, Toronto, Ont.; 31st July, 1912; Annual Meeting, 1916.

Norman Scott Russell, Director, London, England; 18th June, 1913; Annual Meeting, 1917.

David Blythe Hanna, Director, Toronto, Ont.; 18th June, 1913; Annual Meeting, 1916.

Arthur Henry Bowling, Assistant Manager, London, England; 9th February, 1911; No term fixed.

Robert Walter Bartlett, Secretary, London, England; 12th July, 1911; no term fixed.

A Permanent Capital Stock: Total amount authorized £1,000,000; total amount subscribed £750,000, as more particularly set out in Schedule A hereto.

SCHEDULE A.

Class 2.—Fixed and permanent capital stock created by virtue of Joint Stock Companies' Acts or Private Acts.

Description.	No. of Shares.	Par value.	Total amount held.	Total amount paid thereon.	Total remaining unpaid.
		£	£	£	£
Cumulative perpetual preferred shares	250,000	1	250,000	250,000	....
Preferred ordinary shares.	400,000	1	400,000	400,000	....
Deferred ordinary shares..	400,000	5s.	100,000	100,000	....
Totals.............	1,050,000	....	750,000	750,000	....

LIST OF SHAREHOLDERS AS AT 31st DECEMBER, 1913.
(Not printed.)

BALANCE SHEET AS AT 31st DECEMBER, 1913.

Dr.   Capital and Liabilities.

I.—Capital (Liabilities to Stockholders or Shareholders).

A.—Permanent capital stock or shares.

	£	s.	d.	£	s.	d.
1. (*a*) Cumulative perpetual preference shares capital fully called: Total called, £250,000; total paid thereon	250,000	0	0			
2. (*b*) Preferred ordinary shares capital all called: Total called £400,000; total paid thereon	400,000	0	0			
3. (*c*) Deferred ordinary stock capital all called Total called £100,000; total paid thereon	100,000	0	0			
6. (*f*) Reserve fund in respect of (1), (2) or (3)..	117,318	14	6			

C.—Liabilities to Stockholders or Shareholders.

Other than is shown under A, viz.:

	£	s.	d.	£	s.	d.
26. On unpresented dividends—warrants as per list	59	8	0			
				867,378	2	6

Liabilities to the Public.

	£	s.	d.	£	s.	d.
37. Owing to banks (including interest due or accrued)	173,000	0	0			
41. Other liabilities to the public, viz.:						
42. (*a*) Due to associated companies	556,587	16	7			
43. (*b*) Sundry creditors	30,865	17	11			
				760,453	14	6
Total actual liabilities				1,627,831	17	0

II.—Contingent Liabilities.

49. Money for which the Corporation is contingently liable, viz.:

	£	s.	d.	£	s.	d.
50. (*a*) Principal guaranteed	186,745	18	4			
51. (*b*) Interest guaranteed	3,375	2	7			
Total contingent liabilities				190,121	0	11
Gross total liabilities, actual and contingent				1,817,952	17	11

Cr.   Assets.

I.—Assets of which the Corporation is the beneficial owner.

A.—Immovable Property Owned Beneficially by Corporation.

B.—Debts secured by Mortgages of Land.

	£	s.	d.	£	s.	d.
9. (*a*) Debts secured by mortgages of land	7,021	7	0			
11. (*c*) Interest due and accrued on item (9)	40	19	5			
				7,062	6	5

C.—Debts not above enumerated, for which the Corporation holds securities as follows:

	£	s.	d.	£	s.	d.
13. (*a*) Debts secured by accepted bills of exchange	164,552	5	3			
22. (*j*) Debts secured by debentures and shares of railway, electric railway, electric light, gas or water power companies	320,252	1	7			
23. (*k*) Debts secured by debentures and shares of industrial companies	1,896	16	10			
24. (*l*) Debts secured by personal guarantees......	12,101	2	0			
26. (*n*) Interest due or accrued on 14 to 25 and not included therein	2,329	19	1			
				501,132	4	9

BALANCE SHEET AS AT 31st DECEMBER, 1913.—Continued.

D.—Unsecured Debts.

27. (a) Sundry debtors			11,712	1	1

E.—Cash.

		£ s. d.		
31. (a) On hand	7 5 10			
32. (b) In bank	186,021 7 8		186,028 13 6	

F.—Assets not Hereinbefore Mentioned.

37. (a) Investments in debentures and shares of railways, electric railways, electric light, gas or water power companies	651,115 7 2		
38. (b) Investments in shares and debentures of industrial companies	270,781 4 1	921,896 11 3	

Total assets owned beneficially by Corporation	1,627,831 17 0

II.—Assets not Owned Beneficially by Corporation but for which the Corporation is Accountable.

A.—As Guarantor.

(a) Mortgage securities:

43.	(i) Principal	135,376 0 0	
44.	(ii) Interest due and accrued	3,375 2 7	

(b) Other securities:

45.	(i) Principal	51,369 18 4	

Total assets II.	190,121 0 11
Gross total assets I. and II.	1,817,952 17 11

CASH ACCOUNT.

Receipts for the year ending 31st December, 1913.

I.—Received by the Corporation for its Own Use.

A.—Balance from 31st December, 1912.

		£ s. d.	£ s. d.
1.	Cash:		
2.	(i) On hand	. . . .	36 15 10
3.	(ii) In bank	. . . .	190,975 12 6

B.—Sums Received Wholly or Partly on Capital Stock.

4. (a) Calls on joint stock permanent capital	. . . .	66,812 5 0

C.—Receipts on Account of Investments, Loans or Debts.

	(b) On other securities:		
12.	(i) Principal	3,403,580 6 2	7,110,601 2 3
13.	(ii) Interest on dividends	69,181 0 10	69,181 0 10
	(c) Unsecured debts:		
14.	(i) Principal	. . . .	174,322 17 6

CASH ACCOUNT.—Continued.

Receipts for the year ending 31st December, 1913.

E.—Miscellaneous.

18. (a) Commission brokerage (or remuneration as corporate agent, trustee, etc.) 26,879 13 1   26,879 13 1

F.—Borrowed Money.

25. (a) Bank or other advances, discounts or overdrafts 463,000 0 0
29. (e) Borrowed otherwise 2,029,848 12 10

G.—Receipts from Other Sources.

30. (a) Bank deposits withdrawn 82,200 0 0
   (b) Sundries 96 7 0

Totals ... .3,499,641 0 ·1 10,213,954 6 10

II.—Received as Corporate, Trustee, Representative, Guardian or Agent in Trust.

B.—Received on Account of Investments, Loans or Debts.

	£	s.	d.

35. (b) On other securities: Principal, £263,620-12-0; interest, £304-6-2   263,924 18 2

D.—Receipts from Real Estate.

39. (a) Proceeds of issues of shares and debentures 1,110,257 14 2
40. (b) Received to pay interest and dividends on debentures and shares of various companies 317,980 16 1

Totals 1,692,163 8 5

CASH ACCOUNT.

Expenditure for the year ending 31st December, 1913.

	£	s.	d.	£	s.	d.

I.—Expended on Corporation Account.

A.—Sums Loaned on Invested on Capital Account.

1. (a) Loaned on mortgage of realty ......: .... 7,021 ، 0
   (b) Loaned on or invested in other securities, viz.:
2.   (I) Invested in securities of railways, electric railways, electric light, gas or water power companies and industrial companies........ 3,319,427 18 1   3,319,427 18 1
4.   (III) Loans on railways, electric railways, electric light, gas or water companies and industrial companies... .. .. 4,084.417 19 7

CASH ACCOUNT.—Continued.

Expenditure for the year ending 31st December, 1913.

B.—Expended on Stock Account.

8. Dividends paid on permanent stock	34,066	18	8		34,066	18	8
(a) Interest paid on joint stock capital received in advance of calls	75	2	10		75	2	10

C.—Borrowed Money (other than foregoing) or interest thereon paid, viz.:

18. (a) Bank account (principal and interest)	5,691	2	0		295,691	2	0

D.—Management Expenses (other than foregoing).

25. (a) Salaries, wages, fees	7,526	6	2		7,526	6	2
26. (b) Commission on brokerage	32,133	0	3		32,133	0	3
28. (d) Stationery, postage, printing and advertising	3,691	11	1		3,691	11	1
29. (e) Law costs	198	12	6		198	12	6
30. (f) Fuel, rent, taxes and rates	3,495	5	0		3,495	5	0
32. (h) Registration fees	219	0	8		219	0	8
33. (i) Other management expenditure	2,678	11	11		2,678	11	11

E.—Other Expenditures, viz.:

34. (a) Loans repaid (principal and interest).	4,737	11	11		2,115,853	5	4
35. (b) Payments for goods supplied and services rendered to sundry companies ...	.4....	..	..		79,429	12	3
36. (c) Bank deposits	......	..	..		60,600	0	0

F.—Balance.

37. (a) Cash on hand and in banks	......	..	..		167,628	18	6
Totals	3,413,941	1	1		10,213,954	6	10

II.—Expended on Trust or Agency Account.

A.—Loaned or Invested on Capital Account.

42. (b) Loaned or invested on or in other securities, viz.:

43. (1) Invested in debentures of railways, electric light, electric railways and industrial companies	261,810	4	3

B.—Other Expenditures.

52. (c) Debts or obligations wholly or partly paid: Principal, £603,512 0 7; interest, £4,097 10 5	607,609	11	0
53. (d) Remittances of balances of proceeds of issues of shares and debentures ....i..........	820,628	19	3

C.—Balance.

54. (a) Cash on hand (balance not in special banking account, but included among assets shown above) .:................	2,114	13	11
Total	£1,692,163	8	5

1. Amount of debentures maturing in 1914: Issued in Canada, none; issued elsewhere, none.
2. Amount of other existing obligations which will mature in 1914, £173.000.
3. Amount of securities held by the Corporation which will mature and become payable to the Corporation in 1914: £20,000.
4. Average rate of interest per annum paid by the Corporation during 1913: On deposits, none; on debentures, none; on debenture stock, none.
5. Average rate of interest per annum received by the Corporation during 1913:
    (a) On mortgages of realty: (b) On other securities.
        (i) Owned beneficially by the Corporation: (a) 6% per annum; (b) 4 5.8% per annum.
        (ii) Not owned beneficially: (a) none; (b) none.
6. Of the mortgages owned beneficially by the Corporation, none are on realty situate in Ontario, and £7,021.7.0 is on realty situate elsewhere.
7. Of the mortgages not owned beneficially by the Corporation, none are on realty situate in Ontario, and none are on realty situate elsewhere.
8. Loans written off or transferred to real estate account during 1913, viz.:
    (i) Funds or securities owned beneficially, none.
    (ii) Not so owned, none.
9. Number and aggregate amount of mortgages upon which compulsory proceedings have been taken by the Corporation in 1913, viz.:
    (i) Owned beneficially, No., none; amount, none.
    (ii) Not so owned: No., none; amount, none.
10. Aggregate market value of land mortgaged to the Corporation:
    (i) Mortgages owned beneficially, £35,000.
    (ii) Not so owned, none.
11. How often are the securities held by the Corporation valued? One a year for the purpose of annual accounts, and every fortnight for the information of the directors.
12. (a) Specify the officers of the Corporation who are under bond and for what sum respectively: None.
    (b) Are the said bonds executed by private sureties or by Guarantee Companies? None.
13. Date when the accounts of the Corporation were last audited? To year ended 30th April, 1913.
14. Names and addresses of the auditors respectively for 1913 and for 1914 (if appointed):
    For 1913: Robertson, Hill & Co., Chartered Accountants, London, E.C.
    For 1914: The same.
15. What were the dividend days of the Corporation in 1913 and what rate or rates of dividend were paid on those days respectively? Preference dividends were paid on 15th April and 15th October, at 5% per annum. Preferred ordinary dividend paid on May 15th, at 6% per annum, and November 15th at 5% per annum. Deferred ordinary dividend paid on 18th June at 8% per annum.
16. What is the date appointed for the Annual Meeting? Within a period of not more than 15 months after the last preceding General Meeting. Date of last Annual Meeting? 18th June, 1913.
17. Special General Meetings held in 1913: Dates, none.

CAPITAL TRUST CORPORATION, LIMITED.

Head Office: Ottawa, Ont.

CONSTATING INSTRUMENTS.

The Capital Trust Corporation, Limited, was incorporated in 1912 by special Act of the Parliament of the Dominion of Canada (2 Geo. V., C. 81).

Registered on the Trust Companies' Register on the 13th day of November, 1913, to transact business in the Province of Ontario, with powers restricted to the provisions of the Loan and Trust Corporations Act, (2 Geo. V., C. 33 (0)).

ANNUAL STATEMENT

Of the condition and affairs of the Capital Trust Corporation, Limited, of Ottawa, Ontario, at the 31st December, 1913, and for the year ending on that day, made to the Registrar of Loan Corporations for the Province of Ontario, pursuant to the laws of the said Province.

The head office of the Corporation is at No. 115 Sparks Street, in the City of Ottawa, in the Province of Ontario.

The Board is constituted of twenty-four directors, holding office for the term of one, two and three years.

The directors and chief executive officers of the Corporation at the 31st December, 1913, were as follows:

M. J. O'Brien, President, Renfrew, Ont.;	June 26th, 1913;	February,	1916.
Dennis Murphy, Vice-President, Ottawa, Ont.;	"	"	"
Hon. S. N. Parent, Vice-President, Montreal, Que.;	October 9th, 1913;	"	1914.
R. P. Gough, Vice-President, Toronto, Ont.;	June 26th, 1913;	"	1916.
A. E. Corrigan, Vice-President, Ottawa, Ont.;	"		1915.
George C. H. Lang, Director, Berlin, Ont.;	"		1916.
J. J. Seitz, Director, Toronto, Ont.;			"
T. P. Phelan, Director, Toronto, Ont.;			"
J. J. Lyons, Director, Ottawa, Ont.;			
A. E. Provost, Director, Ottawa, Ont.;			"
E. W. Tobin, Director, Bromptonville;			1915.
W. P. O'Brien, Director, Montreal, Que.;			"
M. Connolly, Director, Montreal, Que.;			"
Hugh Doheny, Director, Montreal, Que.;			
Edward Cass, Director, Winnipeg, Man.;			
B. G. Connolly, Director, Ottawa, Ont.;			
Gordon Grant, Director, Ottawa, Ont.;			"
Hon. Wm. McDonald, Director, Glace Bay, N.S.;			1914.
Hon. R. G. Beazley, Director, Halifax, N.S.;			"
W. J. Poupore, Director, Montreal, Que.;	"	"	"
C. P. Beaubien, Director, Montreal, Que.	October, 9th, 1913;	"	"
E. Fabre Surveyer, Director, Montreal, Que.;	"		
L. G. McPhillips, Director, Vancouver, B.C.;	"		

A.—Permanent Capital Stock: Total amount authorized, $2,000.000; total amount subscribed $521,100, as more particularly set out in Schedule A hereto.

SCHEDULE A.

Class 2.—Fixed and permanent capital stock created by virtue of Joint Stock Companies Act or Private Acts.

Calls made in respect of each individual subscription, not in respect of the total subscriptions; installments payable by periodical payments.

Description.	Total amount issued and substit-ing at 31st December, 1913.			Total amount of actual payments thereon.	Total amount unpaid and constituting an asset of the Corporation.
	No. of shares.	Par value.	—		
Instalment stock	5,211	$ 100	$ 521,100 ′	$ c. 155,550	$ c. ....

LIST OF SHAREHOLDERS AS AT 31st DECEMBER, 1913.

(Not printed.)

BALANCE SHEET AS AT 31st DECEMBER, 1913.

Capital and Liabilities.

I.—Capital (Liabilities to Stockholders or Shareholders.)

A.—Permanent Stock or Shares.

8. (h) Instalment permanent stock (payable by fixed periodical payments): Total subscribed, $521,100 on which has been paid	......	$155,550 00
10. (j) Unappropriated profits on (8)	......	2,140 80
		$157,690 80

Liabilities to the Public.

41. Other liabilities to the public, viz.:		
42. (a) Interest reserved to protect guaranteed investments	$9 00	
43. (b) Commissions owing and unpaid on sale of capital stock	1,200 00	
44. (c) Sundry outstanding expense accounts	195 08	
		1,404 08
Total actual liabilities		$159,094 88

II.—Contingent Liabilities.

49. Money for which the Corporation is contingently liable. viz.:		
50. (a) Principal guaranteed	$5,400 00	
51. (b) Interest guaranteed	9 00	
Total contingent liabilities .....,........................		$5,409 00
Gross total liabilities, actual and contingent		$164,503 88

BALANCE SHEET.—Continued.

Cr. Assets.

I.—Assets of which the Corporation is the Beneficial Owner.

B.—Debts Secured by Mortgages of Land.

9. (a) Debts (other than item 10) secured by mortgages of land	$50,000 00	
11. (c) Interest due and accrued on (9) and not included therein	801 37	$50,801 37

C.—Debts not above Enumerated for which the Corporation holds Securities as Follows:

14. (b) Debts secured by Municipal bonds or debentures ..	$39,942 91	
26. (n) Interest due or accrued on item (14) and not included therein	985 75	40,928 66

D.—Unsecured Debts.

27. (a) Accrued interest on bank balances	. . . . .	147 50

E.—Cash.

31. (a) On hand and in bank	. . . . . .	67,217 35
Total of assets owned beneficially by Corporation		$159,094 88

II.—Assets not Owned Beneficially by Corporation, but for which the Corporation is Accountable.

A.—As Guarantor.

(b) Other securities:		
45. (i) Principal	$5,400 00	
46. (ii) Interest due and accrued	9 00	
Total assets II.		$5,409 00
Gross total assets I and II.		$164,503 88

CASH ACCOUNT.

Receipts for the year ending 31st December, 1913.

I—.Received by the Corporation for its Own Use.

B.—Sums Received Wholly or Partly on Capital Stock.

	(Col. 1.)	(Col. 3)	(Total Col. 4.)
4. (a) Calls on joint stock permanent capital	. . . . . .	$155,550 00	$155,550 00
5. (b) Premiums on (4)	$26,500 00	. . . . . .	26,500 00
G.—Receipts From Other Sources.			
30. (a) Bank interest	1,856 80	. . . . . .	1,856 80
Totals	$28,356 80	$155,550 00	$183,906 80

25 L.C.

CASH ACCOUNT.—Continued.

Receipts for the year ending 31st December, 1913.

II.—Received as a Corporate Trustee, Representative, Guardian or Agent in Trust.

D.—Receipts from other sources, viz.:

39. (a) Received from clients for investment..   .... $5,400 00

Total $5,400 00

CASH ACCOUNT.

Expenditure for the year ending 31st December, 1913.

I.—Expended on Corporation Account.

A.—Sums Loaned or Invested on Capital Account.

1. (a) Loaned on mortgages of realty	......	$50,000 00
(b) Loaned or invested in other securities, viz.:		
2. (i) Purchase of municipal debentures	......	39,942 91
3. (ii) Purchase of accrued interest on above	......	540 62

*D.—Management Expenses (other than foregoing).

25. (a) Salaries, wages and fees	......	1,666 65
28. (d) Stationery, postage, printing and advertising	......	255 85
29. (e) Law costs .....:...............................	......	531 50
31. (g) Travelling expenses	......	459 77
33. (i) Other management expenditure	......	2,032 15

E.—Other Expenditures, viz.:

34. (a) Commission on sale of capital stock	......	20,000 00 ·
35. (b) Registration fees	......	545 00
36. (c) Charter fees	......	715 00

F.—Balance.

37. (a) Cash on hand and in bank	......	67,217 35
Total		$183,906 80

II.—Expended on Trust or Agency Account.

C.—Balance.

55. (i) Cash in bank	......	$5,400 00
Total		$5,400 00

*Owing to initiatory stage of this corporation, the expense of management embodies ex-
penses in connection with organization. To this date there is scarcely any distinction to be
noted between the two.

1 Amount of debentures maturing in 1914: Issued in Canada, none; issued elsewhere, none.

2. Amount of other existing obligations which will mature in 1914: None.

3. Amount of securities held by the Corporation which will mature and become payable to the Corporation in 1914, $523.93.

4. Average rate of interest per annum paid by the Corporation during 1912: On deposits, none; on debentures, none; on debenture stock, none.

5. Average rate of interest per annum received by the Corporation during 1913:
   (a) On mortgages of realty; (b) On other securities.
   (i) Owned beneficially by the Corporation: (a) none; (b) none.
   (ii) Not owned beneficially: (a) none; (b) none.

6. Of the mortgages owned beneficially by the Corporation, none is on realty situate in Ontario, and $50,000 is on realty situate elsewhere.

7. Of the mortgages not owned beneficially by the Corporation, none is on realty situate in Ontario, and none is on realty situate elsewhere.

8. Loans written off or transferred to real estate account during 1913, viz.:
   (i) Funds or securities owned beneficially, none.
   (ii) Not so owned, none.

9. Number and aggregate amount of mortgages upon which compulsory proceedings have been taken by the Corporation in 1913, viz.:
   (i) Owned beneficially: No., none; amount, none.
   (ii) Not so owned: No., none; amount, none.

10. Aggregate market value of land mortgaged to the Corporation:
    (i) Mortgages owned beneficially, $164,500.
    (ii) Not so owned, none.

11. How often are the securities held by the Corporation valued? Not yet determined, at least annually.

12. (a) Specify the officers of the Corporation who are under bond and for what sum respectively: Not yet determined, at the end of December, 1913.
    (b) Are the said bonds executed by private sureties or by Guarantee Companies?

13. Date when the accounts of the Corporation were last audited? Just commencing business.

14. Names and addresses of the auditors respectively for 1913 and for 1914 (if appointed):
    For 1913:
    For 1914: J. F. Cunningham, C.A.; M. D. Grant, F.I.A.

15. What were the dividend days of the Corporation in 1913 and what rate or rates of dividend were paid on those days respectively? None.

16. What is the date appointed for the Annual Meeting? February 10th, 1914. Date of last Annual Meeting? None hitherto.

17. Special General Meetings held in 1913: Dates, June 26th and adjournment of that meeting, October, 9th.

COMPARATIVE TABLES

375

COMPARATIVE

Showing Liabilities

Liabilities and Assets.	Loan Companies having only permanent stock.		Loan Compan— minating stock manent stock minating
	1912.	1913.	1912.
Capital Stock.	$ c.	$ c.	$ c.
Capital authorized (permanent)........	99,873,977 19	110,629,102 19	....
Capital subscribed (permanent)...................................	50,595,667 19	52,568,837 19	5,474,220 00
Capital subscribed (terminating)................................	....	....	1,031,308 18
Liabilities.			
Liabilities to Shareholders:			
Permanent.... { Stock fully paid up	28,707,489 10	32,833,549 56	4,644,855 84
Prepaid..	69,176 39	184,431 31	....
Stock paid up in part	8,337,299 39	8,330,363 97	376,109 51
Terminating . { Stock fully paid	....	....	2,550 00
Prepaid...............................	....	....	270,289 09
Instalment stock.	....	....	312,453 50
Reserve fund	15,484,989 82	21,344,964 78	893,000 00
Dividends declared and unpaid..................	887,249 94	1,041,994 68	140,417 12
Contingent fund...............................	134,405 00	139,948 30	11,496 56
Unappropriated profits..........................	1,401,262 66	1,556,213 66	92,416 78
Profits on terminating stock	....	....	90,384 18
Other liabilities to shareholders................	1,895 48	693 40	7,884 10
Total liabilities to shareholders..............	58,008,637 78	65,322,159 66	6,841,265 11
Liabilities to the public :			
Deposits.......................................	20,561,768 33	21,963,964 22	617,580 91
Interest on deposits...........................	209,687 82	220,347 22	10,783 22
Debentures payable in Canada..................	19,203,648 34	20,762,346 66	2,907,187 83
Debentures payable elsewhere..................	65,755,610 37	75,487,328 64	637,078 78
Debenture stock	1,307,888 81	1,232,405 48	....
Interest on debentures and debenture stock	983,162 46	932,907 59	50,783 89
Due on loans in process of completion...........	1,148,671 19	993,949 17	23,179 93
Borrowed on mortgages and on other securities....	7,500 50	13,195 50	....
Owing to banks................................	283,196 56	156,105 82	15,016 89
Other liabilities to public	1,752,481 47	231,713 50	266,534 78
Total liabilities to public....................	110,938,545,77	122,014,166 80	4,528,076 23
Contingent liabilities	....	....	....
Grand total liabilities to shareholders and public ...	168,942,183 55	187,336,326 46	11,369,341 34
Assets.			
Debts secured by mort- { Mortgages of realty	139,512,255 58	151,478,264 41	9,256,201 46
gages of land........ { Mortgaged land held for sale...........	288,100 82	471,725 77	41,863 85
Interest	1,293,990 29	1,414,023 38	96,333 54
Debts secured by :			
Municipal debentures and debenture stock	5,858,369 20	2,328,879 79	136,353 13
Government securities	24,286 80	....	....
Shareholders' stock	609,835 14	766,642 66	168,804 95
Stocks, bonds and securities, other than foregoing	15,408,576 87	19,480,691 90	904,701 96
Office premises	2,070,531 91	2,871,100 13	171,000 00
Freehold land...	288,912 17	204,340 90	156,521 12
Office furniture..	42,071 12	59,200 50	17,052 94
Cash	3,966,368 19	8,106,877 25	395,676 31
Other assets...........	98,584 16	154,379 77	29,882 58
Balance—profit and loss....................................	....	....	....
Total assets owned beneficially.....................	168,942,183 55	187,336,326 46	11,369,341 34
Assets not owned beneficially	....	....	....
Grand total of assets	168,942,183 55	187,336,326 46	11,369,341 34

TABLES.

and Assets.

ies having ter- as well as per- or having ter- stock only.	Loaning Land Companies.		Trust Companies.		Grand Totals.	
1913.	1912.	1913.	1912.	1913.	1912.	1913.
$ c.	$ c.	$ c.	$ c.	$ c.	$ c.	$ c.
....	15,580,000 00	15,580,000 00	34,800,000 00	34,800,000 00	139,302,977 19	160,452,102 19
2,153,850 00	5,473,010 00	5,658,510 00	11,286,500 00	17,764,600 00	72,829,897 19	79,142,097 19
886,118 73					1,031,806 18	886,118 73
1,453,713 81	8,000,000 00	8,865,000 00	2,955,550 00	12,087,710 95	43,307,894 44	50,219,974 32
			908,661 18	69,176 39	1,088,092 49	
361,903 23	1,104,998 49	361,660 16	3,633,601 66	1,954,060 00	12,441,004 05	10,997,986 86
550 00					2,550 00	550 00
214,132 67					270,259 02	214,132 67
307,601 89					312,452 50	307,601 89
658,000 00	2,681,683 83	2,764,408 62	4,780,000 00	6,900,951 12	26,329,563 15	31,568,324 53
51,264 81	50,550 53	50,481 92	232,738 75	230,634 86	1,301,056 84	1,434,326 07
11,436 56	1,52,383 51	60,334 55		33,713 74	189,064 10	245,423 15
53,390 86	931,212 55	837,523 34	806,342 83	1,030,068 84	3,323,141 82	3,478,005 20
119,806 42					90,384 18	119,806 42
354 79			13,068 39		22,273 97	1,048 19
3,235,044 04	7,831,729 44	7,939,667 59	14,412,196 68	23,176,399 99	87,078,828 96	99,670,271 28
394,612 32	409,525 57	445,320 59	241,820 75	748,156 22	21,680,695 56	23,501,063 35
11,394 78	3,467 96	3,865 79		4,543 88	225,969 00	240,051 67
2,222,483 30	719,207 00	908,290 00			22,880,023 17	23,894,129 96
85,896 67	1,315,570 38	1,493,122 14			67,706,359 43	77,066,347 45
	15,062 76	16,080 06			1,307,888 81	1,232,405 48
89,106 27					999,009 13	988,043 92
5,980 00			692,199 94	69,898 09	1,859,051 06	1,069,327 26
4,749 77	1,300,536 37	1,402,397 49	92,316 67	1,519,155 57	1,500,353 54	2,239,498 33
18,832 06				2,836,150 43	373,212 45	3,006,091 41
26,998 22	96,622 43	105,135 64	55,896 46	2,999,678 56	2,171,465 18	3,361,515 92
2,736,068 39	3,769,992 46	4,372,151 71	1,083,163 82	8,177,082 75	120,306,778 28	137,296,464 65
			187,524,581 60	271,293,762 31	187,524,581 60	271,293,762 31
5,967,107 43	11,581,721 90	12,311,819 30	203,018,942 05	302,647,345 05	394,912,188 84	508,262,498 24
5,582,365 53	2,875,588 61	1,752,150 75	6,835,449 60	8,345,732 64	157,979,495 25	167,158,512 33
83,391 47			15,063 63	317,509 56	343,017 80	322,626 80
29,949 87	113,706 50	221,493 87	495,709 42	395,744 48	1,999,788 75	2,061,211 60
2,602 95			192,100 78	274,432 72	5,687,823 11	2,605,915 46
			25,000 00	25,000 00	49,286 80	25,000 00
49,225 80					778,640 09	816,568 46
125,655 04	6,515,687 56	7,194,961 51	4,460,306 26	16,365,878 24	27,392,174 44	43,064,884 69
15,174 35			1,675,585 72	2,656,078 65	3,917,116 93	5,542,353 13
82,296 96	2,086,519 44	2,531,863 50	937,173 92	327,041 97	3,398,925 68	3,095,565 33
7,312 17	766 80	899 59	17,962 59	28,199 21	77,875 68	95,411 37
81,996 55	156,646 51	182,171 07	547,601 61	1,831,870 23	5,066,322 92	10,202,415 10
6,438 74	18,327 22	66,799 05	292,517 69	888,994 94	440,561 65	1,116,612 50
	361,660 16	361,660 16			361,660 16	361,660 16
5,967,107 43	11,581,721 90	12,311,819 30	15,494,360 45	31,353,482 74	207,387,607 24	236,968,735 93
			187,524,581 60	271,293,762 31	187,524,581 60	271,293,762 31
5,967,107 43	11,581,721 90	12,311,819 30	203,018,942 05	302,647,345 05	394,912,188 84	508,262,498 24

COMPARATIVE

Showing Receipts

Receipts and Expenditure.	Loan Companies having only permanent stock.		Loan Compan-minating stock manent stock minating
	1912.	1913.	1912.
Receipts.	$ c.	$ c.	$ c.
Received by the Corporation for its own use.			
Cash Balance 31st December, 1911-1912........................	4,050,226 89	4,049,223 95	403,460 12
Received from shareholders during the year.....................	2,025,080 06	1,402 728 17	95,843 77
Received from borrowers } (principal and interest)............ and investments	85,424,384 36	85,564,632 31	4,235,966 49
Real estate .... { Rents	107,435 68	119,994 80	20,730 77
{ Sales	37,091 83	48,602 14	415,796 65
Bank advances......................................	206,383 64	133,222 25	15,016 83
Borrowed money....................................	8 976 61	9,733 00	5,000 00
Received from depositors during the year..........	55,932,708 22	58,539,665 48	1,107,839 72
Debentures issued during the year.....	12,883,947 07	10,843,034 27	1,490,992 68
Debenture stock	48,666 07		
Bank interest.......................................	57,876 37	89,637 51	15,001 72
Miscellaneous......................................	930,848 45	990,667 01	40,856 21
Terminating converted into Permanent stock............			
Totals	111,693,024 94	111,506,845 89	9,775,505 18
II.—Received as Corporate Trustee, Representative, Guardian or Agent in Trust.			
Cash Balance, 31st December, 1911-1912			
Received from borrowers during the year............			
Real estate .... { Rents			
{ Sales			
Money received for investment......................			
Other receipts......................................			
Totals......................................			
Grand total receipts...........................	111,693,024 94	111,506,845 89	9,775,505 18
Expenditure.			
I.—Expended on Corporation Account.			
Loaned during the year on mortgages	24,021,628 77	19,069,553,67	1,304,072 90
Loaned during the year on other securities	11,799,064 67	10,722,848 04	1,871,460 87
Real estate purchased and incumbrances paid off	92,525 88	539,180 72	66,249 27
Insurance and taxes advanced	66,945 45	87,186 38	209 62
Dividends........ { Permanent...........................	2,399,209 80	2,693,800 03	281,308 96
{ Terminating.....................	2,191 77	....	13,230 07
Repaid bank......................................	58,666 86	281,891 11	35,605 40
Repaid borrowed money............................			
Deposits paid off (principal and interest)...............	56,057,483 80	59,122,525 41	3,254,634 83
Debentures paid off	11,837 236 64	11,384,885 80	1,877,764 87
Debenture stock paid off......................	42,296 82	90,600 65	
Paid for withdrawn, converted, matured or retired stock.......	9,032 05	....	139,067 13
Cost of management................................	1,366,523 19	1,679,063 55	178,571 09
Other	145,721 05	65,418 53	488,664 47
Balance, cash 31st December, 1912-1913....................	3,794,696 99	5,769,492 20	395,676 31
Totals	111,693,024 94	111,506,845 89	9,775,505 18
I.—Expended on Trust or Agency Account.			
Loaned during the year on mortgages................			
Loaned during the year on other securities..............			
Repayment of trust funds..........................			
Real estate purchased and encumbrances paid off			
Other			
Balance 31st December, 1912-1913			
Totals			
Grand total expenditure.............................	111,693,024 94	111,506,845 89	9,775,505 18

TABLES—Continued.

and Expenditure.

ies having ter- as well as per- or having ter- stock only.	Loaning Land Companies.		Trust Companies.		Grand Total.	
1913.	1912.	1913.	1912.	1913.	1912.	1913.
$ c.	$ c.	$ c.	$ c.	$ c.	$ c.	$ c.
104.276 29	288.624 04	158.595 15	567,662 70	1,583,528 78	5,369,973 26	5,843,624 17
88,945 38	....	14,608 22	787,861 42	1,989,797 04	2,857,785 25	5,496,068 81
655,390 47	1,649,294 96	1,840,335 65	9,453,585 05	51,387,201 14	50,763,130 88	89,437,558 57
836 92	136,635 69	158,796 85	151,302 64	196,340 90	418,104 78	475,959 47
7,937 71	417,487 69	540,436 48	402,748 68	18,070 44	1,273,074 84	610,046 77
11,832 06	300,166 78	441,180 98	....	4,191,700 17	521,566 81	4,772,945 41
25,000 00	....	18,000 00	....	10,014,964 47	18,976 61	10,063,567 47
1,142.895 98	587,567 48	656,480 79	522,490 42	4,141,396 10	59,900,805 84	64,290,488 85
852.764 30	188,817 71	449,796 43	....	....	14,478,558 21	12,145,597 00
....	....	....	....	....	48,666 67	....
7,097 25	559 34	804 77	8,296 74	10,968 36	81,324 07	108,637 89
15,416 43	31,311 23	41,285 70	1,887,497 65	2,391,655 51	2,390,013 55	3,389,029 64
15,668 67	....	....	....	....	....	15,668 67
2,927,979 45	3,549,914 83	4,813,817 97	13,031,045 30	75,870,592 91	133,049,490 25	194,618,286 22
....	....	....	10,296,029 89	12, 74,197 07	10,296,029 39	12,574,197 07
....	....	....	43,951,134 70	61,501,308 25	43,961,134 70	61,301,308 25
....	....	....	954,596 75	1, ,670 10	954,596 75	1,065,670 10
....	....	....	2,501,368 57	2,005,255 64	2,501,368 57	2,239,255 64
....	....	....	97,195,875 29	95,398,733 89	97,195,875 29	95,398,733 89
....	....	....	9,357 93	3,716,070 93	9,357 98	3,716,070 93
....	....	....	154,910,264 63	176,290,230 88	154,910,264 68	176,290,230 88
2,927,979 45	3,549,914 83	4,813,817 97	167,941,309 93	252,160,823 79	292,959,754 88	370,908,467 10
368,849 68	447,434 18	595,404 53	3,678,255	5,781,547 14	29,951,391 22	25,815,355 02
66,564 38	966,412 43	922,696 02	5,130,063	47,698,949 74	19,767,001 77	59,410,488 18
14,555 66	176,065 07	1,014,247 09	533,926	371,732 71	1,173,564 80	1,989,716 18
1,112 07	9,853 77	....	94,996 38	138,882 97	173,005 68	227,181 42
107,657 23	277,557 41	296,658 99	682,761 38	1,903,515 56	3,640,837 30	4,101,631 81
30,387 06	....	....	....	....	14,431 84	30,387 06
70,705 15	417,075 00	300,014 45	49,160 99	3,342,082 54	560,508 36	2,894,643 28
5,000 00	64,487 22	18,000 00	439,396 27	10,762,095 69	563,734 29	10,780,095 69
1,088,586 08	515,848 16	635,443 44	97,791 18	3,873,739 89	59,963,757 96	64,730,388 77
867,909 52	158,838 96	183,521 13	....	....	13,273,810 07	12,435,616 44
....	....	....	....	....	43,396 89	90,600 65
187,438 19	132,327 34	101,613 35	1,189,996 27	1,886,585 14	280,926 53	137,438 19
74,380 68	79,684 35	69,945 13	226,696 11	491,833 50	2,814,783 90	3,692,172 72
12,567 20	150,104 46	183,144 83	553,101 61	1,669,738 08	961,185 09	639,164 20
31,996 55	155,785 68	....	....	....	4,899,362 79	7,703,861 61
2,927,979 45	3,549,914 83	4,813,817 97	13,031,045 30	75,870,592 91	133,049,490 25	194,618,286 22
....	....	....	18, ,989 27	18,064,893 88	18,532,969 27	18,064,393 88
....	....	....	31. 08	37,907,744 94	31,583,578 08	37,907,744 94
....	....	....	90, 578 70	109,441,556 56	90,308,355 70	109,441,556 56
....	....	....	1,232 355 16	1,217,888 16	1,253,353 16	1,217,883 16
....	....	....	1,366,980 79	659,577 39	1,309,960 79	659,577 39
....	....	....	11,712,067 63	8,979,074 95	11,712,067 63	8,979,074 95
....	....	....	154,910,264 63	176,290,230 88	154,910,264 63	176,290,230 88
....	3,549,914 83	4,813,817 97	167,941,309 93	252,160,823 79	292,959,754 88	370,908,467 10

COMPARATIVE

Showing Miscel

Miscellaneous.		Loan Companies having only permanent stock.		Loan Compan- minating stock manent stock minating
		1912.	1913.	1912.
Loans written off or transferred to real estate	Owned beneficially	$ c. 53,662 99	$ c. 206,634 96	$ c. 50,982 48
	Not so owned			
Debentures maturing during 1913-1914		11,195,190 29	11,564,842 37	1,190,315 72
Average rate of interest paid on :		per cent.	per cent.	per cent.
1. Deposits		3.4923	3.5050	3.53
2. Debentures		4.215	4.474	4.860
3. Debenture stock		4.0	4.0	
Average rate of interest received on :				
Mortgages of realty	Owned beneficially	6.398	6.505	7.272
	Not so owned			
Other securities	Owned beneficially	5.745	5.633	6.907
	Not so owned			
Number and amount of mortgages enforced	Number { Owned beneficially	268	387	22
	Not so owned			
	Amount { Owned beneficially	$444,744 76	$544,486 68	$39,483 72
	Not so owned			

TABLES.—Concluded.

laneous details.

ies having ter- as well as per- or having ter- stock only.	Loaning Land Companies.		Trust Companies.		Grand Totals.	
1913.	1912.	1913.	1912.	1913.	1912.	1913.
$ c. 4,025 19	$ c. 600 00	$ c. 7,896 80	$ c.	$ c. 2,650 00 15,523 22	$ c. 64,195 47	$ c. 221,306 35 15,523 22 12,517,091 78
664,807 56 per cent. 4.0 5.063	265,683 00 per cent. 3.5 4.13	267,941 80 per cent. 3.5 4.34	per cent. 4.133	per cent. 3.995	12,511,119 01 per cent. 3.7368 4.4350 4.0	per cent. 3.750 4.599 4.0
7.20 ·7.44 2 677 75	6.01 6.37 None None	6.20 6.00 None None	6.794 6.420 5.350 6.788 5 45 $ 6,280 41 65,783 95	6.940 6.674 5.759 5.848 43 193 $ 85,623 23 231,817 57	6.659 6.420 6.213 6.773 308 45 $480,507 95 65,783 95	6.786 6.674 6.307 5.848 432 193 $650,727 60 231,817 57

Orders-in-Council granted under R.S.O. 1897, c. 206, s. 8 (1), empowering the Courts to appoint Trusts Corporations as trustee, administrator, guardian, etc., without security.
[Revised and re-enacted by 8 Edw. VII. (1908), c. 43, s. 2; 2 Geo. V., chap. 34, s. 20.]

Name of Company.

1. Toronto General Trusts Corporation.
2. Trusts and Guarantee Company, Limited.
3. National Trusts Company, Limited.
4. Canada Trust Company.
5. Union Trust Company, Limited.
6. Royal Trust Company.
7. Imperial Trusts Company of Canada.
8. Mercantile Trust Company of Canada, Limited.
9. The Title and Trust Company.
10. Canada Permanent Trust Company.
11. Sterling Trusts Corporation.

List of Loan Corporations whose debentures have been authorized by Orders-in-Council for purposes of investment by Trustees.

Name of Company.

1. Land Security Company.
2. Canada Landed and National Investment Company, Limited.
3. Toronto Savings and Loan Company.
4. British Mortgage Loan Company of Ontario.
5. Midland Loan and Savings Company.
6. Royal Loan and Savings Company.
7. *London Loan Company of Canada.
8. Hamilton Provident and Loan Society.
9. Toronto Mortgage Company.
10. Crown Savings and Loan Company.
11. Oxford Permanent Loan and Savings Society.

List of Loan Corporations whose debentures have been authorized by Order-in-Council for purposes of investment by Trustees and with whom Trustees may deposit trust funds. R.S.O. 1897, c. 130, as amended by 62 V. (2nd sess.), c. 11, s. 32, and by 1 Edw. VII., c. 14, s. 1, and by 3 Edw. VII., c. 7, s. 25, and by 7 Edw. VII., c. 28, s. 1, and by 1 Geo. V., c. 26, s. 28.

Name of Company.

1. Canada Permanent Mortgage Corporation.
2. Guelph and Ontario Investment and Savings Society.
3. London and Canadian Loan and Agency Company, Limited.
4. Industrial Mortgage and Savings Company.
5. Victoria Loan and Savings Company.
6. Landed Banking and Loan Company.
7. Great West Permanent Loan Company.
8. Huron and Erie Loan and Savings Company.
9. Central Canada Loan and Savings Company.
10. Oxford Permanent Loan and Savings Society.
11. East Lambton Farmers' Loan and Savings Company.
12. Lambton Loan and Investment Company.
13. Ontario Loan and Debenture Company.

---

*Name changed by Order-in-Council (Ontario), dated 11th April, 1906, to " The London Loan and Savings Company of Canada."

LIST OF LOAN CORPORATIONS

LIST OF LOAN

Page.	Name of Company	Chief Office in Ontario	Manager, Secretary or *Chief Agent
262	Brantford Trust Company (Limited)....	Brantford	W. G. Helliker .....
	British Canadian Loan and Investment Company (Limited) (a)	Toronto	Ernest S. Ball .....
363	British Empire Trust Company (Limited)	"	*Francis Charles Annesley
96	British Mortgage Loan Company of Ontario	Stratford	William Buckingham.
20	Brockville Loan and Savings Company (Limited)	Brockville ...	L. C. Dargavel ....
99	Canada Investment Corporation	Toronto	Harry Symons, K.C. .
24	Canada Landed and National Investment Company (Limited)	Toronto	Edward Saunders ...
29	Canada Permanent Mortgage Corporation	"	{ John Massey } ..... { R. S. Hudson }
353	Canada Permanent Trust Company	"	{ John-Massey ; } ..... { R. S. Hudson }
278	Canada Trust Company	London	Hume Cronyn ....
34	Canadian Mortgage Investment Company	Toronto	F. W. G. Fitzgerald...
252	Canadian Northern Prairie Lands Company (Limited)	"	L. W. Mitchell ......
369	Capital Trust Corporation (Limited)....	Ottawa	B. C. Connolly ....
39	Central Canada Loan and Savings Company	Peterboro' ...	E. R. Wood (Toronto)
103	Colonial Investment and Loan Company.	Toronto	A. J. Jackson ....
44	Credit Foncier Franco-Canadien, Montreal	"	*W. E. Long ....
49	Crown Savings and Loan Company	Petrolea	Wm. English ....
200	Dominion Permanent Loan Company....	Toronto	F. M. Holland ......
53	Dominion Savings and Investment Society	London	Nathaniel Mills ......
	Dominion Trust Company (b)	Toronto	*N. W. Rowell, K.C. ...
135	Dyment Securities, Loan and Savings Company	Barrie	S. Dyment ....
57	East Lambton Farmers' Loan and Savings Company	Forest	Newton Tripp ....
188	Edinburgh Canadian Mortgage Company, (Limited)	Toronto	Wood, Gundy & Company ....
335	Fidelity Trusts Company of Ontario	London	W. J. Harvey ....
61	Frontenac Loan and Investment Society.	Kingston	Lt.-Col. S. C. McGill..
149	Great West Permanent Loan Company..	Toronto	*William McLeish ....
70	Grey and Bruce Loan Company	Owen Sound..	Wm. P. Telford .....
329	Guardian Trust Company (Limited)....	Toronto	W. S. Morden ....
65	Guelph and Ontario Investment and Savings Society	Guelph	John E. McElderry...
75	Hamilton Provident and Loan Society...	Hamilton	C. Ferrie ....
207	Home Building and Savings Association of Ottawa	Ottawa	C. A. Douglas ....
80	Huron and Erie Loan and Savings Company	London	Hume Cronyn ....
	Imperial Loan and Investment Company of Canada (Limited) (c)..........	Toronto	Gerard Muntz ....
328	Imperial Trusts Company of Canada	"	W. H. Jackson ......
85	Industrial Mortgage and Savings Company.	Sarnia	D. N. Sinclair ......
109	Lambton Loan and Investment Company.	"	James H. Kittermaster
90	Landed Banking and Loan Company	Hamilton.....	C. W. Cartwright ....
236	Land Security Company	Toronto	Alfred H. Cox ......
169	London and Canadian Loan and Agency Company (Limited)	"	William Wedd, Jr. ...
154	London Loan and Savings Company of Canada	London	Malcolm John Kent ..
285	London and Western Trusts Company (Limited)	"	John S. Moore ......

(a) The British Canadian Loan and Investment Company, Limited, having no liabilities, and having disposed of its assets, ceased to transact business on 30th June, 1913.
(b) The Dominion Trust Company was registered on the Trust Companies' Register on the 27th day of February, 1914.
(c) The Imperial Loan and Investment Company of Canada, Limited, ceased to transact business.

CORPORATIONS.

President.	Description of Company	When incorporated	Financial statement for year ending
Christopher Cook	Trusts Co. ...	16th December, 1907	December 31st 1913.
Sir Henry M. Pellatt	Loan Co.	12th April, 1876	"
R. M. Horne Payne..........	Trusts Co. ...	30th April, 1902	"
John McMillan	Loan Co.	5th October, 1877	"
W. H. Cole	"	11th May, 1885	"
Harry Symons, K.C.	....	23rd August, 1889	"
John Hoskin, K.C., LL.D., D.C.L.	.. ....	1858	
W. G. Gooderham	....	1st March, 1855	
W. G. Gooderham	Trusts Co. ...	7th March, 1913	"
Thomas G. Meredith, K.C....	"	23rd July, 1894	"
L. A. Hamilton	Loan Co.	11th August, 1899	"
Hugh Sutherland	Loaning Land Co.	30th May, 1905	"
M. J. O.'Brien	Trusts Co. ...	1st April, 1912	"
Hon. Geo. A. Cox	Loan Co.	7th March, 1884	"
A. J. Jackson	"	14th June, 1900	"
J. H. Thors	.. ....	January, 1881	"
J. H. Fairbank	....	30th January, 1882	"
Hon. J. R. Stratton	....	7th May, 1890	"
Thomas H. Purdom, K.C....	"	20th April, 1872	"
	Trusts Co. ...	1903	
A. E. Dyment	Loan Co.	15th May, 1902	"
James Hutton, M.D........	"	19th December, 1891	"
Sir Andrew H. L. Fraser....	"	24th February, 1912	"
T. H. Purdom, K.C.........	Trusts Co. ...	23rd March, 1910	"
Lt.-Col. H. R. Smith	Loan Co.	13th August, 1863	"
W. T. Alexander	"		
S. J. Parker	....	10th May, 1889	"
Cawthra Mulock	Trusts Co. ...	8th April, 1910	"
Alexander Baine Petrie	Loan Co.	19th January, 1876	"
George Rutherford	"	6th June, 1871	"
John R. Armstrong	.. ....	24th June, 1890	"
T. G. Meredith, K.C.	"	18th March, 1864	"
Douglas A. Burns	"	19th August, 1869	"
James H. Mitchell	Trusts Co. ...	23rd June, 1887	"
John Cowan, K.C.	Loan Co.	20th August, 1889	"
Isaac Unsworth	"	27th March, 1847	"
Hon. Thomas Bain	"	16th December, 1876	"
Geo. F. Little	Loaning Land Co.	29th March, 1873	"
Thomas Long	Loan Co.	1863	..
R. W. Puddicombe	"	2nd May, 1877	"
Sir George Gibbons, K.C.....	Trusts Co. ...	17th September, 1896	"

LIST OF LOAN

Page.	Name of Company.	Chief Office in Ontario.	Manager, Secretary or *Chief Agent.
311	Mercantile Trust Company of Canada (Limited)	Hamilton	Stuart C. Macdonald ..
159	Midland Loan and Savings Company ..	Port Hope	J. H. Helm ....
357	Montreal Trust Company	Toronto	*John F. Hobkirk ...
279	National Trust Company (Limited)	"	W. E. Rundle ....
212	Niagara Falls Building, Savings and Loan Association	Niagara Falls	B. M. Benson ....
	North British Canadian Investment Company (Limited) (d)	Toronto	*Angus C. Heighington
	Northern Trusts Company (e)	"	*Joseph Hatheway King
117	Ontario Loan and Debenture Company ..	London	Alfred M. Smart .....
131	Ontario Loan and Savings Company ..	Oshawa	T. H. McMillan ....
217	Owen Sound Loan and Savings Company	Owen Sound ..	C. A. Fleming ....
164	Oxford Permanent Loan and Savings Society	Woodstock	Malcolm Douglas ....
174	People's Loan and Savings Corporation.	London	A. A. Campbell ......
223	Peterborough Workingmen's Building and Savings Society	Peterborough .	J. Corkery ....
	Port Arthur and Fort William Mortgage Company (Limited) (f)	Port Arthur ..	A. J. McComber .....
242	Provident Investment Company	Toronto	A. H. Cox ....
340	Prudential Trust Company (Limited)..	"	*Edmund Bristol, K.C., M.P. ....
179	Real Estate Loan Company of Canada (Limited)	"	E. L. Morton ....
184	Royal Loan and Savings Company	Brantford	W. G. Helliker ....
304	Royal Trust Company	Toronto	*M. Stanley L. Richey (Toronto) ....
	Scottish American Investment Company (Limited) (g)	.. ....	*W. H. Lockhart-Gordon ....
256	Scottish Ontario and Manitoba Land Company (Limited), Glasgow	"	*Mowat, Langton & Maclennan ....
145	Security Loan and Savings Company ...	St. Catharines	Eugene F. Dwyer ....
113	Southern Loan and Savings Company ..	St, Thomas ...	Jno. Walker Stewart .
139	Standard Reliance Mortgage Corporation	Toronto	H. Waddington ......
347	Standard Trusts Company	"	Alexander Fasken ....
	Sterling Trusts Corporation (h)	"	Col. J. G. Langton ....
228	Sun and Hastings Savings and Loan Company of Ontario	.. ....	W. Pemberton Page .
298	Title and Trust Company	....	John J. Gibson .....
291	Toronto General Trusts Corporation	"	J. W. Langmuir .....
127	Toronto Mortgage Company	::	Walter Gillespie .....
247	Toronto Savings and Loan Company	Peterborough .	W. G. Morrow ....
317	Trusts and Guarantee Company (Limited)	Toronto	E. B. Stockdale ......
267	Union Trust Company (Limited), The ..	"	J. M. McWhinney ....
122	Victoria Loan and Savings Company ..	Lindsay.......	Charles E. Weeks ....
238	Walkerville Land and Building Company (Limited)	Walkerville....	D. F. Matthew ....
193	Waterloo County Loan and Savings Company)	Waterloo......	P. V. Wilson ....

(d) The North British Canadian Investment Company, Limited. This Company is withdrawing from business in Ontario, and for this purpose is registered under 1 Edward VII., chap. 12, sec. 18, as amended by 5 Edward VII., chap. 12, sec. 17, and by 8 Edward VII., chap. 33, sec. 46. The sworn statement of the Chief Agent for Ontario for the year ending 31st December, 1913, shows assets of the Corporation then in Ontario at $22,888.21, consisting of Mortgages, $15,584.32; Stocks, $2,383.00; Investment Loan Account, $307.01; Interest and Arrears Account, $323.99; Cash on Hand and in Bank, $5,269.39; Office Furniture Account, $20.00; that the Company had then no liabilities in Ontario.

(e) The Northern Trusts Company was registered on the Trust Companies' Register on the 17th February, 1914.

(f) The Port Arthur and Fort William Mortgage Company, Limited, was registered on the Loan Companies' Register on the 14th January, 1914.

CORPORATIONS.

President.	Description of Company	When incorporated	Financial statement for year ending
Hon. Wm. Gibson	Trusts Co. ...	12th November, 1906	December 31st 1913.
Wm. Henwood	Loan Co.	5th July, 1872	"
....	Trusts Co. ...	21st March, 1889	"
J. W. Flavelle	"	12th August, 1898	"
R. P. Slater	Local Loan Co.	5th March, 1894	"
	Loan Co.	14th October, 1876	"
George F. Galt	Trusts Co. ...	1st March, 1902	....
John McClary	Loan Co.	26th September, 1870	"
W. F. Cowan	"	12th February, 1873	"
W. A. Bishop	"	1st April, 1889	"
Dr. W. T. Parke	-	27th October, 1865	"
W. F. Roome, M.D..........	....	22nd June, 1892	"
T. B. McGrath	"	17th January, 1889	"
J. J. Carrick, M.P.	"	27th December, 1913	
Hon. G. A. Cox	Loaning Land Co.	3rd November, 1893	"
B. Hal Brown	Trusts Co. ...	19th May, 1909	"
M. H. Aikins, M.D..........	Loan Co.	17th September, 1879	"
Christopher Cook	"	24th March, 1875	"
Right Hon. Lord Strathcona and Mount Royal, G.C.M.G.	Trusts Co. ...	24th June, 1892	"
....		....	....
Robert Anderson	Loaning Land Co.	15th December, 1879	"
Henry J. Taylor	Loan Co.	12th March, 1870	"
Wm. Mickleborough	"	25th November, 1903	"
Nathan H. Stevens	"	14th February, 1873	"
J. T. Gordon	Trusts Co. ...	1st March, 1902	"
....	"	19th May, 1911	....
Whitford Vandusen	Loan Co.	3rd May, 1893	"
E. F. B. Johnston, K.C.....	Trusts Co. ...	25th April, 1905	"
Hon. Featherston Osler, K.C.	"	1st April, 1899	"
Hon. Sir William Mortimer Clark, LL.D., W.S., K.C. ..	Loan Co.	15th December, 1899	"
Hon. Geo. A. Cox	Loaning Land Co.	15th June, 1885	"
James J. Warren	Trusts Co. ...	24th February, 1897	"
Charles Magee	"	7th August, 1901	"
W. Flavelle	Loan Co.	4th September, 1895	
E. Chandler Walker	Loaning Land Co.	22nd October, 1890	"
Thos. Hilliard	Loan Co.	7th April, 1913	"

(g) The Scottish American Investment Company, Limited. This Company is withdrawing from business in Ontario, and for this purpose is registered under 1 Edward VII., chap. 12, sec. 13, as amended by 5 Edward VII., chap. 12, sec. 17, and by 8 Edward VII., chap. 33, sec. 46. The sworn statement of the Chief Agent for Ontario for the year ending 31st December, 1913, shows the assets of the Company then in Ontario at $42,909.31, consisting of Loans secured by Mortgages of land, $21,913.38; sale agreements and mortgages given for balance of purchase money, $20,995.93; that the Company had then no liabilities in Ontario.
(h) The Sterling Trusts Corporation was registered on the Trust Companies' Register on 1st December, 1913.